BAZAINE 1870

SCAPEGOAT FOR A NATION

Quintin Barry

Hardback edition produced in a strictly limited printing
of 500 individually numbered and signed copies.

This is copy number **444** of 500

BAZAINE 1870

Scapegoat for a Nation

Quintin Barry

Helion & Company

To Diana

Helion & Company Limited
Unit 8 Amherst Business Centre
Budbrooke Road
Warwick
CV34 5WE
England
Tel. 01926 499 619
Email: info@helion.co.uk
Website: www.helion.co.uk
Twitter: @helionbooks
blog.helion.co.uk

Published by Helion & Company 2020
Designed and typeset by Mach 3 Solutions Ltd (www.mach3solutions.co.uk)
Cover designed by Paul Hewitt, Battlefield Design (www.battlefield-design.co.uk)
Printed by Gutenberg Press Limited, Tarxien, Malta

Text © Quintin Barry 2020
Images open source unless otherwise stated
Maps drawn by George Anderson © Helion & Company 2020

ISBN 978-1-913336-08-0

British Library Cataloguing-in-Publication Data.
A catalogue record for this book is available from the British Library.

For details of other military history titles published by Helion & Company Limited contact the above address, or visit our website: http://www.helion.co.uk.

We always welcome receiving book proposals from prospective authors.

Contents

List of Illustrations

Key to sources

The Graphic
Illustrated London New
Lindner *Der Krieg gegen Frankreich 1870–71* (Berlin, 1895)
Pflug-Harttung *Krieg und Sieg 1870–71, ein Gedenkbuch* (Berlin, 1895)
Rousset, *Histoire Générale de la Guerre Franco-Allemande (1870–1871)* (Paris, n.d.)
Scheibert *Der Krieg 1870–71* (Berlin, 1914)

List of Maps

Preface

It was not long after I began to research this book that I realised that I had not dealt fairly with Marshal Bazaine in my previous history of the Franco-Prussian war, published in 2007. I found that I had in some respects tended to follow the prevalent opinion of other historians with regard to some aspects of Bazaine's character and general competence; this was inexcusably superficial. This became particularly clear to me when I read the detailed analysis by Generals Ruby & Regnault of the Marshal's career. This was published under the title *Bazaine: Coupable ou Victime?* in 1960, and its thorough research comprehensively demolishes the widely accepted view of the events of 1870 and the part that Bazaine played in them. It is a remarkable work of investigative history, which includes an examination of a number of documents which had only recently seen the light of day. I must acknowledge my very substantial debt to its authors.

I should also mention the only modern book in the English language on Bazaine's life, which is *The Two Marshals*, by Philip Guedalla, published in 1943, which gives a striking account of his career and his trial. Guedalla compares and contrasts Bazaine's career with that of Marshal Petain. I have quoted a number of the vivid passages in which Guedalla conveys the spirit of the times.

The fall of Metz inspired a huge body of contemporary literature on the subject in France, the bulk of which was both ill-informed and profoundly hostile. Although at his trial the more extravagant allegations against him of treason were shown to be absurd, the general belief in France was that he had been justly convicted of surrendering Metz prematurely, and this continued to be the position for very many years. In a telling passage in the preface to the book by Ruby & Regnault, Marshal Alphonse Juin, the distinguished French general of the Second World War, confessed that he had never thought that the trial of Marshal Bazaine called for reconsideration:

> Profoundly affected in my early youth by all the accepted accounts of the war of 1870 which I heard, even those from the mouth of authentic witnesses, I was unable to think that the unfortunate Marshal had been unjustly treated.[1]

---

1   Generals Edmond Ruby & Jean Regnault, *Bazaine: Coupable ou Victime?* (Paris, 1960) p. 7.

I have remarked above that Philip Guedalla's is the only modern book in English on the subject; there were, however, a number of books published at the time by journalists who covered the Franco-Prussian war. Among these, the distinguished war correspondent Archibald Forbes wrote a thoughtful assessment of Bazaine and his story. It is to be favourably compared to a book by GT Robinson, the correspondent of *The Guardian*, who was in Metz throughout its investment, and whose bitterness led him to abandon any sense of fair reporting in a work which must have gone some way to poison British public opinion. His fury at the fall of Metz, for which he held Bazaine entirely responsible, knew no bounds, and was expressed in a flood of intemperate invective and abuse.

With someone who kept his own counsel to the extent that Bazaine did, and who left behind him few reliable clues as to the inner motivation for his decisions, it is bound to be difficult to arrive at a clear understanding of his psychology. Of course, it is possible to see the apparent reason for each of his actions, taken one by one; but it is much harder to pierce the opacity of his overall intention, or even if he had one. Nor is it clear whether, at each stage of the sequence of events as they unfolded, he had really made any forward assessment of the likely outcome. It is entirely possible that because he was in a situation that was unique in its complexity, he simply could not see his way through, and reacted accordingly to each event as it occurred. On the other hand, all that is known of his character points the other way; as General du Barail observed, it could be that he was 'too subtle,' and that his consideration of his situation was too deep for his own good.

Bazaine's motivation therefore is hard to discern, because he did not indulge in philosophical reflection, and does not appear to have confided his innermost thoughts even to his devoted staff. Nor is it easy to look behind the text of his written communications to seek indications of the way he was thinking. All of this makes it difficult conclusively to refute, for instance, allegations of personal ambition, or the extent to which this may have influenced his decisions.

There is an obvious danger in reading into Bazaine's words and deeds more than can be stated with certainty. Many writers, including a number of notable historians, have attempted to evaluate his motivation in this way; and many of them have done so to buttress the convictions which they already held. Bias is corrosive; it destroys the structure of its argument.

It is certainly possible to separate those who were interested only in showing Bazaine as corrupt, cowardly and treacherous, since in this way they could attack the Bonapartist regime. Immediately upon the capitulation of Metz, Leon Gambetta had set the tone of political comment with his cry of treason.

A century and a half after the events with which this book is concerned, passions, even in France, have cooled. Researching and writing this book has been a rewarding and at times a saddening experience. Examining not only the history of great events, but also the private wickedness which led to appalling public consequences, was at times disturbing; this story never could have a happy ending. But I hope that this book may contribute to setting the record straight and do justice to a man profoundly maligned by the nation he did his best to serve.

Acknowledgements

In the Preface I have referred to a number of the books that have been particularly important to me in the writing of this account of Marshal Achille Bazaine and his part in the Franco-Prussian War of 1870-1871. There are of course many others which have been of valuable assistance; of these , I would like especially to record my debt to Sir Michael Howard, whose death last year took from us the historian whose account remains the outstanding study of the war, and which first inspired my lifelong interest in the subject.

I would like to take this opportunity to express my gratitude to my publisher Duncan Rogers, who as ever has been enormously supportive, particularly in his assembly of the images that appear throughout the book; to George Anderson, who prepared the maps; to Tim Readman, who read the book in draft, and made a number of valuable suggestions; and finally, to my wife Diana, who patiently drove me on an extensive and rewarding tour of the battlefields around Metz.

1

Early Career

François-Achille Bazaine was born on February 13 1811 at Versailles, the son of Dominique and Marie Madeleine Bazaine. The couple were probably in fact not married; his father, described in the official records as an engineer in chief, emigrated to Russia where, in 1816, he married a young Russian noblewoman. The young Bazaine came under the protection of Baron Roget, a deputy for the region of Cher. Legend has it that the Baron was in fact his father; at all events, he gave the boy his support, particularly when at the age of 19 he endeavoured to gain a place at the École Polytechnique, one of the special schools for the training of French army officers, the other being St Cyr. When he failed to enter the École Polytechnique, Bazaine opted in the following year to enlist as a private in the 37th Regiment of the Line. Within three months he was a corporal. In 1832 he became a sergeant, and it was in this rank that he applied to join the French Foreign Legion.

Formed in March 1831 by King Louis Philippe, it was initially largely composed of the recently disbanded Swiss and German regiments which he had inherited from the Bourbons. It was expressly provided in its establishment that it should serve only outside mainland France. It was at first divided into six national battalions, comprising Swiss, German, Polish, Italian, Spanish and Dutch-Belgian troops, a system which was not conducive to the development of *esprit de corps.* Disciplinary problems were also to be expected in view of the fact that many of the soldiers were deserters from their own national army. The Legion's initial posting was to Algeria, to strengthen the French forces which had recently occupied the city of Algiers. Its first commander was the legendary Napoleonic veteran Colonel Bernelle, who was renowned for an explosive temper which contributed to an improvement in the Legion's discipline.

It was not until 1833 that Bazaine first saw active service with his regiment, in the countryside around Algiers. He quickly made his mark as a man who would make an excellent officer, and on November 2, 1833 was appointed *sous-lieutenant.*[1] It was the first step on the ladder that would take him to the top of his profession. For the

---

1   Ruby & Regnault, p. 25.

moment, as an officer of the Legion, his principal concern was with Abd el Kader, an Arab chieftain who was consolidating his power as the de facto ruler of a broad swathe of Algerian territory based on Mascara. It was he who was the principal threat to the French possessions in Algeria; but these had been won while King Charles X was on the throne, and in 1834 it was by no means certain that the Orleanist regime of Louis Philippe would continue a policy of conquest in Africa.

In 1835 Bazaine was serving in a force under General Trézel which encountered the army of Abd el Kader in the hills behind Oran, and which suffered a humiliating defeat. Bazaine did well, however, and earned a warm commendation from Trézel in his official report. He also received a promotion to lieutenant, as well as the award of the Legion d'Honneur. He was not, though, destined to remain long in Oran, his current posting; later that year it was decided in Paris to provide military support to Queen Isabella of Spain, at that time engaged in attempting to retain her throne in the face of the Carlist uprising. The support to be given was to consist of the deployment in Spain of the French Foreign Legion. Bazaine sailed with his regiment from Oran to Tarragona, under the command of Colonel Bernelle, who now became a Spanish general; Bazaine was given the local rank of captain. Once more, he was seen to perform his duties well; and when Bernelle was in due course replaced by Colonel Conrad, Bazaine served as the latter's chief of staff. It was a happy relationship:

> The fearless little man was the young captain's dream of what a soldier ought to be. Conrad might not know much about strategy, and he was far too good a soldier to question orders, however injudicious, emanating from superior authority. But when he saw the enemy in front of him, he charged. Bazaine had served with him since 1833 in Africa and in the early stages of the war in Spain. The younger man was utterly devoted to his senior; and in the four years that they had been together he came to regard himself as General Conrad's adopted son. Bazaine had never known a father; but if he had one, this was what he wished him to be like.[2]

The Legion suffered fearful casualties in a battle at Huesca on May 24, 1837, when it formed part of an army commanded by the Spanish General Iribarren, who ordered an attack when, as a historian of the Legion has pointed out, 'it made little sense, either strategically or tactically.'[3] Characteristically, Conrad did not challenge the wisdom of the order, but threw his men forward. Between 350 and 400 legionnaires were *hors de combat* as a result of the battle, including 28 officers. Gravely weakened, the Legion fought another engagement on June 2, occupying the right of the Cristino line. Bazaine wrote an account of what happened when the rest of the line broke under the Carlist assault:

2   Philip Guedalla, *The Two Marshals* (London, 1943) p. 38.
3   Porch, Douglas, *The French Foreign Legion* (London. 1991) p. 46.

Our troops hesitated; confusion began to appear in our ranks. [Conrad] believed that by setting an example through his own courage he could rally them. He went well to the front of the skirmish line, placed his cap on the end of his cane, and shouted 'Forward!' But the men, seized by panic, did not hear his voice. They continued to flee ...

At this point Conrad was killed by a bullet and fell to the ground. Bazaine went on to describe what happened next:

His body almost fell into the hands of the enemy. But thanks to the help of four courageous NCOs and soldiers of the Legion, I got him on to my horse and across the battlefield. However, as we were outflanked on our left I needed a half-hour to get his body out of danger.[4]

Bazaine now assumed temporary command of the battered Legion, extricating it safely and bringing it to Saragossa. For him, the sense of his loss was profound. He next was appointed to take charge of the office at Pamplona of Colonel Senilhes, the French Commissioner at the Cristino headquarters. He threw himself energetically into his new responsibilities, in the absence of Senilhes, who had now crossed the border to return to France. He continued to receive meticulous reports from Bazaine six times a week. The complex political situation in Spain taught Bazaine a lot; as his biographer observed, he was able to provide reports on the situation 'with the shrewd appraisal of the strange workings of the Spanish mind.'[5] By the spring of 1838, however, Bazaine's time in Spain was drawing to a close. His experiences there had taught him that above all an officer of the Legion must at all times display personal courage. He had also learned from Conrad the importance of staff work, and his responsibilities under Conrad gave him a thorough grounding in military administration, as well as the control of operations. In the reports which he later wrote on the officers of the Legion, he spelled out frankly the opinions he had formed:

A devastating candour is the normal idiom of such documents, which are rarely charitable; but the interest of this specimen lies in its revelation of Bazaine's dislikes. His principal *bêtes noires* appear to have been gossips, gamblers and alcoholics. He was quick to note the failings of those who had enjoyed a better education than his own; and a poor opinion of the arts may be disclosed in his comments on one subaltern: *Né pour être artiste et non pour être militaire.*[6]

4   Porch, p48.
5   Guedalla, p. 44.
6   Guedalla, p. 44.

When Bazaine left Spain in June 1838, he reverted to the rank of lieutenant in the 4th Light Infantry Regiment. By the following year, however, he was back in the Foreign Legion with the rank of captain. In 1840 he survived, with some distinction, the ordeal of the prolonged siege of Miliana by Abd el Kader. That year he returned to France where he joined the newly formed 8th Chasseurs á Pied, and in due course returned with this regiment to Algeria. In 1842 he took part in a successful operation which ended with a comprehensive defeat of Abd el Kader's army. His next posting was as chief of the *Bureau Arabe* at Tlemcen. This post involved its holder in a wide range of duties:

> Interpreter, judge, tax collector, and policeman, he administered extensive terri-
> tories of which he spoke the language and explored the politics. His intelligence
> reports on local temper and affairs helped to form policy; his attitude to local
> worthies controlled their rise and fall; and his office became the focus of all
> native life, where anxious greybeards interviewed young officers fresh from St
> Cyr with a profusion of grave Arab courtesy, and the sun went down upon inter-
> minable arguments over innumerable brews of sweet, green tea.[7]

His time in this position continued Bazaine's education in both management and politics, and he discharged its complicated functions with tact and skill. In 1844 he became *Chef de Bataillon* in the 58th Regiment of the Line but continued in his post at Tlemcen. At the end of 1847 the long struggle against Abd el Kader came to an end, when the Emir finally surrendered, officially to the Duc d'Aumale, the younger brother of King Louis Philippe, who was at that time serving as governor general of Algeria. The duke was however not destined to remain long in that office; next year the international upheavals of 1848 saw his brother swept from the throne of France, and France was again a republic. Bazaine's career in Africa continued. On April 20, 1848 General Cavaignac, the new governor general of Algeria, was able to congratu-late him on being made lieutenant colonel; asking him to give up the request which Bazaine had made to return to France, Cavaignac wrote: 'It is a fresh sacrifice which I ask of you, but I know that I do not make this appeal to your patriotism in vain.'[8]

Bazaine was formally attached first to the 19th Light Infantry Regiment, and then to the 5th Regiment of the Line, but remained in his post. He was promoted to full colonel in 1850, and was placed in charge of the *Departement d'Affaires Arabes* for the whole of the province of Oran. He continued to collect the good opinions of his supe-riors; General Patrice MacMahon wrote of him that he was 'a man of great intelli-gence, extremely active and always displaying *sang froid* in face of the enemy.' General Pelissier, Commandant of the division at Oran, wrote that Bazaine was 'by a long way the most brilliant *chef de corps* of the division, and had acquired this position over a long

7   Guedalla, pp. 52–53.
8   Ruby & Regnault, p. 27.

period. He has served in a remarkable way and most intelligently.' Pelissier formally recommended him for promotion to *général de brigade*[9].

Although MacMahon had expressed himself so favourably of Bazaine, the latter's feelings towards his superior were by no means so warm. Bazaine had applied for leave to marry the 17-year-old Maria de la Soledad Indria Gregoria Tormo, the daughter of a hotelier in Tlemcen. McMahon refused to countersign his application on the grounds that it would be prejudicial to Bazaine's career, and this appears

Marshal MacMahon, commander of the 1st Corps, Army of the Rhine, and later commander of the Army of Châlons, painting by Princeteau. (Rousset/*Histoire*)

to have led to an angry scene between the two men. Bazaine was obliged to bide his time; he arranged for Maria to continue her education at a convent in Marseille, and continued with his work at Tlemcen, before succeeding to the command of the 1st Foreign Legion Regiment.

In May 1852 his fresh application for leave to marry was successful; the authorisation from the War Ministry was signed by one Colonel Trochu. The marriage took place at Versailles on June 12, 1852. His wife was at once seen as a great credit to Bazaine, 'remarkably pretty, artistic and intelligent, the young wife adapted herself to a new situation with perfect tact;' and she was most warmly received into the society of the Second Empire.[10] Meanwhile her husband continued in his command of his regiment on the Moroccan border. He left behind his successful career in the *Departement d'Affaires Arabes*, in which he had learned so much, not least to keep his own counsel. Philip Guedalla wrote that his experiences there had 'left him with something of a politician's mind and something of a policeman's.' These attributes were, in his military duties, not immediately relevant, but they may well have played a considerable part in influencing him during his later career.

9   Ruby & Regnault, pp. 27-28
10   Ruby & Regnault, p. 29.

The political earthquakes that had seen the fall of the July Monarchy, the establishment of the Second Republic and then, after a short but violent coup d'état, the Second Empire, had not immediately had any effect on Bazaine's career. But the elevation of Prince President Louis Napoleon to the imperial throne as Napoleon III, for which a huge majority of the French people had voted in a plebiscite, was bound to give the new emperor confidence in conducting a forward policy; and for a Bonaparte, military glamour was an essential part of the imperial regime. Recently the only military glories that France could cherish were those that had been won in Africa in the reign of King Louis Philippe. Guedalla reflected on the contribution to the general perception of France's military reputation made by the generation of French soldiers that, in the course of two decades, had finally conquered Algeria:

> Bronzed, decorated, exquisitely tailored in the martial millinery devised to gladden eyes in France, the heroes of the *jeune Afrique* helped powerfully to restore a feeling that their country was invincible. Hussars were as elegant (if not a trifle more so), Lancers as dashing, and Dragoons as helmeted as anything that the Empire had known; white-aproned pioneers still wore beards and bearskins; and big drum-majors paced majestically under tall tricolour plumes. Algeria added its own embellishments – the scarlet *chéchia* and short blue jacket of the Zouaves, and the red burnous of the Spahis. If appearances counted for anything France was still formidable under Louis Philippe.[11]

Now, with the establishment of the Second Empire, the role of the military was bound to be further enhanced; all that was lacking were some contemporary Napoleonic battle honours.

The first opportunity for military glory for the Second Empire arrived with the international crisis in 1854 which pitched an alliance of Great Britain, France and Turkey into war with Russia. A substantial Franco-British army arrived in the Crimea, of which the 1st Foreign Legion Regiment, with Bazaine at its head, formed part. Soon after its arrival General Carbuccia, the commander of the Foreign Legion Brigade, succumbed to cholera, and Bazaine was called upon to succeed him; Pelissier, the corps commander, observed that no better choice could have been made.

The brigade formed part of the 3rd Division of the 1st Corps, commanded by General Paté. It took no part in the battle of the Alma, but thereafter was heavily engaged in the siege of Sebastopol, where it performed well. Bazaine particularly distinguished himself in an action during the night of May 1, 1855, when he led a column of 24 companies to capture the outer works of the Central Bastion. He was commended for this in an army order. Much later, however, it was alleged by his enemies that during the siege he had been rapped over the knuckles by General Forey, in overall command of the siege operations, for leaving his trench lines to visit his wife,

11   Guedalla, p. 65.

who had accompanied him to the Crimea. It is a story for which there is no supporting documentary evidence, and Generals Ruby & Regnault dismiss it, pointing out that when, in due course, Forey was in command of the French army in Mexico, he raised no objection to the appointment of Bazaine to command a division under him.

Pelissier had meanwhile succeeded to the command of the French army in the Crimea. His high opinion of Bazaine continued, and it is not surprising that when a vacancy arose for a divisional commander, Bazaine should have been chosen to fill it. He continued to do well in the course of the siege, and after Sebastopol fell he was appointed to command the ruined fortress. Pelissier, it was generally noted, also had a high opinion of Mme Bazaine, and he frequently invited her to dine with him.

Bazaine's distinguished service during the siege, and perhaps Pelissier's fondness for his wife, led to his being appointed to the command of a joint Franco-British combined operation to attack the fortress of Kinburn, which lay at the mouth of the river Dnieper. The French and British fleets, under the command of Admirals Bruat and Lyons respectively, accompanied the expedition, which comprised two brigades, one French and one British. After a feint attack at Odessa, they landed at Kinburn, where the fortress came under heavy bombardment from the guns of the fleet. After five hours of this, the Russian artillery had been silenced; when attacked by Bazaine's infantry, the fortress commander at once surrendered and the garrison of 1,200 men was taken prisoner. Pelissier, who appears to have continued to enjoy the company of Mme Bazaine during her husband's absence, wrote to Bazaine on October 21, 1855: 'The news of the capture of Kinburn has brought true happiness to the army. I cordially congratulate you on this fine success, and I beg that you will convey my satisfaction to the troops under your orders.'[12]

His reputation by now well established as that of a coming man, Bazaine returned to France. His first posting was as an Inspector General, but soon after this he took up a divisional command at Bourges, an important military base. There, his wife's usual tact and intelligence brought her immediate success in what, by comparison with Paris, was a closed and narrowminded provincial society.

Soon, however, the war drums were beating again. Napoleon III was determined to do something for Italy, which must inevitably lead to a confrontation with Austria. In conjunction with Cavour, prime minister to King Victor Emmanuel of Piedmont, he succeeded in bringing about a *casus belli* sufficiently serious to justify, to himself at any rate, a war with Austria.

When this in due course broke out, Bazaine sailed in April 1859 from Toulon in command of the 3rd Division of the 1st Corps, which was led by the veteran Marshal Baraguey d'Hilliers. The division consisted of two brigades, the 1st (Goze) of three regiments and the second (Dumont) of two. It disembarked at Genoa on April 29 and made its way to the theatre of war. The 1st Division of the corps was commanded by General Elie Forey, and it was he who on May 21 won an important victory at

---

12   Ruby & Regnault, p. 32.

Montebello when he boldly attacked a larger Austrian force. Helmuth von Moltke, when he wrote the Prussian staff history of the campaign, expressed great admiration for the speedy and decisive action taken by Forey in collecting his division and launching the crucial counter-attack which 'snatched victory out of a threatened defeat.'[13]

A fortnight later the critical battle of Magenta, fought on June 4, saw a significant defeat for the Austrians. Colonel Wylly, in his history of the campaign, observed:

> On neither side in this battle did everything fall out quite as had been arranged or intended, but on the battlefield the French certainly displayed superior fighting powers, as their leaders showed better generalship. On the other side the Austrians were brought piecemeal into action; there seemed at times something almost like a reluctance to engage; and throughout reserves were kept far too much in hand – caution, as on previous occasions, prevailing over enterprise.[14]

Bazaine's division had not been engaged, as the 1st Corps took no part in the battle. Four days later, however, he got the chance to make his mark, when his division went into action at Melegnano. What had happened was that Gyulai, the Austrian commander, had at first intended to renew the fighting at Magenta before realising that the demoralisation of his army made a retreat essential. He was then instructed by the Emperor Franz Joseph to make a stand, and accordingly ordered that the town of Melegnano be put in a state of defence. However, the commander of the division stationed there was ordered to offer resistance only to weak enemy detachments, but to fall back before any real strength. On the evening of May 7 Baraguey d'Hilliers was ordered to advance to Melegnano, and on the following morning he was instructed to capture the place. Bazaine was to advance direct on the town by the main road. It was as late as 6.00 p.m. before he was finally ordered to launch his attack.

Bazaine waited until it seemed that the Austrian artillery fire was slackening, and then deployed three companies of Zouaves on his right, followed by two battalions of the 34th Regiment of the Line, while the rest of the Zouaves, supported by the 33rd Regiment, charged directly towards the strong barricade that had been erected to block the road into the town. There followed some desperate hand-to-hand fighting:

> Bazaine's leading battalions had now made repeated assaults upon the front of the town; driven back more than once by murderous fire from the Austrians in the houses and behind the enclosures, the Zouaves and 33rd returned again and again to the attack; first the cemetery and then the farms were captured and the

13   Quoted Wylly, Colonel H.C., *Magenta and Solferino* (London, 1907) p. 59.
14   Wylly, p. 141.

two main streets were occupied, when Ladmirault, penetrating at the same time from the east, drove in upon Bazaine's men the defenders of that flank.[15]

This action was a precursor to the battle of Solferino, which was fought on May 24. The total strength of the Franco-Italian army was 173,603 men, with 522 guns. The Austrian army, which by now had taken up a position behind the river Mincio, consisted of 189,648 men and 752 guns. Baraguey's 1st Corps, together with the 2nd Corps (MacMahon) and the Imperial Guard (Regnaud de St Jean d'Angély), formed the centre of the Allied line, facing three Austrian corps. Bazaine, with the 3rd Division, followed Forey's 1st Division as it approached the Austrian position. As the battle developed, Bazaine was ordered forward to attack a walled cemetery in the village of Solferino. After a lengthy artillery preparation at close range, Bazaine sent his infantry forward to storm the cemetery which, with the support of Ladmirault's 2nd Division was carried at the point of the bayonet.

Subsequently, a number of Bazaine's detractors looked back at this campaign and were critical of his performance: 'General Palat and others after him wrote that Bazaine threw his infantry six times against the walls of the cemetery without any artillery preparation. In the official texts, one finds no trace of an obstinacy so stupid, which appears suspect.'[16] Ruby & Regnault point out that he deployed two batteries, each of four guns, which opened fire at a range of 300 m, and that their contribution was described fully in the regimental histories of the two regiments concerned.

Baraguey commended Bazaine, with his other divisional commanders, for the zeal and vigour they displayed. Captain Hepp, an officer on Bazaine's staff, later suggested that Baraguey was inclined to minimise his role. He wrote that his chief 'had displayed a calm, a *sang froid* and a presence deserving of the admiration of all, but that he was as admirable for his modesty and self-denial as for his sublime intelligence and courage under fire.'[17]

By the end of the day an important victory had been won; the campaign, however, seemed far from over. It was a surprise to all, therefore, when within a week the treaty of Villafranca, hastily negotiated by Napoleon III and Franz Joseph, brought the war to an abrupt end. Bazaine, on the road to Verona, wrote thoughtfully about the battle from his headquarters to a relative:

> The battle of Solferino was long and hard, but victory soon makes you forget fatigue, and two days afterwards we were fit to start again. I was lucky enough to get through without losing any bits of myself; a bullet went through my left holster and lodged in my saddle quite close to my left leg, and my horse's right

15   Wylly, p. 160.
16   Ruby & Regnault, p. 35, quoting General Bartholemeu Palat, *Bazaine et nos désastres* (Paris 1913) I, p. 10.
17   Ruby & Regnault, p. 36.

leg was grazed. It was lucky to come through so lightly, especially under such a fire … This great battle was really grand! But when the excitement of the fight was over, what a dismal sight is the battlefield covered with dead and wounded. In these days war is really an evil, and the men who drive nations to it are very guilty.[18]

With the end of the war Bazaine returned to peacetime soldiering. For some while he remained in Italy with his division, but in the spring of 1860 he returned to France. His reputation had been considerably enhanced by his performance as a divisional commander. It was not surprising, therefore, that he was earmarked for an important command when that arose. He cannot, though, have expected that it would be a catastrophe on the French financial markets that would take him to the next stage of his career.

18   Guedalla, p. 85.

2

Mexico

There are various reasons that might prompt a Great Power to send its troops to intervene in a foreign country, but an attempt in the middle of the nineteenth century to establish a Habsburg empire in the New World was uniquely ambitious. This, though, was the plan evolved by the fertile brain of the Emperor Napoleon III. Palmerston once remarked that his 'mind seems as full of schemes as a warren is full of rabbits,' but this scheme was one of his most extravagant.

It had its origins in the bankruptcy in 1860 of a Paris financial house of which the proprietor was a Swiss named Jecker. It almost at once caused very considerable international complications. The assets of the business consisted principally of a very large amount of Mexican government bonds issued by the previous government and latterly repudiated by the current President Juarez. The scale of the default led to negotiations for a joint armed intervention by Britain, France and Spain to enforce the honouring of the bonds. An agreement was arrived at that an allied force should in the first instance occupy the port of Vera Cruz. Spain, being in possession of Cuba, had less far to send her forces; she dispatched 6,000 troops. The British furnished a small squadron, carrying about 800 marines, and the French provided a force of 2,000 marines and 500 Zouaves.[1]

The Spanish arrived first, so that when the British and French contingents appeared at Vera Cruz, it was to find the Spanish flag flying over the fortress of San Juan d'Ulua. This immediately caused a dispute, since it had been understood that the contingents would arrive together. The Spanish seem to have had a larger ambition than the honouring of the government bonds, but soon discovered that they were as hated by the population as they had been before Mexico achieved independence. Negotiations with Juarez effectively amounted to the recognition of his government, and a convention was agreed laying down the preliminaries for a meeting to be held in April 1862. By now, disputes among the allies ensured the breakdown of any joint

1   Joan Haslip, *Imperial Adventurer* (London, 1971) p. 160.

Emperor Maximilian of Mexico.
(Private collection)

intervention, and the way was clear for Napoleon III to give effect to the plan that had been forming in his mind.

The French contingent had been reinforced by the arrival of 2,500 further troops and was under the command of General Lorencez; then 2,000 more troops arrived, and with these, he reported to Napoleon, he expected it to be 'only a question of weeks' before he hoped to be in Mexico City. His first step was to march on Puebla where, he said, he had been assured that he would be met 'with nothing but flowers.' His optimistic reports did not however take account of the effect of long forced marches, acute supply difficulties and the outbreak of yellow fever which reduced his effective strength to less than 6,000.[2]

Napoleon, meanwhile, had been making progress with the tortuous negotiations by which he intended to carry out his scheme for the future government of Mexico. His plan was that it should become an imperial monarchy, and the candidate for the throne whom he had selected was the Archduke Maximilian of Austria, a younger brother of the Emperor Franz Joseph. This proposal had originated in a discussion between Jose Hidalgo, an old acquaintance of the Empress Eugénie, who met with her and Napoleon to discuss the possibility of putting a European on the throne of Mexico. The Empress suggested Maximilian as a likely candidate and thought that he would accept.

Maximilian who had enjoyed a successful career at the head of the Austrian Navy, hesitated; his wife Charlotte, the daughter of King Leopold of the Belgians was more immediately favourable. Franz Joseph, though, was extremely doubtful about the wisdom of accepting the proposal as was the Empress Elisabeth. Charlotte's father, cautious at first, saw the prestige that would result from another Saxe- Coburg princess on a foreign throne, and advised acceptance.

All this had been going on behind the scenes; the immediate situation, however, was far from encouraging. Napoleon had written to Maximilian on June 7 to tell him that the news from Mexico was very good, and that 'if the great city of Puebla

2   Haslip, p. 172.

pronounces for us, the odds are that the rest will follow.' This optimistic assessment was speedily destroyed a few days later, when Napoleon received the latest report from Lorencez:

> Puebla de Los Angeles had met the invading army with gunshot instead of flowers. Each Baroque church with its tiled dome had been turned into a fort, and 4,000 Mexicans in shabby uniforms, fighting with obsolete British weapons left over from Waterloo and sold to them years ago by the British government, had succeeded in defeating the finest soldiers in Europe, the veterans of Sebastopol and Magenta, and had added the glorious 'Cinca de Mayo' to the annals of Mexican history.[3]

For Napoleon, this was an extremely disagreeable surprise. It left him, facing a serious blow to his prestige, in a situation in which his first bet having been lost he must necessarily increase his stake. Clearly, the French force in Mexico must be very substantially reinforced. An army corps under General Forey was mobilised and embarked at Cherbourg; its two divisional commanders were to be Bazaine and General Felix Douay. Bazaine's name was put forward by Marshal Randon, the Minister of War; as Guedalla put it, 'when Napoleon III wrote '*J'accepte Bazaine*,' he changed the course of Achille's life and, perhaps, of European history.'[4]

Once committed to this very substantial escalation of the French intervention in Mexico, Napoleon's exit strategy, if he gave thought to it at all, was based on hope rather than anything more concrete. He hoped that, in spite of the defeat of Lorencez before Puebla, the Juaristas could be militarily defeated so comprehensively that no recovery was possible. He hoped that Maximilian might be securely placed on the throne and would be supported by the bulk of the population. And he hoped that the Confederacy, likely to be much less hostile to a Mexican Empire under French domination, might win its independence in the American Civil War. Should, however, the Union prevail, Napoleon could be under no illusion about the policy that the American government would adopt once it was free to deal with the issue. In March 1862, at the beginning of the French intervention in Mexico, when France was operating in conjunction with Britain and Spain, Abraham Lincoln had sent a warning note to the three powers to make the position plain:

> A foreign monarchy set up on Mexican soil in the presence of European naval and military forces would be an insult to the republican form of government, which is most widely spread on the American continent, and would mean the beginning rather than the end of revolution in Mexico. The sympathies of the United States would be on the side of her sister republic, for the liberation of the

---

3   Haslip, p. 172.
4   Guedalla, p. 97.

continent from European control has been a leading feature of American history in the past century.[5]

Bazaine sailed from Cherbourg aboard the 100-gun ship of the line *St Louis*, which had been converted to its new role as a troop transport. With him went a number of key members of his staff, which already included a number of trusted colleagues such as Commandant Boyer, and Captains Willette and Blanchot, who remained with him thereafter through thick and thin. His division consisted of eight infantry regiments, organised into brigades under generals Castagny and Neigre, together with two batteries. Bazaine arrived at Vera Cruz in the middle of September 1862 and was soon in action. Carrying out the kind of sweep with which he was very familiar from his time in Algeria, Bazaine was riding with his advanced guard, when it ran into an ambush, and a member of his staff was killed. Next day, however, a large number of mounted Mexicans were scattered by a fraction of their number, and Bazaine went on to capture an elderly fort.

Meanwhile Puebla still stood in the way of an advance on Mexico City. Although Forey had more than four times as many men as Lorencez had had, he proceeded with great caution. It was not until March 1863 that he felt able to advance to the investment of Puebla. Bazaine covered the south, and Douay the north. The Mexicans had put Forey's delay to good use. The defences of Puebla had been greatly strengthened. A garrison of 18,000 men now held the forts and 80 churches with 175 guns. Outside Puebla, an army of relief, under Comonfort, seized every opportunity to reprovision the city, which was already well provided.

Forey began by moving on Fort Penitencier, to the west of the city, but this was too far out to be effective, and Bazaine advised that Fort Carmen should be the objective. Nevertheless the attack on Fort Penitencier went ahead on March 30; after an hour of artillery preparation, Bazaine sent in four battalions. Blanchot later described Bazaine during the operation as, with a cigar between his lips, close up in the most dangerous points of the attack to inspire his troops, he displayed calm courage and coolness under fire, restraining the impatient and reassuring the timid.[6] The attacks on Fort Penitencier failed; at a council of war, Forey lost his nerve completely, complaining of inadequate resources, and saying: 'I won't accept the responsibility. You can try again if you want.' In Bazaine's view it was necessary to restore morale by winning a victory, and he proposed an attack on the army of Comonfort, which he believed to be in the neighbourhood of San Lorenzo, seven kilometres north-west of Puebla. Forey was unenthusiastic, but finally consented, and Bazaine set off with four battalions, four squadrons and two batteries. Launching a surprise attack, he won a decisive victory; Comonfort retreated, leaving 1,200 dead. French casualties were minimal, with 30 dead and 120 wounded.

---

5   Quoted Haslip, p. 175.
6   Ruby & Regnault, pp. 40-41.

The effect of the battle of San Lorenzo was to demoralise the garrison of Puebla to the point where it capitulated without the need for a final assault. Forey and even Douay acknowledged Bazaine's success, which had greatly enhanced his reputation, not least with Napoleon. Forey congratulated him on the way he had inspired his troops: *son coup d'oeil, son sang froid et sa bravoure entrainante.* General du Barail wrote of Bazaine at this time:

> By day and by night, in the trenches or in camp, he could be seen constantly circulating, without ceremony, without fuss and without an escort, his cane in his hand, good-naturedly chatting with everyone and exchanging pleasantries with the troops, listening, and explaining what was going on, in this way skilfully tending to supplant his chief.[7]

Back in Paris Forey's detractors were quick to assign all the credit for the success at Puebla to Bazaine. Prominent among these was Hidalgo, who wrote scathingly:

> Forey was a bungling fool whose dilatory tactics made a laughing stock of the French army ... In bypassing Puebla, he might have spared hundreds of lives and reached Mexico City three months earlier... The situation had only been saved by Achille Bazaine, who in a brilliant action foiled an attempt to cut off the French army in the rear.[8]

Hidalgo claimed that a number of influential men around Napoleon were working to undermine Forey, including, as he suggested, the Duc de Morny: 'If Forey is created a marshal, things will be much better for us, for then he will return to Paris, and we may succeed in having Bazaine at the head of the army.'[9]

Forey put Bazaine in command of the advance column which marched into Mexico City on June 7, where it was greeted with wild enthusiasm. Forey followed three days later and established his headquarters in the magnificent palace of Buona Vista, which belonged to a rich dissident family. He was not, though, long to remain in supreme command; consoled by the award of his marshal's baton, he was recalled to Paris, and handed over command to Bazaine, who was thus presented with what has been described as 'a Herculean labour.'

> He was now called upon not only to pacify a country three times the size of France, but also to create an Empire, all in the course of a few months, and then to hand it over to a completely inexperienced prince who would arrive from Europe full of preconceived notions and ideas ... Bazaine was full of confidence

7   Ruby & Regnault, p. 43.
8   Quoted Haslip, p. 177.
9   Quoted Haslip, p. 177.

– he was ruthless, energetic and courageous – but he lacked both character and integrity, and instead of regenerating the country he ended in succumbing to the Mexican way of life.[10]

This is a harsh judgment, but for what it is worth it should be kept in mind when considering the later events of Bazaine's career.

From August 1863 until June 1864, when Maximilian arrived in Mexico, Bazaine enjoyed power which was limited only by Imperial instructions, which were wide but lacking in precision. For the moment, the immediate task was to oversee the convening of a hand-picked National Assembly, which obediently proclaimed the establishment of a monarchy. A deputation was sent to Europe to make a formal offer of the throne to Maximilian, while Bazaine settled down to the task of creating the conditions necessary for the security of the new Imperial regime.

The immediate military task was to widen the area under French control, which for the moment covered only the Veracruz-Puebla-Mexico City axis. The pacification of the country was a huge task, given the limited resources available to him, but Bazaine proceeded to undertake it energetically, considerably assisted by his fluent grasp of the Spanish language. He pushed forward a number of columns, composed of both French and Mexican forces, towards the north, and through the huge central plateau. He saw it as important to make use of Mexican regular soldiers to show the national flag. In six weeks these operations were astonishingly successful. President Juarez and what remained of his government retreated to the north to San Luis Potosí and then a further 250 miles to Monterey, from where he sent his family into safe exile in the United States. The commanders of the Juarista forces were scattered in different directions; Doblado was with the president in the far north, Comonfort had been killed and his army dispersed; Porfirio Diaz maintained a position in the extreme south. It was the size of the country rather than the strength of the enemy which Bazaine had to overcome; he now had at his disposal a total of 40,000 French troops and 13,000 Mexicans, while Juarez had a total of no more than 20,000 men.[11]

Ruby & Regnault examined Bazaine's mode of life in Mexico. He had followed Forey in basing himself in the Palace of Buona Vista:

> He lived there simply but generously, with a welcoming table. He did not econo-
> mise there. It would be possible to criticise him for being too modest in the
> outward signs of his command. It was only with difficulty that his staff prevailed
> on him to accept a troop of Spahis as an escort, in a country where pomp was
> regarded as a necessity.[12]

---

10   Haslip, p. 187.
11   Montgomery Hyde, H., *Mexican Empire* (London, 1946), p. 124.
12   Ruby & Regnault, p. 45.

In Austria, Maximilian had been hesitating over whether to accept the crown. News of Bazaine's victories in the latter part of 1863 came as a relief, but there were certainly times when his determination wavered. Charlotte, however, remained convinced that he should accept. When news came of the dispatch of the Mexican delegation, he travelled to Vienna to discuss the position with Franz Joseph; apart from his reservations about the wisdom of accepting the offer of the throne, the Emperor was determined that Austria should not be involved in the project, for instance by providing a guarantee for the proposed Mexican government loan. In March 1864 Maximilian and Charlotte travelled to Paris, to meet with Napoleon, who was determined that the offer of the throne should be accepted, and they were welcomed there with much pageantry. An agreement was reached, known as the Convention of Miramar, regulating the future relationship between France and Mexico. After that, the couple went on to England where they were personally made welcome, though without being given any encouragement for the project. Later, with the Archduke still racked by doubts, they returned to their palace at Miramar, where on April 9 Maximilian and Franz Joseph finally agreed the family arrangements. Next day the Mexican delegation arrived, and Maximilian formally accepted the offer of the throne, and swore to devote himself to the 'freedom, prosperity and greatness of Mexico.'[13] Aboard the Austrian frigate *Novara*, the Imperial party made their way across the Atlantic, arriving at Vera Cruz on May 28. On June 12 they made their state entry into the capital, riding in the Imperial coach, with Bazaine riding at their side, amid scenes of great enthusiasm. It was a day which seemed to justify the most optimistic hopes.

In the months before Maximilian's arrival, Bazaine had shown himself well able to tackle the complex tasks which, as the emperor's viceroy, fell to him. He continued to enjoy military success, applying the tactics which he had learned so well in Algeria:

> Swift, effective, and involving strikingly few casualties, Bazaine's operations wholly justified his method. The well-planned advance of his converging and diverging columns swept the vast country like a dragnet; the Republicans were herded away from market towns and driven out into the wilderness or up into the hills, where they could be hunted down at leisure; and behind his swift moving lines the central provinces of Mexico were cleared and ready to receive the new regime ... The unbroken success of his campaign, coming after the mixed fortunes of his two predecessors before Puebla, showed him to be a brilliant practitioner of the class of warfare that was required in Mexico.[14]

At the same time, while acting as Viceroy, he had been showing a considerable grasp of political realities and the diplomacy necessary to manage the country and its political leaders:

13   Haslip, p. 216.
14   Guedalla, pp. 110-111.

His reign as viceroy of Mexico lasted eight months; and it was a remarkable achievement for an ex-sergeant of the Foreign Legion ... He had few illusions about Mexico, deploring the inertia to which each applicant for public office happily succumbed after obtaining it, no less than the unworthy appetites of certain leaders. But, given wise leadership, he did not despair of the country's future.[15]

By early 1864 Bazaine's personal life had been thrown into disarray when he received the crushing news of his wife's death. This had come about in circumstances which led to scandalous gossip to the effect that she had committed suicide when the wife of an actor with whom she had had a torrid affair found, and sent to Bazaine, a packet of her letters. The story went that she had gone to Napoleon to try to prevent their passage to Mexico and that, failing in this, she took her own life, and that the packet did arrive at headquarters, but was burnt by his loyal staff without Bazaine being aware of it. There was no truth at all in the story, but this sort of thing was grist to the mill of Bazaine's enemies, determined to humiliate him. After looking at the evidence in detail, Ruby & Regnault were able to demonstrate conclusively that it had no foundation whatever. Marie Bazaine had in fact died of pleurisy on October 14 after a short illness. Commenting on the work of one hostile writer, they observed: 'as many words, as many errors. These lines illustrate the worst of the frenzy at the time of the trial in the 'literature' in all its forms.'[16]

An American visitor to the Imperial court took note of Bazaine and described him at this time in the account which she gave of Maximilian's rule:

> A plain -looking man, short and thickset, whose plebeian features one might search in vain for a spark of genius or a ray of imagination, and yet under the commonplace exterior dwelt a kindly spirit and intelligence of no mean order.[17]

Bazaine received his due reward on October 7 with the receipt of a marshal's baton: 'How good the Emperor is!' he exclaimed when he heard the news. This distinction, on which none of his colleagues in France congratulated him, was something to console him for the loss of his wife. By then, unfortunately, Bazaine was obliged in his reports to Napoleon to express his disquiet at the lack of progress in establishing the new Imperial regime. In one such pessimistic report he complained of the absence of any decisions on the great questions which divided the country:

> Confidence is only established under the influence of French bayonets, by which safety is ensured, and under the authority of French commanders, by whom

---

15   Guedalla, p. 114.
16   Ruby & Regnault, p. 51.
17   Sara Yorke Stevenson, *Maximilian in Mexico* (New York, 1897) quoted in Hyde, p. 160.

public and private interests are protected. But it is impossible to leave garrisons everywhere; and I do my best to convince everybody that, when a country desires to save itself, it must help itself and make its own contribution to the work of regeneration.[18]

Outwardly, Bazaine and Maximilian maintained a cordial relationship; the Emperor warmly congratulated Bazaine on his being made a marshal. However, their mutual confidence was not improved when, in response to orders from Paris, Bazaine repatriated general Felix Douay as well as part of the troops under his command. Since Douay was very much at loggerheads with him, and had ambitions to become commander-in-chief himself, Bazaine was not sorry to see go. His absence, however, proved to be only temporary; within a short time Douay succeeded in getting the War Ministry to post him back to Mexico.

Meanwhile, notwithstanding his personal tragedy, Bazaine continue to discharge his responsibilities with impressive efficiency. At the beginning of 1865 he took personal command of the operations against Porfirio Diaz in the south of the country. With a force of some 5,500 men, he surrounded the important fortress of Oaxaca, and swiftly captured it with minimal loss, taking some 8,000 prisoners and 60 guns. Bazaine returned in triumph to Mexico City where he had by now other reasons to be cheerful. He was courting the 17-year-old dark-haired beauty Maria Josefa de la Pena y Barragan y Azcarate (known as Pepita), and on June 26, 1865 they were married in the presence of Maximilian and Charlotte, whose wedding gift to the couple was the Buona Vista Palace, the understanding being that if and when they left Mexico and returned the property to the state, they would be given in compensation a sum of 100,000 piastres.

However, with the final defeat of the Confederacy in the Spring of 1865, Maximilian's prospects were already in serious decline. The United States had never recognised the Empire, and Juarez was now bound to receive more support. As the year went on, this proved to be the case, and the activities of the Republican army became more lively, boosted by the regular supply of arms across the Rio Grande. It had been apparent for a considerable time to Napoleon III that his Mexican adventure was running into troubled waters, and with each day that passed it became clearer that the intervention was going to end badly. By September 1865 he was hopefully urging Maximilian to make use of his limited resources, as a precursor to withdrawing enough of his own troops to respond to complaints from the United States. To Maximilian, he wrote of 'the advantage it would be to everybody if your Majesty were to use your Austrian troops for the organisation of a proper army. In this way I would be able to withdraw the greater part of my troops which would remove all pretext for America's complaints.'[19]

18   Guedalla, p. 122.
19   Quoted Haslip, p. 330.

By now Maximilian had begun to dislike and distrust Bazaine, accusing him in a letter to Napoleon of carrying out a policy 'so sinister that people are beginning to say that the object is to prove the incapacity of the Mexican government.' He went on to comment on the rumour that Napoleon was about to announce the withdrawal of the French army:

> For some time past, the European press has been hinting that your Majesty is contemplating a public announcement to the effect that, in a short time, you will be withdrawing your troops from Mexico... I feel bound to tell your Majesty that such a declaration would undo in a day all the work painfully accomplished in the past few years, and that the announcement of such a measure, combined with the refusal of the United States to recognise my government, would be enough to cause the collapse of all respectable peoples' hopes and destroy all public confidence in the future. [20]

Although still outwardly cordial, the relationship between Bazaine and Maximilian was continuing to deteriorate. Bazaine wrote to Randon that Maximilian was 'more Mexican than the Mexicans, more Juarist than Juarez ...no one has any confidence in his political skills nor in his character, which is that of a German dreamer ... If one is not yet willing to pronounce the word disloyalty, it is necessary to recognise that we are reduced to a ridiculous role, that of the useless adviser.'[21]

As the war went on, it became increasingly vicious. In October Maximilian gave orders that all captured Mexican guerillas were to be shot. Historians have generally accepted that this was largely at Bazaine's instigation, and this would certainly not be inconsistent with his reputation for ruthlessness. One reason for the order was the not inconsiderable number of deserters from the Foreign Legion units; many of these made their way north across the Rio Grande into Texas, but others took up arms against their former comrades. There was a financial inducement for this, as Randon noted in a letter to Bazaine: 'What is very clear is that the profession of guerilla is one of the most lucrative in Mexico, and that the leaders of bands are never bothered about finding soldiers and money – two elements of a war in which the Mexican government is in default.'[22]

Bazaine was by now obliged to evacuate parts of Mexico on the periphery of the territory which he controlled, in order to keep the bulk of his forces concentrated, a policy which Randon approved, reporting to Napoleon his satisfaction with the way Bazaine was conducting operations, as well as the clarity of his political observations. Maximilian's mistrust of Bazaine, however, was entirely justified, although the Marshal's conduct was solely in accordance with Napoleon's orders, which obliged

20   Quoted Haslip, pp. 331-332.
21   Quoted Ruby & Regnault, p 55
22   Quoted Porch, p. 159.

him to resort to extreme duplicity, as a letter which he wrote to the Emperor on January 19, 1866 shows:

> So soon as the troops have received all the reinforcements from France and are so far organised as to be able to undertake a fresh campaign, it is my intention to dispatch them in every direction in the Empire at once, and your Majesty will then see that it is not the military situation in Mexico which ought to cause the greatest anxiety.[23]

In fact, Bazaine's master in Paris had already taken the crucial decision to pull out his troops; in the hands of a Baron Saillard, letters announcing this respectively to Maximilian and to Bazaine were already on their way across the Atlantic.

The order for the withdrawal of the French army meant that Bazaine must supervise its evacuation, which was not going to be an easy task to carry out safely. His proposal was that the troops should leave in three stages, in November 1866, March 1867 and December 1867. At the same time the Legion, which was to remain behind, was to be reorganised and as far as possible so must be the Mexican army. The ability of the Legion adequately to hold the position after the rest of the French had left was extremely doubtful; General Brincourt, offered the command, declined it on the basis that it would not be possible to achieve with 15,000 men a task which had been beyond 38,000.[24]

Bazaine had a clear-sighted view of the possibility that Maximilian, full of bitterness at Napoleon's betrayal, might attempt to do a deal with the Republicans before the French army got away, as Joan Haslip noted:

> The Marshal, who was far more cynical and ruthless than his master, believed it to be more in the interests of France to continue to cooperate with Maximilian and maintain him in power until the embarkation of the French troops. If chaos followed, that would no longer be the concern of France. This was tough, cynical advice, but Napoleon was not sufficiently cynical to accept it.[25]

It was illustrative of the enmity which Bazaine aroused that it was suggested that his wish to avoid Maximilian's abdication was prompted by a desire to make sure of the promised gift to be made on the return of the Buona Vista Palace to the state when he left Mexico; but there is no evidence at all that this was so, and in fact he did not receive a penny.

One of his bitterest enemies was Felix Douay, whose letters to his brother Abel Douay contributed substantially to the rumours that Bazaine had personally enriched

---

23   Quoted Hyde, p. 183
24   Ruby & Regnault, p. 59.
25   Haslip, pp. 407-408.

himself during his time in Mexico. Douay wrote that it was 'difficult to imagine a person so completely deceitful. It was his sole preoccupation to enrich himself amid our disasters. He sacrificed the country's honour and the safety of her troops to ignoble jiggery-pokery.'[26] There was no justification for this; his financial management was examined by the competent authorities, and Prime Minister Emile Ollivier expressly confirmed his integrity. Ruby & Regnault also rely upon a comment made whilst in captivity during the Franco-Prussian War by the upright and straightforward General Castelnau, who had been sent by Napoleon to Mexico to report on the situation there, with particular reference to Bazaine and his conduct, and who had secret instructions to hasten the evacuation: 'As to his integrity we find an unexpected confirmation from the mouth of Castelnau. In the course of a conversation which he had with General von Monts, the governor of Cassel, the general stated forcefully that Bazaine, while in Mexico, had done nothing of any kind to impugn his honour.'[27]

A desperate visit to Europe by the Empress Charlotte failed to obtain from Napoleon any commitment to honour his promises of support. Maximilian was obviously and effectively doomed; Bazaine said of the future of the Mexican Empire that it was *une agonie dans l'impossible.* He had been authorised to return to France in advance of the last contingent of his troops to leave Mexico, but he chose to remain while the evacuation proceeded. It was skilfully conducted; 28,000 men left Vera Cruz in a period of eight weeks and Bazaine left with the last convoy.

As he rode out of Mexico City on February 5 1867, Maximilian watched the Marshal go with a sense of relief, remarking to an aide: 'At last we are free.' In his heart, though, he must have known that his adventure was about to end and that it would end badly. Meanwhile as he made his way to Vera Cruz, Bazaine learned of a disaster to a Mexican force at San Jacinto. This prompted him to send a message to the French minister in Mexico to the effect that there was still time to save the Emperor, and he would wait for a week. It arrived too late; Maximilian had left the capital to take personal command of his troops at Queretaro, north-west of Mexico City. There after a siege of 72 days he was betrayed, and captured by the Juarista army on May 15; and there, after a brief show trial conducted on the orders of President Juarez he was convicted and executed by firing squad.

Bazaine left Mexico with an equivocal reputation. His conduct was both then, and subsequently after the conclusion of the Franco-Prussian War, examined in detail. Not many of those that did so displayed much impartiality. Overall, the suggestion that Bazaine was loyal neither to Napoleon or Maximilian, but only to his own interests, as many alleged, will not stand up. He earned the distrust of Maximilian because he faithfully executed Napoleon's instructions; and his ultimate military failure, inevitable in the face of the active support of Juarez by the United States, was hastened by his inability to establish an effective native army.

26   Quoted Ruby & Regnault, p. 74.
27   Ruby & Regnault, p. 75.

The two key questions which summarised the charges laid by historians against Bazaine were first, that he had sought personal power in Mexico, whether as viceroy or as a kind of dictator, and second that he had tried to prevent Maximilian's abdication. Ruby & Regnault analysed these in detail; their judgements were conclusive:'The answer to the first question is thus simple: Bazaine never sought power; his inclinations, his good sense and his instructions prevented it.' As to the second question, they took note of the letters and reports written by Bazaine on the subject of preventing or delaying Maximilian's abdication. They point out that he had both the right and the duty to express his personal opinions in these: 'Bazaine did not press absolutely for the abdication until he saw the Empire entering into its impossible agony and his army was safely concentrated. A selfish view, one may say? It was he and no one else who would carry the responsibility for a total defeat.'[28]

28   Ruby & Regnault, pp. 68-71.

3

Last Happy Years

When Bazaine returned to France, it was not to receive a hero's welcome. Arriving on May 6 at Toulon, he was informed by the Maritime Prefect that orders had been received from the government that he was to receive no special military honours. A similar instruction had been given in 1856, when Pelissier returned from the Crimea. In each case Napoleon III's feelings about the returning soldier were somewhat equivocal; there was a difference, though, in that Pelissier was then rewarded with a marshal's baton and a dukedom, so that the popular opinion in Bazaine's case that this was a slight that was a manifestation of Napoleon's discontent was understandable if unjustified, and the opposition made much of it. The reason for Napoleon's decision is obscure. It might have been that the Emperor was influenced by the reports from Mexico from Castelnau and the vitriolic correspondence of Felix Douay; on the other hand, it was perhaps simply a prudent political move in the light of the failure of the Mexican intervention. Either way, it was 'an act of injustice to a man who had borne without weakening the heaviest of responsibilities, and to the troops who had carried out their duty.'[1]

At any rate, opposition leaders, for whom Bazaine was already something of a hero, complained that he was a 'victim of imperial ostracism,' arguing that Bazaine had personally done well in Mexico, and that it was the Empire that was wholly to blame for the disaster:

> A Republican named de Kératry, who had served on his staff in Mexico, published abroad (out of reach of the French censorship) a damaging account of the whole episode, which vindicated Bazaine and opened with a glowing tribute from the most brilliant pen among the Liberals to 'a tried servant whose strong hand and calm resolution may shortly render France great service.'[2]

1   Ruby & Regnault, p.77.
2   Guedalla, p.146.

The Orleanist leader Louis Adolphe Thiers asked Lieutenant Massa, an artillery officer who had also served on Bazaine's staff, to speak to the Marshal and ask him for access to documents which would enable him to speak in his defence. In this way, justice might be publicly done to Bazaine's conduct while in Mexico. This approach was rebuffed, Bazaine saying that for him to do so would be to commit an act of indiscipline against Marshal Niel, the recently appointed War Minister. Massa recorded in his memoirs that this refusal deeply impressed Thiers, who commented: 'Voila un vrai militaire.' Thereafter Thiers almost invariably described the Marshal as 'notre glorieux Bazaine.'[3]

Emperor Napoleon III. (Scheibert)

There now began for Bazaine what have been described as his 'last happy years' as he settled down with Pepita in Paris, taking a lengthy and well earned period of leave. Although the Emperor had denied him express public approval by the refusal of special military honours, Napoleon received him warmly both at St Cloud and Compiègne. Bazaine duly took his seat in the Senate, at which ceremony he was formally supported by Marshal Randon and General Mellinet. Then, in the winter of 1867 he was appointed to the command of the 3rd Corps, with his headquarters at Nancy; once again he succeeded to a post previously held by Forey. This was arguably the most important of the six major commands in metropolitan France, covering Alsace and Lorraine. It gave him the opportunity thoroughly to familiarise himself with the region which would be the key theatre if war should break out, in which event he had been designated as commander of the Army of Lorraine. With General August-Alexandre Ducrot, at that time in command of the 6th Military Division based at Strasbourg, Bazaine carried out a lengthy examination of the terrain on horseback. He also inspected the fortresses intended to protect the frontier, and found them to have been badly neglected, as well as being inadequately armed.

Bazaine soon discovered, however, that the reports which he painstakingly compiled for the War Minister did not receive much attention. Many years after the war, reviewing the time he spent in command of the 3rd Corps, he quoted from a letter which he wrote to the War Minister on January 25, 1868:

3   Ruby & Regnault, p.147.

There does not exist at the headquarters of the 3rd Corps any map which provides exact information about the fortification of the various places within my command, and of the terrain around them ... I consider these documents to be indispensable, and urgently needed.[4]

This brought forth no reply.

Nor did he and Ducrot find the entrenched camp at Metz, on which work had begun in 1865, to be in anything like a satisfactory state. It had been created by the army's all powerful engineering committee; the location chosen, however, did not command any invasion route, and both Bazaine and Ducrot would have very much preferred it to have been located between the Meurthe and the Moselle, around Toul, Frouard and the Forest of Haye, where it would cover the Paris-Nancy-Strasbourg axis. But the work was well under way, and there was nothing much that Bazaine could do about it, even to modify some of the most serious deficiencies which he found in the forts under construction.[5] Those to the west of the city, Plappeville and St Quentin, did possess some defensive qualities, but Forts St Julien and Queuleu, on the right bank of the Moselle, were useless. Bazaine's suggestion was that the construction of St Julien should be abandoned, and a new work begun further to the east, at St Barbe. For Queuleu, he suggested substituting a new fort in the valley of the Seille.

In July 1868 Bazaine visited Napoleon at Plombières, spending several days with him. This gave him the opportunity to make known to the Emperor his grave concerns about the poor condition of the eastern fortresses. Napoleon listened with careful attention, noting and accepting Bazaine's views, but to no actual effect. While there, Bazaine was also able to expound his own ideas about the future development of the army, particularly in the light of the stunning Prussian victory at Königgrätz. As with many military leaders of the time, he had become imbued with the conviction that defensive tactics were now superior. This was borne out by his own experiences under fire at Melegnano, Solferino and Puebla, coupled with the crushing effectiveness of the needle gun in 1866.

Bazaine was not part of the inner circle advising Napoleon on military affairs, but he kept himself well informed as to the current state of French military thinking, and was given by Napoleon the opportunity to review the plan of campaign, in the event of war with Prussia, that had been devised by General Charles Frossard. He was very much part of the inner circle, having been chosen as the military tutor for the Prince Imperial. Born in 1807, he had joined the army at the age of 20, and enrolled in the engineers. After service in the Crimea he reached the rank of *general de brigade*, and in 1859, by now a *général de division*, he served as Chief of Engineers in the Army of Italy. His plan reflected his engineering background, and was purely defensive in

---

4   Marshal F-A Bazaine, *Épisodes de la Guerre de 1870 et le Blocus de Metz* (Madrid 1883), p.10.
5   Ruby & Regnault, pp.79-80.

character. His assumption was that a German invasion with some 470,000 men would be directed towards the Moselle Valley and Alsace, but that the French army would be able to resist the advance by taking up a series of *positions magnifiques* which he had identified.[6]

When Bazaine considered Frossard's plan, he did so with a certain diffidence born of a slight inferiority complex when in the presence of military intellectuals, even though these had certainly had nothing like his battle experience.

Nonetheless, Bazaine's annotations, in the margin of Frossard's report, showed his good sense and insight. Coming upon the optimistic remark: 'In the present situation, where the invading army will not be superior in number, and where, after a series of major defeats, we would be opposed by

Marshal Achille Bazaine, commander of the Army of the Rhine. (Bibliothèque nationale)

fresh levies lacking in substance,' Bazaine noted: 'What an illusion!'[7]

At Nancy, Bazaine and his family were installed in a fine house in the centre of the city. Pepita soon established herself in the very conservative provincial society that she entered as an exotic newcomer. The couple were depicted by the lively pen of the young Countess de Martel, on a visit to her grandparents. She described Pepita: 'An admirable skin, of dark complexion with large eyes and incredible eyelashes, charming, gracious, sometimes kind, but somewhat childlike.' She was less complimentary about Bazaine, finding him 'ugly, stout, common and small, but intelligent and sympathetic.' The countess also noted that Pepita was 'ferociously jealous of this husband who was 37 years her senior.'[8]

The subsequent events of the Franco-Prussian war were to lead, inevitably, to the retelling, and embroidery, of countless anecdotes about Bazaine, practically all of which were intended to show him in the worst possible light. One such, for instance, concerned a conversation with a young staff captain who was accompanying Bazaine on one of his trips around the territory, when he was said to have pointed to a small wood, and remarked: 'There, I would put a company of sharpshooters.' The story, like

6   Michael Howard, *The Franco-Prussian War* (London 1961), p.45.
7   Ruby & Regnault, p.82.
8   Ruby & Regnault, pp.82-83.

many others, may well be apocryphal, but it was eagerly circulated, presumably to demonstrate Bazaine's smallmindedness.

During his time at Nancy Bazaine was well able to form an opinion about the shortcomings of the French army, and in particular the way in which it was currently organised, but his influence, even with the Emperor, was limited. Long after the war he spelled out his fundamental view:

> The administration of war in France resembles a superb machine in respect of which all the working parts are kept in separate workshops. When it is proposed to start it up, the task is long and difficult, for it is necessary to collect all the cog wheels and fit them together, or, in a word, to rebuild the machine from the simplest nut to the most complicated piece. Nevertheless, with us, the whole organisation does finally get there, but it has only been by zealous efforts and a great waste of time, so that it arrives too late. There is the whole problem.[9]

Bazaine did, though, enjoy a good relationship with Niel, with whom he maintained a regular correspondence. In July 1869 Bazaine was put in overall command of the annual manoeuvres at the camp of Châlons, and in making his final report highlighted a number of serious deficiencies in the way in which the troops were handled. He was particularly critical of the cavalry, calling for a root and branch reform of the way in which it was employed. He argued that it must be much more mobile, and more focused on the gathering of intelligence by active reconnaissance. Niel approved, writing to Bazaine on July 28:

> I have received the report you sent me, at the end of the first phase of the annual camp at Châlons, on the distribution of the cavalry between army corps and divisions. I have read this with the most careful attention; I share all your ideas and I consider that this work is destined to exercise a most fortunate influence on the spirit of our officers of both infantry and cavalry. I thank you and will hasten to put it before the Emperor.[10]

At the conclusion of the Châlons manoeuvres there was a disagreeable incident, of which an eyewitness account was given by the then Lieutenant Devaureix in his recollections of the war of 1870, published in 1909. Bazaine, he wrote, was anxious to efface the 'semi-disgrace' that he had endured on his return from Mexico, and he hoped that a reception for the officers present at Châlons would achieve this. However, many of them did not attend, and those that did were not forthcoming. Many had drunk far too much, and the reception ended in uproar amid breaking glass and overturned tables. Bazaine was obliged to leave without having been able to express his thanks to

9   Bazaine, *Episodes*, p.xxii.
10   Bazaine, *Episodes*, p.xxxii.

those that had participated in the manoeuvres. This rowdy behaviour was in complete contrast to the rather sycophantic sentiments expressed at the same function by General Feray:

> The Army Corps about to leave Châlons will remember for a long time your command, so skilful, so energetic and so watchful for all... Attached unreservedly to the Emperor and his dynasty, we will all be happy, M le Maréchal, to march under your orders whenever his Majesty calls upon our courage and devotion.[11]

After two years in command at Nancy, Bazaine returned to Paris. 1869 brought with it personal tragedy, with the death of his son Max; but Pepita gave birth that year to a third child, Eugénie, the godchild of the Emperor and Empress. A further indication of the regard in which he was held by Napoleon came with Bazaine's appointment to the command of the Imperial Guard. The Emperor wrote a particularly gracious letter to the Marshal on October 15 in response to Bazaine's application for the appointment, saying that it had arrived at the moment when he was about to write to offer him the command. Napoleon concluded his letter with a warm appreciation of Bazaine's past services and those to come.[12] If Napoleon had felt any reserve towards Bazaine on his return from Mexico, this appointment, and the terms in which it was expressed, demonstrated his complete confidence in him, and was an important statement in the light of doubts that had been raised about his loyalty and his contacts with members of the opposition. Ruby & Regnault remarked: 'It seems that the Marshal kept his distance from politics, and led a very simple life. According to the unpublished memoirs of General de Montarby, his spare time was devoted to the study of the art of war 'with high intelligence, in the right spirit and with sound judgement.'[13]

Thus it was that Bazaine was in command of the Imperial Guard, when in July 1870 the wholly unexpected crisis of the Hohenzollern candidature for the throne of Spain erupted. The subsequent withdrawal of Prince Leopold as a candidate seemed for a moment to have brought the fire under control; but it would burst out again with the absurd act of bravado on the part of the Duc de Gramont in sending Ambassador Benedetti to tackle King William at Ems, to demand an assurance that the candidature would not be revived. Within days of his apparent rebuff, the French would declare war, and her army would then be put to the severest test imaginable.

In order to make a balanced assessment of the events of 1870 it is worth considering Bazaine's reputation and the way in which he was actually perceived before the war. The accounts given of Bazaine written afterwards were in most cases tainted by extreme bias; the evidence of those written before, on the other hand, can more

---

11   Quoted Ruby & Regnault, p.81.
12   Bazaine, *Episodes*, p.xxxiii.
13   Ruby & Regnault, p.83.

readily be accepted as dispassionate. Among those whose testimony is useful is that of General Francois du Barail, who wrote that behind his external bonhomie Bazaine concealed a mind that was 'very astute, and very subtle, too subtle perhaps.' This opinion, which was written when both men were in Mexico, is confirmed both by Trochu and by General Zurlinden, a subsequent War Minister. Emile Ollivier, who in fact did not know Bazaine well before 1870, was rather less flattering; he found the Marshal to be lacking in élan, 'valiant but not heroic,' adding that although able to turn a blind eye to trivial misdemeanours, Bazaine was 'incapable of involving himself in serious wickedness.'[14] The testimony of Colonel Blanchot, who spent many years close to Bazaine, is also useful. He was capable of criticising the Marshal on occasion, but 'retained for him in adversity the same respect which he had felt in happier times,' describing him as 'charming and captivating,' a view shared by Massa, another of his aides.[15]

Historians have devoted a good deal of attention to Bazaine's personal appearance. Michael Howard noted that 'one must try to overlook, as did his contemporaries, his remarkably unprepossessing appearance; the tiny malevolent eyes set in a suety, undistinguished face, the heavy bulldog jaw, the stout flabby body sagging inelegantly on horseback in such marked contrast to the cavaliers with whom he was surrounded.'[16] An entirely dispassionate view of Bazaine in wartime comes from an opponent; Lieutenant von Dieskau, sent by Prince Frederick Charles into Metz under a flag of truce in September 1870, reported on his meeting with the Marshal: 'He is a small man, a little corpulent, who appears to be over 60 years of age, balding, with grey hair cut short. His moustache and beard are black, his eyes black and lively, and his manner is mild, with a benevolent outward appearance.'[17]

Some commentators writing after 1870 saw Bazaine as having retained some of the characteristics derived from his time in the *Bureau Arabe*, such as scepticism, love of intrigue and duplicity. Among those who charged him with duplicity was one of his subordinates in Mexico, Intendant-General Wolf, who observed that he had to be always on his guard against this, quoting Bazaine as having said on one occasion: 'Ah! If you believe everything I say, you've heard nothing yet!' Ruby & Regnault drily observed that Wolf was evidently lacking a sense of humour.[18]

As for Bazaine's military reputation, it has been seen how highly he was regarded by Thiers, and other opposition leaders. Emile Ollivier praised his time as commander-in-chief in Mexico, where he could have done no more with the limited forces at his disposal, adding that his conduct of the retreat 'so orderly, so methodical, will remain as a model in military history.' On the other hand Ollivier suggested that Bazaine was not close to his men, a suggestion at odds with many observers of his conduct in

---

14   Ruby & Regnault, p.84.
15   Ruby & Regnault, p.85.
16   Howard, pp.134-135.
17   Ruby & Regnault, p.85.
18   Ruby & Regnault, p.86.

the Crimea, Italy and Mexico, including du Barail. In this, Ollivier may have been influenced by the ever hostile Felix Douay. All the evidence points the other way; the future General Zédé wrote of Bazaine: 'From the beginning to the end of the campaign he possessed the absolute confidence of the army … From the point of view of military competence, the Marshal seemed to me irreproachable; all his operations were crowned with success, even the last and most difficult, which was the army's retreat.'[19] Bazaine's performance both as a junior officer and higher commander in Algeria, Spain, the Crimea and Italy is more than enough to rebut the suggestion that he was not close to the men under his command. Ruby & Regnault conclude that 'without question Bazaine was a talented divisional general, indifferent to danger and an inspiring leader.' They do note, however, that 'without adopting the absurdities of Douay, one is obliged to recognise that after his marriage the mind of the commander-in-chief was not solely on his mission or on his glory.'

In Mexico, Bazaine's political conduct was determined by the fact that he was obliged to wear two hats, as a result of which his role was extremely ambiguous. On the one hand, as commander-in-chief of the French expeditionary force, he was answerable to Napoleon III; on the other, he was Maximilian's most senior military adviser. Much of the criticism which he faced in this latter capacity is unwarranted, bearing in mind that from the outset he was subject to the strictest instructions from Paris.

In his relationship with Napoleon, after setting aside the unproven allegations of his personal ambition, Bazaine does deserve some reproach. For a long time he failed to keep the Emperor as fully informed as he should of the impossibility of pacifying Mexico without an army of considerable size, and he did not contradict his master's ideas, even when judging them to be purely fanciful. Thus his military reports of 1864 and the first half of 1865 had conveyed a real sense of optimism, but by the end of 1865 this had disappeared completely. His political reports, on the other hand, had never expressed optimism at any time.

On the eve of war in 1870, therefore, Bazaine enjoyed, justifiably, a reputation that was generally high. In a preface to Count Kératry's book on the history of the Mexican intervention, the outspoken Orleanist journalist Lucien-Anatole Prévost-Paradol wrote: 'I congratulate my country on having found in the principal and last chief of this difficult war a trusted servant whose strong hand and calm assurance is destined soon to render great service to France.'[20]

Not, as it turned out, the most accurate of prophecies, but it reflected the fact that Bazaine was the military leader above all others in whom France reposed most confidence as she embarked on a war that would bring with it ruin to the Second Empire, and catastrophe to the nation. Thereafter, with the unwavering hindsight that accompanies all those who would rewrite history, that reputation would be utterly destroyed.

19   Ruby & Regnault, p.87.
20   Quoted Ruby & Regnault, p.91.

4

The French Army

The French army of 1867 to which Bazaine had returned was outwardly extremely impressive. Philip Guedalla graphically described the spectacular review which was staged at Longchamp in June that year to mark the Paris Exhibition. It was attended by Tsar Alexander II of Russia and King William of Prussia, who sat their horses either side of Napoleon III as 30,000 men went by at the salute:

> They saw the marching bearskins of the Guard behind a flaunting drum-major and the beards and axes of white aproned pioneers, the flaring red and blue of the Zouaves, trim shakoes of the Line, and green Chasseurs under the long bayonets, and little *vivandiéres* in their gay regimental petticoats; and then the mounted men came charging straight for the saluting base in an immense line that ran clear across the racecourse – big, burnished Cuirassiers, helmeted Dragoons, light cavalry of every shade in bright accoutrements and all kinds of headgear, furred, frogged, and braided, with sling-jackets and without, all thundering towards them, until the racing horses checked at a shouted order, and all the sabres lifted above the roar of 'Vive l'Empereur' in the June sunshine on a field ablaze with every colour.[1]

The impressive appearance of the French army, and its record of success on the battlefield, concealed grave shortcomings in organisation, training and equipment. Soldiers are inclined to be conservative, and resistant to change, and the French army was no exception to this. The need for reform was not readily perceived by most of its leaders, many of whom actively obstructed attempts to change the way things were. There was also a serious failure of attitude, as noted by General Guillaume Bonnal, who wrote that the army was dominated by 'an all-powerful school, made up of soldiers as fortunate as they were brave who loudly proclaimed their contempt for the military art.'[2]

---

1   Guedalla, p. 145.
2   Quoted Howard, pp. 17-18.

There were of course those who did recognise the compelling need for change, and foremost among them was the Emperor himself. He had always had the deepest interest in military affairs which he understood to be at the centre of his Bonapartist Empire. Even before the fearful jolt to French military opinion caused by Prussia's unexpected victory over Austria in 1866, he had been convinced of the need to adopt the principle of universal military service. The objectionable, even immoral, system that was in force in France was in stark contrast to that applied in Prussia which involved the population as a whole. Among those closest to Napoleon there were perceptive observers of the Prussian army, to whom the battle of Königgrätz was not such a surprise. One such was General Charles Bourbaki, who had been monitoring its development since Helmuth von Moltke had become its Chief of the General Staff. In 1864 he wrote: 'Be as rude as you like about this army of lawyers and oculists, but it will get to Vienna just as soon as it likes.'[3]

What had been made painfully clear was that the Prussian system of recruitment produced a potentially decisive numerical advantage. The problem for the French army was that in spite of the size of the country's population its actual intake was limited by the recruitment laws passed under the Bourbon and Orleanist monarchies. These, although theoretically based on the principle of universal military service, provided for those liable to be called up to be divided by lot into two portions. The first portion, the size of which was determined each year but was usually about 20,000 men, served for a term of seven years; the rest received no training at all until 1860, when the law was changed, and following which they were required to undergo six months basic training. Those who had drawn a *mauvais numéro*, however, were allowed to provide a substitute, and until 1855 individuals were free to find and pay someone to serve in their place. By then, public distaste for such a system had grown to the point at which it was clear that the process must be changed. A public fund was established, to which those who had drawn a *mauvais numéro* could contribute; from this fund, a soldier who chose at the end of his term of service to re-enlist was paid a bonus, and he served in place of the conscript. It was calculated by the historian Joseph Monteilhet that in 1870 the astonishing number of 200,000 soldiers were in fact substitutes. Although this system did provide an experienced and long serving body of men, it did not provide nearly enough of them. The standing army only rarely rose to a total of more than half a million men, and by 1870 it would consist of less than 370,000 men, with something under 175,000 reservists.[4]

The principle of universal military service was thus one which aroused strong political feeling. Adolphe Thiers had successfully led the opposition to the attempt made in 1848 to introduce it after the fall of the July Monarchy. He expressed in strong terms the feeling of the educated classes when he said: 'The society where everyone is a soldier is a barbaric society ... in a country where everyone is a soldier, everyone

---

3   Quoted Howard, p. 29.
4   Adriance, Thomas J., *The Last Gaiter Button* (Westport, Connecticut, 1987) pp 22-23

General Nicolas Changarnier, retired French general. (Private collection)

turns out badly ... without specialisation, the army cannot be.'[5] Napoleon's attempt in 1855 to reform the process of recruitment had not, as had been hoped, succeeded in increasing the size of the army. Military opinion still preferred the older system of informal replacement, and in any case there was a remarkable complacency about the numbers actually required. General Nicholas Changarnier was of the view that three or four corps of 60,000 men, well composed and well commanded, could make war successfully against far greater numbers:

Let us not therefore attempt to raise the number of our soldiers to that of our possible adversaries. Even at the risk of exhaustion, we should not be sure of accomplishing it. But there is no ground of uneasiness. If it is very difficult for 3,000 men to oppose 5,000 with success, it is much less difficult for 60,000 to beat 100,000. The more the proportion rises, the less is numerical superiority to be feared. It may be advantageously compensated by the skill of the general and by the superior character of the troops. Beyond a certain number there is no good army, and no army whose supplies can be secured and whose movements can be well directed.[6]

Chesney and Reeve, who quoted this passage from Changarnier in their book comparing the military resources of Prussia and France, also devoted careful attention to a paper published by a French economist, Pierre Andre Cochut. He had analysed the available statistics which showed what the actual human resources available to France amounted to, taking as his starting point the 530,000 male births recorded in the country in 1843. By 1864, only 325,000 of these were still living; of these, about a third, 109,000, were exempted from service by reason of physical defects. Another 57,000 men were excused service as being the sons of widows or old men, or only

5   Quoted Williams, Roger L., *Napoleon III and the Stoffel Affair* (Worland, Wyoming, 1993) p 13

6   Quoted Chesney, Colonel Charles & Reeve, Henry, *The Military Resources of Prussia and France* (London, 1870), pp. 139-140.

children, or from moral causes. This left only 159,000 as eligible, a number further reduced by the draft for maritime service and by those who broke down during basic training: 'The residue of men really fit to bear arms out of the whole number at the age of 20 in a given year is 132,000... Assuming the facts to be as he states, this result presents a frightful picture of humanity.'[7]

Chesney and Reeve went on to examine the practical consequences of this:

> In the two last wars of the Crimea and of Italy, France could only send to the field and maintain by reinforcements one army not much exceeding one fourth of her nominal effective strength. And from the enquiries we have made we have reason to believe (although the assertion will excite surprise and may perhaps be questioned), that in 1866 during the campaign of Sadowa, and again when the Luxembourg question was supposed to threaten war in 1867, the Emperor Napoleon could not immediately have sent above 150,000 men to the Rhine.[8]

The truth was that France could not have expanded the army substantially without adopting solutions which were unpalatable or politically unacceptable. These could theoretically have been a lowering of the minimum physical requirements; exemptions for family reasons could have been ended; or exemptions for those with *bon numéros* might have been abolished – which of course meant universal military service.[9]

Following Königgrätz, it was plain to Napoleon that the country faced a major crisis, and reforms must be urgently introduced. His first step was to take the important decision to send Major Eugene Stoffel to Berlin. Stoffel, born in 1821, was the son of a veteran of Waterloo, Colonel Baron Augustin Stoffel, formerly a Swiss officer, who took French citizenship. Eugene Stoffel entered the École Polytechnique at the age of 18, and in due course became an artillery officer, reaching the rank of captain in 1854. During the Italian campaign he was attached first to the staff of Marshal Randon, the War Minister, who was serving as *Major General*, or chief of staff, to Napoleon III, who took the field as commander-in-chief. Stoffel subsequently joined the staff of General Niel, the commander of the 4th Corps. During the course of the campaign he was noted as an outstandingly promising officer, but it was the scholarly work which he did in connection with Julius Caesar's conquest of Gaul which brought him to the Emperor's attention. Napoleon was working on a history of Julius Caesar, and he recruited Stoffel to assist him with his research. In 1862, by now officially described as ordnance officer to the Emperor, Stoffel was promoted to major, and he took charge of the excavations at Alise Ste Reine, the site of the battle of Alesia in 52 BC, where Caesar defeated Vercingetorix.[10]

7   Chesney & Reeve, pp. 144-145.
8   Chesney & Reeve, p. 149.
9   Williams, p. 14.
10   Williams, pp. 4-10.

Napoleon wasted no time in dispatching Stoffel to Berlin. In doing so, he may have felt that it was only in this way that he could be sure of getting a true and unedited picture of the Prussian army. He was perfectly aware that he would face considerable resistance from the upper echelons of the army to the reforms which he wished to introduce. Stoffel was attached formally to the French embassy in Berlin with effect from August 2 1866, but he had in the meantime gone via Prague to join the head-quarters of Prince Frederick Charles, where he began an association with the Prussian army that would in due course provide him with a comprehensive understanding of its systems and traditions and its strengths. He also established a close familiarity with very many of its senior officers. As an artillery officer, he formed a particular relationship with Prince Kraft zu Hohenlohe, who had commanded the reserve artillery of the Prussian Guard Corps at Königgrätz.

Stoffel was given an unrestricted opportunity to interview all those to whom he wished to talk, of every rank. It was a freedom which, to the eyes of later centuries, appears astonishingly generous. Napoleon had sent him off with a mission to concentrate in the first instance on the two issues with which he was particularly concerned: the application in Prussia of the principle of universal military service, and the merits of breech-loading rifles in general, and the Prussian needle gun in particular.

While awaiting Stoffel's first report, Napoleon set about the process of preparing the ground for army reform. In late August he gave a lunch at St Cloud attended by Marshal François Canrobert and General Barthélemy Lebrun, both of whom could be counted as likely supporters. He told them that he had not changed his own opinions on the two key issues with which he was especially concerned. They both came back for another lunch on September 11, on which occasion they were joined by Marshal Adolphe Niel, General Adolphe Guiod, Intendant-General Robert and Napoleon's aide-de-camp General Henri Castelnau. The latter read a paper which he had prepared on the Emperor's instructions, which predicted that if France went to war with Prussia any time soon, she would meet the same fate as Austria. This, Castelnau argued, called for the immediate introduction of universal military service. Canrobert and Lebrun, as expected, endorsed this; Niel was noncommittal. Before his guests departed, Napoleon asked each of them to prepare a paper outlining his own view as to how the necessary increase in manpower should be obtained; these papers would be debated at a meeting which would be arranged for early November.[11]

In the meantime the court had moved for its regular September break to Biarritz, and it was there that Napoleon received the first of Stoffel's reports. Dated September 8, and addressed to the War Ministry, it had unaccountably been delayed there, and the Emperor had to call for it to be forwarded to him. In this report Stoffel was in no doubt of the reasons why the Prussian army had been so far superior to its adversary. A key factor in the Austrian defeat had been the incompetence of Ludwig von Benedek, the Austrian commander. Beyond this, however, Stoffel was clear that

11   Williams, pp. 18-19.

the very different national character of Prussia and Austria, and the very different social and political background of their soldiers, accounted for the superiority of the Prussian army at every level. Not only were the Prussian officers far more professional and better educated; their men, recruited on the basis of universal military service, were a genuine cross-section of the Prussian nation, and were far more intelligent and performed far better on the battlefield.[12]

As to the needle gun, Stoffel concluded that it had certainly contributed substantially to the Prussian success, but in his view the outcome of the war would have been the same had both armies possessed the same weapon. He devoted a large part of his report to the detailed first- hand accounts which he had received from officers, not only as to the effectiveness of the weapon, but also to the tactical considerations deriving from its use. One instance of this, he noted, was the fact that the Prussian infantry could resist an enemy cavalry charge without the need to form themselves into the traditional square.[13]

Napoleon's meeting in November at St Cloud was a much more formal affair than the intimate lunches that had preceded it, and both proponents of the need for reform and those opposed had plenty of opportunity to prepare for what was always likely to be a spirited debate. It was attended by all the Empire's marshals and admirals; by three Cabinet ministers (Rouher, Vuitry and Fould); and by Generals Lebrun, Palikao, Frossard and Trochu. The meeting had before it six papers, two bearing Napoleon's signature, and one each from Marshals Vaillant and Niel, and Generals Lebrun and Guiod. Those presenting papers adopted entirely predictable positions. Napoleon called for a scheme that would produce one million men under arms; only with the introduction of universal military service could this figure be obtained. Lebrun and Guiod took a similar view. On the other hand, the 76-year-old Marshal Vaillant, in his paper, was totally opposed. Niel took a rather different view, arguing that the solution to the manpower problem was the creation of a trained *garde mobile* to supplement the regular army; his estimate was that this would produce an additional 400,000 men.[14]

In the ensuing debate Vaillant was firmly supported by the civilians, when he argued that it would be politically impossible to introduce universal military service. The discussion became heated, and Napoleon found it difficult to keep it under control. At the end of the day, however, he announced that he had not changed his own view, and that short-term conscription was the answer. In this he was supported by most of the soldiers although not by Vaillant, Randon and Trochu. A great deal more would soon be heard by the general public of Trochu's opinions on the need for reform; for the moment, though, he lined up with the dinosaurs. Randon, the War Minister, insisted that the key statistic was the actual number of men serving at any one time, and his

12   Stoffel, Colonel Baron Eugene, *Rapports Militaires* (Paris, 1871), pp. 1-8.
13   Stoffel, pp. 9-13.
14   Williams, pp. 33-34.

recommendation was that either the size of the existing draft should be increased or the term of service be lengthened. The politicians were completely opposed to any increase in the size of the army, which they knew would be resisted in the Corps Législatif, and they were concerned by the reports from prefects around the country which confirmed that such an increase would be unpopular in France as a whole.

On the following day a further paper, by General Emile Fleury and Colonel Jean Berthaut, was considered by the meeting, which outlined a scheme for universal military service. It tackled the issues of exoneration and replacement, which it proposed should be abandoned altogether. This had been an option that Napoleon rather wanted to keep open, apparently on political grounds. The case against universal service was now led by Adolphe Vuitry, who produced a potentially conclusive argument that it would be unconstitutional. In the face of an apparent deadlock, Napoleon adjourned the meeting for a week to the Palace of Compiègne to which the court was about to move.[15]

By the time it reconvened, Napoleon, who was subject to considerable pressure, had been compelled to recognise that the opposition to universal military service was so strong that he must find another way. It was a fundamental weakness of Napoleon's management of the government of France that he never felt able to challenge the military leaders on any issue which they regarded as fundamental. This, as well as his constant concern with public opinion, prevented him from dominating the discussion about the need for army reform, even though he could see clearly the right way forward. When the commission reassembled at Compiégne to begin discussions on November 14, its membership had been somewhat increased. In addition to Marshals Vaillant, Randon, Baraguey d' Hilliers, Canrobert, St Jean d'Angely, MacMahon, Niel and Forey, there were eight generals (Palikao, Fleury, Lebrun, Allard, Bourbaki, Leboeuf, Frossard and Trochu); two intendants (Darricau and Pagès); four civilian members of the Cabinet (Rouher, Fould, Chasseloup and Vuitry) and the Emperor's cousin Prince Napoleon.[16]

With Napoleon having somewhat retreated over the principle of universal military service, it was Niel's plan on which the commission's discussion focused. Niel had proved himself both on the battlefield and in times of peace and was one of those military figures in whom Napoleon had particular trust. Like so many of the army's leaders, he was an engineer, and had served successfully in Algeria. By 1853 he had reached the rank of general of division, and in the following year he went with the expedition to the Baltic. In 1855 he was sent to the army in the Crimea, where he served as Chief of Engineers. In this capacity he directed the siege operations which led to the taking of the Malakoff. During the 1859 campaign in Italy he commanded the 4th Corps, which was heavily engaged at Solferino; Napoleon made him a marshal on the battlefield. Niel was one of the ablest men in the French army, and when the conference

15   Williams, p. 34.
16   Williams, p. 55n.

appeared to have reached an impasse, his proposal carried the weight of his reputation to break the deadlock. His plan was to revive the *Garde Nationale*, which had been dissolved in the early days of the Second Empire, and to turn it into something resembling the Prussian Landwehr. His scheme, which he estimated would produce 400,000 men, was for all those liable for military service, including both those who had drawn a *bon numéro* and those who had paid for substitutes, to join the *Garde Nationale Mobile*, and there receive intensive training. Napoleon liked the sound of this, but Randon was still firmly opposed, saying: 'It will only give us recruits. What we need are soldiers.'[17]

The stress and anxiety caused him by this issue was taking its toll of the Emperor's health. Lord Cowley, the British ambassador, had met with him frequently during the difficult days of 1866, and had observed how ill

Marshal Niel. (Rousset/*Histoire*)

he seemed. He saw him again on December 11 at Compiégne, following which he reported on the meeting to Lord Stanley, the Foreign Secretary: 'I am sorry to say that I think him neither well nor in spirits. He says that he is all right again, but he looks shockingly ill.' Appreciating that the issue of army reform had been occupying a lot of Napoleon's attention, Cowley asked him about the meetings which had recently been held:

> He replied that he had formed a plan which he hoped would be successful, that it was based on defensive and not on offensive principles and framed so as to obtain the greatest number of men at the least possible expense. He said that it was the superior military organisation of Prussia which had counted in the late war … He said that his present scheme would give him one million of men, the greater part of which, however, would be a reserve which would only be used for defensive purposes. The annual contingent furnished at present was 100,000 men. He proposed to raise it to 180,000, half to be embodied in the active army, half in

17 Howard, p. 32.

the reserve. Those intended for the reserve would be partially drilled without leaving their homes. After a certain number of years' service they would form part of what he called *La Garde Nationale Mobile*, but would still remain at home, being only called out annually for a few weeks drill.[18]

In the light of Randon's opposition, it was now obvious to Napoleon that he must make a change at the head of the War Ministry, and in January 1867 he called for Randon's resignation. In his place he appointed Niel, who was not only the author of the only plan that seemed to be practicable but was also probably the only senior figure in the army with the clout to carry the reform through in the face of the resistance which it would necessarily encounter. The public announcement of the scheme to increase the size of the army and establish a reserve of 400,000 men in the *Garde Mobile* did not make any reference to the reform commission's discussions.

Even the watered-down version of Niel's plan which was put forward in January 1867 faced opposition from all quarters – from those who favoured an entirely professional army to those who expressed the popular resentment at the extension of compulsory service. Republican speakers were in the forefront of those who condemned the proposals for the *Garde Mobile*; Jules Favre famously protested: 'Do you want to turn France into a barracks?' To this, Niel replied: 'As for you, take care you don't turn it into a cemetery!'[19]

Niel's law eventually came into force in February 1868. It provided for a term of service of five years, followed by four years with the reserve. The annual contingent was still divided into two portions, the system of *bon et mauvais numéros* remaining unchanged. Those in the second portion would serve for five months before joining the reserve. The system of hiring substitutes was restored. The practical effect of the new law was to bring back the scheme of 1832. What remained of Niel's original scheme was the requirement that all those who did no military service should join the *Garde Nationale Mobile*. The training of this force was however, skimpy in the extreme, but it was assumed that this deficiency could be made good during the early days of war. The reluctance to follow through on Niel's original concept for the *Garde Mobile* appears to owe not a little to the belief that it would contain a large number of men actually hostile to the regime; placing arms in their hands might be to invite trouble in the future.[20]

Niel's time as War Minister did, however, see the introduction of a number of other reforms which made an important contribution to the strengthening of the French army's ability to meet the challenge posed by Prussia. Much the most important of these was the adoption of the Chassepôt rifle. This weapon was far superior

---

18   Wellesley, Sir Victor & Sencourt, Robert, *Conversations with Napoleon III* (London, 1939), pp 3.13-316.
19   Howard, p. 33.
20   Howard, p. 34.

to the Dreyse needle gun which had proved so effective in the hands of the Prussian infantry in Denmark in 1864 and against the Austrians in 1866. The introduction of the Chassepôt, which began to come into service in late 1866, was due not least to Napoleon's keen interest in the project. It gave the French infantry an immediate and substantial advantage over their opponents. Sighted to 1,320 yards, the Chassepôt had an effective range of 1,000 yards, compared to that of the needle gun(which was sighted to 660 yards) of 400 yards. It was lighter and easier to handle than the needle gun and could fire more than eleven rounds a minute; the needle gun could manage no more than seven. Furthermore, the Chassepôt bullet was of smaller calibre, and thus lighter, so that the French infantry could carry more of them into battle. When war did break out in 1870 a million Chassepôt rifles had been delivered to the army, which was more than enough to equip the units that took part in the initial battles, though not sufficient to arm all those that later came into existence before the war ended.[21] The French infantry had not, however, received sufficient training in the use of the new weapon, and tended to waste ammunition by firing too rapidly. An inspection report of 1867 commented that the infantry liked the Chassepôt 'because it fires fast, that is to say often; it would be better if they liked it because it fires accurately. Men could then be more easily persuaded to fire accurately rather than often, and thus to conserve ammunition, a thing so important in war.'[22]

Another important innovation was the introduction of the mitrailleuse. This was another weapon in which Napoleon had taken a keen personal interest, funding its early development out of his own resources. It was a machine gun that consisted of a revolving barrel of 25 rifled 13 mm tubes, each of which was detonated in turn by means of a handcrank. It was calculated that a loaded magazine could be fired four or five times a minute, delivering a rate of fire that was close to 150 rounds a minute. It was sighted for 1,320 yards, but in fact its effective range was considerably greater. It was introduced into the army in complete secrecy, a policy that proved, when war came, to be self-defeating. Although as many as 215 of these weapons had been delivered by the outbreak of war, there had been little opportunity for training in their use. It was not at all understood by French commanders, by whom it was utilised as an artillery weapon, sited in the open, where its four-man crews were particularly vulnerable to enemy rifle fire.[23]

One area in which the French army had failed to make sufficient technological progress was in the development of artillery, in spite of the Emperor's particular interest in the subject. Bronze muzzle-loading rifled guns had served the French well, and the cost of their replacement was prohibitive. Attention had been paid, of course, to the steel breech-loaders which had been adopted by the Prussian army, although their performance in 1866 had been disappointing. When the Krupp works, like all

21   Wawro, Geoffrey, *The Franco-Prussian War* (Cambridge, 2003), p. 52.
22   Quoted Holmes, Richard, *The Road to Sedan* (London, 1984), p. 204.
23   Holmes, p. 207.

arms dealers seeking customers wherever it could, endeavoured to sell its steel breech-loaders to the French government, its brochure was filed away in the War Ministry, dismissively endorsed *Rien á faire*.[24] There was no sense of urgency about converting or replacing the existing artillery; when the Corps Législatif denied the necessary funds, this was tamely accepted. In 1870, therefore, the French would go to war with the bulk of their field artillery equipped with 4-pounder muzzle-loaders, which were no match for the Krupp 6-pounders; the latter's greater weight of shot, longer range, faster rate of fire and much greater accuracy gave them complete superiority on the battlefield. Work had begun in France on the development of a new artillery weapon, but it would not come in time for the war of 1870.

Although the French army had more than its fair share of loudmouthed unthinking extroverts, there were many other officers who shared with Niel an understanding of the extent of the reforms needed, and in the four years which followed the battle of Königgrätz there was a continuing debate about what needed to be done. In 1868 General Trochu contributed to this by publishing a critique of the French army entitled *L'Armée Francaise en 1867*.

Trochu had long been seen as a coming man in the French army. As early as 1853, when he was secretary to the military committee which reviewed a plan put forward by Napoleon for regional recruitment, and compiled its report, he expressed the committee's hostility to the concept of a nation in arms when he wrote: 'Such an army would be a national army, and that is what it must not be ... The most perfect military constitution is that which creates an army whose instincts, beliefs and customs make it a corporation distinct from the rest of the population.'[25] Trochu was born in 1815, and after leaving St Cyr received a commission in the état-major in 1837. He saw action in Algeria under Marshal Bugeaud, and was successively promoted for gallantry and outstanding service, reaching the rank of colonel in 1853. In the Crimea he served as aide-de-camp to St Arnaud before being appointed to the command of a brigade. In 1859 he had another good war, commanding the 2nd Division of Canrobert's 3rd Corps. In the following years he served as Inspector General of Infantry, performing his duties very much more thoroughly than had traditionally been the case.[26]

During the discussions at St Cloud and Compiègne, Trochu's was a voice that was listened to. Having first supported Vaillant and Randon in their opposition to universal military service, he had later taken a different position, seconding Prince Napoleon when he made an unavailing last-ditch attempt to revive the Emperor's determination to call for obligatory service. The publication of his book caused an immediate sensation; although appearing anonymously, it was soon apparent that he was the author. Although not referring to the discussions of the reform commission directly, there were passages in the book which clearly came from its report, and it

24 Howard, p. 36.
25 Quoted in Williams, p. 18.
26 Cartier, Vital, *Le Général Trochu* (Paris, 1914), pp. 254-255.

was seen by many in the know as a breach of confidence. Although recognised as an officer of great ability, Trochu was not popular in the army. He had been opposed to the coup d'état; he was seen as particularly ambitious; and his intellectual arrogance was resented. Not, however, by Napoleon; seeing that Trochu was both a reformer and of great ability, he suggested to Niel that if war broke out he should be made commander-in-chief. Niel, reflecting the general opinion in the army, said he would prefer Lebrun.[27] Napoleon had apparently already raised the subject on April 11, 1867 with Lebrun, who believed that Niel should be commander-in-chief, but the Emperor said he could not be spared from the War Ministry. In that case, said Lebrun, his second choice would be Trochu.

Roger Williams concludes that on a reading of Trochu's book both he and his detractors were partly right. However, some of his recommendations were not properly understood, and 'ought to have undermined the contemporary notion that Trochu advocated the military philosophy of the Republican opposition. It would appear that more people talked about Trochu than read him.'[28]

In his analysis Trochu showed himself as very much aware of the mindset of the French army. He was convinced that it simply did not understand how to prepare for war, a process calling for profound study over a long period of time: 'We think that every effort can and must be made with the speed of electricity; it is admitted that a few weeks will suffice to prepare for military operations – even for the least known countries, which are studied summarily and which are several thousand leagues from us.'[29]

Chesney and Reeve noted that the first condition of a good army on which Trochu insisted was to raise its moral and intellectual standard, a condition that directly reflected Stoffel's conclusions in his reports from Berlin:

> It is idle to inflame the imagination of troops by a fanciful conceit of their own superiority; that delusion may be rudely dispelled by the resistance of a powerful enemy; the qualities on which an army has to rely are those which can be found in its own ranks. The unity and mutual reliance of the forces in the hour of danger, the knowledge the men have of the officers and the officers of the men, the moral influence which leads men to overcome their natural instincts, and a general acquaintance with the true principles of war, are the essentials with which a great commander seeks to imbue every portion of the troops under his command.[30]

What was more, wrote Trochu, was that peacetime exercises gave troops no conception of a real struggle in a real war.

27 Williams, p. 41.
28 Williams, pp. 41-42.
29 Quoted in Adriance, p. 8.
30 Chesney & Reeve, pp. 154-155.

Trochu's unpopularity, and his perceived opposition to the Second Empire, meant that not a great deal of attention was paid to his recommendations. He was, though, not the only observer who offered unpalatable advice. Another whose comments were frequently expressed in very forceful terms was General Auguste Ducrot, with whom Bazaine had toured Alsace and Lorraine. He repeatedly warned the government of the threat from Prussia, often exaggerating it to make his point. In 1866, for instance, he asserted that a Prussian invasion was imminent, a suggestion that had no basis in fact whatsoever. In 1868 he was calling for a pre-emptive strike into South Germany.[31]

Meanwhile Stoffel continued to send a stream of thoughtful and significant reports that could have left the Emperor and the French high command in no doubt as to the superiority of the Prussian systems and organisation. One aspect of this to which he drew particular attention was the rising standard of education, as a result of which, he wrote 'the Prussian nation is the most enlightened in Europe, in the sense that education is diffused among all classes of society.'[32]

He watched with mounting concern while Niel struggled to pilot his proposals through the Corps Léglislatif . A letter written in March 1868 by Francheschini Piétri, Napoleon's secretary, in response to one from Stoffel, disclosed the latter's anxiety:'What you said in your last letter is fair enough. But I, like you, do not expect to see the Emperor reconcile himself to such circumstances in the future as he has done, or been forced to do, up to now … We must remain continually alert and work indefatigably to make ourselves the strongest.'[33]

The most disturbing aspect of the way in which the *Garde Mobile* was constituted was the lamentably insufficient training that recruits were required to undergo. It was quite insufficient to create a force that was militarily effective. During his five-year term of service in the *Garde Mobile*, a recruit was liable to only 15 days of training in any year and could not be required to be away from home for more than 24 hours at a time. It was 'organised, trained, armed and equipped in an atmosphere of distrust from soldiers and civilians alike.' In March 1868 there were serious disturbances at Toulouse and Bordeaux when the first groups of *gardes mobiles* were called up.[34]

Niel did his best, setting up a special bureau within the War Ministry to assist commanders in the field in their deployment of *Garde Mobile* units. They would be led by officers who had retired from the army, supplemented by newly appointed officers who were considered suitable. Stoffel was asked by the War Ministry in the summer of 1869 to report on how the law of February 1, 1868, purporting to reform the recruitment to the French army, was perceived in Prussia. He did not mince his words in explaining how poorly it was regarded, adding that he was bewildered that such a senseless measure could be considered by the legislature of a great country.[35]

---

31   Adriance, p. 6.
32   Stoffel, p. 44.
33   Williams, p. 55.
34   Holmes, p. 96.
35   Stoffel, p. 291.

Perhaps, if he had survived, Niel would have been able to make more of the *Garde Mobile* and turn it into a force that might be compared in effectiveness to the Prussian Landwehr; but unluckily for France, he was not long to be at the War Ministry. He died on August 13, 1869 from complications arising from operation for a bladder stone. With his death, the army lost perhaps the only man with the vision of what it needed and the capacity to bring about the necessary reform. His place was taken by the 60-year-old General Edmond Leboeuf, an artillerymen who like so many of Napoleon's generals had made his name in Algeria. In the Crimea he commanded the artillery of the 1st Corps, and in 1859 was in command of the artillery of the Army of Italy, where he was seen as having made a significant contribution to the victory. Leboeuf was not altogether in sympathy with some of his predecessor's views – he was, for instance, contemptuous of the *Garde Mobile* – but he was energetic and popular with the Corps Législatif. Howard reckoned that 'too much importance should not be attached to Niel's premature death.' Leboeuf studied the crucially important issues of mobilisation and frontier defence and had a clear understanding of the threat from Prussia. He did, though, suspend the sittings of the central commission on railway movement, which had been doing valuable work to address what would be a key factor in the mobilisation of the army.[36] In the Spring of 1870 Leboeuf was rewarded for his efforts at the War Ministry by receiving appointment as a marshal.

36   Howard, p. 38.

5

Mobilisation & Deployment

Paris, with the rest of Europe, was enjoying the peaceful days of summer in 1870. Ollivier, President of the Council of Ministers since the previous December, felt able in the Corps Législatif to say that 'at no period has the maintenance of peace seemed better assured.' In London, the incoming Foreign Secretary, Lord Granville, was told by Hammond, the Permanent Under Secretary of the Foreign Office, that 'he had never during his long experience known so great a lull in foreign affairs, and that he was unaware of any important question with which Granville would have to deal.'[1] In Prussia, the holiday season had begun. Bismarck and Moltke had retired to their respective country estates, while King William was taking the waters at Ems. In France, the Emperor was in the process of moving his court from the Tuileries to St Cloud, to escape the worst of the summer heat. In Paris, meanwhile, Marshal Bazaine was continuing to enjoy Pepita's success as one of the stars of Paris society.

Into this peaceful scene, on July 2 in Madrid, the Spanish Premier, Marshal Prim, dropped a bombshell. He broke the news to the French ambassador of the candidature of Prince Leopold of Hohenzollern-Sigmaringen for the vacant Spanish throne. When this information reached Paris next day, the fat was in the fire, and the wheels of diplomacy began to turn ever faster, while in both France and Germany the Press adopted a strident tone about a crisis that was to develop with astonishing speed. The Duc de Gramont, the Minister for Foreign Affairs, told Lord Lyons, the British ambassador, on July 5 that France would not resign herself to such a proposal. It would not be permitted, and France would use her whole strength to prevent it. It was, he said, 'nothing less than an insult to France.'[2] On the following day Gramont, with the approval of the Cabinet, used strong language in the Corps Législatif, claiming that the Hohenzollern candidature 'placed in peril the interests and the honour of France. To prevent it, we rely at once on the wisdom of the German and the friendship of the Spanish people. But if it proves otherwise, then, strong in your support and in that of the

---

1   Fitzmaurice, Lord Edmond, *The Life of the Second Earl Granville* (London, 1905), II, p. 33.
2   Wellesley & Sencourt, pp. 356-357.

nation, we would know how to fulfill our duty without hesitation and without weakness.'[3] Apparently the usually peacefully inclined Ollivier had sharpened this statement of government policy, having told the Austrian ambassador that 'we have had enough of the humiliations to which Prussia subjects us.'

On July 7 Lyons reported to Granville that he did not believe 'that either the Emperor or his ministers either wish for war or expect it.' Behind them, however there were more belligerent influences, of which the most strident was the Empress Eugénie. In 1866 she had encouraged Napoleon to enter

Empress Eugenie. (Private collection)

the Austro-Prussian War. At that time, after hearing from Marshal Randon, the War Minister, that 80,000 troops could be concentrated immediately, with 250,000 more in three weeks, she demanded an immediate invasion across the Rhine. She later recalled: 'I felt that the fate of France and our dynasty's future were at stake.'[4] Now, she believed that France would win the war, basing this on what she later claimed were the assurances she had been given by all the leading military figures in France. She strongly endorsed Gramont's view, as he had expressed it to her: 'Our differences with Prussia cannot be solved merely by the Hohenzollern candidate withdrawing. That is no sort of solution and it is never going to satisfy French public opinion – we should be blamed, and quite rightly so, for having been duped by Bismarck.'[5] Eugénie later claimed that Napoleon had raised no objection to Gramont's demand for guarantees from King William that the candidature be withdrawn and never renewed.

Napoleon, meanwhile, with the strong opinions of the Empress ringing in his ears, seemed to Prince Richard Metternich, the Austrian ambassador, to be in an almost exalted frame of mind: 'He appeared delighted, I might even say joyous.' In the course of their conversation the Emperor told Metternich that the French must be ready,

3   Howard, p. 51.
4   Seward, Desmond, *Eugénie* (Stroud, 2004), p. 169.
5   Seward, p. 222.

because everything would depend on the rapidity of military preparations: 'We must have our eyes open,' he added, 'for I believe that the winner will be the one who can be ready first.'[6]

The need for preparedness for war was, of course, a statement of the obvious. Whether the French army was capable of the necessary speed and efficiency was far less certain. Nor did there exist any clear strategy for the French army to follow. The Emperor and his senior military advisers should have had Stoffel's report of August 12, 1869 particularly in mind if the French army was not to be caught unprepared. This was a report in which Stoffel had returned to the subject of French military recruitment and the *Garde Mobile,* comparing the latter very unfavourably with the Prussian Landwehr. He had gone on to review the likelihood of war, summarising his personal opinions in four key points. First, that war was inevitable and at the mercy of an incident. Secondly, that Prussia had no intention of attacking France and did not want war in the least and would do everything possible to avoid it. Thirdly, on the other hand Prussia was sufficiently farsighted to recognise that war, which she did not desire, would unquestionably come, and she was making every effort not to be taken by surprise. Finally, France, by her unconcern, by thoughtlessness and above all by ignorance of the situation did not have the same farsightedness as Prussia.[7]

Although in 1870 the likelihood of the war to which Stoffel had pointed had seemed not to be substantial, Napoleon had earlier that year been exploring the possibility of an alliance with Austria and Italy. In March and April there had been discussions with the Archduke Albert in the course of a visit which he paid to Paris. As a result of these Napoleon sent Lebrun to continue the discussions in Vienna and see what could be agreed. Before he departed, Lebrun, with Leboeuf, Frossard and Jarras had made it clear that if there was to be a war with Prussia, it was indispensable that all three countries should declare war simultaneously.[8]

With this essential requirement in his mind, Lebrun set off to Vienna to confer with the Austrians, pausing at Berlin, Dresden and Prague en route, and arriving in Vienna on June 6. There, he had a succession of interviews with the Archduke Albert before visiting Budapest on June 10. Returning to Vienna, he had the opportunity to hear Franz Joseph's views at first hand, at an audience with him on June 14. The Emperor made it clear to Lebrun that above all, he wanted peace. He would only go to war if he was forced to do so. As for the suggestion that Austria-Hungary should declare war at the same time as France, that was, he told Lebrun, out of the question. On the other hand, he went on:

> But if the Emperor Napoleon, forced to accept or declare war, should appear with his armies in South Germany, not as an enemy but as a liberator, I would be

6   Wellesley & Sencourt, p. 363.
7   Stoffel, p. 302.
8   Lebrun, General Barthélémy, *Souvenirs Militaires 1866-1870* (Paris, 1895) pp. 72-73.

obliged on my side to make common cause with him. In the eyes of my people I would have no choice but to join my armies with the French armies.[9]

This was the message which he asked Lebrun to carry back to Napoleon, and it was this that was in the forefront of the minds not only of the Emperor but also his advisers during the anxious days that followed the beginning of the crisis.

It had some influence on Napoleon's thinking as, during this period he began to review the way in which the French armies should be organised. It had been the settled intention, for several years, that there should be three armies; one, to be commanded by Bazaine, would be based on Metz, and would consist of three corps; another, based on Strasbourg, would be commanded by MacMahon, and would also consist of three corps; and finally a third, based on Châlons, and commanded by Canrobert, consisting of two corps, would stand in reserve. When the crisis erupted, this disposition still held good, and preparations were put in hand in the War Ministry on this basis. However, on July 11, Napoleon instructed Leboeuf that this arrangement would no longer apply; instead, there would be only one army, comprising all eight corps, which he would command personally. The three marshals previously earmarked for an army command would now each command a corps, albeit that these would be enlarged to consist of three divisions rather than the two previously planned. This was a prime example of the way in which Napoleon tended to interfere in key military decisions. The new structure may in part have been due to the influence of the Empress, who maintained that the Emperor must take command in the field while she headed a Council of Regency in Paris. Leboeuf apparently believed that the change had been made on the advice of the Archduke Albert, who thought that it would improve the flexibility of the command structure, not least if Austria came to France's support.[10] Certainly at this time Napoleon still entertained hopes of this.

The decision that he would no longer be in command of an army may well have come as a disappointment to Bazaine; subsequently, it was suggested that he felt so slighted by the decision that it was a major factor in his overall motivation in 1870. It is not surprising that his post-war detractors made much of this; what is surprising, though, is that it has been so treated by some modern historians, most notably Geoffrey Wawro. Beginning with the statement that Bazaine 'never forgot or forgave' the insult of having been blamed for the failure of the Mexican intervention, Wawro goes on to assert that none of Napoleon's attempts at reconciliation were successful, and that Bazaine 'still burned with resentment at the way in which he had been treated three years earlier.' From this he proceeds to consideration of the deployment of the whole French army under one central command, rather than the structure previously contemplated. He appears to have swallowed whole the suggestion that this

9   Lebrun, p. 147.
10   Howard, p. 65.

was a blow to Bazaine's pride which, in the words of General Fay, was 'annihilating ... It could scarcely have been possible to insult a man more completely.'[11]

General Séré de Rivière, when compiling the report which led to Bazaine's trial after the war, asserted that it must have been a real disappointment; General Bonnal wrote of Bazaine having 'a heart full of bitterness,' which might have led him almost to rejoice at the lack of success at the outset of the campaign. Against these opinions must be set the much more compelling evidence of one who was closest of all to the issue; Leboeuf's testimony at Bazaine's trial was to the effect that he never saw anything in Bazaine's demeanour or conduct to suggest the slightest discontent, saying that Bazaine had taken the matter 'like a soldier. '[12] If one is concerned to find evidence of Bazaine being compensated for the change,and a desire to make use of his military talents, one need look no further than the fact that Bazaine was appointed to take command of the whole army pending Napoleon's arrival.

It would have been quite another matter if, Bazaine having been intended for an army command, had at the last moment been passed over in favour of another, and assigned to a lesser command, but this was not the case. There is no good evidence, as opposed to the ill- intended speculation, to suggest that Bazaine, any more than MacMahon or Canrobert, was affected in the manner claimed by Fay. In my history of the Franco-Prussian war, to which I referred in the Preface to this book, I made the mistake of unthinkingly adopting the position of other writers when I suggested that Bazaine was 'particularly offended' by the new command structure, and I now consider that to be entirely wrong.[13]

Meanwhile in Germany, with the balance tilting more towards war, Stoffel had on July 21 a conversation with his friend Hohenlohe, to whom he made a request to be allowed to attend the next artillery firing practice, due to take place two weeks later. Hohenlohe, slightly surprised, agreed to this, and Stoffel said: 'I have to see how you are going to kill us.' Hohenlohe said that he did not want to talk about that but said that Stoffel must admit that war would be unnecessary. This touched a raw nerve; Stoffel burst out: 'It's the greatest stupidity imaginable! Do you understand that this is something I cannot conceive of! Our Emperor is a calm and reasonable man; and Ollivier is both calm and reasonable and a bit timorous. Yet, these two are making blunders which are going to plunge us, heads up or heads down, into a vast pit.'[14]

That same day, Prince Karl Anton withdrew Leopold's candidature, and by many it was supposed that with this all reason for war was gone; but it was also the day of Gramont's ill-fated instructions to Benedetti to seek from King William an undertaking that the candidature would not be renewed. On July 13, the ambassador made his approach to the King; subsequently Abeken sent his telegram reporting the

11   Fay, General Charles, *Journal d'un officier de l'Armée du Rhin* (Paris, 1875), pp 37-38; Geoffrey Wawro, T*he Franco-Prussian War* (Cambridge, 2003), p. 70.
12   Ruby & Regnault, pp. 95-96.
13   Barry, Quintin, *The Franco-Prussian War* (Solihull, 2007), I, p. 69.
14   Prince Kraft zu Hohenlohe-Ingelfingen, *Aus Meinem Leben* (Berlin, 1897), III, pp. 402-403.

matter to Bismarck; and at dinner that night with Moltke and Roon Bismarck edited it for publication. From Berlin Stoffel continued to watch the progress of events with mounting despair, as the French Cabinet plunged heedlessly over the precipice. On July 14 it received from Leboeuf his express assurance that the army was ready. Mobilisation was ordered. On the following day the Cabinet finally resolved on war, and Ollivier and Leboeuf went off to the Corps Législatif. There, each of them made a remark that would live in history. Ollivier, responding to a question from Thiers, said that he accepted the responsibility for war 'd'un coeur léger;' this phrase would never be forgotten, but history would not remember his qualification that

Otto von Bismarck. (Pflugk-Harttung)

what he meant was 'with a heart not weighed down with remorse, a confident heart.' Leboeuf's reply to a question about the army's preparedness was even more memorable; it was ready, he said, 'down to the last gaiter button.'

On July 16 Bazaine set off to Metz to take up his temporary command of the army as it assembled in Alsace and Lorraine. He had no illusions about the enormity of the problems it would face, remarking as he boarded his train: 'Nous marchons á un désastre.' Bazaine was no coward, but he had seen too much of war to view it with exhilaration:

> Ten years earlier he had recalled the horrors of the battlefield after action, and he had seen more since then. Those actions had all been victorious; and how could he be certain that the battles of the next campaign were going to be victories? After all, he knew as much of the deficiencies of the French army as any of his contemporaries. Had he not commanded the frontier army corps for two years? He had seen its incomplete defences and its defective organisation; and he knew that it was still much as he had left it in 1869. What grounds were there in July, 1870, for feeling that they had any chance of winning? The public might believe it and shout itself hoarse in the belief. But an intelligent professional could be forgiven an overwhelming sense of inferiority, as he confronted the victors of Sadowa with the conquerors of Mexico.[15]

15   Guedalla, pp 155-156

Reservists from the Prussian Guard gather at Berlin. (*Illustrated London News*)

In Germany Stoffel was discharging his responsibilities to the last. On July 16, the day before the formal declaration of war, he reminded the War Minister of his previous report as to the timetable of the Prussian mobilisation:

> One should expect that it will take eight or nine days for the several army corps, mobilised in their respective provinces, to be transported by rail to the designated point of concentration. Thus one can see that after 20 days counting from July 15, Prussia will, at different points on our frontiers, have several armies, each of 100,000 to 120,000 men.[16]

It was to prove a chillingly accurate forecast.

Arriving in Metz, Bazaine established his headquarters in the Hotel de l'Europe, and next day went up the road to Thionville to see how far the place had been prepared for defence. He found that although work had begun, no guns had yet been installed; it was held by a force consisting of 600 untrained men and 90 *douaniers*. In Metz, it was obvious to him that the supply chain was breaking down. On July 18 he reported to the War Minister: 'The result of the meetings which I have had with the Intendant of the 5th Division, and the Intendant General of the Army, is that supplies of all

16   Stoffel, p. 464.

kinds will be insufficient when units reach their effective strength.'[17] Since the regular contractors had let them down, the army was seeing what it could buy in the local markets. Meanwhile the regiments streamed into Metz, many of them arriving without camping equipment, wagons and ambulances.

As was evident from his conversation with the Austrian ambassador, Napoleon perfectly recognised the importance of a speedy and efficient mobilisation in order to gain a first and crucial advantage over the enemy. Leboeuf, who also understood how vital this was, had assured the Cabinet as early as July 6 that it would be possible to commence operations within two weeks of the start of mobilisation, at which point he expected to have 250,000 men in the field. Meantime the decision to organise a single army seriously disrupted the work of the War Ministry, as the staff worked to adapt their plans to the new scheme. Although lacking the careful advance preparation that the Prussian General Staff had undertaken for the task of moving huge bodies of men, the French railway system did better than might have been expected. Even so, the delivery of troops to their concentration areas fell short of Leboeuf's expectations. The War Ministry was in a chaotic state of incapability as it struggled to put in place a coherent order of battle, and the results in the field were painful in the extreme. General Michel's famous telegram to the War Ministry of July 21 perfectly illustrated the situation: 'Am in Belfort; can't find brigade; can't find commanding general; what must I do? Don't know where my regiments are.'[18]

The comparative inefficiency of the French staff system had been the subject of one of Stoffel's earliest reports. It was one to which he had attached particular importance, and he outlined the considerable advantages of having a permanent Chief of the General Staff. In Prussia, the post had been held since 1857 by Helmuth von Moltke, and Stoffel had at once recognised that his enormous reputation was entirely justified. No corresponding post existed in the French army. If war appeared to be imminent, an appointment was made of a marshal or senior general to the

Helmuth von Moltke. (Pflugk-Harttung)

17 Bazaine, *Episodes*, p. 3.
18 Adriance, p. 15.

post of *Major-General*, who served as chief of staff to the overall army commander. The difference was that in Prussia Moltke could supervise the selection and instruction of all members of the General Staff, each of whom he could evaluate personally. Not only did the General Staff serve as the body for providing staff training; it was also responsible for the continuous planning for war as well as supervising an efficient mobilisation. When the Prussian army took the field, Moltke knew that he could rely on the officers of the General Staff to carry out their considerable responsibilities in the manner in which they had been trained.

In France on the other hand, a chief of staff appointed at the last minute would lack all these advantages:

> Whatever may be his personal merit, he will not be sufficiently prepared to discharge the important functions that will suddenly fall upon him. In effect, it is necessary, to be a good *Major-General*, one must possess particular aptitudes, and the fullest understanding that can only be acquired by lengthy study ... In addition he must have a perfect knowledge of all the generals in the army, and in particular the officers of the *État-major*, in order to be able to assemble the *états-majors* of the divisions and those of the army corps. How could a general be capable of carrying out such a task, if he had not prepared for it a long time in advance by study and hard work![19]

In July 1870 Leboeuf was appointed as *Major-General*, with Lebrun and Jarras as his assistants. He did not cease to hold the office of War Minister, but in his absence General Dejean was appointed to carry out his duties, with the title of Interim War Minister, an arrangement which inevitably limited the scope of his authority, not least because it was decided that all correspondence from corps commanders addressed to the War Ministry should be forwarded in the first instance to Leboeuf.

Other key members of the *État-major* were General Gregoire Coffinières de Nordeck, commanding the engineers, and General Justin Soleille, the army's artillery commander. The 59-year-old

General Coffinières de Nordeck, Governor of the fortress of Metz. (Private collection)

19 Stoffel, p. 43.

Coffinières, destined to play a key role in the coming months, had served in Algeria and the Crimea, and had been in charge of the École Polytechnique from 1860 to 1865. Allocating the key unit command appointments was not a particularly difficult task. Bazaine's 3rd Corps consisted of four divisions, commanded by Generals Montaudon, de Castagny, Metman and Decaen, with Clérembault in command of the cavalry division. The Imperial Guard, assembling around Metz, was commanded by Bourbaki; his divisional commanders were Deligny and Picard, with Desvaux commanding the Guard Cavalry Division. To the right of the 3rd Corps, Frossard's 2nd Corps had already been partly organised before the outbreak of war; it consisted of three divisions, led by Vergé, Bataille and Laveaucoupet. The cavalry division was commanded by Marmiet. One of Frossard's divisions was already close to the frontier at Forbach; the rest of the corps was moving up from St Avold. Interestingly, Jarras recorded that in the original command structure drafted by Niel, Frossard was to command the army's engineers, and Leboeuf had intended to stick to this; but Frossard preferred a corps command and after some hesitation Napoleon agreed to this.[20]

The 4th Corps, commanded by General Louis de Ladmirault, was assembling at Thionville. It consisted of three divisions led by de Cissey, Rose and Lorencez and a cavalry division under Legrand. At Châlons, Canrobert's 6th Corps comprised four divisions, commanded by Tixier, Bisson, de Villiers and Levassor-Sorval, with the cavalry division under de Salignac-Fénelon. There were two cavalry divisions in army reserve; these were the 1st and 3rd, commanded by du Barail and de Forton respectively. To the right of Frossard's 2nd Corps, the 5th Corps under de Failly was stretched out from Sarreguemines eastwards towards Niederbronn, a distance of some 30 miles.[21]

In Alsace, MacMahon's 1st Corps, assembling around Strasbourg, consisted of four divisions under Ducrot, Abel Douay, Raoult, and Lartigue, with a cavalry division under Duhesme. The 7th Corps was commanded by Bazaine's old adversary Felix Douay and was scattered from Colmar to Lyons. It was composed of three divisions commanded by Conseil-Dumesnil, Liebert and Dumont; the cavalry division was led by Ameil. There was also a cavalry reserve in Alsace consisting of the 2nd Cavalry Division under Bonnemains.

There was as yet no post for Trochu. He had written to the War Minister in July 11 offering to serve as a divisional commander, notwithstanding his seniority, under whatever corps commander to whom he might be assigned. In reply, he was told that it was in contemplation that he be appointed to command an army of observation in the Pyrenees. Such a pointless diversion of essential manpower was, however, soon abandoned.

The organisational chaos that Michel had described so graphically was matched by the failure of the intendants to provide sufficiently for the army's basic provisions,

---

20   Jarras, General Louis, *Souvenirs* (Paris, 1892), pp. 52-53.
21   Adriance, p. 110.

as Bazaine had reported. There should have been enough provisions available, but the necessary transport for the distribution of supplies was sorely lacking. As a result, many French units were reduced almost from the outset to living off the land. Equipment, too, was slow to come to hand, and in this respect the *Garde Mobile* suffered particularly. Theoretically consisting of 250 battalions of infantry and 125 batteries of artillery, only a small proportion, which included those raised in Paris, had been organised. These last was sent to Châlons, where Canrobert was assembling the 6th Corps, and they caused him severe problems, displaying extreme indiscipline.

From Metz, Bazaine continued to send a stream of reports to the War Ministry, not only on the supply situation, but also on the lack of preparations for war. The forts of Longeville and St Julien were urgently awaiting arms and equipment. The mobility of all the units under his command was gravely hampered by the lack of vehicles. The men actually trained in the use of the mitrailleuses had not arrived, although the weapons themselves had turned up, and there was no one else who knew how to operate them.[22]

All the same, the corps around Metz were beginning to take some sort of shape, and on July 23 Leboeuf was able to send some preliminary orders to Bazaine. After the war, Leboeuf was to tell the Commission of Inquiry that he had expected that the army would undertake an offensive in the first week of August. In the meantime, to take account of the direction in which the enemy appeared to be massing his forces, he instructed Bazaine to concentrate on the axis of the Metz-Saarbrücken road. This would not prevent the French from taking the offensive, but if this was decided on it would have to be north eastwards into the Palatinate, rather than directly east into Baden, which would be the direction to be taken if the Austrians came into the war. If

Marshal Leboeuf, French Minister of War in 1870. (Rousset/*Histoire*)

they did not, 'an offensive eastward across the Rhine would have little to recommend it. Militarily it was far wiser to seek out and disrupt the main German armies as they concentrated for battle before Mainz.'[23]

22 .Bazaine, *Episodes*, pp. 3-4.
23 Howard, pp. 73-74.

Bazaine, meanwhile, had moved the headquarters of his 3rd Corps to Boulay, about 15 miles to the east of Metz, leaving the Hotel de l'Europe as the headquarters of the *État-major*. Leboeuf, with Lebrun, arrived there on the evening of July 24, and from then until the Emperor's arrival effectively took command of the army, although Bazaine was still exercising some authority over the other corps.

On July 25 Leboeuf received information which came as a fearful shock. Commandant Laveuve, who was Lebrun's aide-de-camp, had received a letter from his friend Colonel de Bouillé, the French military attaché in Vienna. In this letter de Bouillé said that the Austro-Hungarian army had not begun to mobilise and that there was no sign that it was going to do so. For Leboeuf and Lebrun this meant the overturning of all their hopes, which had been pinned to the idea of an Austrian intervention. After discussing it, they agreed that Lebrun should return to Paris, both to find out more about that aspect of the situation and to get an update on the progress of the French mobilisation. He reached St Cloud on July 26, knowing that he would find there not only General Dejean but also the Emperor and the rest of the Cabinet. The first of the ministers he encountered was the Duc de Gramont, and he told him at once of the letter that had been received from de Bouillé. Gramont tried to reassure Lebrun, questioning whether de Bouillé knew everything that was going on in Vienna. 'Go on, go on,' he added, tapping Lebrun lightly on the shoulder, 'and be confident.'[24]

Not entirely reassured by this, Lebrun next saw Dejean, from whom he received a discouraging report on the mobilisation, which was in disarray due to the difficulties of conducting it across the whole of the country. Lebrun considered that Dejean was doing all that he could, 'but all his zeal and all his intelligence would not suffice for him to do the impossible,' as he reported to Leboeuf on his return to Metz.

Napoleon had not given up hope of an Austrian intervention, and on July 27 he had a meeting with Metternich, telling him that the French army was now poised to launch an offensive into Germany. One army, under Bazaine, was at Metz; the second, under MacMahon, was at Strasbourg. It was MacMahon's advance into South Germany which would satisfy the condition that Franz Joseph had laid down for Austrian cooperation. Behind these two armies, said Napoleon, Canrobert would move forward with the reserve from Châlons, while the French navy would put ashore a force of Marines on the North German coast. All of this might have been credible, if the French possessed sufficient available resources; but as Leboeuf and his colleagues well knew, they did not.[25]

The Emperor travelled to Metz on July 28, arriving in the late afternoon. Hot and tired, he took up his quarters in the Prefecture. Leboeuf had warned Bazaine of his coming two days earlier and had asked him to come into Metz to be on hand to meet with him. The meeting took place with Leboeuf, Lebrun and Jarras. It did not go well.

---

24   Lebrun, pp. 192-193.
25   Wawro, pp. 73-74.

Wawro concludes that resentment on the part of Bazaine about his treatment, previously referred to, accounted for the frame of mind in which the Marshal took part in the discussion of the army's immediate options. It is, of course, possible that Bazaine was sulky about the reduction of his command from an army to a corps, but it is very much more likely that any ill humour arose from the fact that he thoroughly disapproved of the manner in which the French army was going to war. Nothing that he had seen since his arrival in Lorraine had done anything to alter his view of the overall situation or the probable outcome of the campaign. The account which Jarras gives of the meeting has no doubt some

General Jarras, Chief of Staff of the Army of the Rhine. (Private collection)

basis in fact; he noted that Bazaine was cold and reserved during the discussion and expressed no opinion as to what should be done.[26] In his memoirs, published long after the war by his widow, Jarras touched on the possibility that Bazaine's taciturnity was due to his being assigned only to the command of a corps. However, Jarras did not know the Marshal well:

> Bazaine was there; and as he said very little, the observant Jarras concluded that his relegation to the status of a corps commander was still rankling with the Marshal. But he had never been a talker; and the impassive manner, behind which he had learnt to keep his counsel in the *Bureau Arabe* at Tlemcen, and in Mexico, was new to Jarras.[27]

In his memoirs Lebrun made no reference to the meeting or to Bazaine's demeanour at that time.

It should be added that the venomous Colonel Gaston d'Andlau, a member of the headquarters staff, who published a particularly vehement attack on Bazaine in 1872, went even further than Fay in finding Bazaine's alleged resentment as the motivation

26   Jarras, pp. 58-59.
27   Guedalla, p. 159.

for his conduct. He claimed that Bazaine had complained bitterly to everyone of his humiliation, and that the Emperor had ignored his political importance.[28]

During this discussion Leboeuf, still shaken by the news from Vienna, anxiously asked Napoleon what information there was about the Austrians; negotiations were still continuing, the Emperor replied hopefully. In the meantime, it was clear that something must be done, and the discussion continued next day at the railway station at St Avold, where the Imperial party was joined by Frossard. This gave the latter a further opportunity to urge the merits of the scheme which he had prepared for an immediate advance on Saarbrücken. Although Leboeuf's defensive deployment of the army was militarily prudent, it did nothing to relieve the pressure of public opinion for the army to be seen actually to be doing something. This could not easily be resisted; and in the absence of any clear-cut alternative on which general agreement was possible, it was decided to adopt Frossard's scheme. Its objective would be the disruption of Prussian communications by the seizure of the important rail junction at Saarbrücken.

---

28   d'Andlan, Colonel Gaston, *Metz: Campagne et Negotiations* (Paris, 1872), pp. 8-9; Wawro, p. 69.

6

Saarbrücken

Frossard, in putting forth his proposal for an advance on Saarbrücken, had been increasingly worried by the signs of German activity. In command of the most advanced corps of the Army of the Rhine, he had been receiving some, but not nearly enough intelligence of German movements. He reported on July 26 that 60,000 enemy troops were approaching the Saar from the direction of Cologne. To this, Leboeuf replied that he considered it necessary to take the offensive as soon as possible, adding that this intention had been paralysed by the lack of preparation, which was the perfect truth. Next day, Frossard wrote to Bazaine: 'As for the offensive, we don't yet seem able to have any direction to guide us, so that we can plan ahead in any particular direction.'[1]

Bazaine did not think much of Frossard's Saarbrücken plan; later, he was to criticise it because there were insufficient forces available to follow it up, and because it would serve only to provoke the enemy to attack the scattered French corps. This last suggestion is dismissed by Ruby & Regnault, who point out that 'once concentrated, the Germans would go over to the offensive whenever they wanted, whether provoked or not.'[2] At the time, though, Bazaine was inclined to favour an advance by the left of the army, from Thionville.

At all events, though, it would be Frossard's plan that would be adopted. Bazaine was to be responsible for carrying it out, being given operational control for this purpose of the 2nd, 3rd and 5th Corps. Lebrun signed an order to Bazaine to this effect on July 30. Frossard, with his 2nd Corps, would carry out the operation by advancing on Saarbrücken. Behind him, the 3rd Corps would follow in support, while to his right de Failly's 5th Corps would move towards Saarbrücken from Sarreguimines. Bazaine was to move two divisions from his 3rd Corps through the forest of Forbach and advance towards the Saar by way of creating a diversion. He was instructed to meet with Frossard, de Failly, Coffinières and Soleille at Morsbach, which had been designated as the site of Frossard's headquarters, to concert with them the detailed plans for

---

1   Howard, p. 79.
2   Ruby & Regnault, p. 97.

the operation. In fact, notwithstanding the instructions from the *État- major*, Frossard had preferred to locate his headquarters at Forbach.[3]

Geoffrey Wawro, typically looking for reasons to support his thesis of Bazaine's burning resentment, claims that the Saarbrücken operation 'further corroded' the relationship between Bazaine and the Emperor. He finds that Bazaine had been humiliated by the terms of the order of July 30, whereby the 3rd Corps was 'relegated to a supporting position.'[4] This suggestion is decidedly odd, since the order makes clear that it was to be Bazaine who was in overall charge of the operation, in command of the three corps involved, and that the detailed orders to be issued were up to him. Bazaine's reservations about the scheme had been taken account of in limiting the objective to the capture of Saarbrücken, with no attempt to advance further into enemy

General Frossard, commander of the French 2nd Corps. (Rousset/*Histoire*)

territory. Even so, Bazaine was still dubious about the planned operation, responding to the order by pointing out that he still had no ambulances, and was in need of additional horses and medicines. Similar complaints were coming in from the other corps commanders; Ladmirault reported that the 4th Corps had no draught horses; Bourbaki wrote that the Imperial Guard's transport service was inadequate; and Felix Douay reported simply that the commissariat of the 7th Corps had collapsed.[5]

As a result of the inadequacy of French intelligence about the movement of German troops towards the frontier, neither Bazaine nor Napoleon had any clear idea of the strength of the enemy which the advance on Saarbrücken might expect to encounter. According to Lebrun, it was supposed, on the basis of information which Napoleon had received, that a considerable force might be met with, and that the 2nd Corps should be fully supported both to its right by de Failly and to its left by Bazaine's 3rd Corps.[6]

3   Bazaine, *Episodes*, p. 11.
4   Wawro, p. 91.
5   Howard, p. 80.
6   Lebrun, p. 220.

Meanwhile Leboeuf was becoming profoundly concerned about the severe logistical problems faced by all the operational units of the army which were being reported to him. On August 1 he expressed his anxiety in a letter to Dejean: 'When I took leave of you I thought that by the time I wrote this letter we would have undertaken operations. Unfortunately our administrative organisation holds us back on the frontier, and I am beginning to fear that we shall not have the advantages and honours of taking the offensive.'[7]

The organisational aspect of the situation which was causing Leboeuf particular concern was the slow increase in the effective strength of the Army of the Rhine. The high hopes which he had entertained for the campaign while he was in Paris had been based on a belief that France could draw upon a total of 1,142,000 men. This number was made up of the regular army, amounting to 567,000 men; 500,000 men of the *Garde Mobile*; and the 75,000 men of the 1869 contingent of recruits. By the 14th day of mobilisation he hoped that the units of the Army of the Rhine would have been completed to a total strength of 385,000 men, but by that day only 202,448 had arrived. Three days later, on July 31, the total strength on the frontier had reached 238,188 men, a figure which included the 33,201 men of Canrobert's 6th Corps at Châlons and 20,341 men of Felix Douay's 7th Corps at Belfort. There is in fact some dispute about the precise number of men that were available on each of the days before the Saarbrücken operation was to be undertaken. Lebrun calculated that by August 1 the total number of men available was 235,800.[8] Whatever were the exact figures, it is clear that Leboeuf would have had available for offensive operations around Metz less than 200,000 men, a number which certainly justified the gloomier opinion which he had expressed to Dejean.

Bazaine perfectly understood that there was not going to be much in the operation against Saarbrücken and was content to leave its management in Frossard's hands. Instead, he preferred to accompany Montaudon's division of the 3rd Corps as it undertook a diversionary advance through Werden towards Saarlouis. This decision was subsequently to prompt critical speculation as to Bazaine's motives. Jarras wondered whether it was due to the Marshal's discontent, or whether it was an act of courtesy towards Frossard.[9] Lebrun found Bazaine's absence from the scene inexplicable, whether it was due to a feeling of hostility towards Frossard, or whether it was indeed because he wanted to see for himself the extent of the German threat from Saarlouis. Bazaine subsequently recorded his own comment on the matter:

> When I next saw the Emperor, he made no comment on my actions on August 2, but the Major General said to me: 'You acted as a good comrade in leaving the direction of the engagement to General Frossard.' This appreciation surprised

7   Adriance, p. 98.
8   Lebrun, p. 228.
9   Jarras, p. 63.

Napoleon III visiting the camp of the Voltigeurs of the Imperial Guard at Metz.
(*Illustrated London News*)

me, for I had not acted with that in mind, but simply because I believed that the diversion which I was undertaking on the left with the object of supporting the frontal attack of the 2nd Corps was where it would be best to be, since the enemy had concentrated large numbers around Saarlouis.[10]

What Bazaine did not know at the time, because no one told him, was that not only Leboeuf and Lebrun, but also the Emperor and the Prince Imperial planned to be present during the advance. By the time that he learned of this and had set off at a brisk pace to join the headquarters party, the day's fighting was over, and Napoleon had returned to Metz with his son, after expressing some surprise that Bazaine had not been present, and missing the Marshal en route on the way back to the city.

Not that the fighting had amounted to much. Napoleon chose to watch the advance on horseback, though this caused him excruciating pain. The French advanced to occupy the high ground overlooking Saarbrücken, their artillery shelling the drill ground and the Reppertsberg on the south side of the river. The small Prussian force under Colonel von Gneisenau skilfully retreated across the bridge and through the town to the heights overlooking it on the northern bank:

10   Bazaine, *Episodes*, p 18

Whilst this action was in progress and shells were bursting on the drill ground, Napoleon and the little Prince Imperial ascended the ridge and rode forward to the poplars. Beneath their feet lay the river and the town, and beyond, the long green hill with the darker forest creeping down its slopes … The French, though so easily victorious, showed no disposition either to renew the fight or to attempt the passage of the river. They seemed, on the contrary, apprehensive of attack, for the sappers were soon busy on the ridge, and by sunset a long series of shelter-trenches and epaulments crowned the northern crest.[11]

Lebrun, who rode close to the Prince Imperial and the Emperor throughout the day, watched the engagement with them. He described it briefly:

The affair, which lasted scarcely an hour, consisted almost entirely of an exchange of skirmishing fire. After this ceased, the artillery shelled the railway station, with the intention of setting it on fire and destroying it, but it appeared that the artillery did not have sufficient range … When the firing ceased, the Emperor passed in front of several battalions and several batteries; he put his foot to the ground and then threw himself into my arms, saying not a word before walking slowly to his carriage.[12]

The casualties on each side were few; the Prussians lost 83 men killed and wounded and the French 86.

Napoleon famously reported to Eugènie the Prince Imperial's coolness during his baptism of fire. Predictably, the news of the engagement was hailed in the French press as a brilliant victory, though this was much against the Emperor's wishes. The only aspect of the affair that could be counted as a significant success was the capture of the bridges over the Saar; this gave the French cavalry access to the northern bank, but none crossed the river to reconnoitre the German positions or to ascertain their troop movements.

This was particularly regrettable, because the lack of reliable information about the enemy continued to leave the French headquarters in a state of extreme uncertainty. This was also the frame of mind of the French infantry, who were profoundly apprehensive of the dense woods which surrounded their advanced positions and in which it was feared that the Prussians were stealthily moving forward:

The Emperor and his advisers, shrinking in irresolution before the veil which their own ineptitude had drawn between the frontier and the Rhine, shared the apprehensions of the soldiery. Attack was expected now from this quarter and now from that. Each trifling telegram was productive of the greatest excitement,

---

11   Henderson, Colonel G.F.R., *The Battle of Spicheren* (London, 1891), p. 63.
12   Lebrun, p. 271.

and orders and counter orders, following in rapid succession, harassed and demoralised the troops. Ignorant of the enemy's dispositions, swayed by every alarming rumour or by hopes based on insufficient information and false inferences, Napoleon was incapable of adopting any resolute plan of combination either for attack or defence.[13]

Any prospect of a forward movement disappeared on August 3 with the arrival at headquarters of a report from the chief of police at Thionville that 40,000 Prussian troops had passed through Trier and were marching towards either Saarlouis or Thionville. A reconnaissance in force that Ladmirault was to have undertaken with the 4th Corps was abandoned; Frossard was ordered to fall back to St Avold if substantial enemy forces appeared.

On the evening of August 4, when news of the defeat of Abel Douay's division that day at Weissenberg reached headquarters, fresh consideration was given to the command structure. This effectively resulted in a return to the previous concept of operating in three armies, at least for the purpose of managing any major engagement. Bazaine was to command three corps, the 2nd, 3rd and 4th; in Alsace, MacMahon was to command the 1st and 7th Corps, and the 5th Corps was to edge to its right to join him; the Imperial Guard at Metz and the 6th Corps at Châlons were to remain under the Emperor's direct control. Thus it was that Bazaine's army command was restored to him, a command that was almost at once to be tested in a major battle.

Bazaine's conduct of that battle has been the subject of detailed and critical enquiry by historians. His situation was by no means straightforward; although he and MacMahon were each now nominally in command of an army, their authority was restricted to military operations alone, and each of them remained in command of their respective corps. Leboeuf subsequently explained that this curious restriction was imposed because it was impossible at short notice to create a proper army staff, including the relevant service chiefs of the artillery and engineers. The problems caused by this arrangement did not end there:

> The greatest confusion existed in the high command. The *État-Major-General* still sent orders direct to the army corps, sometimes even to divisions, while paying no heed to the new 'army' structure, which was something which, quite reasonably, exasperated Bazaine, who was unfortunately too well disciplined to lodge a formal protest against this meddling. This manifested itself in particular in directing the positioning of divisions, which was properly the responsibility of corps commanders. The difficulties faced by Bazaine in his new position were exacerbated by Frossard in particular, who did not hesitate to make use of the direct contact with the *État-Major-General* to seek and obtain permission to

13 Henderson, p. 68.

locate his own headquarters at Forbach, without consulting or even informing Bazaine.[14]

Frossard also decided to pull back from the ridge overlooking Saarbrücken. He explained his decision in his memoirs:

> The 2nd Corps was exposed to an imminent attack and at this time was liable to be turned on its two wings, which could not be supported without withdrawing troops from the front. General Frossard resolved to effect during the night a change of position to the rear, which would be for no more than a few kilometres. He met his divisional generals and gave them the necessary instructions.[15]

This manoeuvre was not only exhausting for his troops, but at the same time did nothing for their morale. Carried out very cautiously, it meant that his troops must march slowly through heavy rain, in many instances not reaching their new positions until dawn on August 6. Henderson was sharply critical:

> It is impossible to defend Frossard's conduct in relinquishing a position which so effectively commanded the passage of the river, when he had every expectation of an attempt to force the passage being made. Had he occupied the Saarbrücken ridge with a strong detachment, he would certainly have delayed the Prussian attack for many hours; have gained

Prussian Dragoon trooper, drawing by Becker. (Lindner)

14   Ruby & Regnault, p. 98.
15   Frossard, General C.A., *Rapport sur les Operations du Deuxieme Corps* (Paris, 1872), pp. 30-31.

much needed time for the concentration of the French forces, for the removal of the stores at Forbach and, had a withdrawal to Cadenbronn been ordered, have secured his own retreat from the position whereon he now found himself, and which, whatever may have been his intention in withdrawing to it, he was compelled to defend.[16]

In making his dispositions Frossard posted Laveaucoupet's 3rd Division on the Spicheren heights, with Vergé's 1st Division in the Stiring valley and Bataille's 2nd Division in reserve at Oettingen. Forbach was a key point, because of the substantial depot of supplies there; it was dangerously far forward if a defensive battle was to be fought.

As for Bazaine's 3rd Corps, the positioning of its divisions had been prescribed by an Imperial order of August 4 at 9.00 p.m.

> Tomorrow August 5, you will move Decaen's division to St Avold, where you will have your headquarters and your reserves; likewise, tomorrow you will move Metman's division to Marienthal, Montaudon's division to Sarreguimines and Castagny's division to Puttelange.[17]

On the left Ladmirault's three divisions were ordered to occupy Boulay, Boucheporn and Teterchen respectively. Meanwhile to the right de Failly's 5th Corps continued its move towards Bitsche. These dispositions provided no objective for the army and provided no indication of any manoeuvres that might be undertaken. It is not clear why the Cadenbronn position, so carefully studied over a long period by Frossard in the years before the war, was not selected. Resting on the Rosselle and the Saar, and flanked by Forbach and Sarreguemines, it was one of the *positions magnifiques* which Frossard had so confidently identified. As for the scattering of the 3rd Corps behind the 2nd Corps, 'its absurdity is disconcerting – an absurdity for which Bazaine cannot be held responsible.'[18]

By the morning of August 6, therefore, the 2nd and 3rd Corps were occupying a triangle of which the apex was the area south of Saarbrücken and the base ran from St Avold to Sarreguemines. In this position Leboeuf believed that the French would, in meeting the first attack of the advancing German forces, enjoy a temporary local superiority, and for most of August 6 this was to prove to be the case. Frossard, too, began the day with considerable confidence in his ability to hold the position which his corps had taken up, and Lebrun, like many of his colleagues, felt that this certainly should be so: 'General Frossard knew the Spicheren position perfectly; he had visited it and thoroughly studied it in 1867. He was convinced that his corps

16   Henderson, p. 122.
17   Bazaine, *Episodes*, p. 20.
18   Ruby & Regnault, p. 94.

would be impregnable there, provided that the enemy was not going to attack him with immeasurably superior forces.'[19]

Frossard, in appearance and in character, was very different from Bazaine, to whose command he was now to be subject:

> Very tall, austere, brisk and ice-cold, scholarly in both military and scientific fields, and the outstanding military engineer of his time. He had skilfully directed the siege works at Sebastopol and had shown himself in Italy to be an excellent chief of engineers. Although governor to the Prince Imperial, he was the opposite of a courtier. Even the Empress dreaded his inflexibility and his opposition to her wishes.[20]

During the night of August 5/6 Napoleon had asked Bazaine and Frossard to meet with him on the following day at 11.00 p.m. at St Avold railway station. On learning, however, that the enemy appeared to be moving towards Saarbrücken with the evident intention of crossing the river, he countermanded the instruction, telling both to remain where they were and prepare to meet the attack that was expected during the day.

19   Lebrun, p. 264.
20   Ruby & Regnault, p. 101.

7

Spicheren

On the other side of the hill, the intelligence available to Moltke and his army commanders with regard to the disposition of the French army was also far from complete. However, Moltke's principal anxiety as his armies deployed was rather more with the way in which they were moving than the location or immediate intentions of the French. What was troubling him in particular was the distinct possibility that the headstrong General Karl von Steinmetz, the commander of the First Army, would move altogether too soon, and in the wrong direction. On July 27 he sent a telegram which was the first of a series of orders intended to ensure that the First Army was kept on a tight rein: 'King orders First Army not for the present to pass the line Saarburg – Wadern with its main forces. Trier to be held if attacked.'[1]

By July 31 the leading units of Steinmetz's VII Corps had already reached the Saar, while the VIII Corps was advancing down the Nahe Valley towards Saarlouis. Moltke's early decision to de-train his armies on the right bank of the Rhine meant that the Second Army of Prince Frederick Charles was well back; its leading unit was the III Corps of General Konstantin von Alvensleben. As the days went by it was becoming clearer where the French concentration was being directed, and Moltke was therefore watching developments at Saarbrücken particularly closely. On July 30 he had instructed General August von Goeben, the commander of the VIII Corps, that 'the little band at Saarbrücken must not be sacrificed.' By August 4 Moltke had rumbled the fact that the French movement on Saarbrücken was not the precursor to a general advance. At the same time his anxiety about Steinmetz's movements had deepened, and his exchanges with the headstrong First Army commander were becoming extremely strained. What was worrying Moltke was that the First Army, edging to its left, was intruding on the line of march of the Second Army of Prince Frederick Charles. On August 5 he expressly ordered Steinmetz to cross the Saar below Saarbrücken, reminding him firmly that the road through St Avold belonged

---

1   Moltke, Field Marshal Helmuth von, *Military Correspondence 1870-71*, ed. S. Wilkinson (Oxford, 1923), p. 57.

to the Second Army. This instruction appears not to have reached Steinmetz until the evening of August 6. By then the movement to its left of his VII Corps, commanded by General Dietrich von Zastrow, into the intended path of the Second Army, had brought on the battle.

The leading division of the VII Corps was the 14th Division, led by Lieutenant-General Georg von Kameke. Reaching Saarbrücken, Kameke observed that the French had abandoned not only the town but also the heights overlooking the river, and he became convinced that this meant that the French army was in full retreat, and he applied to Zastrow for permission to cross the Saar in pursuit. Zastrow told him use his own judgment; thus given his head, Kameke sent forward his advanced guard under Major General von François. At the same time Goeben, with the leading troops of the VIII Corps, arrived on the scene, having intended to cross the Saar himself at Saarbrücken. Encountering François's troops ahead of him, he confirmed that he would support the 14th Division if necessary.

There were now three German corps heading for Saarbrücken, since the III Corps of the Second Army was also moving forward to that town. Lieutenant-General von Stülpnagel, commanding its 5th Division, had received orders that if necessary he was to clear any First Army units which he encountered off the road. None of this accorded with Moltke's intention, which was that the role of the First Army should be to support the advance of the Second Army, not to get in its way; one German commentator,

General Konstantin von Alvensleben, commander of the German III Corps. (Rousset/*Histoire*)

General von Steinmetz, commander of the German First Army. (Rousset/*Histoire*)

himself a prominent cavalry commander, described the ensuing battle as coming 'as a complete tactical surprise to the Germans. That this was so must be attributed absolutely to the improper use which already, on the days preceding, had been made of the numerous cavalry of the First and Second Armies.'[2]

Thus, preceded by a dense cavalry screen, the German infantry were on the move to the crossings at Saarbrücken, as Henderson graphically described:

> It was a lovely summer morning, cool and fresh after a night of rain, when the German outposts beyond the Saar broke up their bivouacs in the forest. Before the mists had cleared away von Rheinbaben's cavalry were pushing forward to the Saar, and when at 5 o'clock the infantry divisions of the First and Second Armies began their march, his squadrons were 8 to 10 miles ahead of the advancing columns, and his scouts already riding on the riverbank.[3]

The subsequent movements of the German units approaching Frossard's position were therefore dictated by Kameke's erroneous belief that the French units were in the act of withdrawing. He had reached this conclusion for several reasons. First was the abandonment of Saarbrücken itself and the heights immediately overlooking the river, the Drill Ground Hill and the Reppertsberg. Next, from this position only a small force of French infantry could be seen. Thirdly, the bridges over the Saar had not been destroyed, which suggested a retreat in haste. Finally, and most persuasively, it seemed obvious that given the overall situation, the only thing for the French to do would be to fall back and concentrate their forces to meet the oncoming German offensive. In fact, of course, Frossard had pulled back from Saarbrücken and its ridge in order to take up a much stronger position, while the failure to destroy the bridges had simply been a mistake.

Kameke, after he had joined his troops advancing on the Reppertsberg and studied the French position, could see nothing to change the view which he had formed:

> Beneath them, bathed in glowing sunshine, lay the St Arnaud valley, a few Prussian horsemen riding to and fro across the open fields. Beyond, were the hanging woods of the Spicheren heights; directly in front the red escarpments of the Rotherberg; and further to the right, the Forbach valley, narrowed to a simple clearing by the Stiring Copse. Far over the Rotherberg rose the bare outline of a distant ridge, giving promise of more open ground, but to right, and left, and front, as far as the eye could range, except where the valleys and the red spur intervened, the face of the whole country was covered with a sea of foliage. On the crest of the Rotherberg, where the shadows of the trees lay dark and still, some companies of French infantry were visible. From the saddle in rear,

2   Pelet-Narbonne, General G.F. von, *Cavalry on Service* (London, 1906), p. 3.
3   Henderson, p. 98.

a battery of guns played briskly on the Saarbrücken ridge; and small bodies of troops were observed in the Forbach valley.[4]

On the basis of what he could see, Kameke decided to attack at once. This was after completely inadequate reconnaissance of the French position. If indeed there was only a small rearguard on the Rotherberg, he could have cleared it with his artillery; going forward without confirmation that this was all he faced was an unjustifiable risk, even if Kameke's objective was 'to hang closely on the adversary'as the German official history put it.[5]

During August 5 Frossard had been made aware by Imperial headquarters that it might in due course become necessary to fall back on St Avold, although he was not given the reasoning behind such a withdrawal. He made no preparations to carry this out; instead, he took the decision to abandon the Saarbrücken ridge, and pull Laveaucoupet's division back to the Spicheren position, south of the Galgenberg. Notwithstanding his reputation as an outstanding military engineer, he appears to have called for little preparation to fight a battle in this position. A few key points were entrenched, but he did not survey the position further. Nor did he give Laveaucoupet any instructions as to the placement of the units of his division. Although Frossard was expecting an attack, his failure to employ his cavalry in effective reconnaissance beyond the line of the Saar meant that he must await it in almost complete ignorance of the enemy's strength and movements.

Meanwhile, at St Avold, as he awaited news, Bazaine was no better informed as to the Emperor's plans. He had of course only his own corps staff to support him. He had no idea of what was intended if a major German attack was launched, since neither Leboeuf nor Frossard had apparently given any consideration to this. After the war, Frossard in his memoirs querulously enquired why, since the Imperial headquarters had correctly predicted the oncoming German attack, no orders had been given to Bazaine to concentrate his corps immediately. The 2nd Corps, meanwhile, was deployed, from left to right, with the two brigades of Vergé's division northeast of Stiring Wendel, and west of Forbach respectively; Laveaucoupet was on the Spicheren heights and Bataille's division in reserve at Oettingen, on the plateau, three miles south of Spicheren. This disposition was suitable not only for the defence of the position in front of Spicheren, but also for the orderly retreat towards St Avold which had been suggested by Leboeuf as possibly necessary.

At 9:10 a.m. Frossard heard gunfire; this was when the Prussian cavalry had crossed the Saarbrücken ridge and was in contact with the French outposts. He reported by telegraph to Bazaine at St Avold: 'I hear cannon firing at the front, and I am about to proceed thither. Would it not be well if Montaudon's division were to send a brigade

4   Henderson, p. 108.
5   German General Staff, *Official Account of the Franco German War 1870-1871*, trans Captain F.C.H. Clarke (London, 1874), I, p. 205.

to Grossbliederstroff, and Decaen's division to advance to Merlebach and Rossbruck?' This was followed by a report at 10.00 that strong reconnoitring parties of the enemy had come down from the Saarbrücken ridge but that there was as yet no sign of attack.[6]

Forty minutes later Frossard reported that he had been advised that the enemy were at Rossbruck and Merlebach: 'You ought to have forces on that side.' Bazaine responded to Frossard's three messages at 11.15:

> In accordance with the Emperor's order, I have posted Castagny's and Metman's Divisions at Puttelange and Marienthal. I have no one at Rossbruck or Merlebach. I am sending a Dragoon Brigade in that direction. Although I have but a small force present to protect St Avold, I have ordered Metman's Division to Mackeren and Betting-les-St Avold, Castagny's Division to Farschviller and Théding. I can do no more; but as you have three divisions concentrated it seems to me that the one at Oettingen could very well send a brigade and even more to Morsbach, to watch Rossbruck, that is to say the road from Assoet by Emerveilles to Grossrosselle towards Saarlouis. Our line is unfortunately very thin as a result of these dispositions, and if the enemy offensive is so serious, we would do well to concentrate in the Cadenbronn position.[7]

Given the overall situation as it appeared at that time, this was fair enough, and the only fault that can be found with Bazaine's message was that he did not make the suggestion of a retirement on Cadenbronn as a direct order. This allowed Frossard to decide to stand his ground at Spicheren, a decision which he explained by the need to protect the railway station at Forbach and the large supply depot there. It was this that required the presence of Vergé in the Stiring valley:

> Had Frossard been untrammelled by the necessity of providing for the security of the magazine, he would, in any case, have occupied a far stronger and more concentrated position; or, had he had the wisdom to accept Bazaine's suggestion, have been able to withdraw to Cadenbronn.[8]

Bazaine also had to deal with the situation on his left. At 11.00 a.m. he received a lengthy message from Ladmirault, who believed that he was facing a large Prussian force which was intending to attack him (Bazaine sardonically noted that Ladmirault was naive if he expected the enemy to do anything else). Ladmirault reported that in view of this threat he was modifying the instructions given by the Emperor. He was moving his 1st Division (Cissey) to Teterchen, the 2nd Division (temporarily

6   Henderson, p. 119.
7   Bazaine, *Episodes*, p. 25; Henderson, pp. 119-120.
8   Henderson, p. 131.

commanded by General Bellecourt) to Boucheporn, and the 3rd Division (Lorencez) to Coume. General Grenier, who was due to command the 2nd Division, had just arrived at Ladmirault's headquarters, and he had instructed him to maintain contact with Bazaine by establishing a cavalry patrol at Longueville.[9] Bellecourt, meanwhile, had reported a strong Prussian detachment advancing on Ham-sous-Varsberg. Bazaine concluded from the news reaching him that these various enemy movements were intended to conceal the true direction of their attack.

In this they were entirely successful; reports of German cavalry activity from both his left-wing and from his right at Sarreguemines left Bazaine very uncertain of the enemy's intentions. It must be recorded, however, that neither he nor any of his subordinates made any effective use of their cavalry to try to clear up the position.

General Ladmirault, commander of the French 4th Corps. (Rousset/*Histoire*)

For the moment the principal focus of Bazaine's attention was the German movement on Frossard's position.

The natural features of the Spicheren position were very daunting to an attacker:

> The bold projection of the Rotherberg, lifting its red crest high above the open valleys and flanking every direct approach; the steep faces of the plateau, and the woods which hid the interior both from view and fire; the massive village of Stiring Wendel, perfectly protected from bombardment; the open ground which the enemy must traverse in his advance, and the absence of any commanding position for his artillery, rendered the position to all appearances exceedingly strong.[10]

The position offered three alternatives for the deployment of its defenders. It might be held on a line covering the lower edge of the Pfaffen and Gifert woods, and the crest

9   Bazaine, *Episodes*, pp. 22-23.
10   Henderson, p. 127.

of the Rotherberg; or along the crests of those woods and the Rotherberg; or with-drawn to the ridge north of Spicheren and the Forbacherberg, with the Rotherberg as a forward post. Frossard's account does not indicate the choice he made and the reasons for it, or even if he made a choice, but as the battle developed it was the second of these alternatives which constituted the main French line. Bazaine, of course, was not consulted in the matter.

François, leading Kameke's advance guard, wasted no time in bringing up his artillery, getting three batteries onto the Drill Ground Hill and another on the Reppertsberg. Behind the rest of Kameke's division, von Doring's 9th Brigade was moving forward in support, while Goeben had ordered the rest of his corps to move up. For the moment, though, it was François's troops which advanced to the attack; after progress had been made on both flanks Kameke ordered François to assault the Rotherberg. Pinned down by murderous fire from the defenders, the attack stalled at first on the lower slopes. Seeing progress to the right and left, Kameke ordered François forward again. Sword in hand, François led the assault to the crest; as they reached it, he was hit by five bullets as he urged on another company, but his brigade clung on to the position they had won on the edge of the Rotherberg.

To the right, von Woyna's brigade made progress through the Stiring Copse, reaching the outskirts of the village and the coal pits to the north; a counter-attack, however, drove them back to Drathzug. Goeben's leading troops arrived on the Reppertsberg at about 3.00 and as they moved forward he took over control of the battle. To the left, Laveaucoupet was still holding firm in the Pfaffen wood and Gifert wood and beat off repeated German attacks as Alvensleben's fresh troops came forward; at 7.00 Laveaucoupet launched a counter-attack which drove his assailants back to the edge of the woods. By now, however, he faced a sustained assault on the western slopes of his position in the Spicheren wood. On the other hand, the advance by Vergé's division still gave the French possession of the Stiring Copse, while Bataille's division had come up and was heavily engaged.

At 7.22, however, there was a dramatic change in the course of the battle, announced by Frossard in a telegram to Bazaine: 'We are outflanked by Werden; I am with-drawing my whole force to the heights.'[11] This was not very informative; Bazaine, awaiting further news, telegraphed Frossard at 8.15 to ask what position had been taken up. There was no reply.

What had happened was that Zastrow had directed Lieutenant-General von Glümer to cross the Saar at Volklingen with his 13th Division. Marching unopposed down the road to Forbach, his movement was reported to Frossard by the handful of troops that garrisoned the Kaninchenberg to the west of Forbach. It was at once apparent to Frossard that his line of retreat was seriously threatened, and he ordered Vergé and Bataille to withdraw their divisions to the plateau. Although Laveaucoupet was still

11 Bazaine, *Episodes*, p. 29.

holding off the advance of Alvensleben's troops, there was no choice but to retreat, and the 2nd Corps fell back during the night in the direction of Sarreguemines.

It had been a savage battle, fought in extreme heat, and casualties on both sides were high. The total French loss was 4,078 men, of which nearly half was borne by Laveaucoupet's 3rd Division. The Prussian total loss was even greater, amounting to 4,871. Henderson calculated the numbers actually engaged on either side as 23,679 French infantry with 72 guns and 18 mitrailleuses, and 26,494 Prussian infantry, with 66 guns, making the percentage loss about the same.[12]

The recollections of the various French generals involved cannot be relied on. Whether in the form of their self-serving published memoirs or the evidence given after the war to the inquiry and at Bazaine's trial, the accounts which they gave were neither complete nor accurate. This is particularly true in in connection with any issue involving Bazaine. Lebrun's review of the battle of Spicheren is especially inaccurate in its description of the movements of the divisions of Bazaine's 3rd Corps, while his suggestion that Frossard faced an enemy force three times stronger than his own corps is quite simply wrong. The tone of his account makes no attempt at impartiality.

Frossard, predictably, in the description which he gave of the battle, sought to pass the blame for his defeat to Bazaine. In a report to Leboeuf of August 8, he began with the barely veiled threat that there were many to blame for the course of the battle which he would reveal; now, though, was not the time for recriminations.[13] His conscience might well have led him to be more candid. He justified his withdrawal with the claim that he had been abandoned to his own resources, adding that none of the divisions promised as support had marched to the sound of the guns. This was untrue; both Montaudon and Castagny did so, though halting when the battle appeared to be dying down; what appears clear is that Frossard sent them no messages at all as to the assistance he required. He was not, however, altogether consistent, volunteering at Bazaine's trial that he had 'never reproached' the Marshal for the battle of Spicheren and that he had maintained this publicly at the inquiry.[14]

There seems to have been little criticism of Bazaine at the time but he was the post-war subject of fierce complaint. The otherwise well-respected General Bonnal absurdly suggested that Bazaine, in passing on an inaccurate report to Napoleon did so in order to cause the Emperor anxiety, and thereby 'disclosed part of his perfidious soul.' This, as Ruby & Regnault remarked, was a 'refinement of hatred' that was frightening.[15] It was, unfortunately, not untypical of post-war comment.

There has been some criticism of Bazaine for remaining at his headquarters, which he explained by the need to remain in touch with the Emperor and Leboeuf. A similar complaint was made against Frossard, who throughout the morning remained at his

12   Henderson, Appendix I
13   Bazaine, *Episodes*, p. 40.
14   Ruby & Regnault, p. 105.
15   Ruby & Regnault, p. 105.

headquarters in Forbach. His failure to go to the front of his corps to see for himself how the attack was developing has been severely criticised. His explanation was that he remained there in order to be close to his reserve division, that of Bataille, and to the telegraph. This was also the point at which help might be expected to arrive.[16] Henderson was unimpressed by this, writing:

> But his telegrams to the Marshal prove that almost before a shot was fired he had become convinced that he was seriously threatened, that the engagement would be more than a reconnaissance in force; and under these circumstances his place was assuredly in the midst of his troops, on the commanding situation of the Forbachersberg, where he could overlook the field and make his influence felt.[17]

Reviewing the events of the battle in the light of the evidence given at Bazaine's trial, Henderson concluded that 'the statements are so conflicting that the whole must be rejected, and with it Frossard's narrative except where it is confirmed by outside or hostile testimony.'[18] He went on to consider the telegrams which Frossard sent, and Bazaine's replies, and in particular the latter's advice to fall back on the Cadenbronn position. Bazaine's dispositions, he finds, were well adapted to meet not only an attack from Saarbrücken, but also from Saarlouis, which was a threat which he

French lancers on a reconnaissance, painting by Walker. (Rousset/*Histoire*)

16   Frossard, p. 49.
17   Henderson, p. 152.
18   Henderson, p. 245.

had in his mind all day. Bazaine did not, however, make sufficient reconnaissance in that direction, and it is surprising that a closer watch was not kept on the crossing at Volklingen. There were plenty of cavalry units which could have been employed to approach the Saar in that direction. Volklingen is the same distance from Forbach as Saarbrücken. Since it was at Forbach that Frossard had located his headquarters, and it was there that the important supply depot was to be found, it does seem very remarkable that so little attention was paid to the possibility that the Germans might cross the Saar at Volklingen. It must have been apparent that if they did so they would readily be able to outflank Frossard if he stood on the Saarbrücken ridge, unless of course Ladmirault's 4th Corps was moved forward in that direction. The retreat of the 2nd Corps to the Spicheren position made no difference to this, its flank still being exposed to a turning movement from Volklingen, as in fact duly occurred. But neither Leboeuf, nor Bazaine, nor Frossard nor Ladmirault seems to have taken the threat seriously or taken any steps to meet it, though all were sensitive to the possibility of a movement from Saarlouis, considerably further off.

From the German point of view, it was perhaps something of a missed opportunity. The 13th Division, having covered 19 miles to reach its march objective for the day, was then sent on to Volklingen. Its advanced guard, under Major General von der Goltz, pushed on over the river, but paused when it seemed that the battle was dying down. Moltke, in his history of the war, put it very simply: 'If the 13th Division had struck in with a resolute attack, the battle would have ended.'[19]

Bazaine did not go to the front to see for himself, or through one of his staff, what was actually going on, though it is to be doubted if his appearance at Forbach would have been very welcome to Frossard. This was all that Henderson found in Bazaine's conduct that was in any way worthy of blame:

> In effect, what he did was this. First, at the first alarm, 20,000 men were advanced in support to within 6 miles of the advanced guard; and the advanced guard advised to fall back in line with the support. Secondly, when the engagement was announced as serious, 10,000 men were ordered to support the advanced guard, and 10,000, with the Dragoon Brigade, to march directly to its assistance … It was not his fault that Frossard refused to fall back on Cadenbronn; nor that, when withdrawal was no longer possible, he should have neglected to call up or communicate with the three divisions that had been sent up to support him.[20]

Nor could Bazaine be blamed for the late delivery of his telegram to Montaudon, or that his messenger to Castagny took three hours to find the division. Frossard could perfectly well have communicated with either of them direct and Bazaine expected

19   Moltke, Field Marshal Helmuth von, *The Franco-German War of 1870-71* (London, 1907), p. 23.
20   Henderson, pp. 246-247.

him to do so. Nor did Frossard keep Bazaine well-informed, sending no reports after 2.00 until prompted by Bazaine at 4.45. As for the relatively slow movement of Bazaine's divisions towards the front, the contrast with the energy shown by the German divisional commanders is striking.

In his own account of the day, which he describes as 'sad and regrettable,' Bazaine lets the telegrams which he exchanged with Frossard speak for themselves. They suggest that Frossard's grip on events was imperfect; although the struggle for the Spicheren heights had been going on since soon after 12 noon, he was by 5:45 reporting that it was dying down, though it would no doubt flare up again next day. Within minutes, however, he was announcing that his right wing had been obliged to withdraw, and that he was gravely threatened: 'Send me troops, very quickly, and by any means.' Bazaine replied at once that he was sending a regiment up by rail to Forbach from St Avold. Then, at 7.22, Frossard sent his panicky and obscure message that he had been outflanked but gave no reply to Bazaine's enquiry as to the position he intended to take up.[21] Throughout the day Bazaine had kept Napoleon well-informed of the position, so far as he understood it. He outlined the steps he was taking to support Frossard, and that evening reported that he expected to be able to hold the Cadenbronn position, to which would go the divisions of Montaudon and Castagny to join the 2nd Corps there.

It is depressing to find, when one comes to read Wawro's account of the battle, that he believes it probable that what he sees as Bazaine's failure to get a brigade from each of the divisions of Decaen and Montaudon further forward 'had more to do with a lack of acuity or just plain spite: the Marshal did not like Frossard, who was the Imperial family's favourite general.' It is an opinion without foundation and can only be explained as deriving from its author's relentless determination to impugn Bazaine's character and ability.[22]

The battle of Spicheren was not one which Moltke had intended should be fought, and he had no input into the way it was conducted, first by Kameke, then by Goeben and finally by Alvensleben. The French had in the end got away in reasonably good order, and by itself the battle had decided nothing. However, as Howard wrote, 'though Moltke's grand strategy was ruined by the premature and inconclusive engagement, a blow was also struck at the precarious equilibrium of the French high command from which it was never to recover.'[23]

21   Bazaine, *Episodes*, pp. 28-29.
22   Wawro, p. 118.
23   Howard, p. 84.

8

Commander-in-Chief

For a long period of time during the crucial day of August 6, there was a good deal of optimism at the Imperial headquarters, to such an extent that the staff there were working on plans for an offensive by the whole army, which was to be concentrated for this purpose at Bitche. As the day wore on, though, and it became apparent that Frossard was heavily engaged, the problem then became one of disengaging the 2nd Corps. Nevertheless, even after he was obliged to retreat, there was a general feeling of confidence that the position at Cadenbronn was one which could be securely held.

For his part Moltke had considered that it would indeed be the best move for the French to take the offensive, as he wrote to Blumenthal, the Third Army Chief of Staff, on August 7:

> The most appropriate course for him would perhaps be a general offensive against the Second Army. This army, of which the head is still on the move, has not yet been able to concentrate all its units. However, the French would run into superior forces, and so resolute a decision is unlikely, having regard to the attitude they have so far shown.[1]

By then, however, events had dramatically changed the position in which the French army found itself.

Any lingering optimism at the Imperial headquarters was swept away by the arrival of a laconic telegram from MacMahon in Alsace: 'I have lost a battle; we have suffered great losses in men and materiel. The retreat is presently in progress, partly on Bitche, partly on Saverne, and. I shall try to reach this point, where I shall reorganise the army.[2]

MacMahon and Ducrot had watched the defeat of Abel Douay's division at Weissenberg from the crest of the Col de Pigeonnier. The threat from the advancing Third Army was all too apparent, but it was still MacMahon's intention to resist the

---

1   Moltke, Field Marshal Helmuth von, *Correspondance Militaire* (Paris, n.d.), I, p. 258-259.
2   Howard, p. 117

enemy by taking up the strong position at Wörth which he had previously identified. On August 5 he had been given operational control over General Pierre de Failly's 5th Corps, in addition to his own 1st Corps and Felix Douay's 7th Corps. This last was still strung out across Alsace, much of it not yet having left Belfort. MacMahon at once called on Failly to move to join him in his position at Wörth. In the event Failly, still anxious about the threat from the other side of the Saar, managed to send off only one division towards MacMahon, and this did not arrive until the afternoon of August 6, too late to take part in the battle. Of the 7th Corps, only Conseil-Dumesnil's division arrived in time to join the 1st Corps.

The position at Wörth was a strong one. It rose up to the west from the swampy valley of the Sauer. The western slopes commanded the eastern along the whole of its length; the key to the position was the village of Froeschwiller. However, not a great deal been done to strengthen it for defence. MacMahon commanded a total of some 48,000 men with which to hold the position. Although he had been optimistic that he could do so successfully, he began at the last minute to have second thoughts about the wisdom of attempting to do so. One of his concerns was that after Weissenberg his cavalry had completely lost touch with the enemy's advance. In discussion with Ducrot he came to the conclusion the better course would be to withdraw into the Vosges, and he had in fact issued orders to this effect when the sound of gunfire told him that fighting had begun, and he cancelled the orders. MacMahon had not been expecting that any engagement would begin before August 7 – which had also been the expectation of Blumenthal and the staff of the Third Army.

As it was, though, the initial contacts between the leading units of the Third Army with the French outposts gradually drew more and more German units into the battle, which became bitterly contested. As at Spicheren, it was ultimately the German artillery that proved decisive; its greater range, accuracy and rate of fire overwhelmed the French gunners. Before the end MacMahon was reduced to the desperate expedient of sacrificing his cavalry in an attempt to extricate his beaten army, which fell back with a loss of over 20,000 casualties. German losses were about 11,000 men. MacMahon's troops had become scattered, and units intermingled as they retreated, narrowly escaping being surrounded. The flight became disorderly; most of the army took the road via Bouxviller to Saverne; only a few troops went to Bitche. The cavalry reached Saverne in the early hours of August 7, but the infantry did not arrive till much later, having marched throughout the night. Lespart's division of the 5th Corps had reached Niederbronn at 5.00 p.m. on August 6 and endeavoured to cover the retreat before itself falling back in two columns, one towards Bitche and the other on Saverne. When Failly heard the news of Spicheren and Wörth, he ordered his two remaining divisions to fall back from Bitche and Rohrbach, taking the mountain roads, and displaying a good deal more effort in this operation than had been made to join MacMahon.[3]

3 Du Cane, Brigadier General J.P., *The Campaign in Alsace* (London, 1912), p. 164.

One of Failly's brigades, left behind at Sarreguemines, joined Bazaine; the rest of the 5th Corps, and the 1st Corps and the division of Conseil-Dumesnil made their way to Lunéville and thence to Neufchâteau and Chaumont, before moving by rail between August 14 and August 16 to Châlons. For the moment they were off the chessboard altogether.

During August 7 Napoleon and Leboeuf went to St Avold to discuss the situation with Bazaine. It was a fraught and emotional meeting:

> When the Marshal heard the news of MacMahon's defeat at Wörth, Leboeuf saw his eyes fill with tears. The two men had quarrelled violently 20 years before over Bazaine's application for official leave to marry a dark Spanish girl at Tlemcen; and his enemies preferred to think that Bazaine always viewed his colleagues' ill success with satisfaction. But there was no trace of it that morning at St Avold.[4]

Bazaine's initial reaction was to propose that the whole army should concentrate for a stand in front of Nancy, but the suggestion did not appeal to Napoleon and Leboeuf, who continued to issue orders for a retreat on Metz.

A more detailed report of the battle of Wörth arrived from MacMahon at the Imperial headquarters during the evening of August 7. It set out in painful clarity the extent to which it had been the German artillery that had been responsible for crushing the French troops. This provoked a violent outburst from Lebrun, which he remorsefully recorded in his memoirs:

> On reading this passage of the report, in which the Marshal explained the inferiority of our artillery, I could not resist the first wave of anger which it aroused in me. I stormed into the room where my trunks were kept; I took up the ledger into which I had copied the report written by Commandant Berge, following my visits to the Bonscoet firing range. Returning to the Emperor's office, I put the report in front of the Major-Général. 'Look,' I cried, 'did I not tell you the truth in 1867?' 'Do you believe,' he exclaimed in his turn, 'that I did not know that the Prussian guns were superior to ours? But where could one have found the money necessary to transform our artillery? Wasn't it the Corps Législatif that would never give it to me?'[5]

Lebrun at once regretted his outburst, recognising the truth of Leboeuf's response. The failure of the French to improve their artillery to match that of the enemy was to be one of the defining reasons for the outcome of the war. In his memoirs Lebrun, after sorrowfully recording this exchange with Leboeuf, went on to list the mistakes that, in a few short days, had already been made since the outbreak of war, many of

---

4   Guedalla, p. 167.
5   Lebrun, pp. 258-259.

which had already become apparent. One example of gross inefficiency was Failly's handling of the 5th Corps. Had one of his divisions succeeded in joining MacMahon in time to take part in the battle it would, he considered, have made all the difference at Wörth.[6]

It was at this point that there arrived the elderly General Changarnier, who had decided of his own accord to join the Imperial headquarters. Long since retired, the 77-year-old Nicolas Changarnier had enjoyed a brilliant career in Africa before returning to Paris where he stood unsuccessfully for the office of President in 1848, coming bottom of the poll. He was, however, influential in the politics of that time as commander of the National Guard and of the army in Paris. He was dismissed in January 1851 by reason of his opposition to President Louis Napoleon, and after the coup d'etat in December of that year was exiled from France. He returned after the general amnesty, living quietly at his estate until the outbreak of war in 1870. After his arrival at Metz he acted as a strong support to the ailing Emperor.

The pressing question now, though, was what should be done to recover the situation. The news of the two simultaneous defeats at Spicheren and Wörth had thrown the headquarters into 'a state of stupor and indignation,' as Lebrun put it, not least because of the general awareness of how the news would be received across France, especially in Paris; there, the revolutionary press would blame it all on the Emperor. Conditions in Metz for the staff were not in any case conducive to the maintenance of high morale:

The officers of the general staff were distributed in four sections which,

A veteran French infantryman, drawing by Röchling. (Lindner)

in different terms, corresponded to our actual permanent bureaux. They were camped out in the Hotel de l'Europe, mingled with officers passing through, with journalists and with foreigners. The staff were eventually located close to the Prefecture and installed in a hastily furnished Orangerie.[7]

Brooding on the effect that the two defeats would have on the public perception of the Emperor, and aware that at that moment he would be alone in his office, Lebrun knocked on his door. He had, he told Napoleon, come to see him in such a grave situation out of his duty to his conscience and of his personal devotion to him. Asking that he might be permitted to speak perfectly frankly, he went on to say that he must tell him that his continued presence with the army was a source of great danger. The Emperor must, he said, look at it from both the military and the political perspective. It was imprudent to continue in command with no certainty that fresh misfortune might not overwhelm the army; while from the political standpoint such a situation would be dangerous in the extreme.

All this was very difficult for Lebrun to say. Napoleon listened with his habitual calm, though profoundly distressed by Lebrun's words, and the thought of leaving the army at so unfortunate a time. He made no comment while Lebrun was with him then, but that evening he sent for him. Taking his hand, Napoleon told him that he had thought all day of what Lebrun said, but that he had reached the conclusion that having left Paris at the head of the army, it would be impossible for him to return without it. Lebrun sadly accepted this decision; if it was irrevocable, he said, he had only one thing to add: 'I truly fear that great misfortunes may lie ahead.'[8]

The Emperor's poor physical condition, aggravated by the stress of the army's first defeats, could not be concealed any longer. There were many that shared the views which Lebrun had expressed. Piétri, Napoleon's confidential secretary, wrote to the Empress on August 8 to express his concern, echoing Lebrun's comments of the previous day:

> I have said to him that it would be better for him to go to Paris to reorganise another army and sustain the national will, with Marshal Leboeuf as War Minister, leaving the command of the army to Marshal Bazaine, in whom he has confidence and who we believe has the power to turn things around. If then we have another defeat, the Emperor would not have all the blame. This is also the advice of his true friends.[9]

The suggestion was anathema to the Empress, who demanded that Napoleon consider what would be the consequence if he returned to Paris under the shadow of two defeats. It was a view that Napoleon felt obliged to accept.

7   Ruby & Regnault, p. 111.
8   Lebrun, pp. 280-283.
9   Ruby & Regnault, p. 111.

Turning it over in his mind, Napoleon came up with an alternative to a shamefaced return to Paris. Instead, he could go to Châlons and there organise a fresh army to move forward to resist the raiders, giving up as he did so the command of the Army of the Rhine. That, of course, meant that the difficult question which must then be decided was the choice of a commander-in-chief. It was a decision into which came considerations of seniority and popularity as well as competence.

For the moment, however, the immediate task was to redeploy the army in front of Metz. This should, of course, have been Bazaine's job if he was really in command of the three corps assigned to him; but true to form, the Imperial headquarters intervened directly. On the night of August 6/7, Bazaine had reported to Napoleon that he had ordered Ladmirault to close on him, but at 4:15 a.m. on August 7 a direct order in the Emperor's name was issued to Ladmirault: 'Retire on Metz after you have rallied all your divisions.' This being the latest order that he had received, Ladmirault told Bazaine that he must comply with it.[10]

Bazaine pointed out to Leboeuf the loss of time that resulted from the giving of such direct orders to subordinate units. He received a soothing reply on August 7 that it was he alone who should give the orders, which having regard to the recent practice of the Imperial headquarters he was unlikely to find convincing. In the same dispatch, Leboeuf told him to return the Imperial Guard to Metz, unless he regarded a battle as imminent, and that in any case he should order Ladmirault to cover his flank. Advising Bazaine of the movements of MacMahon and Failly, Leboeuf added hopefully that 'the news from Paris is good.'[11]

The issue of whether the army should remain in front of Metz, with its back to the Moselle, and there offer battle, or fall back to Châlons to regroup, was discussed at a meeting on August 7. Present were Napoleon, Leboeuf, Soleille, Coffinières and Jarras. The Emperor recommended the Châlons option, urging that the army should cross to the left bank of the Moselle as soon as possible. Coffinières thought that the effect on morale of an abandonment of Lorraine without firing a shot would be very serious. The enemy, he said, although superior in numbers, would be disorganised by the pursuit. He advocated offering battle in the strong position of Mercy-le-Haut, with the option of retiring if necessary on the forts of Queuleu and St Julien, and ultimately on Metz itself. The Army of the Rhine was strong enough not to fear a blockade, and the existing bridges, and those that could be added, would enable it to cross the Moselle swiftly. This did not convince the Emperor, and the decision was taken to fall back across the river. Lebrun and Jarras set to work to prepare a scheme for a march in the direction of Verdun.[12]

The habit of maintaining a direct relationship between the Imperial headquarters and individual corps commanders was, however, incurable, and it is no surprise that

10   Bazaine, *Episodes*, p. 30.
11   Bazaine, *Episodes*, p. 35.
12   Jarras, pp. 67-68.

Frossard should have addressed his report of the battle of Spicheren, dated August 8, direct to Leboeuf. In that letter he also offered his views as to the future conduct of the campaign; he suggested that French strategy should be based on the establishment of two large fortified camps at Metz and at Langres.[13]

Fortunately for the French, the German cavalry had lost touch with both of their defeated armies, to Moltke's considerable frustration. This, coupled with the need to sort out the various units involved in the two battles, obliged the Germans to allow the enemy a few days breathing space. Leboeuf wrote again to Bazaine on August 8 to tell him that Frossard, whose 2nd Corps was that moment en route from Puttelange to Nancy, had been ordered after repeated advice to bring his corps to Metz to join the rest of Bazaine's forces retreating from St Avold.[14] Bazaine himself, in the days immediately following Spicheren, was acting as the corps commander which he still was, overseeing the retreat of his four divisions as they trudged wearily towards Metz in driving rain.

In Paris, news of the defeats of August 6 inevitably caused a major political upheaval. On August 9 the ministry led by Emile Ollivier fell from power, to be succeeded by a ministry led by the Comte de Palikao, who as General Cousin de Montauban had led the French expedition to China of 1860. Another casualty was Leboeuf, for whose dismissal there had been public clamour for days, and who was ousted as War Minister; Palikao took that office himself. At Metz, the news, though not unexpected, was ill received. Jarras was present in

General Count Palikao, President of the Council. (Pflugk-Harttung)

Leboeuf's office when the dispatch from the Empress announcing what had occurred arrived at headquarters:

> Consternation was written on their faces. The Emperor, impassive, watched and waited. Marshal Leboeuf, appalled, complained bitterly of the injustice of man; General Changarnier, who passed his time between the Emperor's office and

13 Bazaine, *Episodes*, p. 41.
14 Bazaine, *Episodes*, p. 35.

that of the major-général, deplored the measure ... Of which, according to him, the significance was evidently revolutionary.[15]

It was the first time that Jarras had seen Changarnier since his arrival at Metz, and he was very surprised to find him ensconced in the Prefecture as a guest of the Emperor.

Dismayed by the loss of Leboeuf as major-général, Napoleon asked Lebrun for his opinion as to which of MacMahon or Bazaine would be best fitted to take his place. Lebrun replied that both were needed at the head of their troops; but if, as he suspected, Napoleon was inclined to appoint one of them as commander-in-chief, then it would suffice to appoint a less senior general to act as chief of staff; in that case he thought that Jarras would be the right man. He was, said Lebrun, 'capable, intelligent, with a strong character, straightforward and loyal, which were all the qualities needed.'[16]

Before he turned to the question of appointing a commander-in-chief, Napoleon had a painful meeting with Leboeuf, who asked him that he be given the command of an infantry division; the Emperor replied that he hoped soon to be able to do this. Lebrun, who had been present at the start of the meeting, tactfully withdrew. While pondering the difficult situation, which he was sure would result in Bazaine's appointment, he met Jarras outside Napoleon's office. He told him that without doubt it would be he who took over as chief of the staff under Bazaine. Jarras protested that he must decline the position, but Lebrun insisted that it was his duty to take it. When, subsequently, Jarras was called in to a meeting with Napoleon and Leboeuf, at which Changarnier and Lebrun were also present, he protested again that he should not be appointed. Asked if his objection was due to any difficulty in his personal relationship with Bazaine, he replied that they had always got on well. After some flattering remarks from Napoleon, he felt that it was indeed his duty to accept the post.

In considering what to do about the post of commander-in-chief, the Emperor's preferred candidate would have been Leboeuf, but in the existing state of public opinion that was out of the question. Of the other actively serving marshals, MacMahon had just lost a crucial battle at Wörth, while Canrobert made it clear that he would not consider the post, as usual declining to accept a responsibility which he knew was beyond him. By a process of elimination, therefore, Bazaine must be the selection. He was popular with the general public as a man who had risen from the ranks and had demonstrated his physical courage, and he had previously been a successful commander, albeit not of any force as large as the Army of the Rhine. Furthermore, the troops had faith in him. In any event he was the only candidate of whom the Empress and Palikao would have approved.

In the situation in which he found himself, Napoleon concluded that he had no alternative but to appoint a commander-in-chief immediately, and thus it was that

15   Jarras, p. 75.
16   Lebrun, p. 287.

a letter went to Bazaine on August 12 formally appointing him. This also conveyed the decision to appoint Jarras as état major-général of the Army of the Rhine. Bazaine was not consulted about this, and indeed he would, if he could, have made a different choice, such as Manèque, his present chief of staff. A separate letter explained that in the circumstances the post of Major-General of the army as a whole had effectively become redundant, and that Leboeuf would accordingly step down from the post.

Bazaine received these letters during the afternoon, and at once made his way to Metz. He found the Emperor in his office with Canrobert and Changarnier. It was an awkward meeting for all of them. Although both Napoleon and Bazaine were noted for maintaining an impassive countenance, behind the mask each was trou-

Marshal Canrobert, commander of the French 6th Corps, Army of the Rhine. (Rousset/*Histoire*)

bled with profound emotions. For the Emperor, he was facing a situation in which it was all too plain that he might not only be about to lose a war, but that it might also cost him his throne. Bazaine was confronted by an appointment that would require him to take charge of an army many times larger than previously in his experience, and to do so moreover in an extremely unpromising situation.

Bazaine protested against his appointment, saying that both Canrobert and MacMahon were senior to him, and better fitted to discharge the functions of the commander-in-chief. Canrobert raised no objection to what Bazaine was saying but made it plain that he would not be prepared to accept the command. Changarnier made no comment, apart from observing that it would not be possible for the army to reach Verdun unless it retreated swiftly. Napoleon was adamant, saying to Bazaine:

> Public opinion, as well as that of the army, points to you as my choice; MacMahon has been unfortunate at Froeschwiller, and Canrobert has suffered damage to his prestige at the camp of Châlons. There is no more to be said, and it is an order which I am giving you.[17]

17   Bazaine, *Episodes*, p. 44.

During his trial Bazaine gave his own account of the circumstances of his appointment:

> I received word of my appointment during the afternoon. I at once went to see the Emperor and told him that there were marshals both more senior and more capable than I of taking over command in the difficult situation in which we found ourselves. I had been given no other details; no statement of further intentions, no word about the retreat of the 1st, 5th and 7th Corps, no intelligence regarding the enemy. The chief of staff who was present at this meeting had nothing to add. There had been no mention, none whatever, at this meeting of the concentration of troops at the camp of Châlons. The chief of staff should have informed me of the orders which had been given to Marshal MacMahon. He did not do so.[18]

Given all that was later to be written and said about Bazaine's motivation, Ruby & Regnault pose the very pertinent question of whether Bazaine really wanted the position of commander-in-chief:

> Bazaine is thus placed at the head of an army inferior in numbers, with weakened morale, dominated technically and tactically. If one adds that the strategic situation is agonising, it is necessary to accept that a victory would require a miracle. Can one, in these circumstances seriously argue that the Marshal sought the honour of the supreme command? Would it not be more accurate to say that honour and fidelity compelled him to make this supreme sacrifice?[19]

18   Ghio, A. (ed.), *Procès du Marechal Bazaine* (Paris, 1874), pp. 18-19.
19   Ruby & Regnault, p. 119.

9

Borny – Colombey

On August 9 Leboeuf's plan had been to concentrate the army behind the Nied, and await attack there while, as he hoped, MacMahon would so order his retreat to enable him to join the Army of the Rhine. MacMahon, however, completely ignored the suggestions that he should do so, moving further and further away to avoid contact with the Crown Prince's Third Army. Nor was Leboeuf much more successful in getting the rest of Douay's 7th Corps to join the main body as it came up from the Belfort area. The morale of the Army of the Rhine as a whole had been badly shaken by the events of August 6, and by the marches that they had been compelled as a consequence to make. Ladmirault wrote to Leboeuf on August 9: 'My men have been marching for five days, yesterday under drenching rains. We have had little sleep, and the horses and gun carriages are horribly worn out by all the mud and exertions. We need a long rest in a peaceful camp under the walls of Metz.'[1] In these circumstances the arrival at Metz of Canrobert with the 6th Corps was a welcome relief.

This had not been the original intention. The plan had been for the 6th Corps to move from Châlons to Paris, but in response to alarming intelligence reports that a German attack with 300,000 troops was imminent, it was rerouted by rail down the Mosellele valley to Metz. This line was extremely vulnerable to attack, as an officer on the staff of General von Voigt-Rhetz's X Corps reported. He had been sent forward in response to a complaint from Rheinbaben that his outposts at Faulquemont were dangerously exposed:

> After having seen the French at large today I cannot take this view. The enemy is greatly depressed. I think, on the contrary, that the more we stick to the enemy's heels the more prisoners we shall make … I think it would not be a difficult task to cut the railway from Nancy to Metz. It could be done with certainty.[2]

---

1   Quoted in Wawro, p. 144.
2   Pelet-Narbonne, p 159

A Prussian cuirassier, drawing by Becker. (Lindner)

The movement by rail of the 6th Corps was therefore fraught with danger; although most of its infantry did arrive safely in Metz on August 9, the line was cut before the cavalry, artillery and other service troops could get through.

With MacMahon hastening as far out of the way as fast as he could, there was nothing much to hold up the advance of the Third Army to the Moselle. Nancy was occupied on August 14, and the line of the Moselle was now largely in German hands. Approaching Metz, Moltke eschewed any attempt to envelop the Army of the Rhine in the manner which had been suggested to him by Frederick Charles, and instead had given orders for the First and Second Armies to move forward to a line between Boulay and Faulquemont. However, on August 11 he received information that the French were falling back from the Nied, apparently to Metz.

Without the additional support from MacMahon and Douay which had been hoped for, it had become clear to Leboeuf and Napoleon that the position on the Nied could not be held, and orders were given for its abandonment. As a result, Bazaine inherited on his appointment a situation with very few options. Napoleon, perfectly correctly, was uneasy about the oncoming advance of the enemy on either flank of the Army of the Rhine, and wrote to Bazaine: 'The more I think about the position occupied by the army, the more critical I find it; for if one part of it was driven back, and we had to retreat in disorder, the forts would not prevent the most appalling confusion.'[3]

Advice of this kind, however well-intentioned and however soundly based, did not help Bazaine to get a grip on his command or to feel that he really had the necessary authority to take decisions. Napoleon's continued presence with the army was having just the kind of effect that Lebrun had foreseen. It is hardly surprising that it should unsettle Bazaine, or that he should grumble about it; he remarked to an aide, who had arrived at his headquarters with a message outlining the Emperor's suggestions, that on the previous day these would have been orders but now they were wishes – 'the same idea in different words.' Nevertheless Bazaine was doing his very best to get the army into a position from which it could make the crossing to the left bank of the Moselle in an orderly manner. The problems which this entailed were not his fault, arising as they did from the very limited space in which the army was operating. To these problems was now added another serious setback when the heavy rains resulted in a rise in the level of the Moselle, which swept away or damaged all the pontoon bridges which the engineers had been erecting.

Bazaine's headquarters were still at Borny. Leboeuf had wanted him to establish these at Metz, which he was disinclined to do. There were, he wrote later, several reasons for this, of which two were the most important. First, he was reluctant to be too close to the Emperor while he was trying to exercise his command. Secondly, he was very mindful of the close proximity of the enemy at the time he was trying to get the army across the Moselle.[4]

He estimated that he had under his orders some 170,000 men, with 456 guns and 84 mitrailleuses; of these, he calculated that 122,000 men were infantry, 13,000 cavalry, 10,000 artillery and 25,000 engineers, administrative services and *gardes mobiles*. In addition to this number there were a further 8,000 troops of Laveaucoupet's division, which had been earmarked by Napoleon to remain behind for the defence of Metz. The rest of the army was to be set in motion at once. However, Coffinières, who had been designated as the governor of Metz, had warned that in spite of every effort the bridges would scarcely be ready by the morning of August 14.

Napoleon was becoming extremely agitated about the time it was taking to get the army across the river to relative safety, in the light of the ominous movements which the enemy appeared to be making. On August 13 he wrote anxiously to Bazaine: 'The Prussians are at Pont á Mousson, 300 are at Corny. On the other hand, I hear that Prince Frederick Charles is making a turning movement towards Thionville. There is not a moment to lose before making the necessary movement.'[5] The threat to Thionville was largely imaginary, as no German move had been made in that direction; but the need for haste was in any case obvious.

3   Bazaine, *Episodes*, p. 62.
4   Bazaine, *Episodes*, p. 67.
5   Bazaine, A., *L'Armée du Rhin depuis le 12 aout jusqu'au 29 Octobre 1870* (Paris, 1872), p. 50.

Bazaine was perfectly aware of this, as he was of the extreme difficulty which he faced in getting the army over the river at all, let alone if the Germans interfered. He told Napoleon that his preference would be to stand his ground for the moment. Indeed, it was his view that the best course would be to go over to the offensive, and drive the Germans back over the Nied, before executing a withdrawal to take up a position at Haye, west of Nancy between Dieulouard and Toul, where the whole army could be concentrated.[6] Such a move would put the army in a position to interpose between the oncoming Third Army and its route to Paris, while at the same time threatening the left flank of the other two German armies. As Lebrun pointed out, if the army fought and was beaten at Metz, it might have to take refuge inside the city under the protection of the forts, whereas if it was beaten in the suggested position at Haye it would at least have a secure line of retreat towards Châlons.[7]

The option had been discussed at length at the headquarters of the Army of the Rhine; in addition to Lebrun, another strong proponent of the Haye position was Changarnier. It was, however, ridiculed by Bonnal in his history of the campaign, who was scornful of Bazaine's support for the proposal, which he contended was a reversion to an 18th century concept of a war of positions. Bazaine, he considered, was profoundly ignorant of the way in which the wars of Frederick the Great and Napoleon had transformed the art of war, if he thought he could balance the German numerical superiority by the positions he took up.[8] Bonnal was one of Bazaine's severest critics, and went on to write of his 'narrowmindedness and childishness' as displayed by some of the observations which he made after the war. As noted above, however, the belief that moving to the Haye position would have been the right course was by no means confined to Bazaine.

As it was, whatever might have been its merits, it was in the event plainly no longer a valid option. Bazaine accepted that he must execute the retreat across the Moselle, and he began to issue the necessary orders. Wawro suggests that he was dilatory in doing so: 'The Marshal let an entire week pass before he ordered the first troops out of Metz on August 14.'[9] Since Bazaine was not in command until August 12, and he was issuing orders on the following day, the charge is entirely without foundation, though not unexpected from a historian whose view of every action of Bazaine is uniformly critical.

It was in response to his suggestion that it would be preferable to take the offensive that Napoleon forwarded to him the dispatch from the Empress, from which he had learned of the turning movement which Frederick Charles was supposed to be making. But whatever might be the truth of that, plans were in hand for the crossing as soon as possible. It would commence on the morning of Sunday, August 14; the

6   Bazaine, *L'Armée du Rhin*, p. 50.
7   Lebrun, pp. 293-294.
8   Bonnal, General H., *La Manoeuvre de St Privat* (Paris, 1904), I, p. 362.
9   Wawro, p. 144.

2nd Corps and 4th Corps would cross first. The crossings would be covered by the 3rd Corps, the command of which had now been entrusted to General Decaen.

Beginning with this retreat over the Moselle, Bazaine has been pilloried for failing to make effective use of Jarras. His decision to keep his headquarters at Borny, rather than with the staff at Metz, has been treated as an indication of his reluctance to take full advantage of Jarras's administrative skills, and his orders for the retirement have been seriously questioned. The truth is somewhat different. Guedalla observed that 'his directions for the march were detailed and practical,' and he notes, not unreasonably, that 'when Bazaine is found attending to small matters his critics have elected to discern a limited intelligence rather than a Napoleonic sense of detail.'[10] An example of the careful orders which he gave is to be found in his instructions to General Decaen, the newly appointed commander of the 3rd Corps, on August 13, which went into considerable detail. They were also circulated to the whole of the Army of the Rhine.[11]

Even more compelling, however, is the disclosure by Ruby & Regnault of the instructions which he gave to Jarras, which set out, albeit untidily, what Jarras was to do. After summarising the terms of this document, they go on:

> No doubt whatever is possible. It is a document which we would today call 'A note for the *Chef d'état-major.*' Jarras could find there all the elements of an authentic order. He contented himself merely with re-copying it and in this form sending it to the army corps and supporting services. These simple indications were sufficient for any *chef d'état-major* worthy of the name to draft a coherent march instruction. If any doubts occurred to him it was easy for him to go to Borny to resolve them. Such an initiative did not occur to Jarras.[12]

When at dawn on August 14 the retirement got under way, the situation soon became chaotic. As the baggage trains led the way they were held up by traffic jams in the city, which in turn held up those behind waiting to cross. The two cavalry divisions could not move until the afternoon, when they were followed by the infantry in six columns converging on the bridges. Further movement was hampered by the build-up in the approaches to the bridges. It was while the infantry had been standing around for six hours in the broiling sun that the ominous sound of artillery could be heard in the rear.

Steinmetz, after all the trouble he had got into during the first days of the campaign, had gone into his shell, and the First Army was moving forward very cautiously. In particular its cavalry made no attempt to probe the area to the north of Metz, which was the movement that the French particularly feared. By nightfall on August 13, on the right of the First Army, General Edwin von Manteuffel's I Corps was on the

---

10   Guedalla, p. 174.
11   Bazaine, *Episodes*, pp. 50-51.
12   Ruby & Regnault, pp. 132-133.

French Nied, with the 1st and 2nd Divisions close to the Saarbrücken and Saarlouis roads respectively. On the left, the VII Corps had also reached that river, with its 14th Division principally at Domangeville. The 13th Division was mainly at Pange, where the 25th Brigade and most of the corps artillery bivouacked for the night. The advanced guard, consisting of von der Goltz's 26th Brigade, with a rifle battalion, three squadrons of hussars and two light batteries went into bivouac west of Villers-Laquenexy. The 3rd Cavalry Division was on the Bouzonville road, principally at Vry, with outposts between Ste Barbe and Sanry. This was not a position in which the division could do much good, except to cover the right flank of the First Army against a threat which was never going to materialise.

The orders which Moltke issued on the night of August 13 reflected his understanding that the French had halted on the eastern side of the Moselle, and he took steps to prepare for either their retirement or the launching of an attack. The First Army was to remain in position and observe the movements of the French by pushing forward advanced guards. For the Second Army, he decreed that the III Corps should advance only to a point abreast of Pagny, while the IX Corps went to Buchy, 'where, at a distance of 5 miles, they will be prepared by a well-timed march to take part in a serious action before Metz.' The rest of the Second Army was to continue its westward march to the Moselle and beyond. He was discontented with the efforts of the German cavalry thus far and made a point of emphasising that the cavalry of both armies was 'to push forward as far as possible and molest any retreat of the enemy along the road from Metz to Verdun.'[13]

At 12.50 p.m. Bazaine reported on progress to Napoleon:

> Generals Frossard and Ladmirault have commenced their movement across the Moselle. The 3rd and 4th Corps will follow the route to Conflans; the 2nd and 6th Corps the route to Verdun. The Guard, and the reserve artillery under General Canu also follow that route. I hope that the movement will be completed this evening. The corps have orders to camp alongside these roads in order to follow them tomorrow morning and the staff of each are to make the necessary reconnaissances.[14]

As early as 10:45 p.m a cavalry patrol sent forward by von der Goltz reported that Colombey had been evacuated and that on the basis of other observations, 'a slow retirement of the whole line … seems to be the only conclusion.' The patrol kept the enemy under constant watch and by 3.00 p.m. reported that all doubt had been resolved, and that long columns could be seen on the roads leading to Metz. When he read this, von der Goltz was clear what must be done. During the morning he had had a visit from Colonel Karl von Brandenstein, one of Moltke's most trusted staff officers,

---

13 *Official History*, Vol. I, p. 300.
14 Bazaine, *Episodes*, p. 67.

and this had confirmed in his mind the importance of preventing the French from getting away. The only way to stop them doing so was by launching an immediate attack. Without more ado, he issued orders for his force to advance, notifying the rest of Zastrow's VII Corps, and Manteuffel's I Corps on the right, asking for immediate support.

Manteuffel was ready himself to give such support. He had ridden forward to his outposts at about 2.00 p.m., and as a result of what he could see he applied for permission from Steinmetz to advance. This was refused; but in case the French movements presaged an attack on either his corps or the VII Corps, he ordered both his infantry divisions to stand to arms. For his part, von der Goltz had not thought it necessary to seek permission from either Glümer, his divisional commander, or Zastrow, to launch his attack.

General von Manteuffel, commander of the German I Corps. (Pflugk-Harttung)

Covering the retreat, the 3rd Corps was spread out along a wide front. Montaudon's division was at Grigy, with Metman at Colombey, Castagny at Montoy and Aymard at Nouilly. In the rear of the corps stood the Imperial Guard, with one brigade between Fort Queuleu and Grigy, and the remainder west of Borny.

Von der Goltz's advance thus began a battle which the leadership of neither side had expected. The German Official History described the plateau of Metz on which it was to be fought:

> It gradually ascends from the south in the direction of Ste Barbe. The conspicuous church tower of this village forms an excellent landmark in the surrounding district. The latter is generally noticeable by its broadly swelling ridges, the view over which, especially in the northern parts, is little interrupted by the villages, which, as is general throughout Lorraine, lie mostly in the open. On the other hand, in the southern part are found numerous parks and other small copses between the larger woods of Ars Laquenexy and Failly. Of exceeding importance is the generally deep valley which at first tends northwards by Colombey, and afterwards bends away as the bed of the Vallières brook, in a westerly direction towards the Moselle. The entire plateau is divided by it into a smaller southwestern and larger north-eastern half, which may be designated briefly from their main features as that of Borny and Ste Barbe. Of the brooks which flow from the east and north-east into the Colombey and Valliéres valley, that coming from Ste

Barbe and flowing between Servigny and Noisseville is of special importance. The vine clad slopes of this watercourse are contiguous to the northern bank of the Valliéres brook as far as the Moselle. The deep bottom of the brook coming from Ste Barbe separates the plateau of that name into a west and east position.[15]

It was a terrain well suited to defence, and the French were to make the most of it.

When he heard the German guns begin to fire, Bazaine was furious, assuming that his troops were engaged in a skirmish with a handful of German cavalry. He rode up, complaining that they were wasting ammunition, insisting that he would not have a battle, and that the retreat must go on.[16] It soon became apparent, however, that a full-scale German attack was under way.

Von der Goltz had moved out from his bivouac at Laquenexy at about 3:30 p.m. His advance speedily took Château Aubigny and carried on to occupy the village of Colombey. Having driven back Metman's division, he had to face an immediate counter-attack launched by Castagny, and he soon found himself hanging onto the ground that he had gained only with the greatest difficulty. Von der Goltz now committed all the rest of his advanced guard, but could make no further progress as the French were strongly posted on the heights west and north of Colombey as far as the Saarbrücken road.

Help was, however, at hand. As soon as he had learned from von der Goltz of his intention to attack, Manteuffel had ordered his whole corps to move forward, led by the advanced guard of each division. Meanwhile Glümer, the commander of the 13th Division, had also arrived on the scene, and he put the rest of his division in motion, while at the same time applying to Zastrow for permission to attack. The latter was extremely doubtful whether this could be said to be within the spirit of the orders which he had received from Steinmetz, which had been to stand where he was. However, he also made his way to the front and when he arrived at about 5.00 p.m. realised that the battle was now so serious that it could not be broken off. He not only authorised Glümer to launch an attack but brought up the 14th Division as well.

To the north, Manteuffel's advance stalled in the face of French reinforcements. Ladmirault, whose 4th Corps had begun to cross the Moselle at Chambière, turned back to reinforce the left of the French line, and held firm against a series of determined German assaults. By now Bazaine, in his natural element as soon as the fighting began, was among his frontline troops, moving battalions, siting batteries and giving them the range. In the course of this he was hit in the shoulder by a shell splinter.

The French, taking advantage of their superior numbers in men and guns, and with the benefit of a strong natural position, were able to pin down von der Goltz's troops. On the left, the arrival of Ladmirault's corps enabled the French to occupy the village ·of Mey, from which they were able to threaten Manteuffel's right flank. To the east

---

15 *Official History*, I, p. 307.
16 Guedalla, p. 175.

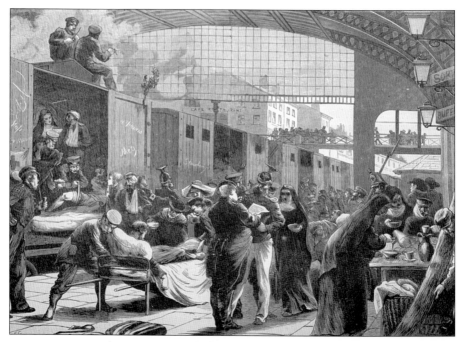

A train arriving with German wounded. (*The Graphic*)

of the village there was a bitter struggle for the possession of a small wood which continued after night fell.

Steinmetz, coming up at about 8.00, was furious at the way in which the battle had developed, and issued peremptory orders to both Manteuffel and Zastrow to pull their troops back to the river Nied. Neither was disposed to comply with such an order, which would have meant abandoning the battlefield to the enemy and acknowledging defeat. Mindful of the feelings of their exhausted troops, they preferred to remain in the positions they had gained. Nor did von Wrangel's division of the IX Corps, which had advanced from Peltre towards Grigy, withdraw from the ground it had occupied. Steinmetz's reaction to all this was recorded in a history of the operations of the First Army: 'He could not but express disapprobation that so serious an action had been engaged in without orders from a higher authority, and that it had been permitted to develop to such an extent, when the role of the First Army was essentially defensive.'[17] Steinmetz could not have been pleased, either, to discover that the actions of his subordinates were expressly approved by higher authority, or that King William had ridden forward on the following day to congratulate his troops.

17   Schell, A. Von, *The Operations of the First Army under General von Steinmetz* (London, 1873), p. 86.

Casualties in the battle had been high on both sides. Total German losses in killed and wounded amounted to 4,870; the heaviest casualties had been sustained by the 2nd Brigade from the I Corps and the 26th Brigade. French losses were 3,408; among them was General Decaen, who was mortally wounded. He died several days later; command of the 3rd Corps passed to Marshal Leboeuf, whose wish for an operational command had thus been speedily gratified.

Philip Guedalla described the scene as Bazaine made his way to Longeville to report to Napoleon:

> The streets of Metz were packed with slowly moving troops under a waning moon as the Marshal picked his way across the congested town, riding on slippery pavements and up echoing sidestreets. When he reached Longeville, the sick man was in bed; and Bazaine reported on the day's events. He said that he was anxious in case the Germans, who evidently were feeling for them, got across their line of march; and as his wound was painful when he rode, he asked to be relieved of his command. But Napoleon patted his shoulder with its shattered epaulette, telling him it was nothing, and that it would be better in a day or two, and that he had 'broken the spell.'[18]

The Emperor particularly emphasised that Bazaine should take no unnecessary risks, telling him that there should be 'no more reverses.' Bazaine, habitually cautious, needed no such advice; but the situation of the army was nevertheless still extremely perilous. Although neither side could unequivocally claim a victory, Bazaine was realistic about the outcome: 'in delaying our passage from one bank to the other the Germans had obtained the result which they sought; they won the day which we lost, and took the offensive at several points, particularly in the front of the 4th Corps..'[19]

What is plain is that Bazaine, no matter how reluctant he was to see the fighting break out, had no choice whatsoever but to resist the German advance. If, as is generally accepted, von der Goltz's attack led to the imposition of a 12 hour delay in the retreat of the Army of the Rhine, there was nothing that Bazaine could have done about it. A retreat under the guns of the relatively ineffective forts to the east of Metz would have been to invite disaster. Given the situation that arose, it cannot rationally be suggested that Bazaine was acting in any way in breach of Napoleon's instruction. And to suggest, as Wawro does, that 'he halted the French retreat on 14 August and fought a half-hearted battle on the right bank of the Moselle at Borny' is to pervert the facts altogether.[20] Now, however, it was Bazaine's task to get the army on its way before Moltke's pincers closed around it.

---

18   Guedalla, p. 175.
19   Bazaine, *Episodes*, p. 69.
20   Wawro, p. 146.

10

Retreat Across the Moselle

It had been a tough and physically demanding day for Bazaine. After leaving the Emperor he set off to return to his headquarters. On his way out, he met a group of officers on Napoleon's staff; one called out to him: 'You're going to stir up a hornets nest for us, M le Maréchal!' To this he replied that he would certainly do his best to do so.[1]

Arriving at his headquarters at about 1.00 a.m. Bazaine snatched a few hours' sleep before Jarras came to him with a report of the movements of the various units of the army as they marched westwards out of Metz. Officers were sent to each of these to urge them to keep moving, and to pass on the necessary orders to the corps commanders. Even now, however, when a fatal delay had been imposed on the French by the battle of Borny, there was a lack of urgency as the army, some 140,000 strong, made its way up the steep road by the Rozerieulles heights to the plateau of Gravelotte.[2]

Laveaucoupet's division of the 2nd Corps was to remain to garrison Metz. Of the rest the 4th Corps, on the right, concentrated at Doncourt, with the 3rd Corps behind it on the Vernéville heights. On the left the 2nd Corps, which had passed the night at Rozerieulles, was to press on to Rezonville and thence to Mars la Tour after the 6th Corps arrived at Rezonville to take its place there. Frossard had been reinforced by the brigade of the 5th Corps which had become detached after Spicheren. The Guard, in the wake of the 6th Corps, was to bring up the rear, posting a rearguard at Point du Jour. The two cavalry divisions of Forton and Valabrègue were to cover the flanks.

The 2nd Corps, having reached Rezonville, did not go on to Mars la Tour; Frossard later claimed to have received a counter order that he should suspend its movement. Neither Bazaine nor Jarras, however, had issued such an order; Frossard's failure to move forward left his bivouacs crowded together with those of the 6th Corps, and this was to have an unfortunate effect on the following day.[3]

---

1   Bazaine, *Episodes*, p. 71.
2   Howard, p. 145.
3   Ruby & Regnault, p. 132.

Bazaine's wound was still troubling him and he had it checked by a doctor before leaving his headquarters on August 15. It was, the doctor reassured him, no more than a bruise. Meanwhile that morning the Emperor demonstrated that he still exerted some authority when nominating Leboeuf to take Bazaine's place at the head of the 3rd Corps. Reporting to the Marshal, Leboeuf said: 'My dear Bazaine, if the Emperor had listened to me, you would have been appointed commander-in-chief six days ago, and I would have been commander of the 3rd Corps.' At noon, realising that the 4th Corps had still not moved, Leboeuf took the decision to reverse the order of march, and put the 3rd Corps at the head of the right-hand column. He took the road through Lessy; by nightfall, however, the heads of his columns had only reached Vernéville.

At the 4th Corps, matters were still worse. Ladmirault had asked Bazaine if his corps could stay where it was all day; when this was refused, he asked if he could use the Lessy road, and this was permitted. Lorencez's division set off, but the road was so congested that Ladmirault asked instead to move the rest of his corps through Woippy and St Privat; Bazaine refused. After the war, Ladmirault boasted that he had taken this course contrary to Bazaine's instructions and that the Marshal had then acquiesced. This was not the case; in fact the 4th Corps spent the whole of August 15 to the north of Metz. General Bonnal, not a writer usually sympathetic to Bazaine, observed that 'in not obeying the instructions of the Marshal, Ladmirault had committed a serious breach of discipline,' which should have been cracked down on with the utmost rigour.[4]

Disobedience of this kind did not make Bazaine's task any easier, but he was plainly at fault in not doing more to accelerate the retreat of the army towards Verdun. In his defence, it may be said that he had a particular concern to keep his army concentrated, fearing that the enemy were getting around him both to the north and the south. He was given a sharp reminder of the potential seriousness of this threat, when on the morning of August 15 4 Forton's cavalry division, covering the southern flank of the army's march, was suddenly assailed by gunfire from German horse artillery batteries on the hills to the south. By 11.00 a.m. von Redern, the commander of the 13th Cavalry Brigade had his troops well in hand and wished to push on to the Verdun road, and thus stand in the path of the retreating army of the Rhine. Rheinbaben, his divisional commander, not for the first time in this campaign, bungled the chance by refusing permission for Redern's move. Forton, meanwhile, fell back on the main body of the French army.

On the French side, this incident also resulted in the loss of an opportunity. First, du Barail, having at first marched towards the sound of the guns, changed his mind and retreated to Doncourt. Then Frossard, who had been at the head of the 2nd Corps looking for news of the enemy, met Forton and encouraged him to fall back on the 2nd Corps, bivouacking alongside its cavalry division under Valabrègue. Bazaine was sharply critical:

---

4   Bonnal, Vol. II, p. 82.

It is difficult to understand why three cavalry divisions were not able to take the offensive when they were closely supported by the 2nd and 6th Corps echelonned behind them. This offensive would have avoided the battle of August 16. The cause was the inertia of General Frossard.[5]

An attack might not in fact have prevented the battle, but with the odds so heavily in their favour, the French cavalry lost a possible chance of inflicting a reverse on Rheinbaben's division – although in practice it would probably have been the case that Redern would have slipped away before the attack could develop.

This was not the only incident that contributed to Bazaine's anxiety about his flanks, and thus to his desire to keep his corps concentrated at the expense of a speedier retreat to Verdun. To the north of Metz, a detachment of the German 6th Cavalry Division had boldly advanced under the cover of the morning mist and surprised Tixier's division of the 6th Corps which had been stationed between Longeville and Moulins. The German horse artillery was overcome by the guns of Fort St Quentin, but in the course of the engagement the French army lost one of its most distinguished officers, the well-known military writer Colonel Ardant du Picq, who was mortally wounded. Not surprisingly Bazaine, when this engagement was reported to him, began to fear a German thrust on his northern flank, and he ordered that the bridge over the Moselle at this point should be blown up. It was, however, protected by the guns of Fort St Quentin, and its destruction was to handicap the defenders of Metz. As Ruby & Regnault point out, however, it was a decision that demonstrated that Bazaine had no intention at this time of returning to Metz.[6]

The move through and out of Metz had been gravely hampered by the convoys which totalled over 2,500 laden wagons. At 11.00 Bazaine ordered that these be unloaded and taken back into Metz, with the exception of those belonging to the 2nd Corps, to the reserve cavalry divisions and to the general staff. It appears, though, that the rest, held back at Ban St Martin, were not unloaded.

During the afternoon of August 15, Bazaine made his way to visit the Emperor, who was now at Gravelotte:

> Napoleon was sitting on a chair outside the little inn at the crossroads; and an endless stream of marching men went by in a depressing silence. As it was August 15, the *fête* day of the Empire, Bazaine had brought a few flowers from his garden; and his little offering was graciously received. Then Napoleon enquired if he had better leave at once; and Bazaine replied that as he did not know what was going on in front of them, it would be as well to wait.[7]

---

5   Bazaine, *Episodes*, p. 76.
6   Ruby & Regnault, p. 135.
7   Guedalla, p. 176.

Later that night, when he saw Napoleon again, the Emperor told him that he had decided to leave at dawn the next day. Howard observes that 'there can be no doubt that Bazaine was heartily glad to be rid of the Emperor,' citing his depressing fatalism, his tendency to interfere and the burden of the huge convoy of the Imperial household. Bazaine wrote later that it had been his wish that the Emperor should remain with the army, but that 'he knew better than me where his presence would be most useful.' And this is borne out by the letter which he wrote to his wife August 15 telling her of the outcome of the battle of Borny and adding: 'The Emperor intends to leave the army. I shall regret this, because the responsibility would become too heavy, the more so as all that has been done up to now has gone on quite apart from me – I have only been consulted as a matter of form.'[8]

At dawn on August 16 Bazaine made his way at the gallop to Gravelotte, where he found Napoleon and the Prince Imperial sitting in an open carriage. His baggage, escorted by a battalion of Grenadiers, had left during the night. 'I have decided,' the Emperor told him, 'to leave for Verdun and Châlons', adding that Bazaine should get the army on the road to Verdun as soon as possible. According to General de Béville, the Emperor's aide-de-camp, he told Bazaine, repeating the instruction he had previously given, that he should take no risks with the army, bearing in mind the possibility of an intervention by Austria. Massa, standing by the door of the carriage, heard Napoleon add: 'I entrust you with France's last army; think of the Prince Imperial.' With this sad farewell, he shook Bazaine's hand, and, escorted by a squadron of Lancers, the Imperial procession moved off down the road to Conflans en route to Verdun.[9]

Returning to his headquarters, Bazaine found that the general staff appeared to be depending almost entirely on the mayors of the villages of Gorze and Ars for information, but that there was no news of the enemy, and that the army had in consequence been able to pass an entirely untroubled night. It was still his intention that the army should, by making a forced march, get ahead of the enemy and take up the defensive position at Fresnes which had been identified, and from which it would be able to disrupt the German move westward. Only now, however, was he given by Jarras a crucial letter from Leboeuf, sent at 11:05 p.m. the previous night. In this, the new commander of the 3rd Corps pointed out that the 4th Corps, which should have been ahead of him, had not moved the previous day, and was still, when he wrote, in Metz. What was more, two of his own divisions had been delayed. Leboeuf suggested that it would be wise if the army did not move until it had been entirely concentrated.

In his memoirs Jarras makes no mention of the letter from Leboeuf, so there is no explanation for his delay in passing the important information which it contained to Bazaine. A less lenient commander than Bazaine would have seriously rebuked Jarras for this failure. What Jarras does record, though, is Ladmirault's request through an

---

8   Howard, p 148; Ruby & Regnault, p. 139.
9   Ruby & Regnault, p. 142.

aide-de-camp he sent to Bazaine during August 15 to be allowed to take the road out of Metz towards Woippy and St Privat, a request which Bazaine curtly refused, adding that the corps should use the roads to Plappeville, Châtel St German and Lorry to Amanvillers. Ladmirault's aide complained that these roads were not wide enough for the passage of vehicles, but Bazaine was firm in his refusal.[10] He did not want the 4th Corps, when it finally got under way, to detach itself from the army by taking the road north-west towards Briey. In the event, Ladmirault again disobeyed a direct instruction, and did make use of the Briey road.

With Napoleon's parting words in his mind, which could only serve to reinforce his natural caution, Bazaine agreed that the march should not begin until the afternoon. It was a decision which, later, proved grist to the mill for Bazaine's enemies when they were vying with one another to identify instances of his conduct which supported the preposterous allegations of his treachery. This postponement of the march was suggested by the profoundly malevolent d'Andlau as an indication of Bazaine's determination to make the army independent of any authority but his own. For this absurd suggestion to be put forward, let alone believed, is illustrative of the grotesque perversions that were in due course to swirl about the Marshal's head. As Ruby & Regnault point out: 'It is contradictory to depict Bazaine as an indecisive leader, burdened by the weight of his responsibilities, and at the same time to suggest that he wanted to take charge of everything.'[11]

In pursuing a retreat towards Verdun, with the ultimate object of reaching Châlons, it was hoped that it might be possible for the army to reach Fresnes en Woevre in time to be able to take up a position to bar the German movement to the west. Escape through Verdun was always a vain hope, as Bonnal pointed out:

> For us, following calculations having as their basis the opposing tactical doctrines, if the Army of Lorraine, slow to move, had set off from the outskirts of Metz on August 15, it would have reached Verdun if not detained by August 17; but it would then have suffered, on August 20 or 21, between Dombasles and Clermont en Argonne, a disaster of the kind which obliterated the Army of Châlons on September 1 at Sedan.[12]

This assessment Guedalla found 'more impressive than the invective of Bazaine's contemporaries in the first bitterness of defeat' Written in 1904, it was by a man who was neither a politician or a contemporary soldier on the defensive but a well-qualified military expert of a later generation. His conclusion in *La Manoeuvre de St Privat* was that ' Marshal Bazaine's solution was the only wise one, given the inadequacy of the

10   Jarras, p. 94.
11   Ruby & Regnault, p, 139; d'Andlau, p. 66.
12   Bonnal, General H., 'La Psychologie de Bazaine' in *Revue des Idées*, February 15 1904; quoted Ruby & Regnault, p. 162.

high command and the waste of time between August 7 and 12'– before, that is to say, Bazaine assumed responsibility. The Marshal was perhaps unduly impressed by the firepower of modern weapons which he considered so substantially strengthened the defensive, and he preferred to fight such actions near the frontier rather than deep in the heartland of France.[13]

Moltke's first reaction after the battle of Borny was to take a cautious view of the possibility that the French might launch a counter-attack on the First Army, and he telegraphed Frederick Charles early on August 15 to restrain the Second Army's forward movement, concluding with an injunction that pursuit along the Metz-Verdun road was important. The Second Army commander had planned a movement into the Moselle Valley by the X Corps with the III Corps advancing to Cheminot and the XII Corps to Nomeny. After the receipt of Moltke's telegram, the III Corps was ordered to halt, and the X Corps to send forward the 5th Cavalry Division to find out whether the French army had retreated from Metz or was in the process of doing so. By 11.00 Moltke was more confident, telegraphing Frederick Charles to release him:

> French completely thrown back into Metz, and probably by this time in full retreat to Verdun. All three corps of the right wing (III, IX and XII) are now placed at the free disposal of the army commander-in-chief. The XII Corps is already on the march to Nomeny.[14]

The stage was thus being set for what proved to be a crucial encounter battle, and at 6.30 p.m. on August 15 Moltke ordered that the Second Army should advance on Verdun, through Fresnes and Étain.

Frederick Charles, however, was convinced that the French retreat had progressed much further than was in fact the case, and the orders which he issued that evening for the following day's operations reflected this. Rather than the northward advance which Moltke had prescribed, the bulk of the Second Army was to move to the west towards the Meuse. On the right of the army, Alvensleben was directed to take the III Corps towards Vionville; to its left Voigts-Rhetz was to march with the X Corps to Fresnes. The IX Corps was to follow the III Corps while the

Prince Frederick Charles, commander of the German Second Army. (Pflugk-Harttung)

---

13   Guedalla, p. 181.
14   *Official History*, Vol. I, p. 344.

remainder of the army marched westwards. Frederick Charles had made an under-standable mistake; it was reasonable to expect the French to have reached Verdun by August 16. The consequence was that on the following day it was only the corps of Alvensleben and Voigts-Rhetz that were in a position to do battle with the whole of the French army.

As dawn broke on August 16, the most westerly French unit was Forton's cavalry division, encamped at Vionville. To the east, at Rezonville, lay Frossard's 2nd Corps and Canrobert's 6th Corps, either side of the Verdun road. Leboeuf, with the 3rd Corps, was about 4 miles to the north at Vernéville; Bourbaki, with the Guard, was at Gravelotte and Ladmirault, with the 4th Corps, was still in Metz. Voigts-Rhetz had one division at Thiaucourt, with the other some way behind; Alvensleben, across the Moselle at Novéant, was making for Gorze. The First Army, and with it Manstein's IX Corps, was still east of the Moselle. Only Rheinbaben's 5th Cavalry Division, at Puxieux, 2 miles to the south of Mars la Tour, was close to the French line of retreat.

The battlefield of August 16 was a broad plateau, across which ran the main road from Metz to Verdun. To the east and south-east were large connected woods, particularly on the upper slopes of the heights falling away towards the Moselle. To the north of the main road, the ground sloped up to a line of smaller woods extending along the Roman road. A mile or so to the west of Vionville, a road ran off the main road south-west to Tronville and thence through Puxieux towards St Hilaire; the main road continued west through Mars la Tour. The woods masked to some extent the movement of troops; otherwise, the open plateau, especially on the ridges which crossed it, gave an extended view in all directions. There was not much cover, except in the gentle undulations of the ground, and the large hollows in which lay the villages of Rezonville, Flavigny, Vionville and Mars la Tour. A key position was that between the rising ground above Tronville to the north of the road and the plateau of Bruville and St Marcel to the north. From Vionville there was at first a gentle depression towards the Roman road, but it deepened along the northern edge of the Tronville copses. The open fields of the plateau were given over to cattle grazing. A historian of the battle of Mars la Tour, describing the battlefield, makes the point that although descriptions of the fighting often refer to 'the heights' or 'the hills,'in fact there are only gentle undulations of the ground; 'yet the ground, with its quiet contours, its re-entrants, and its woods, provides a surprising degree of concealment.'[15] It was a terrain that was particularly favourable to the defence. For an army advancing towards the Verdun road, it meant debouching from the woods to the south into the bare fields beyond. These woods were the Bois des Ognons, Bois de St Arnaud and Bois de Vionville.

When, after seeing off the Emperor, Bazaine returned to the headquarters, there to receive from Jarras the letter from Leboeuf, he was determined to keep his army concentrated at all costs. This, rather than a reluctance to leave Metz, was the reason for the order which he issued permitting a delay in the army's westward march:

15   David Ascoli, *A Day of Battle* (London, 1987), p. 115.

Since our own returning patrols have reported that the enemy is not in any strength in the vicinity, permission is given to pitch tents again. We shall probably resume our march during the afternoon as soon as I know that the 3rd and 4th Corps have completed their arrival on the plateau. Further orders will be issued in due course.[16]

Bazaine's willingness to accept the lack of information about the German movements was wishful thinking and was due to the failure to insist on thorough reconnaissance to the south, from which it must have been obvious to him that the main threat must come. It should have been the responsibility of Forton's division, as the unit furthest to the west, to be scouting for signs of the enemy, but as it settled down to breakfast early on August 16 it was blithely unaware that the enemy was close at hand.

Redern, as the commander of the most advanced brigade of the 5th Cavalry Division, had sent forward three squadrons of hussars and a battery of horse artillery as an advanced guard, which discovered that Murat's cavalry brigade of Forton's division lay just west of Vionville and was cooking breakfast. The horse artillery unlimbered on a height north-east of Vionville, and opened fire on the unsuspecting French camp at a range of 1,200 yards. Taken entirely by surprise, the French brigade panicked, and abandoned its camp, fleeing eastwards, not stopping in its retreat until it was safely to the east of Rezonville.

Redern's advance had come about when the cautious and unimaginative Rheinbaben received a direct order to push forward and attack the French at Vionville. Rheinbaben, unlike Voigts-Rhetz, did not think that the French troops on the main road were the rearguard of the army that had reached Verdun, and needed a good deal of persuading. Voigts-Rhetz sent his Chief of Staff, the able Colonel Leo von Caprivi, to Rheinbaben to get him to move. Caprivi in fact was of the same view as Rheinbaben and believed that the bulk of the French army was yet to pass Mars la Tour. For him, though, this was a compelling reason to attack as soon as possible; it was essential to delay the French westward movement.

16   Ascoli, p. 119.

11

Vionville – Mars La Tour

The first shells of Redern's horse artillery rained down on Murat's camp at Vionville at around 9:15 a.m., and the news reached Bazaine as he sat down to breakfast. Ordering the Guard to stand to, in position either side of the main road, he was soon on his way to find out what was happening. As he made his way along the main road, he encountered the ruins of Murat's brigade streaming to the rear. By the time he reached Frossard's 2nd Corps around Rezonville, he found that it was heavily engaged, and had deployed to meet the German attack. Bataille's division comprised Frossard's right wing, and had succeeded in occupying Vionville and Flavigny, in the face of hostile artillery fire, with Poulet's brigade which was supported by five 4 pounder batteries. To its left, facing south-west, stood Bastoul's brigade; it had no artillery support. Next came Vergé's division, facing the northern edge of the Bois de Vionville and the Bois de St Arnould, with the divisional artillery in support. The extreme left of Frossard's position was occupied by Lapasset's brigade, which had been placed under his orders, and which stood on the Gorze road, facing South

Frossard had received information from the mayor of Gorze during the night that columns of enemy troops had crossed the Moselle. At Bazaine's trial, he claimed that he had notified the commander-in-chief of this, and that there were between 20-25,000 enemy troops there. Jarras recorded that Frossard's memory was at fault, because the information available to Bazaine actually came from a report from Captain de France, of the general staff, who had visited the headquarters of the 2nd Corps. There, early on August 16, when he asked what was happening in the front of the corps, he was told by Frossard that about 4,000 of the enemy were at Gorze, lacking artillery. De France went on to Canrobert, who had no news of any enemy movements.

North of Frossard, Canrobert had got into a position for defence, situating his corps facing westward, but to the rear of Frossard, immediately north of Rezonville. On his left stood Lafont's division; in the centre the 9th Regiment, which was the only element of Bisson's division which had reached Metz before the railway was cut, and on the right Tixier's division, fronting towards St Marcel. The division of

Levasseur-Sorval was in reserve, drawn up in a position parallel to the main road.[1] Du Barail's cavalry division was on the northern road from Metz to Verdun, at Doncourt, in advance of the 3rd Corps, the heads of which had reached a position a mile north-east of St Marcel. The 4th Corps had begun to extricate itself from Metz, and was in rear of the 3rd Corps.

Bazaine's state of mind as he prepared to fight a battle crucial to the survival of his army has been the subject of detailed examination, not only in the fevered atmos-phere of France after the war, but by historians exploring every aspect of the course of events after he took command. Looking at the situation from Bazaine's point of view, Guedalla pointed out his fears of the steps that the Germans might now be taking out of the sight of his army:

> Bazaine was haunted by the unpleasant possibility that they might have crossed the river south of Metz in order to attack his host in rear. That notion haunted him all day; and his first instinct was to strengthen the portion of his line nearest to Metz. His later critics diagnose a fatal fascination exercised by the unfinished fortress upon a timorous commander. But though Bazaine was cautious (and he could hardly overlook the Emperor's injunction that the army was not to be unduly risked), it would have been criminally reckless to leave his rear exposed and to drive blindly forward in the direction of Verdun.[2]

Bazaine made no secret of his concern for his line of communications with Metz, and the threat which he perceived to the 2nd Corps. Noting that the German action on his right against Canrobert's 6th Corps was for the moment confined to artillery fire, he wrote in his dispatch of August 22:

> It was evident the enemy was going to make a great effort on our left from the woods which sheltered his men, and to cut us off from any line of retreat on Metz. Although I saw the meaning of this attack, I was anxious that our right should be solidly supported.[3]

In order to strengthen Canrobert, he ordered Forton to take his cavalry division to a position in rear of the 6th Corps 'with orders to charge the enemy at any opportune moment.'

To reply to the German artillery, which was firing with deadly effect on both the 2nd and 6th Corps, Bazaine ordered up seven batteries of the army's reserve artil-lery. Schirmer's horse artillery battery had opened proceedings from a position on height 901, putting Murat's cavalry brigade to flight as it did so. It was reinforced

1   Ascoli, p. 133.
2   Guedalla, pp. 180-181.
3   Ascoli, p. 369.

by three more horse artillery batteries; the gun line thus formed was under the command of Major Körber, the horse artillery commander of the X Corps. Seeing at about 500 yards to the west of Vionville that there was rising ground from which an extensive view in all directions was to be had, Körber had brought up his guns to this position, from where they fired on the infantry of Frossard's corps advancing towards Vionville.[4]

Körber was of course well ahead of the main body of the X Corps. The orders given to Voigts-Rhetz on the evening of August 15 had been to advance through Thiaucourt and thence to St Hilaire. Von Schwarzkoppen, with the bulk of the 19th Division, had moved off from Thiaucourt at 7.00 a.m. The 20th Division (von Kraatz-Koschlau) reached Thiaucourt at 11.30 and pushed on in the direction of Verdun. The distant sound of artillery could be heard by

General von Voigts-Rhetz, commander of the German X Corps. (Rousset/*Histoire*)

the 19th Division, and it was assumed that this indicated that Rheinbaben was in action with the French rearguard, but in order to see for himself what was going on Voigts-Rhetz rode forward to Jonville. There he received a report from Caprivi, and he went on at once to Tronville, where he found a major action in process. As the morning progressed, Kraatz-Koschlau could also hear the sound of artillery, and he sent forward officers to find out the situation. News which reached him from Caprivi led him at once to change direction.

It had been the artillery of the III Corps which could be heard. Alvensleben's orders from Frederick Charles had been to move on Gorze; no enemy units had been found by patrols in that village, and the assumption was that the bulk of the French army was well on its way to Verdun. Alvensleben could expect to encounter, therefore, only the tail end of the French rearguard. On the right, preceded by the 6th cavalry division, the 5th Infantry Division (von Stülpnagel) had since 7:30 a.m. been making its way along the valley road from Novéant to Gorze, with the intention of advancing from there to Vionville. On the left the 6th Division (von Buddenbrock) had moved off earlier from Arnaville, marching through Onville and Buxières in the direction of Mars la Tour. The divisional and corps artillery marched ahead of Buddenbrock's infantry. The two roads being taken by the III Corps were narrow

4   *Official History*, Vol. I, p. 59.

country lanes winding up the escarpment from the valley through vineyards and thick woods.

Stülpnagel deployed his two brigades in their advance northward with the 9th Brigade (von Döring) on the right moving up the road to Rezonville, while the 10th Brigade headed for Flavigny. Reports from the patrols of the 6th Cavalry Division had indicated that French forces were moving along the Rezonville plateau towards Gorze. When the main body of the division emerged onto the lower slopes of the plateau near the Bois de Vionville, it was met with a violent bombardment from Vergé's division which was located along the ridge south of Rezonville, and the Prussian troopers retreated to the cover of the copse to the west of the Flavigny road. Stülpnagel now advanced all his divisional artillery, four batteries of 24 guns under Major Gallus.

Alvensleben's advance was of course an enormous bluff, since he was attacking, with just two infantry divisions, the whole of the French army. Apart from the III Corps, and on its left, to the west of Frossard's position, there were for a considerable time only Körber's guns and Rheinbaben's troopers. Inside Royal headquarters at Pont à Mousson, where it was appreciated that the III Corps would be heavily engaged, there was a general feeling that Alvensleben would be the man for the job: 'The task which he might be called upon shortly to undertake would involve, in all probability, some fighting under very difficult conditions. But General von Alvensleben enjoyed such a high reputation as a leader of troops that he was looked upon as capable of coping with the most difficult situations.'[5]

If it was not at first immediately apparent to Alvensleben that he was facing the whole French army, it soon became entirely clear that his situation was indeed most difficult. He was undaunted by the task before him; he wrote later: 'Bazaine might beat me, but he would not be rid of me for a long time.'[6]

Alvensleben had ridden on ahead of 6th Division and when he reached Tronville the magnitude of his task became apparent. With the 5th Division heavily committed south of Rezonville, it was clear that he must shift the advance of Buddenbrock's division to its right, aiming for Vionville rather than Mars la Tour. It was also clear to him that it must launch an immediate attack, as he later wrote: 'I had to take the battle area for better or for worse as I found it and make the most of it. This meant that I had to match the physical inferiority of my numbers by the moral superiority of my offensive action.'[7]

Accordingly, at 10.30 as Buddenbrock's division came up to the high road, it wheeled to its right, abreast of Tronville. The 64th Regiment, part of the 12th Brigade, crossed the high road to come on Vionville from the north-west. Within an hour the village was in German hands; Buddenbrock brought up his reserves to strengthen his left and then pushed on from Vionville along the road towards Rezonville. By now the

5   Verdy du Vernois, Colonel Julius von, *With the Royal Headquarters* (London, 1897), p. 70.
6   Quoted in Ascoli, p. 150n.
7   Quoted in Ascoli, p 145.

farm buildings of Flavigny, which was a key point in Frossard's defensive line, had been set on fire by the German artillery. Buddenbrock's infantry pressed forward over the open ground, while on his right units of the 5th Division also advanced, and Frossard's battered troops abandoned Flavigny and fell back towards Rezonville. They were followed up by the two cavalry brigades of Rauch and Grüter but successfully beat them off and retired in reasonably good order.

Artillery was going to be the key to this battle. It had been Bazaine's first thought, correctly, to bring up his artillery reserve, and numerically the French had far more guns available than their adversaries. As the German artillery became engaged, however, they were soon able to assert their dominance over the French gunners, due not only to the quality of their weapons and their range, but also to the tactical doctrines employed. It has been calculated that by the evening of August 16 the Germans had had 210 guns in action, and that during the course of the day these had fired nearly 22,000 rounds.[8]

Bazaine, after meeting with Frossard and Canrobert at Rezonville, had ridden north, where he met Leboeuf, who had assembled three of his divisions south-west of Vernéville, advancing towards St Marcel. After this he returned to Rezonville, where it was plain to him that Frossard's corps was under the greatest pressure. Already Bazaine was throwing himself into the battle with his customary enthusiasm:

> When some infantry began to waver, he was there talking to the men and ordering the drums to beat; he trotted for 200 yards in front of two field guns, which he sited to his satisfaction; then he was off leading a battalion of infantry into action with a cheerful 'Allons, mes enfants, suivez votre maréchal.' He seemed to find a sardonic satisfaction in taking his staff under fire at a walk, though once he ordered Jarras and his cavalcade to keep clear of him.[9]

Combat always brought out the best and worst in Bazaine. His extraordinary energy and physical courage was noted even by d'Andlau, who observed:

> He involved himself in every detail, siting individual batteries here and there, showing battalions the positions which each should occupy. He was everywhere, not sparing himself for a moment, but entirely confusing his responsibility as a commander-in-chief with the more modest duties of the general or even an ordinary colonel.[10]

The criticism is just; but in fact in these early stages of the battle there was not a lot else he could do until he saw how the German attack developed. What was clear to him

---

8   Ascoli, p. 136.
9   Guedalla, p. 182.
10   Quoted in Ascoli, p. 144.

was that he must beat off that attack before the army could either resume its march to Verdun or take another course.

Another observer of Bazaine during the battle reflected on the tranquillity with which he faced danger: 'Bravery takes many forms; that of Marshal Bazaine was a kind of unconscious indifference to danger, entirely as if his long experience had left him able to ignore its existence.'[11] There can be no doubt that in this way Bazaine was a source of huge inspiration to his men, as he perfectly understood; when reproached by an officer for his rashness, he replied that it was necessary to keep up the morale of the troops.

By noon, following the fall first of Vionville and then of Flavigny, Frossard was becoming desperately concerned about the ability of his corps to hold the line, and the indications that Alvensleben was going to push his advance to the east of Flavigny. He asked permission to launch the 3rd Lancer Regiment, which formed part of Lapasset's brigade, in an immediate assault. To this request, Bazaine agreed, and made available as support to the Lancers the Cuirassier Regiment of the Guard, from du Preuil's brigade. It was said that the commander of the cuirassiers objected to charging unbroken infantry, to which Bazaine was supposed to have replied: 'It is vitally necessary to stop them; we must sacrifice a regiment.'[12] It was, predictably, a disaster.

Without any preparation, the 3rd Lancers assembled to the south of Rezonville, launching themselves on a line parallel to the main road against the enemy infantry that had reoccupied Flavigny. Broken up by the wire fencing that was scattered across the terrain, the charge fell into the void. Better positioned, the Guard cavalry, whose cuirasses were adorned with white aiguillettes, all mounted on black horses, charged a little further to the south. Pushed to the limit, the charge cost this magnificent regiment half its effectives.[13]

Bazaine reckoned, however, that it had achieved its purpose, stabilising the line until the artillery, and the Grenadier Division of the Guard arrived. Frossard claimed that the cuirassiers had ridden between the Prussian infantry and artillery, 'where they sabred several gunners.' As it was, the survivors were driven back to their own lines by Redern's hussars and dragoons. Bazaine was caught up in the ensuing melee:

> The Marshal stood his ground and drew his sword in a storm of pounding hoofs and pistol shots; and presently he found himself riding alongside an excited French subaltern. 'Allons, jeune homme,' the older man remarked, 'du calme. Voyons, vous n'êtes plus un enfant. Ce n'est rien.' Then he walked his horse away and found himself near Frossard. Pointing to a cloud of dust, he said that it was Steinmetz trying to cut them off from Metz.[14]

11   Colonel Fix quoted in Ruby & Regnault, p. 147.
12   Howard, pp. 155-156.
13   Ruby & Regnault, p. 147.
14   Guedalla, pp. 184-185.

Once he had escaped from the cavalry conflict which had surged around him, it was clear to Bazaine that the 2nd Corps had been so knocked about during the morning's fighting that it could no longer be depended on to hold the left flank of the army, and he pulled back the division of Bataille (who had been seriously wounded), and the brigade of Valazé. These he withdrew to Gravelotte, replacing them with Picard's Grenadier Division of the Imperial Guard, supporting it with Deligny's Voltigeur Division which covered the exits from the Bois des Ognons. Bazaine had a substantial numerical advantage on the battlefield and now, with this rearrangement of his line, Alvensleben faced fresh troops. The III Corps, which had been fighting all morning in the fierce heat, was barely able to hold the positions which it had taken, and but for the effectiveness of its artillery might not have been able to resist a determined attack. Even before it came into action, Buddenbrock's division had marched 15 miles in five hours.

North of the high road, the French artillery posted along the Roman road were keeping Vionville under extremely heavy fire, and in order to ensure its continued occupation a further advance eastward was launched by the 20th Regiment, while the 64th Regiment pushed forward along both sides of the road. The struggle here became intense, and casualties mounted rapidly. In this sector of the battlefield, Bazaine was especially strong. Not only was Canrobert's corps in position around Rezonville north of the high road; by noon Leboeuf's 3rd Corps had come into position beyond the Roman road, and although Alvensleben may have been unaware of it, Ladmirault's 4th Corps had passed Malmaison a mile or so north-west of Gravelotte, heading to take up a position on Leboeuf's right. Canrobert was becoming aware that the German line in his front was perhaps not so strongly held as he had thought, and he began a movement intended to recapture Vionville.

It was now evident to Alvensleben that, to maintain his bluff until relief could come from the X Corps marching towards the battlefield, he must do something very quickly. Not only was Canrobert preparing what might be a fatal assault; on his right Leboeuf's corps offered a further threat. He had no further infantry reserves with which to resist Canrobert's advance. All that he did have were the 5th and 6th Cavalry Divisions; the force most readily available to him was von Bredow's 12th Cavalry Brigade.

It is almost impossible to do justice to what followed, although many writers have attempted to do so. The task confronting Bredow was, on the face of it, almost as impossible as that which had, only shortly before, led to the destruction of the French lancers and cuirassiers. It was entirely likely that it would lead to a catastrophe similar to that which had engulfed the French cavalry at Morsbronn 10 days earlier or to that of the Light Brigade at Balaclava. Bredow's objective was to be Canrobert's gunline, securely protected by infantry, a target which was most definitely not one that should be demanded of even the most audacious cavalry commander. Alvensleben was under no illusion about what he was asking, but Bredow did not demur, though he took time to make careful preparations before launching his attack. He had only two regiments with him, the third having been detached to form part of the exiguous force to the north of Mars la Tour. It was with the 804 men of the 7th (Magdeburg) cuirassiers

General von Bredow receives the order to
attack, drawing by Becker. (Lindner)

and the 16th (Altmark) Uhlans that he now prepared to advance. At 1:58 p.m. he led
his brigade from its position south-west of Flavigny past Vionville and along a narrow
track sheltered from the sight of the enemy to a point east of the Bois de Tronville
where it dropped to a shallow valley.

The French could see Bredow now, and it was under increasingly heavy fire that he
wheeled to the right and then, with the cuirassiers on the left and the uhlans on the
right, gave the order to advance. The German Official History described the charge:

> Under an overwhelming artillery and infantry fire poured in at close range, the
> brigade dashes forward in line, Major Count Schmettau with the 7th Cuirassiers
> on the left and Major von der Dolen with the 16th Lancers on the right, against
> the nearest masses of the enemy. The first French line is ridden over, the line
> of guns broken through, teams and gunners put to the sword. The second line
> is powerless to check the vigorous charge of horse; the batteries on the heights
> further to the rear limber up and seek safety in flight. Eager to engage, and
> thirsting for victory, the Prussian squadrons charge even through the valley
> which descends from the Roman road to Rezonville, until at length after a career
> of 3,000 paces they are met on all sides by French cavalry.[15]

The French cavalry which now came up and surrounded the brigade were from
Forton's division, anxious to efface the memory of their flight in the early morning
and also from Valabrègue's division. Bredow sounded the recall, and what was left
of his brigade fought its way back to the German lines. It was estimated that some
3,100 French cavalry were engaged. Bredow's men had suffered terribly, losing a total

15   *Official History*, Vol. I, p. 387.

A study of the cavalry battle at Mars-la-Tour, painting by Hunten. (Rousset/*Histoire*)

of 370 men; but they had inflicted a serious check on Canrobert's advance, and given Alvensleben a crucial breathing space.

Meanwhile Bazaine had, during the cavalry melee in which he had been involved south-west of Rezonville, become separated from Jarras and the rest of the staff. Jarras, in his account, said that the separation was for about an hour; one of Bazaine's orderly officers, Captain de Mornay-Soult, put it at much longer, and it seems that Jarras was not particularly assiduous in finding out where the Marshal had got to. Asked by de Mornay if he was going to rejoin Bazaine, he gave an answer which came as a surprise: 'That's a matter for you, Mr Orderly Officer.' It was a reply which Jarras indignantly denied at Bazaine's trial; although not able to recall their conversation precisely, he said that de Mornay was completely wrong. In fact, he said, he had been sending out in all directions to find the Marshal.[16] This apparent indifference on the part of Jarras was confirmed by Colonel Fix, who had himself become separated from the staff. When he rejoined it, he asked Jarras if he knew where the Marshal was; the reply was: 'I know nothing,' to which Fix observed that in that case it would be necessary to look for him, and off he went, finding Bazaine without difficulty in front of Rezonville in command of some artillery.[17]

When Fix caught up with him, Bazaine merely commented: 'Ah, ça, ces bougres-là vont me laisser seul en l'air,' and he sent Fix to tell Leboeuf that he need not hurry his advance, for he should wait for Ladmirault. When other members of his staff rejoined him and urged him to order the army to move at once in the direction of Verdun, his response displayed again the caution that he might be walking into a trap: 'Mes amis,

16   Jarras, p. 109.
17   Ruby & Regnault, pp. 148-149.

vous ne savez donc qu'ils nous attendant avec leurs forces réunies sur le plateau de Fresnes-en Woevre, et que ce serait se jeter dans leur gueule.' He was of course not to know that the bulk of the Second Army was actually marching away from him; but it was not unreasonable to suppose that if he got as far as Fresnes he might indeed find that he had walked into the lion's mouth.[18]

Another staff officer was with Bazaine during the period of his separation from Jarras. Baron Berge wrote later:

> I spent nearly half an hour with the Marshal; I found that he was scarcely acting as a commander in chief, but was cheerful, active, appearing in good humour, and expressing a number of very apposite ideas. He said that he had no news of Ladmirault, but that when the moment arrived for him to come up, he would sweep all away.[19]

All accounts of Bazaine at this time record not only his unwavering courage, but also his absolute calm, to which both Canrobert and Bourbaki would testify at his trial. His confidence that when Ladmirault appeared he would be able to drive the German left off the battlefield was not without good reason, as subsequent events were to show. As the advance of the 4th Corps was developing, Bazaine had a further meeting with Leboeuf to whom he gave instructions for the 3rd Corps to advance southwards.

In general, though, Bazaine had throughout August 16 more or less delegated the conduct of operations on his right wing to the individual corps commanders involved, which meant that it would be down to them as to how to arrange to cooperate with each other. Mutual support, during the course of the Franco-Prussian war, was not something at which French commanders were very good, although at times during the battle of Vionville-Mars la Tour there does appear to have been some useful cooperation between them. For Bazaine, whose concern with his left wing never eased, it was enough to trust his corps commanders to march to the sound of the guns and attack the enemy which they encountered. It proved to be one of his more serious lapses of judgment.

It was the decisive moment of the battle. The Germans had committed all their immediately available resources, to the last man and the last gun. There were at least five hours of daylight left, and the French had four intact divisions ready to advance:

> An offensive launched from the woods of St Marcel and Rezonville and from the Bois de Tronville must bring victory. It did not take place. Bazaine, whose plan it was, made it subject to the arrival of Ladmirault. Had he already given up on victory? Was there some serious motive for delaying this counteroffensive?[20]

---

18   Guedalla, p. 185.
19   Ruby & Regnault, p. 149.
20   Ruby & Regnault, p. 151.

A fragment of de Neuville's panorama of Mars-la-Tour. (Rousset/*Histoire*)

Ruby & Regnault discovered that Bazaine's motives were not in the least mysterious. First, the extremely aggressive stance of the enemy had deceived him, as with the other French commanders, as to the strength of the opposition which they faced. The German artillery had not let up, and between 2.00 and 3.00 had inflicted colossal damage on the French batteries between Rezonville and the Bois des Ognons. Secondly, at about 3.30 Bazaine received a dispatch from Coffinières sent from Fort St Quentin at 2:19 p.m.to the effect that considerable columns of enemy troops had been seen behind Augny, moving towards the Bois de Jouy and the Moselle, which was a serious threat both to Gravelotte, to the French rear, and to the convoys held up behind the combat units. Finally, the situation caused by the retreat of the 2nd Corps at Rezonville had only been partly resolved. Bazaine, who was personally close to the endangered sector, was perhaps devoting too much attention to it. But were the steps which Bazaine was taking due to a concern for his centre, motivated by the need to resist powerful and dangerous attacks or, as is generally supposed, by his desire not to be cut off from Metz? For Ruby & Regnault the distinction is unimportant; they point out that having condemned Bazaine to death at his trial, his judges qualified it by reference to the strength of his determination to maintain the centre of his line on August 16.[21]

21   Ruby & Regnault, p. 152.

On the French right wing Ladmirault's advance was having a telling effect. Grenier with his leading division was driving the German infantry out of the Bois de Tronville, pushing them to the south of the main road to Tronville, while du Barail's cavalry division was able to reoccupy Mars la Tour as the German cavalry fell back. Now was the moment for the 4th Corps to 'sweep all away.' At this critical moment Grenier's nerve failed. He believed he should wait for more support and Ladmirault, whose 2nd Division under Cissey was moving up, thought he was right. It would only be half an hour before Cissey could be deployed in Grenier's support.

It was a delay that was to prove crucial. Ever since early morning, the infantry of Voigts-Rhetz's X Corps had been on the march. In spite of the intense heat, they had maintained a ferocious pace. The 38th Brigade (von Wedell), in the lead and heading for St Hilaire in accordance with orders, would cover more than 27 miles in less than ten hours, and the 20th Division nearly 25 miles in eight hours, ultimately going straight into battle with scarcely a break and with no cooked meal.[22] Lehmann's 37th Brigade, which had set off behind the 38th Brigade, but which, alerted by Caprivi's warning message had turned towards the sound of the guns, had reached Puxieux by noon, and had been committed by Alvensleben into the Bois de Tronville. Although ultimately unable to resist the advance of Ladmirault's men, it had provided a solid support to Alvensleben's left wing for several vital hours; and its arrival on his right may have caused some concern to Bazaine at a time when his own left seemed to be crumbling.

Voigts-Rhetz, when he got Caprivi's message, realised that Alvensleben was in trouble, and he switched the 20th Division from Thiaucourt up the road to Chambley, sending his corps artillery on ahead. Schwarzkoppen, whose 37th Brigade had already anticipated the situation, was ordered to turn east along the main road to Mars la Tour as soon as he reached it. Voigts-Rhetz galloped on ahead to find out exactly what had been happening with the III Corps, meeting Alvensleben soon after Bredow's charge. The decision to send the X Corps artillery on ahead paid dividends immediately; taking up a position south west of the Bois de Tronville, it opened fire at 3:48. Ladmirault, in the face of what he considered to be a serious threat, now pulled Grenier back to the Bruville slope.[23] This exposed the flank of Aymard's division of the 3rd Corps, and Leboeuf felt obliged to order it to fall back from the position it had gained at the Bois de Tronville.

By 5.00 the X Corps was heavily engaged. The 40th Brigade, from Kraatz's division, which had formed up at Tronville half an hour before, had succeeded in reoccupying the Bois de Tronville. To the Germans, Grenier's withdrawal seemed surprising:

> This rapid change, the retreat of a far superior force of the enemy in front of a few fresh battalions, can only be perhaps explained by the simultaneous

22   Ascoli, p. 181.
23   Ascoli, p. 183.

cooperation of other causes. The vigorous attacks of the Prussians from the direction of Vionville had caused Marshal Bazaine to reinforce the 6th Corps west of Rezonville in the manner already alluded to; his chief solicitude was, however, still directed to his own left wing, and he consequently remained there in person, in order to be able to meet in good time any turning movement of the German forces in the woods on the left bank of the Moselle. Less apprehensive about the right wing of the army, he had about 5.00 merely sent orders to Marshal Leboeuf to maintain (de maintenir fortement) his position in conjunction with the 6th Corps.[24]

The official historians thought that in addition to this order, Leboeuf's decision to hold back from attacking Tronville at this time might also have been affected by news of additional German troops approaching from Hannonville, to the west of Mars la Tour.

This was Wedell's 38th Brigade, which had reached a position south of the main road and then turned east, with the divisional commander Schwarzkoppen riding at its head. Reaching Suzemont, he received an order from Voigts-Rhetz informing him of the difficult situation in the Bois de Tronville; but by the time the brigade had reached a point south-west of Mars la Tour the situation had changed for the better. This led Schwarzkoppen to make a serious error of judgment; he resolved to send the brigade forward north eastwards from Mars la Tour to attack the position occupied by Grenier's division.

The brigade moved forward under intense rifle and mitrailleuse fire, advancing in rushes of 100 to 250 yards. As it came down the slope it encountered an obstacle which, properly reconnoitred, should have led to the attack being aborted. A steep ravine, nearly 50 feet deep, faced the charging infantry. Undaunted, they climbed the opposite slope, to face a withering file fire at short range. The French superior numbers were overwhelming, Cissey's division having come up on Grenier's right, and Wedell's shattered brigade fell back.[25]

The brigade's losses were appalling; out of a total strength of 4,641 officers and men, 2,614 casualties had been sustained; well over half its men had been lost, including many senior officers killed or seriously wounded. The ruins of the brigade poured back over the road towards Tronville, where Caprivi hurriedly gave orders for all the X Corps documents to be burned. It was a catastrophe which presented Ladmirault with a colossal opportunity to smash the German left wing.

Once again, he hesitated. His 3rd Division had still not come up, and he feared that making a further advance might be to lose the victory which he seemed to have gained. Bazaine, in his dispatch of August 22, wrote: 'General Ladmirault recognised that Tronville was too strongly occupied to be taken with two divisions, and he

---

24   *Official History*, Vol. I, p. 396.
25   *Official History*, Vol. I, p. 407.

contented himself in occupying temporarily the enemy, and in establishing himself on the ground which he had gained.'[26]

Voigts-Rhetz, though, was made of sterner stuff. Summoning the Guard Dragoon Brigade under Count Brandenburg, which had accompanied Wedell's brigade along the high road, he ordered an immediate attack. With three squadrons of dragoons and two of cuirassiers, Brandenburg charged northwards into Cissey's infantry just as they emerged from the valley in which the 38th Brigade had been destroyed. Although they stood their ground, their advance was halted, and the opportunity had passed. Ladmirault ordered Cissey to return to his previous positions. It was 5:30; although Brandenburg's brigade had lost about half of the 600 men engaged, it had succeeded in destroying what was left of Ladmirault's nerve.

By now the commander of the 4th Corps was becoming seriously concerned about the safety of his own right flank, which rested on the road running north from Mars la Tour towards Jarny. He summoned his own cavalry commanders, telling them that his right wing was menaced by enormous masses. Bodies of fresh enemy infantry were preparing to advance again from Tronville: 'This will be the moment to make a charge. Clear these masses away from me, and my right wing will be saved.'[27]

With three years to consider his conduct during the battle of Vionville-Mars la Tour, Ladmirault came to Bazaine's trial with an account of how he saw the situation, in terms which were somewhat different:

> At this moment, I wished to exploit my advantage. My corps had suffered some 2,000 casualties. I had only two divisions in the line: Cissey's, which had taken part in the earlier attack, and Grenier's, which had been fighting throughout the afternoon. My third division, Lorencez's, which had left Metz on the 15th, had not arrived. I sent aide-de-camp after aide-de-camp to urge him to expedite his arrival on the battlefield. He did not arrive until 10.00 p.m..[28]

Ladmirault had a large force of cavalry at his disposal; the cavalry division of the 4th Corps, commanded by General Legrand and the reserve cavalry division of du Barail, while the cavalry division of the 3rd Corps (Clerembault) was also on hand. The latter came up too late to take part in the engagement which followed; but the first two of these divisions charged over the open country west of the Yron, their immediate target being Rheinbaben's division. The French had some 800 yards to cover and reached the German column in some disorder. By the time that the bulk of the French cavalry had been prepared to charge, it seemed to du Barail that the most favourable moment had passed and he said as much to Legrand. 'It's all the same to me,' the latter replied: 'I have been ordered to charge and I will charge,' and he gave orders to Montaigu,

26   Quoted in Ascoli, p. 191.
27   Bazaine, *Episodes*, p. 85.
28   Anon., *Proces du Marechal Bazaine* (Paris, 1874), p. 109.

commanding the light brigade of his division, to charge without delay. To Colonel Carrelet, the commander of the 2nd Hussars, who asked if before doing so the front rank should deliver a salvo with their carbines, he gave an abrupt reply: 'Non, au sabre!'[29] As Howard wrote: 'More and more squadrons, French and German, charged into the gigantic melée until over 40 were involved, Chasseurs, Uhlans, Dragoons, Hussars, in a confusion of dust wherein it became difficult to tell friend from foe.[30]

The outcome of this engagement was described by a German historian:

General Legrand, commander of the Cavalry Division, French 4th Corps, killed at Mars-la-Tour. (Rousset/*Histoire*)

> The Prussian cavalry rallied on the plateau which they had won, and then retired into the line of battle of the infantry, who had in the meantime re-formed near Tronville, and were prepared for fresh resistance. Darkness fell on this phase of the combat. This action has been called, by critics who condemned it, an unnecessary cavalry duel ... But it was by no means without result. The Prussian cavalry had the advantage. Owing to the excellence and the number of the enemy's cavalry, he did not suffer a serious defeat, but he was driven back in the end, and the Prussians held the field of battle. The result was that we obtained all we wanted to obtain. Our infantry was enabled to reform itself.[31]

Bonnal, who gave a detailed account of this cavalry battle, pointed out that in fact it divided into two separate melées. That to the north involved 1,400 Prussian cavalryman and 1,500 French, while that to the south involved 1,300 Prussians and 900 French. Bonnal observed that cavalry tactics had not significantly changed since the days of Seydlitz and Zieten. He was unimpressed with the quality of the leadership of

29   Quoted, Bonnal, II, pp. 421-422.
30   Howard, p. 159.
31   Hohenlohe-Ingelfingen, Prince Kraft zu, *Letters on Cavalry* (London, 1889), pp. 29-30.

The arrival of Prince Frederick Charles, painting by Freyberg. (Rousset/*Histoire*)

such as Rheinbaben; and noted that in the decade after the war both the German and French armies reviewed the whole basis of their cavalry tactics.[32]

Casualties during these cavalry battles were high; the Germans lost 359 out of 3,040 men engaged; the French lost 434 out of 2,820. In each case, the losses among officers were very much greater. These included the death of Legrand and severe injuries to Montaigu; 28 percent of the Prussian officers were killed or wounded, and 35 percent of the French.

Meanwhile the commander of the Second Army had been on the scene for some time. It was only at about 1.00 p.m. that Frederick Charles had heard of the fierce struggle in which Alvensleben's corps was engaged, and he soon resolved to go and see for himself. Before setting out from Pont à Mousson, he ordered von Manstein, the commander of the IX Corps, to get his leading troops over the Moselle as soon as possible, and march to Alvensleben's support. Frederick Charles reached the battlefield at about 4.00, and his first thought appears to have been an order to Voigts-Rhetz to advance on his left against Ladmirault, an order which it would have been impossible to execute.[33] Thereafter, for some time he left it to Alvensleben and Voigts-Rhetz to continue to direct the battle in which their corps were so heavily engaged; it was evident to him that it would be some time before Manstein could come up in support. And although elements of the VIII Corps from the First Army were also approaching the battlefield, it would be some time before their influence could be felt.

When the 32nd Brigade came up through Gorze, at about 5.00, Alvensleben at once committed it to the struggle on the edge of the Rezonville plateau where, facing the overwhelming strength of the French there, it soon began to suffer heavy casualties. But its appearance on the French left served to reinforce in Bazaine's mind his concern that the Germans intended on this sector of the battlefield to cut him off from Metz.

Although his numerical advantage here meant that Bazaine's left was in fact reasonably secure, there were moments when his concern was justified. At about 5.30 two batteries of the Voltigeur Division of the Guard, coming under heavy German artillery fire, precipitately retreated. This, coupled with the death of General Marguenat, commanding a brigade of Levasseur-Sorval's 4th Division of the 6th Corps, caused a panic first in the 26th and then the 25th Line Regiments, which fell back rapidly towards Rezonville. Bazaine ordered Montaudon, the commander of the 1st Division of the 3rd Corps, to fill the gap thus created, and the line held.[34] There were other instances of such abrupt withdrawals; Canrobert, at about 7.30, was obliged to order two squadrons of Chasseurs of the Guard 'to prevent the retreat of the infantry.' The troops concerned may have been reservists, but

General Count Brayer, commander of the 1st Brigade, 1st Infantry Division, French 4th Corps, killed at Mars-la-Tour. (Rousset/*Histoire*)

such incidents were not confined to units which were largely composed of these; there were other such occasions when this was not the case.[35] When panics of this kind occurred, they created a strong impression on the mind of witnesses, even to experienced soldiers like Bazaine and Canrobert. In addition they caused a weakening of the structure of their units, and damaged discipline to the point for instance where troops at the least occasion abandoned their packs:

> After the complete disorganisation of the 2nd and 6th Corps during August 16, it is not surprising that it caused breakdowns during the evening. Only exhaustion and the fall of night prevented an exodus all the way to the gates of Metz. This depressing spectacle certainly had an appreciable effect on the decision that would be taken by the Marshal.[36]

34   Bonnal, II, pp. 462-463.
35   .Ruby & Regnault, p. 156.
36   Ruby & Regnault, p. 156.

Bazaine's sense of his vulnerability was increased by a decision now taken by Frederick Charles, who at about 7.00 ordered a final attack on Rezonville. His intention was that it should be launched by both Voigts-Rhetz and Alvensleben, but the former was quite unable to mount any sort of offensive. It was carried out by Buddenbrock's 6th Division and part of Stülpnagel's 5th Division. It was checked by heavy artillery fire; but Frederick Charles followed it up with an attack by the 6th Cavalry Division. Although suffering heavy casualties, including the death of Grüter, the commander of the 14th Cavalry Brigade, it came as a surprise in the gathering gloom, and drove back the French outposts into Rezonville. Moltke did not approve:

> It was clearly most unadvisable to challenge by renewed attacks an enemy who still outnumbered the Germans; which action, since no further reinforcements could be hopeful, could not but jeopardise the success so dearly bought. The troops were exhausted, most of their ammunition was spent, the horses had been under the saddle for 15 hours without fodder; some of the batteries could only move at a walk, and the nearest army corps on the left bank of the Moselle, the XII, was distant more than a day's march.[37]

David Ascoli takes a different view, arguing that the unexpected advance so late in the day had the effect of confirming Bazaine's belief that he was opposed by a greatly superior enemy:

> That this was not so, had never been so, and would not be so for another 48 hours is irrelevant. When a commander abdicates supreme responsibility and allows a resourceful opponent to dictate his course of action, figments of imagination become useful substitutes for true facts. It is for this reason that Moltke was wrong and Frederick Charles – for all the wrong reasons – was right.[38]

Ascoli's opinion was shared by Hohenlohe, who firmly rejected Moltke's view, and ascribed Bazaine's decision on the following day to retreat to a conviction that the boldness of the attack could only be explained by the arrival of strong reinforcements: 'Thus the indecisive battle became a victory, while for this victory the army owed almost as many thanks to the courage and daring of its cavalry, as it did to the heroic endurance of the infantry and artillery.'[39]

It may however be argued that this brings speculative hindsight to a decision to launch an assault that was quite unnecessary. Bazaine no doubt all day believed that he was facing stronger opponents than was in fact the case, but his anxieties as he rode slowly away from the battlefield that night were dominated by the perceived

---

37   Moltke, p. 45.
38   Ascoli, pp. 206-207.
39   Hohenlohe, p. 33.

threat to his left. The late attack on Rezonville had been beaten off and had not affected the French position there; and the characteristically competitive instincts of Frederick Charles had merely served to increase the total of casualties suffered by his exhausted units.

The losses on both sides had been extremely heavy. The German Official History put the total French casualties at 17,007, a figure which included the many French wounded who were abandoned when the French army retreated; the Germans lost 15,799.[40] It is no surprise that each side should have claimed a victory; there was no realisation on the part of the French that their movement on Verdun had been effectively halted by four divisions of infantry and two of cavalry. Leboeuf believed that they had been opposed by sixteen divisions. Letters written that night enthusiastically reported a victory. Jarras wrote in his memoirs:

Colonel Ardant du Picq, a noted writer on military affairs who was mortally wounded on the eve of the Battle of Mars-la-Tour. (Rousset/*Histoire*)

> I do not think that a single voice could be heard challenging the success of the French army. It remained the master of the battlefield, that is to say it occupied, that evening, the ground on which it had fought all day; in other words, it had won a defensive battle.[41]

The question of the outcome of the battle was explored at Bazaine's trial, when the president of the court put to each of the corps commanders on the French right and in the centre the question of whether after the battle the army was in a situation in which it could have reoccupied Mars la Tour and Vionville, and then inflicted a defeat on the enemy sufficient to enable it to resume its march on Verdun:

> The response of Canrobert was unexpected: 'why retake areas in our possession?' The president did not press him. And Canrobert, whose corps had been

40   *Official History*, Vol. II, p. 421.
41   Jarras, p. 113.

completely disorganised, declared that he was ready to resume a struggle which was, nevertheless, dangerous. Leboeuf was dubious about the possibility of success or of resuming the march. Ladmirault, on the other hand, was full of confidence. He would attack on August 17 without hesitation – this, which he had not been inspired to do on the previous day, when he had all the cards in his hand. According to him, this would have brought a victory which would have made the retreat unnecessary.[42]

Bazaine was questioned as to whether, reinforced by the two divisions that he had not used, he could have taken the enemy positions on August 17, and was emphatic in his reply: 'I did not think so for a moment … We were not sufficiently coordinated, we had not yet reformed the individual units, and we had suffered heavy losses.' He wrote later:

> The enemy had suffered but remained in his positions from which he threatened our left flank for each step which the army took towards Verdun. How could a march be attempted in these tactical circumstances? It would be to lead the army to a certain defeat. My experience and my conscience forbade it.[43]

Whatever the view that might be taken as to claims of victory, or the immediate consequences for the respective armies, it had been a day of the most intense fighting, and of the most fearful losses on each side. The German Official History depicted the scene as the battle drew to a close:

> It was now past 9 o'clock before the contest had ceased at all points. Deep silence then reigned over the broad expanse upon which since 9 o'clock that morning death had been reaping so terrible a harvest. The hot summer's day was succeeded by cool night, and after superhuman efforts the warriors snatched a short rest in their bivouacs. Across the plateau of Rezonville, so hardly won in the fight, stretched in a broad bow from the Bois des Ognons to the Tronville copses, the line of Prussian outposts, which on the rising of the moon was extended by the cavalry of the left wing over the bloodstained field of Mars la Tour as far as the Yron brook.[44]

---

42 Ruby & Regnault, p. 160.
43 Bazaine, *Episodes*, p. 91.
44 *Official History*, Vol. I, p. 421.

12

August 17

As Bazaine made his way back to Gravelotte, to the inn in which Napoleon had spent his last night before leaving the army, he encountered crowds of stragglers who had been sidling all day from the battlefield. It was a discouraging experience, reinforcing in his mind the conviction that the position was unfavourable. To his orderly officer Captain de Mornay-Soult, he said that he must not say that it was a victory. As the staff collected at Gravelotte, he remarked: 'Notre situation n'est pas brillante,' as a check on the euphoria which some were exhibiting.[1]

And it certainly was the case that there was a general conviction that the French had won the battle. General Bonnal observed:

> Reading the official reports produced on the day after the battle of Rezonville gives the almost total impression that, in the French camp, it was believed that they had been victorious ... If they had not advanced they had not retreated either. The illusion of a belief in victory consisted of holding one's position and sleeping on the battlefield and had its origin in the campaign of 1859 during which the success of each combat or battle did not go beyond the limits of the field of conflict. And then, the extraordinary disorder observed during the night of August 16/17 around Rezonville and towards Gravelotte hardly bothered the colonels and generals who recalled the same spectacle on the evening of Magenta and Solferino.[2]

At 10.00 p.m. that night Bazaine retired to a small room to consider what must be done, and to issue his orders for the following day. Captain Fix described the scene:

> The room was furnished with several chairs and was lit by two candles placed on a round table. There were few present: Jarras, two staff officers and the Marshal's

---

1   Guedalla, p. 186.
2   Bonnal, II, pp. 487-488.

nephews. Scarcely had he entered before Bazaine took note of three telegrams that had arrived during the day, via Châlons. They came from Palikao and from MacMahon, then at Joinville. MacMahon, who was reporting his situation for the first time to his superior, announced that he would concentrate the 1st and 5th Corps at Châlons by August 19. The Minister spoke of the combinations to be expected between the two armies. Then Colonel Vasse Saint-Ouen, chief of staff to General Soleille, the commander of the artillery, arrived; the general, bruised by a fall from his horse, wished to report to the Marshal that the expenditure of ammunition during the day had been enormous, amounting to a third or half of that supplied, and that the army was in a 'disquieting shortage.'[3]

This was true of the 2nd and 6th Corps, and of the Guard, but greatly exaggerated for the rest of the army. At the same time Captain de France arrived with alarming news about the army's provisions.

It was enough; Bazaine took his decision. In a subdued voice, pausing from time to time to look at his map and to reread, he dictated his orders for the next day. In spite of his robust constitution, he was obviously exhausted. 'He's asleep,' murmured Jarras. Bazaine's decision, in the situation in which his army now found itself, was clearly going to be difficult. It would scarcely be possible to sort out the shambles around Rezonville in time to launch an assault on the following morning; any such advance would have to be led by the 4th Corps and perhaps part of the 3rd Corps, and although Bazaine has been pilloried for his concern with his line of retreat to Metz, he obviously could not ignore the fact that the German pressure there must necessarily increase as fresh troops came up.

It was doubtful if, by taking another road to Verdun, by Étain, to the north of the Vionville road, he could do so without the Germans falling on his flank and rear. Indeed, if that was the option he chose, it would not be long before Frederick Charles swung his left wing around to reach Étain before he did. The breakdown of his supply organisation meant that it would be extremely difficult to feed his troops, while Soleille's warnings about ammunition stocks could not be ignored.

These considerations had, as we have seen, been sufficient to preclude the option of fighting his way through to Verdun, though Moltke had by no means ruled out the possibility, and overnight issued orders which allowed either for a French attack or a retreat. He did not know, of course, just how anxious Bazaine was about his connection with Metz. The orders which Bazaine now dictated were for the army to fall back to a position running from Rozerieulles to St Privat, on the Amanvillers plateau. The 2nd Corps was to take up a position between Point du Jour and Rozerieulles; on its right, the 3rd Corps would hold the heights of Châtel St Germain; the 4th Corps was to prolong the line to Montigny la Grange, while the 6th Corps would stand at Vernéville. Du Barail's cavalry division would follow the 6th Corps as it moved to its

3   Ruby & Regnault, pp. 156-157.

position, while Forton would follow the 2nd Corps. The Guard would take up a position in reserve at Lessy and Plappeville, where Bazaine would establish his headquarters. Somewhat optimistically, he decreed that these movements should begin at 4.00 a.m. on August 17; the retreat would be covered by Metman's division at Gravelotte.[4]

Once he had finished his dictation, Bazaine lifted his head, and said: 'It is necessary to save the army, and, for this, to return to Metz.' He added, as an afterthought which was apparently addressed to Jarras: 'If anyone can think of anything better to do, let him speak.' Jarras made no comment, believing that Bazaine's orders were the result of interviews with the corps commanders:

> I assumed that these general officers, in reporting on their respective situations, had made known the sad state of things. I was convinced also that the Marshal had had confirmation of these reports from the general commanding the artillery, and by the army's Intendant General, both of whom he was able to see at a moment's notice.[5]

His orders issued, Bazaine telegraphed at 11.00 p.m.to report the day's fighting to the Emperor at Châlons:

> At 9.00 this morning the enemy attacked the head of our columns at Rezonville. The battle lasted until 8.00 this evening. It was an extremely bitter engagement; despite considerable casualties we have held our ground. Our main problem now is that our expenditure of ammunition and supplies has been such that we should have difficulty in getting through another such day. I therefore feel obliged to fall back to the line Vigneulles – Lessy to replenish my stocks. The wounded had been evacuated to Metz. According to the information I have regarding German troop concentrations, I think I shall be obliged to take the northern route to Verdun.[6]

Apparently this did not reach the Emperor at first, but it was in Napoleon's hands by the afternoon of August 17.

Although he was later to be criticised for it, Bazaine's decision to withdraw to a strong defensive position outside Metz was perfectly reasonable. It would give the French army an opportunity to inflict heavy casualties on the enemy if he chose to assault that position. Bazaine's subsequent explanations for the decision have been found, for instance by Ascoli, to be contradictory. In 1871 in evidence to the Commission of Enquiry, in terms which he repeated in his *Episodes de la Guerre 1870*:

---

4   Ruby & Regnault, p. 157.
5   Jarras, pp. 116-117.
6   Ascoli, p. 212.

'The previous battles had shown me that by fighting one or perhaps two defensive battles in positions which I felt to be impregnable I would wear down my adversary's strength, forcing him to sustain heavy losses which ... would weaken him enough to allow him to let me pass without serious opposition.' And then, at his trial two years later, he said: 'I believed, and the Emperor also believed, that in giving time for the Army of Châlons to be organised, it would be possible to assemble a considerable force which would be able to move to disengage us.'[7]

The two concepts are not, in fact, really contradictory; if he was able so seriously to damage the enemy as to permit him to move safely to join MacMahon, well and good; if not, his defensive battles would buy the time necessary for the army of Châlons to reach a strength sufficient to enable it to advance to his relief. It is, though, almost certainly the case that neither of these objectives was at the time the direct reason for Bazaine's decision, although it is perfectly possible that he had given some thought to the way in which the campaign would subsequently develop. Howard remarks 'it is hard to believe that either of these statements was more than wisdom after the event, or that Bazaine on August 17 had any plans at all.'[8] In fact, on that day, he was as he said concerned with saving the army and taking up the position which he had selected was the best way to do so.

That position was extremely strong. The plateau north and west of the Moselle, with hills and valleys extending in every direction, forms several long ridges in front of Metz, which provided extremely favourable defensive positions. On the left of the French line, the southernmost sector was especially strong. A deep ravine which carried the Mance stream southwards from the dense Bois de Genivaux passed between the thick woods of the Bois des Ognons and the Bois de Vaux before it reached the Moselle at Ars. To the east of the ravine, and west of the village of Rozerieulles, there lay three extremely defensible sets of farm buildings. These were Point du Jour, St Hubert and Moscou. The Verdun road, which crossed the Mance ravine to the east of Gravelotte, climbed eastward up the slope, past St Hubert farm, which commanded it completely. The road then continued past Rozerieulles, after which it joined the road which ran north along the ridge towards Amanvillers. The Verdun road continued towards Longeville. East of the junction was the height of Mont St Quentin, behind which lay the little village of Plappeville.

Moving northward, the French line ran past the Leipzig farm and La Folie, before passing to the east of Montigny la Grange. Beyond Leipzig, the nature of the terrain was somewhat different. The Mance ravine levelled out, and it ran through the thick woods of the Bois de Genivaux, and beyond this, overlooked by the defensive positions of the French, there were open fields which provided an attacker with little or no cover. North of Montigny la Grange lay Amanvillers, to the west of which, below

7   Ascoli, pp. 213-214.
8   Howard, p. 164.

the slopes which stretched down from the village, was the Bois de la Gorce. Finally, north of Amanvillers stood the walled village of St Privat, which represented the end of the French line. There was an outpost here to the west of the main position at the village of St Marie les Chenes.

The farms along the ridge which overlooked the Mance ravine had been turned into formidable strong points, loop-holed and barricaded, and linked by lines of trenches supported by emplacements which had been prepared for the artillery. Almost throughout its length of about 7 miles the position commanded the long open slopes over which an attacker must come and provided its defenders with a magnificent field of fire for their chassepôts and mitrailleuses.

The news that they were to retreat bewildered and angered the French troops, whose discipline had already begun to fray during the preceding ten days. Loud complaints were heard, and the general indignation was expressed in extensive looting and a considerable number of desertions. As the troops marched back to their new positions, they seized all the food they could carry from supply convoys and dumps, in spite of all that the intendant staff could do to prevent them.

The rearward movement, which for most of the French units meant a march of no more than three or four miles, was chaotic. There had been no time for Jarras and his staff to work out detailed routes and march tables for each of the columns, with the result that the confusion was even worse than it had been prior to August 16. Jarras, though, denied that this was so, and claimed that the retirement went well:

> From dawn on August 17 the army was on the move. In accordance with the Marshal's intentions, I had sent to each corps commander a senior staff officer to indicate the route that should be taken. The march was carried out without incident, and soon the positions indicated had been occupied.[9]

It is understandable that Jarras should put the best face he could on the movement, since it was, above all, a staff responsibility; but in fact some units took over eight hours to reach their assigned positions, arriving there only later that night. The problem was compounded by the selection of the positions to be taken up by each of the corps. Whatever the staff officers sent by Jarras to supervise the retirement were able to do, they could not prevent serious traffic jams, as for instance when the 6th Corps, heading for Vernéville, crossed the line of march of the 3rd Corps as it made for its positions at St Hubert and Moscou. This, in turn, obstructed the movement of the 4th Corps from Bruville to Amanvillers. Similarly, Montaudon's division ran into Metman's division which was endeavouring to cover the army's retreat from between Malmaison and Gravelotte. Meanwhile Ladmirault, true to form, disobeyed the order to march at 4.00 a.m.; the 4th Corps did not set off until 11.00.

---

9   Jarras, p. 118.

Contents

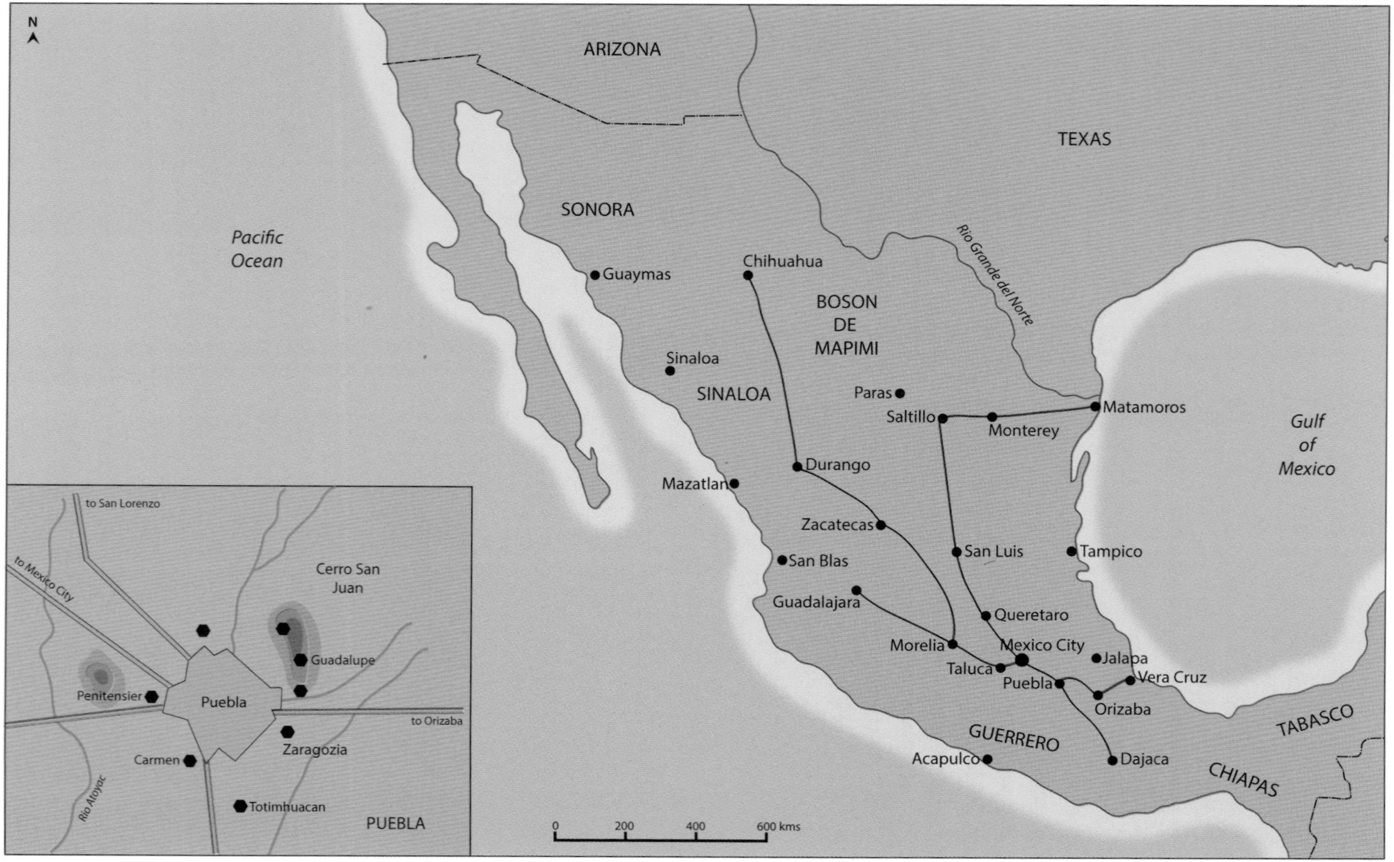
N
ARIZONA
TEXAS
SONORA
Pacific
Ocean
Guaymas
Chihuahua
BOSON
DE
MAPIMI
Rio Grande del Norte
Sinaloa
SINALOA
Paras
Saltillo
Monterey
Matamoros
Gulf
of
Mexico
Durango
Mazatlan
Zacatecas
San Luis
Tampico
San Blas
Guadalajara
Queretaro
Morelia
Mexico City
Jalapa
Taluca
Puebla
Vera Cruz
Orizaba
GUERRERO
TABASCO
Acapulco
Dajaca
CHIAPAS
0
200
400
600 kms
to San Lorenzo
to Mexico City
Cerro San
Juan
Guadalupe
Penitensier
Puebla
to Orizaba
Zaragozia
Carmen
Rio Atoyac
Totimhuacan
PUEBLA

Map 1 Mexico.

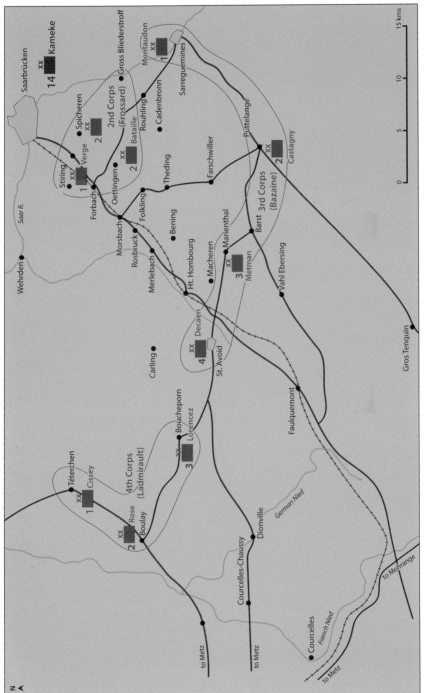

Map 2 Spicheren, August 6 1870. Situation 12 noon.

III

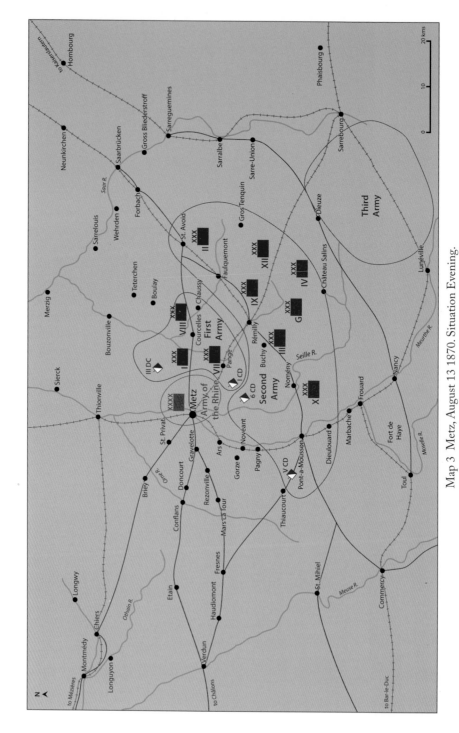

Map 3 Metz, August 13 1870. Situation Evening.

IV

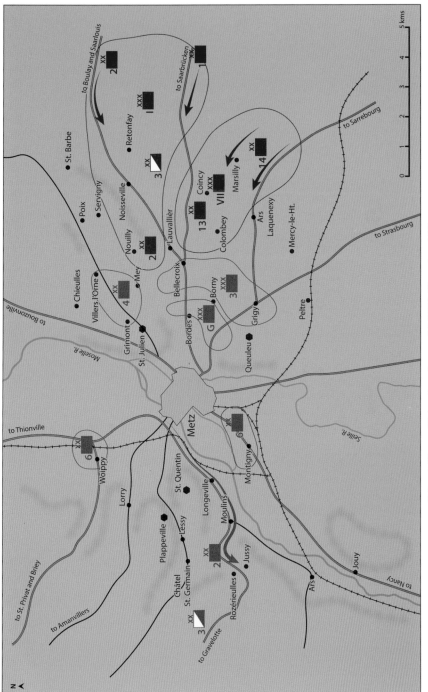

Map 4 Borny–Colombey, August 14 1870. Situation 6.30 p.m.

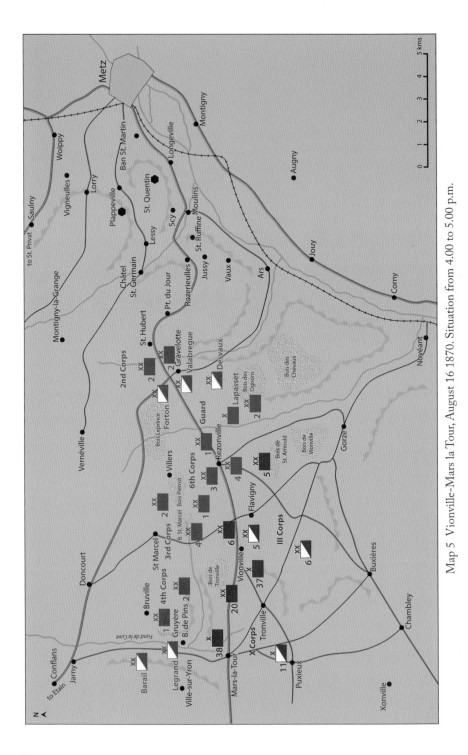

Map 5 Vionville–Mars la Tour, August 16 1870. Situation from 4.00 to 5.00 p.m.

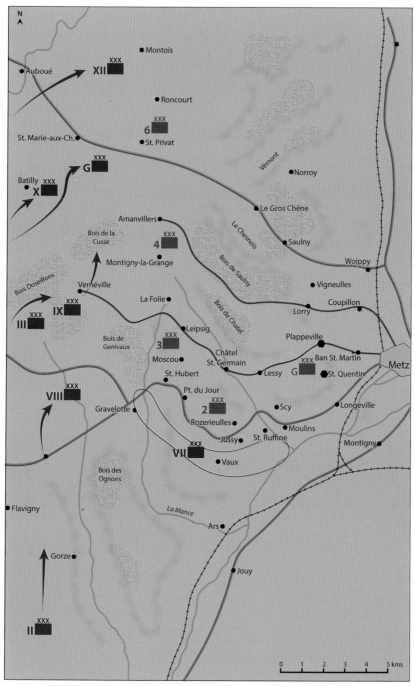

Map 6 Gravelotte-St Privat, August 18 1870. Situation towards 12 noon.

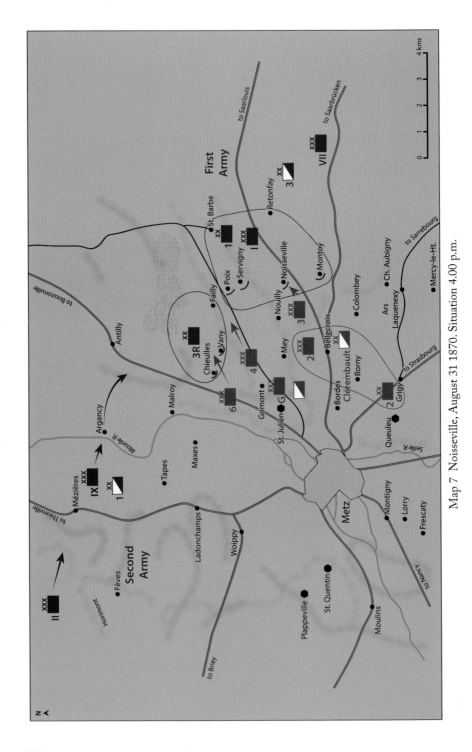

Map 7 Noisseville, August 31 1870. Situation 4.00 p.m.

VIII

French camp at Gravelotte, near Metz. (*Illustrated London News*)

Howard commented that Bazaine had some reason to consider the position which he had selected to be impregnable, and that it did credit to his topographical skill. Ascoli speculates that it had always been Bazaine's intention to fight a battle there: 'The detail of the French dispositions on the Amanvillers line suggests strongly that it was a preconceived plan. It could not possibly have been worked out in the bare hour between the staff meeting at Gravelotte and the issue of the order itself.'[10] There is really no evidence at all to sustain the suggestion. Ascoli does not indicate when this 'preconceived plan' was supposedly worked out, or by whom, and there is for instance nothing that supports the suggestion in the account which Jarras gave. Nor does Ascoli explain why, if a detailed plan had previously been worked out, no one mentioned it, then or later. Bazaine always had a good eye for country, and it was a demonstration of his defensive skills that he was able to choose a position in which to fight a battle which only the interruption of his retreat to Verdun had made necessary.

Bazaine's original orders had assigned the 6th Corps to a position at Vernéville, well forward of the rest of the French line. Canrobert was extremely discontented with this position, flat and shut in by woods, and he asked Bazaine if he could not instead locate his corps around the village of St Privat, on the crest of the ridge to the north of Amanvillers with an excellent field of fire. Bazaine was always conscious of the seniority of the other marshals – Canrobert was 10 years his senior in the rank – and he readily acquiesced. Senior or not, it was probably the correct decision; St Privat provided a more readily defensible position. It meant, though, that the French line was almost 7 miles long, and on August 18 the battle that was fought was effectively in two halves.

10 Howard, p. 167; Ascoli, p. 221.

The move was discussed at the hearings of the Commission of Enquiry, at which Bazaine remarked that he regretted that Vernéville had been evacuated. Put to Canrobert, it appeared to the latter that Bazaine was trying to fasten on him the blame for the army's subsequent defeat on the following day. Canrobert was not having that and drew from his pocket the letter from Bazaine authorising the move, which led to a vigorous exchange between the two marshals. Writing many years later Bazaine still considered the move to have been a mistake, because it enabled the Germans to occupy Vernéville, and it facilitated their great turning movement on the French right.[11]

Soleille was still, incorrectly, warning gloomily of the shortage of ammunition. Bazaine was asked at the Commission of Enquiry why, during the night of August 16/17, he did not take steps to equalise the amount of ammunition available to each corps by transferring stocks from those units which were well provided. It was, he said an astonishing question from general officers; perhaps, he thought, they had forgotten the sort of thing that occurred during a battle:

> How, after 12 hours of combat, in the middle of the disorder into which the divisions of the various army corps had fallen by reason of the manner in which they had become engaged, by reason of the considerable extension of our battle line, would it have been possible during the night of August 16/17 to carry out such a complex undertaking? It was an impossible operation.[12]

It was a fair point.

In order that the natural strength of the Amanvillers position should be further augmented, it was necessary that, once the various corps arrived, they should at once take steps to fortify it. The engineering experience of Frossard led him to set about the task at once:

> Since we were expecting a battle on the following day, the rest of August 17 was occupied in strengthening our positions, by the digging of trenches and epaulements for the batteries, notably around the two houses at Point du Jour, which were loop-holed, and which were linked by an earthen parapet and other works.[13]

Similar work was put in hand along the front of the 3rd Corps and the 4th Corps. However, in assigning the 6th Corps to its post on the extreme right of the French position, Bazaine had made an error of judgment. As a result of its belated and hurried journey to join the Army of the Rhine at Metz, it had become separated from its engineers. It was therefore the unit least well-equipped to execute Bazaine's orders to

11   Bazaine, *Episodes*, pp. 96-97.
12   Bazaine, *Episodes*, p. 96.
13   Frossard, p. 103.

strengthen the position as much as possible, and since the right of the position was in the air, was the worst choice to cover that flank of the Army of the Rhine against the German turning movement. It appears that Canrobert was content merely to loophole the stone buildings of St Privat. If that was because his men had no suitable equipment to fortify the position to any greater extent, it must be said that he seems to have made no effort to obtain any from local sources.

Properly strengthened wherever possible, Bazaine was indeed entitled to think that the position which he had taken up was more or less impregnable. Looking back at the orders he had given, he wrote that he could not have emphasised more firmly the instruction which he gave that the French lines must be 'trés solidement fortifiées.'[14] From his headquarters established in the Villa Bouteiller in the little village of Plappeville, Bazaine telegraphed the Emperor with confirmation of his brief report during the previous night. In this, he wrote:

> I have established the Army of the Rhine in a position between St Privat la Montagne and Rozerieulles. I think that I shall be able to resume my march the day after tomorrow by taking a more northerly route … The Ardennes railroad is still open as far as Metz, and this indicates that the enemy's objectives are Châlons and Paris. One hears of the junction of the armies of the two princes. We have before us Prince Frederick Charles and General Steinmetz.[15]

Having received at 5:10 p.m. an enquiry from the Emperor about his situation, Bazaine followed up his telegram with a more detailed report in a letter sent the same day, in which he dwelt on the shortage of ammunition. He enclosed a note from Soleille on the subject; the ammunition intended for Metz must, he supposed, have been sent to Bourges. This letter, with copies of the previous telegrams, was taken by Commandant Magnan to Châlons via Thionville, where he arrived in company with Intendant Preval on the morning of August 18. Preval's mission was to concentrate all the resources he could at Longuyon and Montmédy, a clear enough indication that at this time Bazaine genuinely intended to leave Metz. Magnan also carried with him a request that Jarras be replaced by General Manèque, who had served as Bazaine's chief of staff of the 3rd Corps, and that Frossard be replaced by General Deligny, the commander of the Voltigeur Division of the Guard.[16]

Away to the west in Châlons, the Emperor had convened a crucially important meeting. He had reached the city on the afternoon of August 16, and next morning he called MacMahon to him to discuss what next should be done. Also there were present Trochu, who had been appointed to command the 12th Corps, and Schmitz, his chief of staff; the meeting was also attended by General Berthaut,

14   Bazaine, *Episodes*, p. 99.
15   Bazaine, *Episodes*, p. 99.
16   Ruby & Regnault, p. 168.

the commander of the unruly and unreliable *gardes mobiles*, and by Prince Napoleon. The Prince took the lead in the ensuing discussions to such an extent that Trochu later observed that he was now the only Napoleon that counted. The Emperor was profoundly depressed and sat silently listening to the debate. In the end, it was agreed that Trochu should hand over command of the 12th Corps to Lebrun and proceed to Paris to take over as military governor of the city; he was to be accompanied by the *gardes mobiles,* and would be followed by MacMahon's army, when its reorganisation had been completed.

After being appointed to command the Army of Châlons, MacMahon sent an aide, Commandant Broye, on the afternoon of August 17 with orders to seek instructions from Bazaine, under whose authority he had been placed. MacMahon supposed Bazaine to be on the point of reaching Verdun. However, when news arrived from Bazaine of his true position, MacMahon recalled Broye before he could set off on his journey. Bazaine later pointed out that if MacMahon had sent him on by the rail route through the Ardennes, he could have reached Metz, and the two marshals would have been aware of each other's plans, and of the movements of the enemy. MacMahon later seemed uncomfortable about this, entirely failing to mention the incident in his deposition given before Bazaine's trial.[17]

It was Bazaine's first message that had led MacMahon to recall Broye. It spoke of the repulse of the German army on August 16 but also reported the decision to retreat to Metz, which suggested that all was not well. Napoleon sent off an anxious telegram appealing to know with greater clarity the actual situation of Bazaine's army, 'so that I can act accordingly.' That night a further telegram reached Napoleon, which compounded his irresolution. Palikao, Ollivier's successor as President of the Council, was horrified by the decision to retreat to Paris, believing that it would be seen as a desertion of the Army of the Rhine: 'Could you not make a powerful diversion against the Prussian corps, already worn out by several engagements?'[18] On the following day Commandant Magnan arrived with Bazaine's further dispatches, confirming his intention to make an early move in the direction of Châlons by taking a more northerly route, which led to further debate. By then, however, Bazaine's army was already in action. The Battle of Gravelotte-St Privat had begun.

17   Bazaine, *Episodes*, pp. 100-101.
18   Howard, p. 186.

13

Gravelotte – St Privat

On Wednesday, August 17 Frederick Charles was the first of the German leaders to visit the battlefield of the previous day, riding up the steep slope from Gorze to the Flavigny height at about 4.00 a.m.. He was joined there by Moltke and the King, who arrived at about 6.00. At that time it was not yet certain what the French were doing, beyond the fact that they were retiring from the battlefield. It still seemed to Moltke that it was not impossible that Bazaine might make an attempt to resume his march. He wrote later: 'The reports to headquarters sent in until noon by the reconnoitring cavalry were somewhat contradictory; they left it uncertain whether the French were concentrating towards Metz, or were pursuing their retreat by the two still open roads through Étain and Briey,'[1]

It was another blazing summer's day, and the air was uncomfortably hot. As time went on, white lines of *tentes d'abri* could be seen on the heights which the French had occupied, which certainly indicated that they intended to fight a defensive battle in front of Metz. It had been Moltke's first thought that the battle might be resumed on August 17, but it soon became clear that the concentration of the Second Army would not be completed in time for that to be possible.[2] After a conference with Goeben, who had ridden on ahead of the main body of his VIII Corps, Moltke confirmed that no attack on the French should be made that day.

By noon Moltke was clear that an assault should be launched on the French position on the following day, although the reports from his cavalry patrols still gave him insufficient information about the actual positions taken up. The movements of the contending armies had created an unusual situation, in that both would now have to fight with a changed front, and break up their lines of communication, a circumstance which meant that the effects of victory or defeat would be materially increased.[3]

Moltke's orders were characteristically brief:

1   Moltke, p. 47.
2   Verdy, p. 73.
3   Moltke, p. 48.

The Second Army will be formed at 5 o'clock tomorrow morning, the 18th, and advance in echelon from the left between the Yron and Gorze brooks (generally between Ville sur Yron and Rezonville). The VIII Corps will accompany this movement on the right flank of the Second Army. Upon the VIII Corps will devolve, in the first instance, the duty of protecting the movements of the Second Army against any hostile enterprises from the side of Metz. His Majesty's further arrangements will be dependent on the measures of the enemy. Reports will, for the present, be sent to his Majesty on the heights south of Flavigny.[4]

Having issued this order at 2.00, Moltke and the King returned to Pont à Mousson.

Bazaine had spent the whole of that Wednesday in his headquarters at Plappeville immersed in a large number of administrative functions. For this, he has been severely criticised; but he was the commander-in-chief, and such tasks were required of him. It was regrettable, though, that he did not find time to visit Canrobert and inspect the right of his defensive line. Since this rested in the air, it was obviously going to be a vulnerable point. Moreover, it appears that he had no detailed map of the country around St Privat.

One matter which continued to be of extreme concern to him was the question of the army's supply of ammunition. Soleille reinforced the warning that he had previously given Bazaine, sending him a note during the morning of August 17:

> I have come from visiting the Arsenal at Metz. There are no resources there with which to re-provision the army, and it can produce only 800,000 rounds of ammunition for the infantry. I ask with the greatest urgency that the necessary supplies be sent by rail through Thionville during the course of tomorrow. Marshal Bazaine should cover the railway with cavalry during the day, against their arrival at Thionville.

General Soleille, commander of the artillery in the Army of the Rhine. (Rousset/*Histoire*)

Consumption during August 16 has been enormous, the army is in a disturbing shortage of ammunition.[5]

A copy of this was sent to Paris by telegraph.

Meanwhile Jarras was taking a very passive view of his responsibilities, endeavouring, he said, to transmit the orders which he had received as quickly as possible. Later, in his memoirs, he explained his attitude as he had seen it:

> One thought, however, crossed my mind. Since the Marshal judged it absolutely essential to re-provision himself with munitions and supplies, would it not have been better to remain in the positions which we held, and to send into Metz for all the army needed, rather than effect a retreat of which the moral effect on the troops would be damaging? But this question was exclusively the province of the commander-in-chief, and up to now he had so completely abstained from involving me in such decisions that it was impossible for me to make the slightest observation. Moreover, time was pressing to get out the orders, and it was important not to waste it in discussions which I considered could have no result.[6]

Having taken up the kind of defensive position from which he might inflict the maximum number of casualties on an enemy launching an unsuccessful assault, which was the whole basis of his decision to occupy the line of Amanvillers, Bazaine was confident that the Germans would oblige him by launching just such an attack. What he did not know was just how soon that attack would come, and early on Thursday morning all was, for the moment, quiet. Another blazing August day was in prospect. It is frequently suggested that, on the eve of battle, so great was Bazaine's anxiety about his left, and his potential line of retreat on the fortress of Metz, that he focused his attention on this sector virtually to the exclusion of all else.

That this was not the case, and that he had much in mind the situation on his right, may be judged from the text of an important letter which he wrote to Canrobert at 10.00 a.m. on August 18, at a time when Leboeuf had reported the movement of substantial German forces in his front and in the direction of 6th Corps:

> Establish yourself as firmly as possible in your positions and keep your touch of the right wing of the 4th Corps. Troops must encamp in two lines and on as narrow a front as possible. You will also do well to cause a reconnaissance to be made of the roads which lead from Marange towards your right wing; to General Ladmirault I recommend the same as regards the roads from Norroy le Veneur. Should it appear that the enemy is extending before our front, so as to attack St Privat la Montagne from the west, then take all the necessary steps to maintain

5   Bazaine, *Episodes*, p. 94.
6   Jarras, pp. 117-118.

your position there, and give your right wing the opportunity of undertaking a change of front, with a view to occupying, if necessary, the rearward positions which are now in course of being reconnoitred.[7]

Notwithstanding Bazaine's evident intention to defend St Privat in depth by massing the whole of the 6th Corps there, there had been two important decisions taken during the course of the corps' deployment. To the north of St Privat, the French line was extended by locating a brigade under General Péchot at Raucourt; while in front of the main position an outpost had been located at Ste Marie aux Chênes. Bazaine's idea in concentrating the 6th Corps at and behind St Privat was to create a readily available reserve between the village and the Bois de Jaumont, and with this to meet any turning movement. Since the 6th Corps had been deprived of its cavalry division by reason of its late arrival at Metz, Bazaine detached Bruchard's cavalry brigade from the 3rd Corps, and assigned it to Canrobert.

The 6th Corps only completed its move into the new position authorised by Bazaine on the morning of August 18. Meanwhile the Guard had been located close to Bazaine's headquarters at Plappeville, together with the reserve artillery. The cavalry reserve was posted in the Château-St Germaine ravine; Bazaine considered that the state of its forces was such that a period of rest was essential. The cavalry divisions attached to each of the corps would undertake reconnaissance, and also protect the railway line to Thionville. These dispositions were intended to facilitate the reprovisioning of the army during the morning of August 18.

Fritz Hönig reviewed Bazaine's dispositions:

The Marshal wished neither to be torn away from Metz nor to be driven back into that fortress, but simply to remain connected to it on political and other grounds (ammunition, supplies, sick and wounded), and to protect and strengthen himself, while relying upon and supported by it. Do his dispositions correspond with these objects? The French position was by nature very strong along the entire front, and was undoubtedly strongest ... on its left, though the right also was capable of being energetically defended. The Marshal should certainly therefore have considered the possibility of the latter flank being turned; in fact, as we have already shown, he did reckon on this. On the other hand, there was comparatively little reason for him to fear for his left flank. When the Marshal, nevertheless, placed the reserve of his army in rear of his left, this disposition (especially when considered with regard to the support already afforded to him at that point by the forts of St Quentin and Plappeville) distinctly shows his politico-strategic object. He was determined not, under any circumstances, to be cut off from Metz. But the second task which he set himself, namely, not to be thrown back upon the fortress, is in direct contradiction to this disposition

---

7   *Official History*, Vol. II, p. 104; Bazaine, *Episodes*, pp. 102-103.

of his troops; thus, as we have here shown, it was impossible to carry out both of these tasks.[8]

Hönig concluded, though, that even had he posted his main reserve in time to support St Privat, it would merely have postponed his defeat until the following day

Not all the corps commanders realised the imminence of danger. Leboeuf, 'who seemed to have given himself the task of putting behind him the responsibility which he had incurred as Minister,' acted throughout the day decisively and loyally. He had actively strengthened the position occupied by the 3rd Corps with extensive field works. On his left Frossard, whose ardour had been somewhat cooled by his experiences during the battle of August 16, had marched his corps in good order into a position that was naturally extremely strong. As has been seen, he had also carried out some work to augment it:

On the other hand Ladmirault had not done as much as he might to strengthen his position. The 4th Corps was in some disorder; Lorencez's division was facing towards Metz, while Cissey's two brigades were located back to back.

On the right, the situation at the 6th Corps was, if anything, rather worse. Some of the units which had only arrived during the morning had not been fed, and the soldiers looted the farmhouses. They also assailed Canrobert with demands for food. He was not amused, and pompously apostrophised his officers: 'You allow your soldiers to demand of a Marshal of France that they be given food! You should yourselves have informed the intendant or your chief of staff.'[9]

Howard thought it possible that the reason that not much was done to strengthen the positions of the 4th Corps or the 6th Corps might have had something to do with the long open fields of fire available to the defence, making Ladmirault and Canrobert feel that extensive works were unnecessary.[10]

During the morning the assistant chiefs of staff of each corps had gathered at Château- St Germaine to reconnoitre the positions to be taken up if a retreat became necessary. These were on an intermediate line between the Amanvillers position and the line of Forts Vignerolles and Lessy. The discussions were broken off when the sound of artillery fire recalled the staff to their respective units. Bazaine's letter of 10.00 a.m. to Canrobert had not been to authorise an immediate change of position of the 6th Corps, but to set out the alternative position to which he could retire if necessary – if, that is, Canrobert discovered that the enemy was enveloping the army's right flank. He wished Canrobert to anticipate any such move, adding: 'I do not wish to be forced there by the enemy.'

Bazaine, therefore, not having sufficient forces to prolong his position northwards as far as the Orne, was in this way being careful to prepare for the eventuality of a

8   Hönig, Fritz, *Twenty Four Hours of Moltke's Strategy* (Woolwich, 1895) p. 23.
9   Ruby & Regnault, p. 171.
10   Howard, p. 164.

turning movement there. At the other end of the line he was in a much more secure position, with the Guard at Plappeville with the army's artillery reserve, and with his flank covered by Mont St Quentin and protected by the river.

At noon, having become aware that contrary to his orders the corps had not been restocked with ammunition, Bazaine sent a warning note to each of the commanders. At the same time, his staff were still engaged in the process of making promotions, made necessary by the enormous losses which had been suffered in the battles of Borny-Colombey and Vionville-Mars la Tour. This process has been criticised as a pointless bureaucratic exercise; but the work was essential, in some instances regiments being under the command of captains. There were other important duties to be carried out:

> It was necessary above all to send to each corps one or two liaison officers with a sufficient number of couriers. If the Marshal did not think of pointing out the need of this elementary precaution, it was because he assumed that the staff would discharge this duty without further instruction.[11]

It was just such a turning movement around Bazaine's right flank that Moltke contemplated, although in issuing his orders he still had in his mind that the Marshal would put his army in motion towards the north in a further attempt to get away. If so, the advance of the German left wing, which was to wheel to its right through Doncourt, would enable it to attack and detain the retreating French army, while the right wing came up in support. Conversely:

> In case the enemy should be remaining about Metz, the German left wing was to swing eastwards and outflank his farthest north position, while the right was to hold his left closely engaged until this movement was accomplished. The battle, under these circumstances, probably could not be decided until late in the day, owing to the wide sweeping movement of a portion of the army.[12]

This movement of the German army, across the front of the Army of the Rhine was, of course, soon apparent. It gave the French, in theory at least, an opportunity to launch a flank attack, which might have caught the Germans at a severe disadvantage. But this would have meant abandoning the almost impregnable Amanvillers position, and in the improbable event of the French being lured down into an attack on the marching German columns, the numerical superiority of the latter would almost certainly have meant a crucial defeat.

As the Second Army moved forward, the XII Corps (Crown Prince Albert of Saxony) took the direction of Jarny. Next came the Guard Corps (Prince August of

---

11   Ruby & Regnault, p. 171.
12   Moltke, p. 48.

The chateau at Vernéville, occupied by the German IX Corps. (Rousset/*Histoire*)

Württemberg), marching through Doncourt. Setting off an hour later from between Vionville and Rezonville, the IX Corps (Manstein) was furthest to the right, moving in the direction of Vernéville. Behind these three corps came the X Corps (Voigts-Rhetz) and the III Corps (Alvensleben), for the moment held in reserve after their exertions of August 16. The First Army stood opposite the French left, though Moltke had removed the VIII Corps from Steinmetz's control, much to the latter's disgust; it was to be held ready for an advance on the French position when and if Moltke judged it expedient. Zastrow's VII Corps was intended to be the pivot of the great eastward wheel of the army. Steinmetz had been directly instructed that he was not to take offensive action unless expressly ordered to do so.

In the centre, Manstein, whose direction of march would bring him soonest of the corps of the Second Army into close proximity with the enemy, was as early as 10.00 a.m. ordered by Frederick Charles that if contact with the right wing of the enemy was made, he was to open proceedings by launching, in the first instance, an artillery attack on Montigny and La Folie. Hönig points out that this almost certainly meant that Manstein would be attacking alone; but he excuses Frederick Charles; an attack in succession by the corps of the Second Army was, in the known state of affairs, almost unavoidable: 'How could anyone hope to begin an attack simultaneously with such masses, when no one was very sure as to what 'simultaneously'meant?'[13]

13   Hönig, p. 50.

Although good deal of activity on the part of the French could be seen, it was not immediately apparent what this meant. As late as 9:30 a.m. the Royal headquarters was notifying the Second Army that the troops which could be seen on the heights towards Metz appeared to be moving northward, presumably towards Briey. Soon after this, however, reports indicated that the French might after all, be staying put, and at 10.30 Moltke felt able to issue specific instructions for the imminent battle. Frederick Charles was ordered, if the enemy should retreat, to attack him at Ste Marie aux Chênes; if not, he should be attacked in the Amanvillers position. 'The attack must take place simultaneously, by the First Army from the Bois de Vaux and Gravelotte, by IX Corps against the Bois des Génivaux and Vernéville, and by the left wing of the Second Army from the north.'[14]

Frederick Charles had begun the day convinced that the French would be retreating, but by 10.00 was coming to realise that this was not the case. Soon after he received Moltke's order of 10.30, at about 11.00, a report was received that French troops had been seen at St Privat, and it was understood for the first time that the French right extended well beyond Amanvillers. Aides were hurriedly sent off to the IX Corps to order the postponement of any attack until XII Corps and the Guard Corps could get into position. They were too late. Manstein had seen an opportunity to take Ladmirault's 4th Corps by surprise, and he sent forward his artillery into the fields beyond Vernéville: 'The carelessness of the French seemed to him to be tactically so tempting that he nevertheless determined to act contrary to the spirit of the order, and to surprise him in his camps by suddenly opening a fire of artillery.'[15] It was noon; the battle of Gravelotte-St Privat had begun.

Bazaine had been working with Jarras at about 9:30 when Leboeuf's dispatch arrived, reporting the enemy movements. His reply, sent orally by the officer of Leboeuf's staff who brought the dispatch, was to say that the 3rd Corps was occupying a very strong position, the defence of which should be straightforward. Meanwhile the work of fortifying it should be continued. Bazaine went on to discuss the situation with Jarras, saying that the position taken up by the army was secure against enemy attack, and he did not believe it would be seriously attacked; if it was, the attack would fail.[16] Bazaine displayed the same confidence throughout the morning, remarking several times to the liaison officers at his headquarters from the various corps: 'You have excellent positions, defend them!'

When the sound of Manstein's opening salvos could be heard, Jarras ordered that their horses be saddled, expecting Bazaine to be ready to leave the headquarters; the Marshal, though, was convinced that the attack was not serious, and he told Jarras that he and the staff should continue with their work. Towards 1:30 p.m., a staff officer from the 6th Corps arrived at Plappeville. Canrobert reckoned that an attack was

---

14   *Official History*, Vol. II, p. 16.
15   Hönig, p. 51.
16   Jarras, p. 122.

A German artillery gun line, drawing by Becker. (Lindner)

imminent, and called for infantry reinforcements, a battery, and munitions. In reply Bazaine assured him that a division of the Guard, two batteries of 12 pounders and ammunition wagons would be sent. Somewhat later, no such reinforcements having arrived, Canrobert sent another officer, Captain Chalus, to repeat his request. Bazaine did not follow up his promise of a division of the Guard, apparently having received reassuring information about the situation on his right wing; it is not known from whom this emanated. Soleille was, however, instructed to send up the two batteries as well as 20 caissons of ammunition.[17]

At 2.00 Bazaine decided that the time had come for him to leave his headquarters and see for himself what was happening. He left Jarras at Plappeville, however, saying that there was no need for both of them to go.[18] He painfully mounted his horse, and rode off with several officers to St Quentin, where a good view of the southern section of the battlefield could be had. He spent a large part of the afternoon there before riding to the Col de Lessy, where he met, at about 5.00, Captain Beaumont, who was attached to Bourbaki's escort. To him, Bazaine gave a verbal order for Bourbaki, the terms of which were later to be the subject of minute enquiry during the course of Bazaine's trial: 'According to Bazaine and his aide-de-camp Mornay-Soult, it was to tell the commander of the Guard to remain in his positions, to put himself in

17   Ruby & Regnault, p. 172.
18   Jarras, p. 123.

communication with Canrobert, but to avoid becoming engaged without very good reason.'[19] The prolonged enquiry into the precise terms of the order was in any case pointless, since after Beaumont had rejoined Bourbaki the Guard had already become involved in trying to cover the army's retreat, and continued to do so throughout the night.

By 5.00 Bazaine had reason to feel not dissatisfied with the way that the day had gone. He had not visited the right of his line, but in his centre and on the left his troops had been putting up a very stout defence indeed. Manstein's precipitate attack on the 4th Corps had exposed his artillerymen to a withering fire from the French infantry, and after

General Bourbaki, commander of the French Imperial Guard. (Rousset/*Histoire*)

an hour of this, during which they sustained heavy casualties, they retreated to the shelter of the woods. Manstein restored the situation by bringing forward his infantry, but Ladmirault remained entirely secure in his position. On the right, the combined artillery of the First Army had moved up at about 1.00. Moltke had sent a further order to Steinmetz forbidding any offensive action beyond counter battery work; but as it turned out it was Goeben who brought on the battle on this flank when advancing into the Bois des Génivaux.

As the battle developed, Steinmetz cast aside his instructions and launched his infantry forwards. Although the farmhouse of St Hubert was taken, the ensuing assault on the heights of Point du Jour and Moscou was disastrously unsuccessful. The Germans were beaten back with heavy casualties. Steinmetz persevered; losses mounted, and a further attack was tumbled back into the Mance ravine. Steinmetz compounded his folly by ordering the 1st Cavalry Division forward to make a desperate and futile attack on the unbroken French positions. As the day was drawing to a close, Fransecky's II Corps came up. The shambles that Steinmetz had created was all too evident. The King became convinced that the II Corps should be launched in a fresh attempt to carry the heights. Moltke strongly protested, but his advice was ignored. In his later account, in a rare though oblique criticism of his royal master, he famously wrote:

19   Ruby & Regnault, p. 174.

St Hubert Farm. (Rousset/*Histoire*)

It would have been more proper if the Chief of the General Staff of the army, who was personally on the spot at the time, had not permitted this movement at so late an hour of the evening. A body of troops, still completely intact, might have been of great value the next day; but it could hardly be expected on this evening to effect a decisive reversal of the situation.[20]

In the event, the assault of the II Corps soon broke down; it got within a few hundred yards of Point de Jour, but as it pushed forward it became involved with the masses of broken units pinned down by the French fire.

Meanwhile to the north the Guard Corps had begun the battle at about 3.00 by taking, in conjunction with the XII Corps, Canrobert's advanced post at Ste Marie aux Chênes. Thereafter, an immensely powerful gun line, with the artillery of the XII Corps to the north and of the Guard Corps to the south of the village, together with that of the IX Corps and the III Corps still further south, came to dominate this sector of the battlefield. The French artillery was effectively silenced, and 180 German guns concentrated their fire on Canrobert's infantry. Further north, the infantry units of the XII Corps, seeking to turn the flank of the French army, moved on Roncourt.

It was at about 5.15 that Prince August judged that the time had come for an infantry assault on the main French positions at St Privat and Amanvillers. It was a catastrophically mistaken decision. Although the French artillery had fallen silent, Canrobert's infantrymen, with a clear field of fire for their Chassepôt, were well placed to inflict fearful casualties as the Guard Corps advanced up the slopes towards

20   Moltke, p. 58.

The attack of the Hessian infantry on the Champenois Farm, painting by Röchling.
(Rousset/*Histoire*)

St Privat. By 6.15 the battered German infantry had struggled to within half a mile of the main French position, but were there pinned down. Relief came only when the developing attack of the XII Corps swept through Roncourt and on up to St Privat. Subjected to the concentrated fire of 24 German batteries, the village was reduced to a flaming ruin. A desperate cavalry charge ordered by Canrobert in an effort to relieve the situation was broken up before it had covered 50 yards. At 7.30 the Saxons of the XII Corps and the Prussians of the Guard Corps stormed into St Privat. Canrobert's shattered corps retreated in disorder down the road to Woippy.

Bazaine had previously warned Bourbaki of the danger to which Canrobert was exposed, and the commander of the Guard had moved up towards the battle line Picard's division. This consisted of one regiment of Zouaves and three of grenadiers, together with its artillery; to this was added two batteries from the general reserve. By 4.00 these forces were established at Gros-Chêne, astride the road from Plappeville to St Privat, and there for some while it remained. Earlier in the day Bazaine had ordered Bourbaki to send a brigade to support Frossard's 2nd Corps. This he did, though protesting at the commitment of the reserve piecemeal. To this Bazaine, in response, left it to Bourbaki to recall the brigade if he thought fit.[21] At about 6.15 two officers from Ladmirault's staff arrived with a plea for assistance; Bourbaki was hesitant, but he set off towards Amanvillers.

21   Howard, p. 177.

The Prussian Guard Fusiliers attacking Sainte-Marie-aux-Chênes, painting by Röchling.
(Rousset/*Histoire*)

Bourbaki was not having a good day : 'Nervous, hesitant, disorientated one knows not why, about an imaginary danger that might appear to the north of Metz, he was influenced by the panic of the 6th Corps, did not want to'assassinate' his grenadiers, and refused to launch a counter-attack.'[22] It was not long before any counter-attack had ceased to be feasible, as was readily apparent to Bourbaki, who raged at his guide: 'You promised me a victory; now you've got me involved in a rout. You had no right to do that! There was no need to make me leave my magnificent positions for this!'[23] Bourbaki pulled back; his retirement panicked elements of the 4th Corps as well as the retreating troops of the 6th Corps, and the Guard units themselves were swept back. Only its artillery was able to check any attempt by the Germans to pursue.

News soon began to reach Bazaine of the collapse of his right flank. One after another, two officers from Canrobert's staff and an aide-de-camp from Ladmirault came to report the gravity of the situation, and the decisions taken to retreat. Bazaine received the news calmly and sympathetically, saying, in words which were later criticised: 'You should not feel saddened [*attrister*] about this retreat,' adding that it would have had to be undertaken on the following morning in any event.

It was clear to him that the Amanvillers position must now be abandoned. In an order signed by Colonel Lewal, he gave instructions to the various corps as to the positions which they should now take up. The 2nd Corps was to retreat towards Longeville, the 3rd Corps to Plappeville and Lessy, the 4th Corps to Lorry and Coupillon and the 6th to Saint-Saëns. The Guard was to remain where it was, while

22   Ruby & Regnault, p. 173.
23   Howard, p. 177.

the cavalry conducted reconnaissances on either flank, du Barail towards Thionville and Forton in the direction of Ars:

> But General Henry, Canrobert's chief of staff, wrote later that he had received this order at the height of the battle, before 4.00. It must be admitted that Lewal had dictated this to the assistant chiefs of staff in the course of their morning briefing. But in this case, why had Canrobert, in receipt of the order, not carried it out? Perhaps the disintegration of his units did not permit it.[24]

A much less charitable view of Canrobert's proceedings was taken by General Cissey, whose division of the 4th Corps had immediately adjoined the position of 6th Corps:

> When the Marshal judged that the battle had gone on long enough, he calmly ordered the movement on Metz without warning anyone, least of all General Ladmirault. When he had commenced his retreat, his pretext was a lack of cartridges. However two regiments at least of his corps had not fired a shot. These troops, compressed into too narrow a space, had never been seriously engaged. After 6:30 p.m. one of Canrobert's divisional generals arrived at the Château de Woippy where he dined in tranquillity before enjoying a good night's rest.[25]

General Cissey, commander of 1st Division of French 4th Corps. (Private collection)

It was not necessary, that evening, for the 2nd and 3rd Corps to retire from the positions which they still occupied, at least not immediately, but Bazaine acquiesced in Frossard's wish to fall back to the line of the forts. Meanwhile at the Royal headquarters, there was considerable concern at the position; no news had been heard from the Second Army for several hours, and it was necessary for Moltke to insist to the King that orders must be given for the renewal of the battle next day. After what he had seen of the horrific losses of the First Army in the Mance ravine, Moltke might have been permitted some dismay at the situation, but he remained perfectly calm:

> When the victorious message of Prince Frederick Charles arrived after midnight, the Chief of the General Staff received it with his peculiar outward equanimity; and, as if he had been sure of it all along, at once drew up the dispositions for reaping the fruits of the great success, so that the whole situation was ready to be laid before the King in the early morning of the 19th.[26]

In considering Bazaine's conduct of the battle, it must be accepted, as Ruby & Regnault recognise, that Bazaine had been taken by surprise at the extent of the battle and, badly informed, had erred in a number of instances. He failed to order the 2nd and 3rd Corps to follow up their success in repulsing the attack of the First Army; he did not launch the Guard to restore the situation on the right; 60 guns of the reserve artillery remained unused at Plappeville; he made no use of his cavalry, which might have been employed in holding up the German turning movement; and the retreat was not well conducted, even though contingency plans had been put in place.

Bazaine's judges, his contemporary critics, and later historians were unbridled in their comments on his performance. Various explanations were put forward for his failures; the motivation for his actions suggested, invariably speculative and almost universally hostile, ranged from the possible to the ludicrous. His failure to provide adequate support for Canrobert's corps, for instance, was absurdly put down to the fact that he saw the Marshal as a rival; there was no evidence whatever to sustain this accusation. Most of his critics believed him to been mesmerised by the attraction of Metz as a place of safety. Alfred Duquet, in *Les Grandes Batailles Autour de Metz*, observed: 'If he had wished to leave Metz, he would not have allowed the crushing of his right at St Privat.'[27] Ruby & Regnault find especially disconcerting the ill-natured and speculative comments of the French Official History: 'perhaps the Marshal was counting on a lack of success to justify a retreat which he had already decided to undertake.'[28] Apart from anything else, this suggestion is completely at odds with the testimony of General Jarras. The chief of staff was in no doubt on the point:

> I do not believe that, in whatever form, the Marshal had ever expressed the intention to retreat with his army into the fortified camp of Metz, and this intention, if it had existed, would have been completely irreconcilable with the

---

26 Hönig, p. 177.
27 Duquet, Alfred, *Les Grandes Batailles Autour de Metz* (Paris, 1888), p. 305.
28 Ruby & Regnault, p. 177; *Service Historique de l'Armée, Guerre de 1870-1871* (Paris) III, p. 305.

boundless confidence which he never ceased to display about the solidity of the line of Rozerieulles, Amanvillers and St Privat.[29]

It must be conceded, though, as is apparent from his memoirs, that Jarras never understood Bazaine at all, and that Bazaine never had much of an opinion of him. From the start of what was a crucial partnership for the Army of the Rhine, they were an ill matched pair.

D'Andlau, at once the most malevolent as well as the most profoundly unreliable of Bazaine's accusers, put into the Marshal's mouth words to suggest that a straightforward defensive battle did not need any intervention by the commander-in-chief, and that this explained his absence from the battlefield, adding, 'If there was a defeat there, the blame must fall on the troops who failed to hold the lines which I had charged them to defend.'[30]

In their review of Bazaine's conduct of the battle of Gravelotte- St Privat, Ruby & Regnault put forward one plausible explanation:

> He had pulled back his army to a well-chosen position upon which he could, with some chance of success, deliver battle. This battle he was obliged to to accept, since the enemy had the initiative. If he succeeded, he could again take the road to Verdun. If defeated, the retreat to an intermediate position would permit him, before he became cooped up in Metz, some space and a certain freedom of action. We should not forget that the Amanvillers – Norroy position to some extent covered the railway to Thionville, a vital interest. The retreat to this intermediate position could not be carried out, because Canrobert had not understood his chief's intentions, which had been, it is true, only briefly explained.[31]

In his final account of the Army of the Rhine, Bazaine set out in full his letter to Canrobert outlining those intentions, explaining the movements which each corps should make to the intermediate position which he had previously selected if it should become necessary to fall back. For the 6th Corps, he directed that it should take the Briey road in moving to its new position, with its left on Sansonnet and its right projecting north of Fort Moselle; it would have on its left the 4th Corps. In front of the positions to be taken up by each of the corps, defence works, covered trenches and breast works must be put in hand with the greatest urgency, as soon as the movements had been completed.[32] Quoting this letter, which had similarly gone to all the corps commanders, Bazaine protested that it had been used to prove that he did not want to

29   Jarras, p. 131.
30   D'Andlau, p. 99.
31   Ruby & Regnault, pp. 177-178.
32   Bazaine, *Episodes*, pp. 106-107.

move away from Metz: 'It proves nothing of the kind, but only that the slanderers did not know of the regulations for service in the field.' As he pointed out, these regulations expressly required the commander-in-chief to prescribe in advance the dispositions to be followed in the case of defeat. He was certainly entitled to object to the 'absurd and malicious nonsense' emanating from such ill informed critics.

An alternative explanation for Bazaine's management of the battle was put forward by his son. If the Marshal did not appear on the right of his line, and maintained part of his reserves at Plappeville, it was because he was anxious

King William on the evening of the battle of Gravelotte, drawing by Becker. (Lindner)

for the security of his left flank. Significant enemy forces, in the shape of Manteuffel's I Corps, remained on the right bank of the Moselle. It had pushed forward its artillery to Ars-Laquenexy, Mercy le Haut and Peltre, and from 5.00 until 6.30 had directed a heavy fire on Fort Queuleu and the outskirts of the city. In this situation the French army was exposed to the risk of being outflanked on both wings and cut off from Metz. This, apparently, was a move which the Germans had considered. This threat alone justified the retention of the reserve at Plappeville. So runs this argument, which is not without merit; Ruby & Regnault, though, join the majority in seeing an actual and violent attack on the right wing as being more urgent than a mere threat to the left.[33]

33   Ruby & Regnault, p. 178.

French prisoners following the Battle of Gravelotte-St Privat, painting by Dupray.
(Rousset/*Histoire*)

Acknowledging that Bazaine, in sending part of his reserve to support Leboeuf, while keeping the rest to cover a possible threat to his left, was in error, Ruby & Regnault conclude that Jarras must bear a large part of the blame. He failed to discharge the proper functions of a chief of staff. He was well aware that Bazaine's condition was such as seriously to impair his mobility. But though orders might have gone to Bourbaki to come forward sooner on the right, and this might have achieved some local success, it would not have been for long; the Germans might have been briefly held up, but they had four corps moving forward.

Overall, the conclusion reached by Ruby & Regnault was firm and compelling:

> It is laughable to reproach Bazaine for having envisaged, before the battle, that he might break off the battle and withdraw his troops to an intermediate line, and that in doing so he might lose control of the last road to Verdun. On August 18 he could no longer be concerned with Verdun unless an improbable victory gave him the freedom to move on that road, and doubtless others. For the moment, it was necessary above all to preserve the army, as he had understood two days before.[34]

Bazaine's sympathetic biographer, Philip Guedalla, put Bazaine's military situation in these terms:

34   Ruby & Regnault, p. 179.

He had not been disposed to risk his last reserve, the Imperial Guard, in support of Canrobert, since he judged St Privat to be a point of secondary value in comparison with the road to Metz. For if that were cut, they would all be disarmed and starving; but if St Privat went, they could still fall back and kill more Germans in another defensive position nearer Metz.[35]

35   Guedalla, p 192

14

Blockade of Metz

The battle of August 18 had been a German victory, which in due course would be seen as decisive in the context of the war as a whole, but it had been dearly bought. Total German casualties were 20,170, of which 5,238 had been killed; French losses are less certain, but the incomplete and approximate return put the figure at 12,273.[1] Heavy though were the losses his armies had suffered, Moltke was in no doubt what must be done. The victory had given him the opportunity effectively to take the Army of the Rhine off the board by blockading it in Metz, and he took immediate steps to this end. It had not been part of his original intention; he had expected that it would be necessary only to observe the place while the main army passed it enroute to Paris.

Now, however, a complete reorganisation of the forces comprising the First and Second Armies was necessary. Prince Frederick Charles was assigned the task of blockading Metz, for which he was allocated the three corps previously comprising the First Army (I, VII and VIII Corps), and the II, III, IX and X Corps of the Second Army. A new army, the Army of the Meuse, was constituted, under the command of Crown Prince Albert of Saxony, consisting of the Guard, IV and XII Corps. Frederick Charles would also have the 3rd Reserve Division, which had been originally earmarked to watch Metz, together with the 1st and 3rd Cavalry Divisions. Crown Prince Albert was assigned the 5th and 6th Cavalry Divisions.

The Army of the Meuse would have a total strength of 86,275 men, leaving behind for the blockading army approximately 150,000 men; this figure, it was appreciated, might be no more numerous than the army it was intended to blockade, which it was assumed would make an effort to break out to the west. Frederick Charles, therefore, was instructed to keep the bulk of his forces on the left bank of the Moselle. Moltke wasted no time in issuing the orders necessary to effect this reorganisation, which went out by 11.00 p.m. August 19.[2] He was determined to retain the initiative; while

1   *Official History*, Vol. II, Appendix 2; Howard, p. 181.
2   Moltke, pp. 64-65.

The French Imperial Guard at Metz. (*Illustrated London News*)

Frederick Charles kept Bazaine immured in Metz, the Third Army and the newly formed Army of the Meuse would go after the French forces assembling at Châlons under the command of Marshal MacMahon. The new organisation had the effect of placing Steinmetz under the orders of Frederick Charles, an arrangement which was unlikely to last very long before the wilful First Army commander committed some further offence which would justify his removal. An incident involving Royal protocol duly ensued; Frederick Charles took offence, King William was furious, and Steinmetz was appointed as Governor of Posen and relieved of his command of the First Army on September 7.

Bazaine's adversary during the investment of Metz was by no means enthusiastic about the task which he had been given. Moltke, in pointing out what seemed to him to be the most likely direction of a breakout, wrote to Frederick Charles on August 22 to encourage him:

The difficulties and the disagreeable features of the very important task which has fallen to your Royal Highness are clearly understood but may perhaps be of short duration. If the enemy succeeds in breaking out, it will probably be attempted in the direction of Nancy, when the investment will at once become a campaign in the open field. Since, in this case, we can count on an effective and vigorous pursuit, the other two armies would, in my opinion, continue their march. If the French army in Metz is unable to break out, it cannot without relief exist long there. Your Royal Highness will achieve, in its capitulation, one of the greatest successes recorded in military history.[3]

One of Bazaine's first duties on August 19 was to report the outcome of the previous day's battle to the Emperor:

The Army fought all yesterday in its positions from St Privat la Montagne to Rozerieulles, and held them until 9.00 p.m., when the 6th and 4th Corps changed front to meet a turning movement of large enemy forces on our right, seeking to take advantage of poor visibility. This morning, I have pulled back the 2nd and 3rd Corps, and the Army is in position on the left bank of the Moselle from Longeville to Sansonnet, forming a curved line passing behind the forts of St Quentin and Plappeville. The troops are exhausted by this incessant fighting, which gives them no chance to recover; it is indispensable that they have two or three days' rest. The King of Prussia was this morning at Rezonville with General von Moltke, and everything indicates that the Prussian army intends to feel out Metz. I still intend to take a northerly direction and then to cut across via Montmédy on the road from St Ménéhould to Châlons, if it is not too strongly occupied; in that case I will continue towards Sedan and Mezières in order to reach Châlons.[4]

It was perhaps not the most comprehensive or candid account of the situation of his army on the morning of August 19, but it could have left no doubt that the Army of the Rhine had suffered a serious defeat.

Bazaine said later, of the situation in which he now found himself: 'I wished to act only when I was certain,' and that meant taking no risks, as Guedalla observed:

For the essential, as he saw it, was to preserve the army in order that it might live to fight another day. Those had been the Emperor's instructions; and in retrospect it is not easy to find fault with them, although contemporaries could hardly be expected to applaud the strategy by which their main army was immobilised in an encircled fortress after two indecisive battles. But what else was there to

---

3　Moltke, *Correspondance Militaire*, I, pp. 307-305.
4　Bazaine, *Episodes*, pp. 107-108.

do? MacMahon's defeat at Wörth had let the Germans into France. And how else could the war be kept away from the defenceless centre of the country, whilst an army was concentrating in Champagne for the defence of Paris?[5]

Bazaine had left his headquarters at Plappeville at 2.00 p.m. on the morning of August 19, without apparently notifying Jarras. The chief of staff had not remained with him, and apparently spent part of the night looking for him. The Marshal made his way into Metz through large crowds of retreating troops from the 4th Corps and 6th Corps which were in a state of complete disorganisation. This depressing spectacle brought from him the mournful comment: 'What can one do with troops like these!' It was all too clear that their morale had progressively deteriorated during the previous days, not least because the army's supply system had practically broken down. On all sides the cry was heard: 'They are leading us to the butchers!'[6]

The problems which had faced Bazaine on assuming command of the Army of the Rhine had been, it was at once obvious to him, enormously difficult from the outset; now, a week later, they had increased immeasurably. In the space of five days, the army had fought three major battles, in the course of which it had suffered over 37,000 casualties, or more than 20% of its strength. The 2nd Corps had been badly knocked about on August 16; the 6th Corps, and a large part of the 4th Corps, likewise on August 18, and in these units the decline in morale had been particularly marked. Of all the units in the Army of the Rhine, however, it was the artillery that had suffered the most, overborne as it had been by the ruthlessly efficient German artillery. It was estimated that the losses of the French artillery during the three battles amounted to 1,430 men and 1,442 horses; and these figures excluded the casualties suffered by the artillery reserve.[7]

Bazaine selected for his new headquarters the imposing Villa Herbin, in the suburb of Ban St Martin; the staff were accommodated in a rather more modest building some distance away. The old city of Metz lay within a bend of the river Moselle. Ever since 1866 the French War Ministry had been endeavouring, not altogether successfully, to strengthen its defences. These had been the subject of severe criticism by Bazaine himself after his tours of inspection before 1870.

The positions initially taken up after the battle of Gravelotte-St Privat were for the most part on the left bank of the Moselle. The 2nd Corps was disposed in several lines on the south and south-east slopes of Mont St Quentin; Lapasset's brigade, which had formed the rearguard during the retreat, was at Longeville, with Forton's cavalry division. The 3rd Corps was to the west of Plappeville with, on its right, the 4th Corps on the Coupillon ridge. The 6th Corps, with du Barail's cavalry division, was engaged in

---

5   Guedalla, p. 194.
6   Ruby & Regnault, p. 183.
7   Kunz, Hermann, *Le Maréchal Bazaine pourrait-il en 1870 sauver la France?*(Paris, 1896), p. 146.

Fort Bellecroix during the siege. (Rousset/*Histoire*)

the process of sorting itself out in the ground to the north of the forts. The Imperial Guard was concentrated to the east of Plappeville. The artillery reserve was at Ban St Martin. During the course of August 20 the 3rd Corps withdrew to a position behind Forts Plappeville and St Quentin and then, two days later, crossed over to the right bank of the Moselle.[8]

The defence of the entrenched camp of Metz was based on four forts, Plappeville and St Quentin on the left bank of the river, and St Julien and Queuleu on the right bank. Work on the forts was still incomplete when the investment began, but within a short time they were considerably reinforced with earthworks. Steps were also taken to strengthen the whole of the French position on the left bank of the Moselle, which faced the bulk of the army of investment. Extensive abattis were prepared in the south eastern sector of the woods of Chatel and Vigneulles, while batteries were thrown up along the ridges of Mont St Quentin and Coupillon, near the Plappeville quarries, and also in the valley of the Moselle south of Woippy.[9]

Bazaine's disposition of the army around Metz was the subject of particularly severe criticism by Alfred Duquet. His complaint was that the French army had been pulled back unnecessarily close to the fortress, thereby losing the greater breathing space it might have had. 'Bazaine,' he wrote, 'allowed the besiegers to approach as close as they wished; he did not dispute any important position; St Barbe, Courcelles sur Nied, Mercy le Haut were abandoned.'[10] Each of these was, however a considerable distance from the line of the forts, and it was unrealistic to hope to retain possession

8   *Official History*, Vol. II, p. 479.
9   *Official History*, Vol. II, p. 480.
10   Duquet, p. 4.

of villages so far out from the fortress. Their garrisons would have been at constant risk of being cut off by the enemy. While pushing out the defences to create such a huge ring around Metz would considerably stretch the resources of Frederick Charles, he could in practice have moved closer in whenever he chose, and it would also have extended the defence lines to breaking point. Duquet is not to be regarded as a reliable commentator; throughout, his work displayed the most extreme hostility to Bazaine, verging at times on hysteria. He adopted unquestioningly many of the more absurd canards which the Marshal's enemies delighted to repeat.

On the day that Bazaine established his new headquarters, there occurred an incident which, at the time, occasioned no remark. Debains, a former secretary at the French embassy in Berlin, who was attached to the staff of the Army of the Rhine, published a communiqué intended to reassure the general public, and which appeared in the local Press, in the course of which he wrote:

> One of France's armies is today concentrated around Metz, in the positions ordered by the Marshal Commanding in Chief after the battle of August 18. It can be said that the plan of the enemy for the battle did not succeed. In holding a position around Metz, the army of Marshal Bazaine has confronted strategic and political necessities.[11]

Much later, the inclusion of the word 'political' in this statement was seized on as connoting some hidden objective in Bazaine's mind. In vain, Debains protested, in the course of the Marshal's trial, that he had received no directive whatever from Bazaine as to this statement, the wording of which had no special significance. It was, though, all grist to the mill for those who suspected Bazaine of ulterior motives.

The besiegers had wasted little time in ensuring that any attempted breakout would meet with effective resistance. Although Moltke had suggested to Frederick Charles that militarily the wisest move for Bazaine was to head south to Nancy, the concentration of the French army on the left bank of the Moselle suggested that it might be in the opposite direction, northwards towards Thionville, that the first move might be made. Initially, therefore, it was the left bank of the Moselle that must be the focus:

> As regards the right bank of the Moselle, only a close interception of all communications and the defence of certain especially important points was in contemplation. Any sally on the part of the enemy along the left bank was to be prevented at all hazards, and consequently a continuous line of works was to be thrown up from the very commencement.[12]

11   Ruby & Regnault, p. 184.
12   *Official History*, Vol. II, p. 173.

The defensive perimeter around the city was some twenty five miles, and the work of making it as close to impregnable as possible was put in hand at once. Roads were barricaded; villages fortified and linked by communication trenches; woods were blocked by abattis or in some cases cleared to ensure a field of fire. Covered trenches were dug; batteries prepared for the artillery; additional bridges erected over the Moselle, and a telegraph network established. Observation posts were set up at intervals around the line. [13]

To achieve the freedom of movement necessary if he was to reach out towards the Army of Châlons, Bazaine knew that whatever route he took, he would find his way barred by the enemy. Certainly, if it was to be attempted, the breakout must be launched as soon as possible, whatever the state of the army's intelligence about MacMahon's intended movements. In preparation for this, Bazaine called for detailed reports from each of his corps commanders. These, which he received on August 20 and 21, were surprisingly bullish. Frossard noted that in spite of the privations suffered by the troops of the 2nd Corps, they were generally in good health. Morale had dipped due to the high casualty rate among officers; many companies had only one officer, while the 8th Line Regiment, among others, was led by a captain. Leboeuf reported that the morale of the 3rd Corps was excellent, particularly among the soldiers; 'The officers, very dedicated and very brave under fire, are naturally a little inclined to be critical, but without bitterness, each having his own ideas about the campaign.' The corps had suffered 4,000 casualties in the three battles, but was presently about 40,000 strong. [14]

Ladmirault, too, gave a good report of the 4th Corps, though like Frossard he was concerned about the casualty rate among his officers. As a body of men, they left nothing to be desired, and the health of the soldiers was good. The corps was, he wrote, capable of making a supreme effort. In his report, Canrobert looked back at the haste with which the 6th Corps had been sent to join the Army of the Rhine, and the consequent partial loss of its artillery and engineers. He too was concerned about the level of casualties among his officers, but overall their morale and that of their men inspired him to feel great confidence. Bourbaki reported that the troops of the Imperial Guard were in excellent condition, and had been fully supplied with munitions. Their morale was high, and their greatest wish was to take on the Prussian infantry. [15]

All this was, in terms of planning the breakout, most encouraging. The crucial question was to determine the direction to be taken. Westwards, the most direct route towards the army of Châlons, an advance would run head on into the bulk of Frederick Charles's investing army. In the north, a lengthy and circuitous route might be taken to reach the northern fortresses, and from there to turn west. Certainly Bazaine must

---

13   Howard, p. 258.
14   Bazaine, *Episodes*, pp. 153-154.
15   Bazaine, *Episodes*, pp. 155-156.

The Porte des Allemandes, Metz. (*Illustrated London News*)

expect to be closely pursued in this direction. Eastwards, the investing forces were weaker; only Manteuffel's I Corps and the 3rd Reserve Division stood in the way. It was to be expected that they would be able to hold up an advance until troops came over from the left bank to their support. Finally there was the possibility, the very bold possibility, of a stroke southwards across the German lines of communication, seen by Moltke as Bazaine's best move. It would not take him to Verdun, of course, but it would seize the initiative, and seriously disrupt the German armies' march across France. But if it offered the most results, it was even riskier than the other alternatives.

The truth was that, if preserving the army was the first priority, remaining within the forts was the safest course. But preserving it for what purpose? True, it would pin down Frederick Charles and his large army; but France needed more than that. And, as Moltke had observed, Metz could not hold out for very long. So work began to plan the breakout. Crucial to this was all the available intelligence about the state of the Army of Châlons and its intended strategy. MacMahon was in a similar position, needing to know as much as he could of Bazaine's plans in deciding what to do with his army. Coordination of the operations of the two armies was always going to be extremely difficult; as it turned out, it was impossible. Communication between them, such as it was, ultimately had little influence on the decisions that were taken, but the correspondence between Bazaine and MacMahon, subsequently minutely pored over, became the subject of controversy. This was perhaps not surprising. Later, the parties to the correspondence, as well as many others, had axes to grind in putting forward their own accounts of the situation as it actually appeared at the time, and the effect of each message on events as they unfolded.

In his first message after the battle of Gravelotte – St Privat previously referred to, Bazaine had spoken of his intention to take a northerly direction and proceed via St Ménéhould to Châlons. For MacMahon, the idea of taking his army eastwards always seemed very dangerous, and on August 18, well before he knew of the outcome of the battle then raging outside Metz, he was having grave doubts. The Emperor's presence with his army did nothing to encourage him in planning such a move; insofar as his opinions still carried any weight, Napoleon remained of the view that a retirement on Paris was the proper course. Since Bazaine was nominally his superior, on the following day MacMahon sent him a dispatch to express his concerns: 'If, as I believe, you are forced to beat a retreat very soon, I do not know, at the distance which I am from you, how to come to your assistance without uncovering Paris. If you judge differently, please let me know.'[16] On August 19 Bazaine had not yet received this message when he sent a telegram to MacMahon later in the day, but it gave MacMahon his answer: 'I am too far from the centre of your operations to indicate to you the movements you should undertake. I leave it to you to act in accordance with your own judgement.'[17] In all the circumstances, each of these messages was entirely reasonable, but they did not take forward the strategic questions that must be answered.

While MacMahon hesitated, time was not on his side. A lively anxiety about the threat posed by the German cavalry, spreading out across the plains towards Châlons, in advance of the Crown Prince's Third Army, could not be ignored. MacMahon's army would be safer in Reims, while consideration was being given to the strategy to be pursued. If necessary, a retreat towards Paris would be perfectly feasible from there, and it would put MacMahon on the northern flank of the Crown Prince's march. Accordingly, on August 21 the army took the road to Reims. Meanwhile in Paris the Council of Ministers had reached the firm conclusion that MacMahon must advance to the relief of Bazaine, whatever risk that entailed, and on the same day Eugene Rouher, the President of the Senate, set off to Reims to tell MacMahon what had been decided. When he heard this, the Marshal was appalled, having now concluded that a relief operation must fail, as he told Rouher: 'It is impossible to rescue Bazaine. He has no munitions, no supplies, he will be forced to capitulate and we shall arrive too late.'[18] Rouher was entirely convinced by the force of MacMahon's arguments, which he completely accepted, and agreed to go back to Paris to report accordingly.

It was at this point that Bazaine's message of August 19 arrived, which appeared to put a very different complexion on the matter. If his intention was, as he said, to take a northerly direction and then move via St Ménéhould to Châlons, it suggested that perhaps a meeting of the two French armies was a possibility. And even if it

16   Ruby & Regnault, p. 187.
17   Ruby & Regnault, p. 187.
18   Howard, p. 189.

Metz, from the Thionville road. (*Illustrated London News*)

did not really mark a significant change in the military situation, it certainly altered the moral position. In the light of Bazaine's message, it became extremely difficult for MacMahon to stick to his resolution not to move east. Accordingly, he changed his mind, issuing orders for the Army of Châlons to set off on August 23 towards Montmédy. This would be a safer course at any rate than to march head on towards the Third Army. MacMahon duly notified Palikao of his change of heart, and he also informed Bazaine, sending a telegram at 10:45 a.m. on August 22: 'Received your dispatch of 19. Am at Reims. Will be on the Aisne tomorrow afternoon, where I will act according to circumstances to come to your aid.' He sent the text of this to the commandants of Verdun, Montmédy and Longwy. If he had sensed the misgivings in Bazaine's message, he passed over them.[19] The news of MacMahon's changed decision came of course as a profound relief to Palikao and to the Council of Ministers, which had already heard Rouher's report and rejected it, insisting that the Army of Châlons must move eastward.

During the night of August 22/23 another message arrived from Bazaine which in due course was to provoke yet another controversy. On the face of it, it did not add a great deal to his previous dispatch. Sent on August 20, it read as follows:

19   *Guerre 1870-1871, Armée de Châlons* (Paris), Docs. Annexe, p. 136.

I have had to take up a position near Metz, in order to rest the soldiers and resupply them with rations and munitions. The enemy continually increases around us and I shall follow, very probably, in order to re-join you, the line of the northern fortresses. I shall inform you of my march, if, that is, I can undertake it without compromising the army.[20]

A good deal of effort had gone into getting this message to MacMahon. It was one of three copies sent by Bazaine on August 20 and transmitted by wire to Thionville. From there, they were taken as hard copies by a police commissaire named Guyard to Longwy. The commandant there, Colonel Massaroli, handed them to two police inspectors named Rabasse and Miès, who were working for Colonel Stoffel, who was himself assisting the intelligence staff of the Army of Châlons in a supernumerary capacity. From Longwy, the contents of the messages were sent by telegraph to Rethel, and Rabasse and Miès then set off to take the hard copies to army headquarters. They were obliged to take a roundabout route through Belgium, and it was not until the evening of August 25 that they arrived at Rethel. There, they handed them to Colonel d'Abzac, an officer on MacMahon's staff, who later, at Bazaine's trial, they convincingly identified as having received them. Handing back the dispatches, d'Abzac observed: 'We have known these things for two days; that's what you telegraphed.'[21] Next morning the two inspectors saw Stoffel at breakfast and gave him the originals. Rabasse and Miès assumed that Stoffel had seen the telegraphed copies of the dispatches, which appears not to have been the case, and so made no comment when he merely put them in his pocket. The Duc d'Aumale, presiding at Bazaine's trial, expressed incredulity that Stoffel should so carelessly have pocketed them. It was a question about which Stoffel was closely examined. General Séré de Rivières, who conducted the investigation which preceded the trial, suggested that Stoffel had deliberately suppressed the dispatches on the instructions of the Emperor. This so enraged Stoffel that he burst out in a denunciation of Seré de Riviéres, saying that he shared the sentiments of the entire army and felt for him only 'contempt and disdain'.[22] Refusing to retract, he was later charged with slander, and spent three months in prison as a result.

MacMahon, when originally asked about it, said that he had not received the dispatch and would not have forgotten a message of such importance. Later, after the evidence at Bazaine's trial pointed firmly to his having received it, he somewhat revised his evidence, telling the court: 'I do not recall having received this dispatch, and I find it impossible that I could have overlooked it as it would have justified halting my movement towards the east if circumstances seemed to require it.'[23]

20   Bazaine, *Episodes,* p. 163; quoted in Roger Williams, *Napoleon III and the Stoffel Affair* (Worland, Wyoming, 1997), p. 131.
21   Williams, p. 146.
22   Williams, p. 153.
23   Williams, p. 147.

MacMahon's memory was, however, to put it mildly, somewhat selective, as his account of the fate of a later dispatch, which very probably did not originate from Bazaine, was to demonstrate. Transmitted from Thionville on August 27, it read: 'We are cut off, but only weakly. We can break through when we want. We shall await you.[24] This unquestionably did reach MacMahon at Raucourt by the hand of a M. Hulme, the owner of a spinning mill near Mouzon, who delivered it to him personally, yet the Marshal still sought to deny receiving it. He said he could not recall being given such a dispatch, noting that if it had reached him after his decision to move east, such a message would surely have struck him.

So there it was. On the balance of probabilities, it seems very likely that the accounts given by Rabasse and Miès were correct, and that it was indeed into d'Abzac's hands that Bazaine's message first came. Why he should deny it is a matter for speculation, but if he did receive it, there can be little doubt that MacMahon did as well. Perhaps they both felt that admitting its receipt would reflect badly on the decision to continue the eastward march. MacMahon's revised and carefully worded, not to say shifty, statement was essentially made to support d'Abzac. The suggestion that Stoffel received the message and suppressed it at the behest of Napoleon is beyond belief, not least because the Emperor in any case opposed the eastward march. If the message contained anything new at all it was merely a reservation about the Army of Metz being able to undertake the suggested march. For Roger Williams, MacMahon's conduct in relation to the dispatch brought by Hulme raised several questions; perhaps he failed to perceive the implications of the dispatch; or perhaps he had become so reconciled to the government's insistence that he should move east to relieve Bazaine that having ordered the march he was indifferent to any information which suggested the wisdom of calling it off.[25] This last seems the most probable explanation, consistent as it was with his failure to react to the dispatch of August 20.

MacMahon's initial instinct had been correct; the decision to march to the east was a desperate mistake, not least because as an organisation the Army of Châlons was incapable of moving fast enough to evade the enemy. Apart from this, the *intendance* system proved completely powerless to cope with the army's need for supplies. As early as the first day's march from Reims, discipline began to break down, and hungry troops pillaged the countryside as they marched. It was almost immediately apparent that the army's line of march must be altered, to bring it to a railway line through which it could be resupplied. This involved a move to its left towards Rethel, causing further delay, although the unexpected change of direction at least had the effect of shaking off the ubiquitous German cavalry for a couple of days.

Meanwhile in Metz plans were put in hand for a breakout, which it was intended should take place on August 26. In the absence of any definite news from MacMahon,

24   Williams, p. 158.
25   Williams, p. 161.

the decision had to be made without taking the Army of Châlons's movements into account; the sector chosen for the assault was the north-east of the fortress, down the right bank of the Moselle. Notwithstanding the bullish reports which Bazaine had received from the corps commanders, however, the planned breakout was plainly going to be an extremely hazardous operation.

15

A Council of War

According to Colonel Lewal, Bazaine's decision to launch a breakout from Metz was prompted by the receipt of a message from MacMahon. At the Marshal's trial, the colonel testified that the message arrived rolled in a cigarette, and that Bazaine read it out in a loud voice in the presence of another witness, Mornay-Soult. Bazaine, however, denied it. He dealt with the question expressly in his first book, suggesting that Lewal's recollection may have related to a much later incident on August 30.[1] Certainly he never mentioned it to his staff or to his senior commanders. Since the alleged message spoke of MacMahon's projected march to Stenay it would have been a huge responsibility to remain silent about it. Jarras, not one of Bazaine's warmest admirers, dismissed the suggestion out of hand, writing that it was beyond belief that 'a Marshal of France, Generalissimo of the armies charged with driving the enemy out of the country, could have left his lieutenants in ignorance of so important a message, at a time when he believed it necessary to consult them about the greatest part of what he intended to do.'[2]

Characteristically, Bazaine began his consideration of the point at which to launch an attack with a discussion with Lewal rather than Jarras. It was his thought that, even if the breakout failed, it would have the effect of pinning down a large number of enemy troops which would otherwise be available to confront MacMahon. Lewal advocated a much wider offensive, with the cavalry pouring down the Saarlouis road, but Bazaine opted for an attack on a narrow front of 5 kilometres. He was, though, prepared to use his cavalry to exploit any success gained, and had created a cavalry corps under General Desvaux consisting of the cavalry division of the Imperial Guard and that of Forton.[3]

Bazaine's conclusion that the attack should be made northwards on the right bank of the Moselle, rather than the bolder thrust southwards which Moltke thought

---

1   Bazaine, *L'Armée du Rhin*, pp. 304-305.
2   Jarras, pp. 164-165.
3   Ruby & Regnault, p. 197.

The arsenal at Metz. (*Illustrated London News*)

would have been more promising, reflected his preference for taking the line of the northern fortresses if he could. In following that route he could hope to pick up supplies and ammunition not only at Thionville, but also at Longwy and Longuyon. It was a manoeuvre full of uncertainty; but it was possible. On August 23 he managed to send out a message to Napoleon which more or less repeated his dispatch of August 20, in which he informed the Emperor that he intended 'undertaking the march I spoke about before, through the northern fortresses, in order not to run any risk.'[4] The advance was to be led by Leboeuf's 3rd Corps, which had been on the right bank of the river for several days. It was to concentrate on the morning of August 26 between the Saarlouis road and the Mey copse. The remaining corps would cross the river during the morning; Bazaine ordered Coffinières, as commandant of the fortress, to throw two additional bridges over the Moselle at the island of Chambière.[5] The intention, once they had got across the river, was for the 6th Corps to operate on the extreme left, facing north, with the 4th Corps to the left of the 3rd Corps and the 2nd Corps in its rear. The Guard and other reserve formations would remain for the time being on the left bank. The trains were to be assembled on Chambière Island. Orders for the operation were duly issued on the evening of August 25.

4   Howard, p. 260.
5   *Official History*, Vol. II, p. 483.

In some respects a good deal of progress had been made in restoring the battle-worthiness of the units that had been so heavily engaged. By August 22 all the field artillery and ammunition parks had been completely resupplied. In addition to the 140 rounds of Chassepôt ammunition provided for every infantryman, there was a general reserve of over one and a quarter million rounds. Meanwhile the 540 guns of the fortress had all been restocked with a sufficient store of ammunition.

The garrison of Thionville, with a total strength of some 3,500 men (of whom about 2,000 were *gardes mobiles*) and 209 guns had been largely left alone by the Germans after an unsuccessful *coup de main* on August 15, but by August 22 Moltke felt it necessary to allocate resources for its investment. On both banks of the Moselle infantry battalions, supported by cavalry, were posted to contain the fortress, but no significant operations were undertaken.

When he read the orders for the breakout, Coffinières was gravely concerned. In the deposition which he was later to give to the *Enquête Parlementaire*, he described how early next morning he had gone to the army headquarters and there encountered General Soleille. He already knew at this time, he said, that there was a question of MacMahon marching towards Metz, not officially, but rumours of this had been circulating. To Soleille, he said:

> The Marshal has ordered a sortie, but we do not know the situation of the troops which are coming to the rescue of Metz; we do not know where they are, or what route they are following. I believe, for my part, that it would be wiser to await accurate news, to know in what direction they are arriving, for several days at least, to hold on and to use the time to strengthen the forts.[6]

Soleille warmly agreed with him, saying that their situation was not so bad; they held a position on the flank of the enemy from which at the right moment they could make a major effort, if MacMahon was on the march. The position was, he said, analogous to that of Napoleon I after the battle of Arcis sur Aube. He thought Coffinières was wise; they should in the meantime, over a period of several days, harass the enemy and strengthen the fortifications until they knew when MacMahon would come.

Accordingly the two generals made their way to Bazaine to make their views known to him. The Marshal at first was unimpressed: 'It is possible that you are right, but too bad; my movement is prepared, and I am going to carry it out'.[7] He declined to cancel the operation, but he convened a meeting to take place later that day at the Château de Grimont, in front of Fort St Julien, at 2.00 p.m.. In the meantime, the initial phase of the operation got under way, with an exchange of rifle fire with the Prussian outposts which continued most of the morning. This was pursued with sufficient vigour to oblige the outposts of the 1st Division at La Grange aux Bois and Colombey to pull

6   Bazaine, *Episodes*, p. 159.
7   Bazaine, *Episodes*, p. 159.

back; the village of Noisseville was occupied by the French after the garrison of the place fell back to Servigny. In the front of the 3rd Reserve Division, substantial bodies of French troops were observed at the Bois de Grimont, which pushed forward a line of skirmishers. The signs of an imminent offensive had not gone unnoticed, and the redeployment of the German forces on the left bank of the Moselle was put in hand in accordance with prearranged plans. It was the intention of Frederick Charles that while the First Army remained in its positions, the Second Army should move around the fortress to the north to block any French advance on Thionville, and at 1:30 he issued the necessary orders.[8]

To support the 3rd Reserve Division at Malroy, about 4 kilometres north of Fort St Julien, 10 battalions of the X Corps crossed over the river to Argancy on the right bank. Additional support was available from the 25th Division a little further north at the bridge of Hauconcourt. Meanwhile Manteuffel ordered the I Corps to close up behind Servigny. In the event of the French army being able to push aside these forces, and make for Thionville, Frederick Charles was confident of intercepting it with the II, III and part of the IX Corps.[9]

General Boyer, aide de camp to Marshal Bazaine. (Private collection)

Heavy rain had seriously delayed the movement of the French army to the left bank, and it was still pouring down when the five corps commanders arrived at the Château de Grimont for their meeting with Bazaine. It was also attended by Soleille and Coffinières, and by Bazaine's principal aide-de-camp, General Boyer, who took the minutes of the meeting. Bazaine briefly summarised the situation and then asked Soleille to speak.[10] The artillery commander had a lot to say. He was an interesting personality. Born on the Ile de Bourbon in the Indian Ocean, of indifferent health and a gloomy outlook, he was technically very sound and was intelligent and well-informed. He had already misled Bazaine and the War Ministry on the subject of excessive consumption of munitions on August 16. His was an opinion likely to carry considerable conviction with his colleagues.

---

8   *Official History*, Vol. II, p. 484.
9   Moltke, p. 102.
10   Bazaine, *Episodes*, pp. 164-167.

Soleille began his exposition by repeating his comparison of the army's situation with that of Napoleon I in 1814; but whereas the Emperor's plan then could not be realised, the situation was now different, because Paris was fortified. The Army of the Rhine, on the flank of the enemy's communications, must cause him great anxiety. The army had a great role to play, politically as well as militarily. If the government was obliged to negotiate, the possession of Metz would carry great weight. He went on to say that the army had sufficient munitions for only one battle; an attempted breakout would consume a large part of them. He added that the army need not be inactive since from Metz it could harass the enemy's lines of communication.

Frossard shared Soleille's opinion absolutely. The army was discouraged, which was easy to understand. Its morale could not survive a defeat, and it would be an army in a state of dissolution. Canrobert went along with the views of Soleille and Frossard, adding that morale could only be maintained if the army remained active and constantly showed its claws. Ladmirault reckoned that it was impossible to proceed without munitions. Leboeuf, when it came to his turn to speak, spent a good deal of time warmly denying any responsibility for the situation of the army, or for the want of preparation for the war. No one, he said, had consulted him on anything, nor had anyone listened to him about the deployment of the army on the frontier. He did make one good point, though: 'To preserve the army intact is the greatest and best service that could be rendered to the country; but what is it going to live on'?

Bourbaki accepted that it was clear that nothing could be done without munitions; oddly, Wawro regards it as merely 'probable' that he argued for a run to the Vosges; in fact, Boyer's record shows that he expressly described this as 'mon désir le plus vif'.[11] Coffinières, who later wrongly told the *Enquête Parlementaire* that he did not speak at this Council of War, was the last to do so. He said that he shared Soleille's opinion. The fortress was not yet in a state to defend itself for more than a fortnight against a formal attack. He said that the army should remain at Metz, and he described the works that he would put in hand to strengthen it.

Bazaine wound up the meeting by raising the question of using companies of 'partisans' to attack the enemy, and it was agreed that this should form the basis of the limited operations to be undertaken. Having heard what his senior commanders had to say, it is not surprising that at 4.00 Bazaine gave orders to abort the operation. As the rain continued to teem down, the weary, muddy troops retraced their steps; chaos ensued as the leading units endeavoured to return down roads crowded with those still moving up. It had not been a happy day for the Army of the Rhine, as the correspondent of the *Manchester Guardian* observed:

> All that very wet day did those poor troops stand draining themselves as best they could on the long clayey slopes of St Julien, right in face of the enemy. For more than thirteen hours stood many of those regiments there without an order

11   Wawro, p. 197.

to move; some of the cavalry were fifteen hours in the saddle that day, and then had to return to broken up quarters, to pitch tents as best they could in muddy lakes.[12]

What was surprising during this discussion was the failure to consider the principal issue raised by Soleille and Coffinières, when they visited Bazaine early that morning, which was the lack of clear information about the efforts being made to relieve the Army of the Rhine. Even if, as Coffinières claimed, it was only in the form of rumours that anything at all was known of MacMahon's movements, it is astonishing that none of those present raised the matter during the Council of war, since all of them must have been aware of the rumours.

That night, Bazaine wrote a message to the War Ministry:

> Still around Metz, with sufficient artillery ammunition for only one battle. Impossible to force the enemy's entrenched lines in these circumstances. No news of Paris, nor of the national morale. Urgent to receive this. Will act effectively if an offensive movement forces the enemy to beat a retreat.[13]

This is, of course, entirely contradictory to the message which reached MacMahon at Raucourt from the hands of M. Hulme, which was almost certainly not composed by Bazaine.

12   Robinson, G.T., *The Fall of Metz* (London, 1871), p. 153.
13   Ruby & Regnault, p. 200.

16

Noisseville

MacMahon had been under no illusion as to just how hazardous an attempt to relieve Metz must be. After his march northwards to resupply the army, he turned east again, but all the indications which he was receiving of the movements of the German armies heightened his concern. He sent an anxious message to Bazaine, which seems not to have arrived: 'I do not think I can move much further East without having news of you and knowing your plans, for if the Crown Prince's army marches on Rethel I shall have to fall back.'[1] By the evening of August 27, at La Chesne, his mind was made up; the army must retreat. He dictated to Colonel Stoffel a telegram to Palikao to tell him what he was doing. In this, he pointed out that there was one German army on the right bank of the Meuse and another marching on the Ardennes:

> I have no news of Bazaine. If I advance to meet him I shall be attacked in front by a part of the First and Second German armies, which, favoured by the woods, can conceal a force superior to mine, and at the same time attacked by the Prussian Crown Prince cutting off my line of retreat. I approach Mézières tomorrow, whence I shall continue my retreat, guided by events, towards the west.[2]

MacMahon showed the telegram to General Faure, his chief of staff; having read it, Faure sagely advised him not to send it yet, saying that if he did he would get an answer which would perhaps prevent him from adopting his preferred course; it would be better to send it next day, when the army would be well on its way.

'Send it', said MacMahon; and at 1:30 next morning Faure's intuition was proved right. Palikao's response, which had been dispatched at 11.00 p.m. was addressed to the Emperor. It was emphatic:

---

1 *Guerre: Armée de Châlons*, I Docs, annexes, p. 251.
2 Hooper, George, *The Campaign of Sedan* (London, 1908), p. 252.

If you abandon Bazaine, revolution will break out in Paris, and you will yourself be attacked by the entire enemy forces. On the other hand, Paris will defend herself; the fortifications are complete. It appears to me urgent that you are able to move quickly towards Bazaine … You have at least thirty six hours over [the Crown Prince of Prussia], perhaps forty eight; you have before you only a weak part of the forces blockading Metz and which, seeing you retire from Châlons on Reims, was moved towards the Argonne. Your movement on Reims has deceived the Crown Prince. Here everyone has felt the necessity of relieving Bazaine and the anxiety with which your movements are followed is extreme.[3]

When he read this, MacMahon went to Ducrot, whose opinion he trusted, to ask him what he thought about continuing the march to Montmédy. Ducrot was doubtful but thought that by pushing forward the cavalry on the right it might be possible to halt the advance of the enemy, enabling the army to reach Bazaine. Just as MacMahon and Ducrot were parting, another and even more direct dispatch arrived from Palikao: 'In the name of the Council of Ministers, and the Privy Council, I request you to bring help to Bazaine, profiting by the thirty six hours advantage which you have over the Prussian Crown Prince. I am directing Vinoy's corps to Reims.'

In the face of this MacMahon considered that he had no alterna-

General Ducrot. (Rousset/*Histoire*)

tive, and he cancelled the instruction to move on Mézières, substituting an order for the whole army to march towards the Meuse. Later, MacMahon had an interview with Napoleon, who was horrified at the decision to continue the eastward move and appealed to the Marshal not to comply with Palikao's request. The minister's dispatches were not orders, he said, and MacMahon was free to act as he thought fit; he should think very carefully before he gave up his decision to retreat in order to cover Paris. The advice was clearly militarily sound, and MacMahon must have been able to see that, but he did not believe that he could refuse to carry out the operation demanded of him, notwithstanding the huge risks involved.

3   *Guerre: Armée de Châlons*, I Docs, annexes, pp. 278-279.

Napoleon later sent General Pajol of his staff to say that he regretted MacMahon's decision; to him, the Marshal replied that after much careful consideration it was impossible for him to countermand the orders he had given. For the Army of Châlons, the die was cast.

At Metz, meanwhile, there had been little aggressive activity on the part of either side. On the day after the abortive sortie, Moltke, in anticipation of MacMahon's possible advance, had ordered Frederick Charles to release the II and III Corps from the investment, and post them at Damvillers, from where they would be well placed to join any action against the Army of Châlons if this was necessary. As a further precaution Moltke had suggested that if necessary the investment on the right bank could be lifted temporarily; the abortive attack of August 26, however, suggested that the opposite policy would be wise, and Frederick Charles transferred the 28th Brigade to the right bank to strengthen the defences there. Further resources for the investment were becoming available; a newlyformed corps under the Grand Duke of Mecklenburg-Schwerin was shortly to arrive and was directed towards Les Etangs. Fifty heavy 12-pounders, with five companies of fortress artillery also arrived. One aspect of the proceedings of August 26 had led to a good deal of concern; this was the occupation by the French of the village of Noisseville as they deployed in readiness for the sortie. A hospital had been established there, and the arrival of the French infantry caused great dismay both to the doctors and their patients. As soon as the French retired, the village was reoccupied and the hospital transferred to the Château Gras. Thereafter Noisseville was to be included in the defence line of the 1st Division, and it was garrisoned by a battalion of infantry.

In anticipation of another sortie, a number of steps were taken by the French. On August 28 it was ordered that at all times the troops should be provided with three days' rations. Coffinières was ordered to strengthen the two temporary pontoon bridges over the Moselle that had been constructed before the intended sortie of August 26, and also to build a third bridge in order to speed the crossing from the left bank. Steps were also taken to improve the approaches to the bridges and the ascent to the height of St Julien.[4]

There had been little doubt in anyone's mind that a fresh sortie would take place sooner rather than later, and Bazaine's staff had been working on the plans for this. On August 29 a message reached Metz which at once raised the prospect of another attempt at a breakout. Forwarded by Colonel Turnier, the commandant of Thionville, it read: 'General Ducrot, commanding the 1st Corps should be by tomorrow, the 27th, at Stenay, on the left of the army. General Douay on the right of the Meuse. Hold yourself ready to march at the sound of the first cannon shot.'[5]

Bazaine appears to have been at first in some doubt as to the authenticity of this message; but next morning one of his own agents, who had made his way through the

---

4   *Official History*, Vol. II, p. 490.
5   Ruby & Regnault, p. 192.

German lines from Verdun brought a message from Napoleon. It was a copy of the message dispatched by MacMahon on August 22 in reply to that from Bazaine dated August 19. Although undated, it had evidently been sent before that forwarded by Turnier, and it certainly served to confirm the sense of that message: 'Received your dispatch of August 19. Am at Reims. I am marching in the direction of Montmédy. I will after tomorrow be on the Aisne, where I will act according to circumstances in order to come to your aid. Send me your news.'[6] If MacMahon was going to have been on the Aisne on August 23, and according to Turnier's message would have reached Stenay by August 27, it was plain that the army had been able to make remarkably good progress towards the relief of Metz. In the light of this information, Bazaine at once gave orders that the sortie should be launched on the following day.

In the drafting of the orders, some lessons had been learned from the débacle of the abortive attack on August 26. Bazaine's staff were conscious of the need to ensure that the process of bringing over to the right bank the units of the army that were to lead the assault should be completed as quickly and smoothly as possible. Officers from the army's general staff would be assigned to each of the bridges to supervise the crossings, while staff officers from each corps and division would be on hand to ensure that their units got over the river quickly and in good order. Lieutenant-Colonel Charles Fay, an officer on Bazaine's staff, noted sadly that if such an efficient use had been made of the staff on August 15 and again on August 17, much of the disorder and exhaustion of the troops on those occasions would have been avoided.[7]

In spite of these precautions, however, the deployment of the army into its assigned positions was much delayed. Much later, at his trial, Bazaine was to suggest that the delay in getting over the river was partly intentional, in that his object was to draw as large a part of the enemy as possible over to the right bank, in order in this way to reduce the pressure on MacMahon's approaching army. This does sound very much like an afterthought, and an improbable one at that, but it seems certainly to be the case that when, during the morning of August 31, d'Andlau pointed out the long dust columns that could be seen to the north and the south of the city, Bazaine's response was to say:'That's good, those are the troops coming over from the left bank.'[8] Later, on the day of the capitulation of Metz, Bazaine had a conversation with Frederick Charles. The Prince asked him why he did not bring his army over to the right bank of the Moselle during the night. Bazaine replied that the large number of reservists in the Army of the Rhine made night marches extremely difficult.[9]

The plan for the concentration of the army was substantially the same as that for August 26. Fay found this astonishing, since everyone knew of what had been intended; but secrecy would in any case have been to no avail, since the German

6   *Guerre: Armée de Châlons,* I Docs, annexes, p. 136.
7   Fay, Colonel Charles, *Journal d'un officier de l'Armée du Rhin* (Brussels, 1871), p. 135.
8   D'Andlau, p. 151.
9   Ruby & Regnault, p. 201.

outposts and observation towers could not fail to see the preparations for a sortie, wherever it was planned to take place. From the left bank, Ladmirault's 4th Corps would be the first to cross, followed by Canrobert with the 6th Corps; then would come the Guard, and the artillery reserve, and finally the newly constituted cavalry corps. These were to join the 2nd and 3rd Corps already on the right bank. It was with the latter that Leboeuf was to take the lead in the assault. He was to leave one division in Metz which would take up a defensive position in front of Fort Queuleu facing Grigy; the other three divisions would advance towards Noisseville, with their right wing resting on the road and their left on the heights between Mey and Nouilly, a front of just under two kilometres.

The 4th Corps, on Leboeuf's left, was to advance from a position in front of the Château de Grimont which was at right angles to the road to St Barbe; its left would stretch to a point about 1,200 metres from Villers de l'Orme. The 6th Corps was to come up on the left, with its right wing in touch with the 4th Corps, while its left was bent back as far as the height opposite Thury. The Guard and the artillery reserve would be concentrated between the Bois de Grimont and Fort St Julien; the trains would remain on Chambiére Island. The cavalry divisions of the 2nd and 3rd Corps were assigned to skirmish on the right flank of the 3rd Corps; they were to be pushed forward in advance of the front. Bazaine's intention was to conduct the battle from Fort St Julien.[10]

The orders for the sortie were worked out by Colonel Lewal; once again Jarras played little part in drafting them. Perhaps understandably, he was critical of those officers closest to Bazaine, upon whom the Marshal placed the greatest reliance, and who had effectively supplanted him in his position as chief of staff. Jarras was also censorious in his view of how Bazaine discharged his duties as commander-in-chief. In his opinion the Marshal was far too pliable in the hands of those officers. He observed that, 'partly by nature and partly by design, Marshal Bazaine was unable to bring himself to exercise the command with a firm and vigorous hand.' Too often, Jarras thought, his orders lacked precision; indeed, in many cases he wondered whether they were deliberately equivocal.[11]

Jarras was one of those who questioned whether even a successful breakout towards Thionville would have enabled the army to take the necessary further steps towards Montmédy, Sedan and Mézières which would have permitted it to reach the interior of France and take part in the national defence. His own conviction was emphatically in favour of striking south, and taking the direction of Château Salins, Lunéville and the Vosges. This, he considered, would give the best chance of saving all or at least part of the army.[12]

---

10   *Official History*, Vol. II p. 491; Fay, pp. 136-137.
11   Jarras, p. 190.
12   Jarras, p. 188.

Although, if necessary, and as proved to be the case, Frederick Charles could bring substantial forces over from the left bank of the Moselle to stiffen the defences, the planned assault would fall on Manteuffel, who with the I Corps and the 3rd Reserve Division was holding the investment line in an arc from the Moselle on his right to beyond Mercy le Haut on his left. This was, in other words, about one third of the circle of investment around Metz. The ground selected for the assault was largely that over which the battle of August 14 had been fought, and principally involved most of the same troops.

The route out of Metz in a north-easterly direction, which runs towards Thionville, Saarlouis and Saarbrücken, crosses a plateau which is broken by a series of valleys and of which the high point is at St Barbe. Barring the most northerly of these, the road to Thionville, was the 3rd Reserve Division under Lieutenant-General von Kummer, in position behind the villages of Malroy and Charly. His left rested on the almost impenetrable Bois de Failly, while his right was directly on the Moselle. In front of the position, artillery was posted at Rupigny, from where it could take in flank an advance towards St Barbe from Villers de l'Orme.

Manteuffel's 1st Division (Lieutenant-General von Bentheim) directly covered the approach to St Barbe in a position of considerable strength on the higher ground between Poix and Servigny. The 1st Brigade (Major General von Gayl) was in the front line of the defence between Failly and Noisseville, with the divisional artillery to the east of Poix, and the 2nd Brigade (Major General von Falkenstein) was with the corps artillery in reserve between Vremy and St Barbe. On the flanks of this position, however, the conditions were much less favourable to the defence, because both the view and the ranges were limited by the extensive vineyards on both slopes of the ridge. Neither of the villages of Failly, on the right, and Noisseville on the left, was easy to defend. At Failly, the houses straggled down to the foot of the northern slope. At Noisseville, now garrisoned by one battalion since the abortive operation of August 26, the château at the northwest angle of the village projected like a bastion from the surrounding border. About 300 yards in front of the low walls of this, a shelter trench had been dug, but the possibility of successfully defending the position depended on holding the large brewery buildings on the left.[13]

South of Bentheim's division, Manteuffel's line was held by the 2nd Division of Lieutenant-General von Pritzelwitz. His troops were spread out in a long line, occupying advanced positions at Ars-Laquenexy and the western edge of the copses between Colombey and Mercy le Haut. Pritzelwitz's line was, therefore, not strong; but the indications were that the French assault would be in a north-easterly direction. It would, of course, have been a different matter if the views of such as Bourbaki and Jarras had prevailed, and the sortie from Metz had been directed southwards.

Bazaine's intention was that the 4th Corps and the 6th Corps should begin their march from the left bank of the Moselle at 6.00 a.m. Leboeuf's 3rd Corps was to commence the assault by opening fire at 8.00. Although it did so, driving back the German outposts in front of Colombey, nothing further happened. The German Official History noted that activity on the part of the French had been observed for some time:

> Considerable uproar and the incessant clanging of military bands in the positions of the invested army had attracted the attention of the Prussian watch posts as early as the evening of August 30. During the early hours of August 31 these conspicuous proceedings were repeated, and in the grey of the morning considerable movement was apparent in the enemy's camps, which were still partly enshrouded in mist. As the light of day waxed it was seen that several bivouacs west of the Moselle had been abandoned, that large bodies of troops were assembled at Fort St Julien, and that others were following thither from the left bank.[14]

Manteuffel and his men, therefore, knew exactly what to expect. The 1st Division stood to arms at 7.00 and the rest of his troops followed suit shortly after. The French preparations for an assault had come as no surprise at all, but the failure of it then to materialise most certainly did. To their amazement, the Germans could see that French troops had piled their arms and were settling down to cook a midday meal. The principal reason for this delay was the slow progress of the deployment of the units coming over from the left bank.

Naturally, Bazaine was extremely unhappy about the delay in launching the assault; he had expected that by noon all the troops on the left bank would have crossed and be ready to attack. He did not propose to commit his troops piecemeal. While waiting for all to be in place, at about noon he convened a meeting of the corps commanders in front of Fort St Julien. To them he read the two messages which he had received which appeared to indicate the progress which the Army of Châlons was making to the relief of Metz. He went on to give instructions for the coming battle; he had previously been reluctant to go into detail because of the climate of insecurity and indiscretion which prevailed within the city. The attack would commence with the firing of a signal gun from Fort St Julien, when the remaining troops had come up.

During his meeting with his corps commanders Bazaine emphasised the crucial importance of the planned attack:

> I drew the attention of these gentlemen to the gravity of the situation, the necessity that the attack should succeed. I indicated that the objective would be to take, with a maximum force, the position of St Barbe, the intention then being, if successful, to reach Thionville via Bettlainville and Kedange with the 6th, 4th and 3rd Corps, with the Guard and the 2nd Corps following on the Malroy road.[15]

---

14   *Official History*, Vol. II, p. 494.
15   Bazaine, *Episodes*, p. 169.

Bazaine ordered Leboeuf to advance on the left of the St Barbe position, and then to take the heights of Bois de Cheuby. The 4th Corps was to advance through Villers de l'Orme on Failly and Vremy against the right of the St Barbe position, aiming for Sancy les Vigy. The 6th Corps would advance beyond Chieulles towards Charly and Malroy, and then move upon Antilly. Behind the 3rd Corps, and protecting its right flank, would come the 2nd Corps, which Bazaine placed for the moment under Leboeuf's orders.

As the afternoon wore on, while the remaining troops were getting into position, Bazaine ordered the construction of emplacements near the St Barbe road, into which were to be installed fifteen heavy guns taken from Fort St Julien. It was his intention that this powerful artillery reinforcement should be in position to support the infantry as soon as the attack was launched, but the work proceeded only slowly and it was not completed until approaching 4.00.

The delay in launching the assault had produced one beneficial side-effect, since it convinced the Germans that after all there would be no attack that day. The lull in the action, while the build-up of French troops from the left bank of the Moselle was continuing, suggested that a serious attempt at a breakout was intended but only for the following day. Accordingly Frederick Charles decided that in order to rest his men, he would withdraw the reinforcements which he had ordered up to Manteuffel's support. He gave instructions that the II Corps and the 1st Cavalry Division should return to the positions which they had previously occupied; those parts of the X Corps which had crossed the river were to return to the left bank; and the III Corps at St Privat and the IX Corps at Roncourt were told to remain where they were for the night, as was the 25th Division at Antilly, behind Charly.[16]

At 4.00 Bazaine gave the order for the signal gun to be fired, and the batteries on the St Barbe road opened a vigorous bombardment of the positions held by Bentheim's 1st Division. Soon, the artillery of the 4th Corps and the guns of Fort St Julien joined in. Leboeuf now sent forward his infantry, with Metman's division to the north of Nouilly, and Montaudon's division and that of Bastoul (from 2nd Corps) to the south of the village. Aymard's division followed in the rear of these. The advance was supported by the 3rd Corps artillery, located on either side of the Vallières brook. Meanwhile Ladmirault's 4th Corps deployed in front of the German positions between Poix and Servigny.

It was immediately clear to Manteuffel at St Barbe that this advance was indeed a determined attempt at a breakout. The immediate question which he and his staff must decide was where and how to meet it. The more cautious view was that the defence line should be established on the rear part of the St Barbe plateau. Alternatively, the more advanced position occupied by the 1st Brigade could be held. This was risky; although it might more effectively hold up the French advance on the broad ridge, it was more vulnerable to being taken in flank. Nevertheless, this was the option urged by Major

---

16   *Official History*, Vol. II, p. 498.

General von Bergmann, commanding Manteuffel's artillery, and by Colonel von der Burg, the chief of staff, and this view prevailed.

The defence line accordingly ran from in and near Failly, through Poix, in front of Sevigny, and extended to Noisseville and the brewery. Seeing the strength of the French advance, Manteuffel ordered Kummer's 3rd Reserve Division to move to St Barbe to support the 1st Division. He directed the 25th Division, which had been placed under his orders, to move forward from Antilly to take Kummer's place at Malroy and Charly. Manteuffel warned Frederick Charles that it was likely that he would need to move the 25th Division to St Barbe, in which case further reinforcements must be brought over from the left bank of the Moselle.

It was, though, the artillery on which Manteuffel was principally to rely to stop the French advance, and within a short time he had a gun line of ten batteries, or 60 guns, posted some 800-1000 yards in front of the infantry positions:

> The adversary's batteries appeared unable to cope with the powerful effect of these 60 guns. They were at all points rapidly reduced to silence, and even the forward movement of the enemy came to a standstill. It was only in the sinuosities of the Valliéres brook that the skirmishers of the divisions of Montaudon and Metman gradually approached the neighbourhood of Noisseville and of the great Prussian line of guns, which suffered great annoyance, especially on the left flank, from the fire of the chassepôts in Nouilly bottom.[17]

The fighting began to extend southwards; Memerty's 3rd Brigade had come up to cover Bentheim's left flank, and by doing so threatened the right flank of Leboeuf's advance. Montaudon detached a brigade in the direction of Montoy to cover this, and this was followed soon after by Bastoul's division. Clinchant's brigade, from Montaudon's division, was heavily engaged in front of Noisseville and the brewery, while Metman's division remained held up at Nouilly.

At about 4.45 the French put in a major assault on Noisseville and the brewery. After a bitter struggle, the extensive buildings of the brewery were captured, and what was left of its garrison retreated into the village. This now came under heavy fire, and although reinforcements were expected, the commander of the battalion holding Noisseville felt obliged to pull his troops out of the blazing buildings.

Although the dominant German artillery had been successfully holding up Ladmirault's advance on Servigny, the achievements of Leboeuf's 3rd Corps at Noisseville materially changed the situation. Now advancing on Servigny from the south, the French infantry compelled Manteuffel to pull back his gun line, enabling Ladmirault's men to surge forward into the outskirts of the village. The French were fighting with great determination, and their considerable numerical advantage was

---

17 *Official History*, Vol. II, p. 501.

An impression of a skirmish near Metz, by de Neuville. (Rousset/*Histoire*)

beginning to tell. Although of course Manteuffel could expect substantial reinforcement, his outnumbered troops were steadily forced back.

Meantime the French had also been enjoying success on their right at Montoy. Occupied at first with little difficulty by the French infantry, a vigorous German counter attack succeeded in retaking the village. In response, a renewed attack by the 1st Brigade of Montaudon's division, and by Bastoul's division, succeeded in driving out the Prussian troops with heavy loss. After this, the French pushed on, intending to advance on Retonfay, but were held up in front of Flanville, where a stalemate ensued.

Still further south the French had advanced on Colombey, which they occupied in great strength. Here they arranged the buildings of the château for defence to such effect that an attempt by the Prussian 45th Regiment to recapture them broke down with heavy loss. Following the success the French took Coincy, and Lapasset's brigade pushed on towards Château Aubigny. After a brief struggle, the Germans also had to abandon this key position, and their line was forced all the way back to Marsilly, where they managed to beat off an attack before the fighting died down in this sector at about 7.00.

It still continued, however, further north, where following the retreat of the German artillery Ladmirault was pressing hard on the position between Poix and Servigny. He had deployed Cissey's division on his right and Grenier's division on his left, with Lorencez's division in the rear of these. To its right, the advance of the 4th Corps was supported by Metman's division of the 3rd Corps. Explaining the initial delay in the progress of Ladmirault's advance, the official French report noted:

> Noisseville held out longer than was expected; it was captured at 6:30 o'clock, and not until this was effected could our columns advance against the Servigny position. The 4th Corps, the movement of which was to conform with that of the 3rd, had up to that time been obliged to remain under heavy artillery fire, awaiting the moment to attack.[18]

The German Official History, observing that there was nothing in Bazaine's orders requiring Ladmirault to postpone his attack until after Noisseville had been taken, concluded that it was indeed the German artillery that was responsible for holding up the advance.

In any case, the French were making good progress. On the south side of Servigny Potier's brigade of Metman's division led the way, driving back the German infantry. A brief counter attack held up Potier's advance for a while, but the French were still poised on the southern outskirts of the village when Cissey's division launched an assault on its western side, capturing the cemetery and several of the houses.

To Ladmirault's left, Canrobert's 6th Corps had not been enjoying much success. It was not until 6.00 that Tixier's 1st Division and La Font de Villers's 3rd Division deployed, to the south-west of the villages of Vany and Chieulles. Behind them came Levasseur-Sorval's 4th division, on the Kedange road. Had Canrobert's advance in this direction been pursued, it would have fallen on the 25th Division, which had occupied the position previously held by the 3rd Reserve Division when this, in accordance with Manteuffel's orders, had moved off to St Barbe to reinforce the 1st Division there.

18   Quoted in *Official History*, Vol. II, p. 505n.

However, before Canrobert's advance got under way, Bazaine ordered him to direct his corps on Failly, while holding back his other two divisions pending the outcome of this attack. Failly was only weakly held, but when at about 7.30 Tixier's assault went in, it succeeded only to a limited extent, and the village itself remained in German hands. Meanwhile Kummer's 3rd Reserve Division had been held back by Bentheim on the high road south of Vremy. Hearing, incorrectly, that Failly had been taken, he sent forward two landwehr battalions with orders to recapture it. Finding it still in German hands, these now reinforced the garrison of the village, which successfully beat off further French attacks. Canrobert, leaving Tixier's division in front of Failly, gave up any further attempt to take the place.

At 9.00, when in other parts of the battlefield fighting had more or less died down, Leboeuf ordered Aymard's division forward in an attempt to seize Servigny. After a bitter hand-to-hand fight with the bayonet, Aymard's men succeeded in capturing the place, with the exception of a walled vineyard to the south of the village, in which a company of Prussian infantry, unobserved by the French, still held out.[19] The local German commanders were at first unaware that the French had taken Servigny; in the course of the savage battle for its possession, not a shot had been fired. As soon as Gayl, the commander of the 1st Brigade, realised its loss, he ordered a counter-attack. Reinforced by troops from the 2nd Brigade, Gayl's men stormed into the village, at which point the troops in the vineyard rose up and joined in the attack. Aymard was obliged to pull his troops back to the western edge of the ridge on which the village stood.

To the south Memerty launched an attack on Noisseville; it was now getting dark, and the enemy's position could only be made out from the rifle flashes. After a brief struggle, the Germans once more took possession of the village. Soon after this, though, Memerty received a report that the French had advanced as far as St Agnan, and he felt obliged to pull back his troops to Château Gras. The French again occupied Noisseville, and a further attempt to regain it failed.

Frederick Charles had throughout been watching the battle from the Horimont, a height near Feves, on the left bank of the Moselle. From here, he had a clear view of the way in which the action was developing, and it seemed evident to him that the French would renew their attack on the following day. With this in mind, he ordered Manstein, a large part of whose IX Corps was at Roncourt, to move off at once, and to march via Marange to cross the river at Hauconcourt, and thence proceed to St Barbe to support Manteuffel. The I Corps commander was likewise in no doubt that the French would try again in the morning, reporting this view to Frederick Charles.

As usual, once the fighting commenced, Bazaine had been up in the front line with his troops, leading the 73rd Regiment of Goldberg's brigade in the course of Cissey's attack on Servigny. Determined as ever to inspire his men, the Marshal exposed himself recklessly. It was what he did best, of course, but it meant that for the time

19   *Official History*, Vol. II, p. 510.

French wounded being brought into Metz. (*Illustrated London News*)

being he was not in control of the battle. However, at this point it probably made little difference; the objectives of each of the corps had been clearly defined, and the French infantry was heavily engaged all along the front. Jarras, too, was in the thick of it; at about 6.00, riding alongside Bazaine, he had his horse killed under him when a shell burst beside them.[20]

Bazaine remained on the battlefield until well after dark, only leaving it at about 10.00. When he did so, as he wrote much later, he was entirely convinced that the day had gone well. He rode back to Villers de l'Orme to get news of the rest of the army and gave orders that all his units should bivouack in the positions they occupied. After this, between 11.00 and midnight, he rode to the village of St Julien, where he snatched a few hours' sleep.

17

Sedan

Next morning, before dawn, Bazaine met with Jarras to issue his orders for the corps commanders for the day's operations. Never one to count his chickens before they were hatched, Bazaine was characteristically cautious. He was well aware of the resources which Frederick Charles could call upon to strengthen the forces immediately engaged with the Army of the Rhine:

> If the dispositions which the enemy may have been able to make opposite you permit, we should carry on the operation undertaken yesterday, which should first lead to the occupation of St Barbe, and secondly facilitate our march on Bettlainville. In the contrary case, we must have hold onto our positions, consolidate them, and this evening we shall then retire under St Julien and Queuleu.[1]

He gave instructions that this order was to be taken personally to each of the corps commanders by the four colonels on Jarras's staff – Colonels Lewal, d'Andlau, Lamy and Ducrot. Jarras dictated the order to them, and then each wrote the text of it before setting off to deliver it.

Having dictated his battle order to Jarras, Bazaine went on to read to him two messages which he had prepared to send to Napoleon. In what was intended as a report of the outcome of the sortie, he was similarly cautious. The first of these messages was to be sent if the operation had been successful. The second, alternative, message was to go if the sortie failed. He told Jarras that he proposed to send immediately from the battlefield whichever was appropriate, adding that it would be necessary for it to be taken by the hand of a reliable emissary, who should take advantage of the inevitable confusion that followed a battle to slip through the enemy lines. In the first of these messages, Bazaine conveyed the news that the army was marching on Thionville; the alternative, going into much greater detail, informed the Emperor that the sortie had failed and that the army was returning to Metz. He added that there was 'little

---

1   Quoted in Howard, p. 265; Jarras, pp. 182-183.

reserve of field artillery ammunition, meat or biscuit,' and that the army was operating in sanitary conditions which were far from ideal, as the fortress was full of wounded.[2] Jarras did not know if this dispatch was ever actually sent, but Bazaine said that it was.

Bazaine has been heavily criticised for what is seen as the pessimistic tone of his orders. However, the performance of the French armies in the field since the outbreak of war had hardly been good enough for him to feel confident that the operation to break out of Metz would succeed. Nor had the leaders of the Army of the Rhine covered themselves in glory. On the other hand, the ordinary French soldier had on occasion displayed real fortitude, entitling Bazaine to feel hopeful that the success achieved on the previous day would on September 1 be followed up with a breakthrough.

In his memoirs Jarras, although no great admirer of Bazaine, was usually fair-minded in reviewing the later allegations against the Marshal. He dealt firmly with the suggestion that Bazaine had no serious intention of breaking through the German lines, and had all along intended to take the army back into Metz. Jarras wrote that he had 'seen nothing nor heard a single word, before or after September 1 which would support such a suggestion.'[3]

While Bazaine was dictating his orders, and as dawn was breaking, the battlefield was shrouded in a thick mist, hampering the opposing commanders in assessing the actual situation on the ground. It was only just before dawn that Manteuffel learned that in the fighting after dark the French had hung on to Noisseville, and he had at once resolved to make an immediate attempt to retake the village. He had a meeting with Manstein, who had ridden over to St Barbe to report that at 4.00 a.m. the 18th Division of his IX Corps had reached Antilly, behind the Bois de Failly, after a night march. The two men concerted their plans for an all-out attack on Noisseville. Now that the whole of the IX Corps had become available to strengthen Manteuffel's position in front of St Barbe, the disparity in numbers was significantly reduced, and he could make his preparations for the assault with greater confidence.

Meanwhile the French were also preparing to launch a further attack. In spite of the mist, as early as 5.00 strong bodies of French infantry could be seen between Montoy and Flanville. Memerty, the German commander in the sector, brought up the artillery of the 3rd Brigade in order to check the threatened advance. Manteuffel, who had seen himself the French movement in this direction, reinforced Memerty's artillery so that by 6.45 24 guns were bombarding the French troop concentrations. Memerty also felt strong enough to push troops towards Noisseville in support of the attack which Manteuffel was developing there. At the same time, in the face of heavy fire from the village and the adjoining vineyards, the Prussian infantry broke into the eastern and northern edges of Noisseville. Once into the village, however, they were received with such a murderous fire that their advance stalled, each building having to be taken separately. Further troops worked their way round to the western side of the

2   Howard, p. 265; Jarras, p. 183.
3   Jarras, p. 184.

Advanced Prussian outpost outside Metz, Mercy le Haut. (*Illustrated London News*)

village but fell back when a vigorous counter-attack by Clinchant's brigade retook the whole of Noisseville. A fresh German attack broke down in the face of concentrated chassepôt fire. For the moment, after this, attempts to capture Noisseville ceased, and Montaudon's division remained in its positions there and at Montoy.

In front of the Poix-Servigny position Ladmirault was waiting for Leboeuf's corps to come up on his right. He had replaced Cissey's division in his front line with that of Lorencez. At this time, he confined himself to bringing forward and deploying a number of batteries and advancing a skirmishing line of tirailleurs in an effort to suppress the German artillery. Bentheim, who had been preparing to launch a fresh assault on Noisseville, for the moment also limited his activity on the Poix-Servigny line to artillery action. It was Manteuffel's intention to smash any prospective French advance by the use of his guns, and before 9.45 he had assembled a line of no less than 114 guns under Bergmann's direct supervision.

A fierce artillery duel had also developed at Flanville. Von Woyna's 4th Brigade had advanced from Coligny through Ogy and Puche at 6.00, aiming to launch an attack at Flanville. Before sending forward his infantry, Woyna deployed two batteries in front of the village. Supported by the left of Bergmann's gun line Woyna's artillery effectively silenced the French batteries in this sector. With Flanville now in flames, the French infantry began to pull out of the village, falling back to Montoy and Coincy, and Woyna's troops were able to take possession of the place.

German pressure was mounting; the 28th Brigade now deployed on either side of the Metz-Saarbrücken high road. As a result Bastoul's division was obliged to fall back. This provoked a major dispute between two of Bazaine's corps commanders. As soon as he learned of Bastoul's retreat Leboeuf scribbled a pencilled note to Bazaine, who received it at about 10.00. It read as follows:

> Bastoul's division having retreated an hour ago, contrary to my orders, my right flank is entirely uncovered. I am enveloped both by the fire of the enemy, and his attacking columns in front and flank. After having held my position to the last moment, I have been obliged to beat a retreat.[4]

Bazaine, dismayed by this withdrawal which uncovered Noisseville, demanded explanations. Bastoul had been operating under Leboeuf's orders, but since he was part of Frossard's 2nd Corps, the latter felt obliged to defend one of his divisional commanders, writing angrily to Bazaine next day:

> In accordance with your instructions, General Bastoul is going to your head-quarters, to give you the explanations for which you have asked as to what occurred yesterday. It is an enormous exaggeration. The movement of 500-600 metres in rear, that General Bastoul made in good order and slowly could not have the consequences you suppose. It was not any retreat, and only took place on seeing the division of Montaudon (the 1st Division of Leboeuf's Corps) retire precipitately. It retook its position immediately and continued to hold it. Marshal Leboeuf gave his own orders to it throughout the action. He got before a Prussian battery, had his chief of staff Manèque, killed, and then the retreat of his right wing ran all through the force.[5]

During the fighting in this sector it appears that Bazaine had given orders that Castagny's division, which had been posted near Fort Queuleu, should move up to support Bastoul, but this seems not to have happened, and this division took no part in the fighting on this day.

Further to the right of Bazaine's army, some progress had initially been made. Under the cover of a heavy bombardment, advancing French infantry had forced the Prussians back, retreating at about 10.00 from the position which they had held at Mercy le Haut. A counterattack briefly regained possession of this village, but further detachments of French troops advancing from La Grange aux Bois again recaptured it.

4   Franklyn, H.B., *The Great Battles of 1870 and the Blockade of Metz* (London, 1887), p. 235; Bazaine, *Episodes*, p. 172.
5   Franklyn, p. 235; Bazaine, *Episodes*, p. 173.

On the west side of the Moselle, at his headquarters at Malancourt, Frederick Charles had been keeping in mind the possibility that the Army of Châlons might be on its way towards Metz, although he had no up-to-date information as to its situation. From about 6.30 he had been able to hear the distant rumble of artillery in a westerly direction. At about 8.00 he went off with his staff to his vantage point on the Horimont, leaving behind at Malancourt a staff officer with instructions to monitor the sound of artillery from the west. As he rode towards the Horimont, he could hear that the battle on the right bank of the river had already flared up, and when he reached that point he was handed a telegram from Manteuffel, sent at about 7.30, reporting that he was heavily engaged with a superior force. This, Frederick Charles could now see for himself, and as a precaution he gave orders that the III Corps should move one of its divisions, together with the corps artillery, to Maizières, from where it could, if necessary, move to beef up the forces engaged on the right bank of the Moselle.

Those closest to the river faced Canrobert's 6th Corps, but it made no move to advance in a northerly direction. Instead, Canrobert's immediate objective was to push forward on the left of Ladmirault's 4th Corps and renew the attack on Failly. At about 8.30 Tixier's division advanced on the village, but its first attack was short lived. About an hour later Tixier launched a further assault in greater strength, but this was again repulsed. At the same time as Tixier's first attack, Canrobert had opened a heavy bombardment of the village of Rupigny, which he followed up by launching an infantry assault. By now, however, the Germans also had in line von Wrangel's 18th Division, and its 35th Brigade took up a position between Rupigny and Failly, supported by the divisional artillery which had deployed between Charly and the western edge of the Bois de Failly.

At 11.00 Tixier made a final assault on Failly, this time endeavouring to work round to the north of the village. By now, though, the 36th Brigade had also come up, into a position from which it completely commanded the plateau and took the advancing French infantry in flank. The French were driven back, and Wrangel, following them up, forced them still further back. With the defeat of this effort, Canrobert abandoned any further attempt to advance, thereafter contenting himself with holding the line immediately south of the Chieulles brook.

The heaviest fighting during the morning had of course been the struggle for Noisseville, in which the dominant German artillery was beginning to prove decisive:

> The combined fire of the German batteries south of Servigny, which had been unremittingly directed since about 9.00 against Noisseville, produced an effect far above what could have been expected. The village was in flames, the brewery buildings were riddled with shot, all the enemy's guns in action in that neighbourhood were reduced to silence, while his repeated attempts to bring up fresh troops to the threatened point had each time ended in failure.[6]

6   *Official History*, Vol. II, p. 527.

At 1030 Manteuffel judged that the time had come to make a fresh attempt on Noisseville, and the 6th Landwehr Brigade accordingly advanced on either side of the Vallières brook towards the village. For some time the advance was held up by a party of French troops holding a stone wall around a vineyard, but a charge by a landwehr battalion succeeded in driving its defenders back into Nouilly. As the advance towards Noisseville continued, it became apparent that the French were pulling out of the village. Leboeuf's order to withdraw was in response to the developing threat to his right flank, and the whole of both the 3rd and the 2nd Corps slowly retreated.

The breakout had failed. Bazaine ordered Ladmirault also to retreat to the shelter of Fort St Julien, and at noon Canrobert was ordered to give up his position along the Chieulles brook, and to retreat to the security of Metz. Practically all the French units engaged were able to fall back in good order. Manteuffel followed them with artillery fire but saw no reason to expose his infantry to the risk of further, and needless, loss.[7]

It had been a bitter struggle, and the casualty figures reflected this. Total French losses amounted to 3,547; among the killed was General Manèque, the chief of staff of the 3rd Corps, who was the man whom Bazaine would have preferred as his own chief of staff rather than Jarras. The German losses were also considerable, at a total of 2,978 killed, wounded and missing.

Colonel Fay recorded his impression of the feelings of the army as it made its way back into Metz:

> The discontent was very great among all ranks; it was said that an army like ours, attacking at a specific point on the circumference of the enemy's position, must succeed in breaking through, if it had the will to do so; but that it was essential, to succeed, to take the enemy by surprise and to advance without the baggage. This was clear to everyone; in addition, the reason for our lack of success was questioned: 'Was there a real intention to succeed?'[8]

Fay's account was of course published much later, when the furious campaign against Bazaine was at its height. It is also worth remembering that, in any army that had suffered a defeat, there would be a lot of grumbling to be heard, usually directed at the leaders seen as responsible for that defeat.

D'Andlau, seeking to ascribe to Bazaine the worst possible motives to explain his conduct of the breakout, suggested that the battle of Noisseville was merely 'a theatrical diversion to calm the army's impatience', and that Bazaine had launched a sortie with no serious intention that it should succeed, leaving MacMahon to fend for himself. According to d'Andlau, Bazaine considered the situation in the light of a number of alternative scenarios for the fate of the Army of Châlons. First, if MacMahon retreated, he would give battle in front of Paris, and Bazaine would continue to

7   *Official History*, Vol. II, p. 529.
8   Fay, p. 151.

pin down the forces of Frederick Charles around Metz. Secondly, if MacMahon fought, and was beaten, there would be peace, a revolution, and a change of regime. In that event both Bazaine's army, and his reputation, would remain intact. Finally, if MacMahon fought and won, Bazaine would have have a rather better chance of operating to good effect against Frederick Charles.[9]

Considering this, Michael Howard observed that it was 'not necessary to look so far for an explanation of Bazaine's hesitant and ambiguous leadership on August 31 and September 1.' He suggested that the Marshal would have realised that even if the breakout succeeded, the task of avoiding a defeat as the army headed for a

Beacons of the Prussians before Metz.
(*Illustrated London News*)

junction with MacMahon would be almost impossible. If on the other hand he failed to break out, and kept his army intact, he not only avoided disaster, but he might, with luck, have the opportunity to make an effective military contribution. 'This cautious but hopeful fatalism seems a more probable guide to Bazaine's actions than the cold-blooded little calculations attributed to him by his accusers.'[10]

Jarras, as we have seen, dismissed the suggestion that Bazaine was less than half-hearted in launching the sortie. However, following through d'Andlau's ill-natured speculations, in an apparent effort to demonstrate that the accusation had some merit, the prosecution brought evidence at Bazaine's trial to suggest that the German

9   D'Andlau, pp. 172-173.
10   Howard, p. 263.

defensive works were of little value, one witness claiming that they had been dug little more than 50 cm deep, while engineer Colonel Villenois dismissed the 'much vaunted German defences' as of no account.

Generals Ruby & Regnault effectively demolished this aspect of the prosecution's case by citing rather more significant evidence. Canrobert, for example, spoke of the successive German positions as having had their natural strength considerably augmented by entrenchments and the positioning of numerous batteries. Bourbaki, too, when subsequently on his way to England, was able to take note of the formidable abattis and fortifications strengthened with wire, even in the sectors that were least strongly defended. Intendant Lejeune was present among a group of officers with Ladmirault watching the retreat of the 4th Corps; he recorded that when one of them commented on the possibility of breaking through, the general replied simply: 'C'est impossible.'[11]

As the defeated and exhausted French troops trudged mournfully back into the environs of Metz on September 1, they were not to know that the possibility that the Army of Châlons would come to their rescue had, that day, been extinguished. While the struggle for Noisseville had been raging, at Sedan, some 50 kilometres to the north-west MacMahon's men were fighting a hopeless battle that would end in catastrophic defeat, condemning them, as well as the Emperor Napoleon, to captivity.

Just over a week before, on the day that MacMahon had taken the decision to march his army to the east, Moltke's forces had on August 23 begun the movement that would end at Sedan. At first, Moltke had found it difficult to believe that MacMahon really would head eastward, but, as always, he prepared for all eventualities. By the evening of August 25 there were clear indications that MacMahon was indeed on his way. It might, of course, be an elaborate attempt to deceive, but Moltke was now prepared to take the chance that it was true, and he wheeled the Army of the Meuse and the Third Army towards their prey.

By August 27, indeed, MacMahon knew beyond doubt that his quest was hopeless, and had decided to abandon it, only once again to reverse his decision under pressure. On August 29 Moltke, scarcely able to believe his luck, realised that he could now safely take the offensive. On that day there was a clash between Failly's 5th Corps and the left wing of the Saxon XII Corps. Following this the French fell back towards Beaumont, where on August 30 Failly suffered a severe defeat and was driven back to Mouzon.

Next day MacMahon retreated with his whole army to the small *declassé* fortress of Sedan. That evening, he had a conversation with Douay, the commander of the 7th Corps, to whom he announced his intention on September 1 'to manoeuvre in front of the enemy.' Douay was unimpressed, saying: 'M le Maréchal, tomorrow the enemy will not give you time.'[12]

11   Ruby & Regnault, p. 204.
12   Bibesco, Prince Georges, *Belfort, Reims, Sedan* (Paris, 1872), p. 124.

Reviewing his situation, MacMahon concluded that even if the Germans tried to cut off his retreat, they would be too tired, and the forces available would be of insufficient strength to prevent him. That being the case, he thought that next day could be a rest today for the whole army. Bazaine would later face recurring criticism of what was contended as his failure to move more promptly. On August 31 MacMahon deserved, but did not receive, the same excoriation.

Next day, as Douay had foreseen, the Germans closed in on the hapless Army of Châlons. On the left, the Third Army pushed the XI Corps over the Meuse to shut off any retreat to the west. On the right, the Army of the Meuse drove remorselessly forward. During the course of the morning MacMahon was wounded in the leg by a shell burst, and he passed over the command to Ducrot, whose immediate response to the situation was to prepare to force a way out to the west. Before the movement could get properly under way, however, General Emmanuel Wimpffen, who had arrived to take over the command of the 5th Corps from the discredited Failly, appeared at headquarters. He presented a secret order from Palikao designating him as MacMahon's successor, should the need arise. He immediately reversed Ducrot's decision and determined to launch an attack in an easterly direction. The consequence was inevitable. By noon the German circle around Sedan had been completed. The French fought on, with desperate courage, but their situation was utterly impossible. By the late afternoon Napoleon, an anguished spectator of his army's sufferings, had seen enough, and ordered that the white flag be hoisted. Moltke accordingly sent one of his key staff officers into Sedan to find out the position; Colonel Bronsart von Schellendorff was, to his amazement, shown into Napoleon's quarters, and returned with the Emperor's famous letter surrendering his sword to King William, a document memorably described by Michael Howard as 'not the least of the title deeds of the Second German Reich.'[13]

It was some days before the appalling news of Sedan, and of the revolution in Paris which had toppled the Second Empire, finally reached Metz. The first hint that all might not be well with the Army of Châlons came with rumours of the battle of Beaumont. On September 3 the sight of distant dust clouds on the northern horizon prompted further rumours of great events. Then, on September 6, Frederick Charles took the opportunity, in arranging the exchange of 500 Prussian prisoners with a similar number of French soldiers, to send in prisoners taken at Sedan rather than from those taken in the fighting around Metz. Their interrogation on their arrival in the city left no doubt that MacMahon's army had ceased to exist. News came a few days later of the events in Paris which told Bazaine and his men that the Second Empire was no more, and that they now represented the only remaining symbol of Imperial power in France.

Frederick Charles no doubt hoped that by providing unimpeachable news of MacMahon's defeat he would thereby erode the morale of the Army of the Rhine.

13   Howard, p. 218.

This, however, proved not to be the case; Jarras observed that in fact it had had little effect on the morale of the troops.[14] It did, however, leave their commander with an almost impossible problem to solve.

14   Jarras, p. 204.

18

Regnier

Bazaine was no fool. Nor was he just a simple soldier – he had for a lengthy period exercised a considerable political power in Mexico. And after having been in the upper echelon of the army following his return to Paris he was entirely familiar with the complexities of both domestic and international politics. With France now facing military defeat, its lawful government overthrown, and the army's ability to hold Metz patently time-limited, he faced a uniquely difficult situation. Cut off from the rest of France, the burden of decision rested solely on Bazaine. Naturally he could consult with his senior commanders, but whatever view they took, his would be the responsibility, and it is not altogether surprising that in the circumstances he frequently chose to keep his own counsel.

Reviewing his options, it was plain that for the moment he was politically paralysed. He certainly could not himself embark on any kind of negotiations with the Germans, at least for the moment. He must, for as long as he dared, wait and see, and in the meantime keep the army intact. Beyond this, he must consider his military situation.

Plainly, he must keep open the possibility of making a fresh bid to break out of Metz. That, though, was certainly going to be even more difficult than his defeated attempt at Noisseville. With every day that passed, the Germans were strengthening their lines around the city. Although not expecting a further immediate sortie, fresh attacks were anticipated sooner rather than later:

> The works of fortification along the entire front of investment proceeded almost without intermission. The 3rd Reserve Division increased their shelter trenches between Malroy and Rupigny and threw up in the real fighting position some more gun emplacements, part of which fronted towards the left bank of the Moselle. In the same manner the I Army Corps strengthened the line of defence of its right wing, now stretching from Failly as far as Noisseville, as well as the ground south of the Saarlouis high road, which was hitherto entirely unfortified and only watched by cavalry. In the latter position the villages of Montoy and Coincy, in addition to the brewery, were arranged for defence and connected

by means of shelter trenches. A large number of gun emplacements served to command the ground on the west side of the fortress, more especially the roads leading from Metz.[1]

Since it was entirely possible that a different sector would be chosen for the next sortie, work was steadily put in hand all round the rest of the circumference of the investment. Fifty heavy guns had arrived to reinforce the field artillery and these were gradually brought into position behind strong cover on commanding heights. A comprehensive network of telegraphs was completed, and additional bridges were thrown over the Seille and the Moselle.

To increase the pressure on the garrison there was, on September 9, a heavy bombardment of the French camps and the suburbs of the city:

> The enemy's outposts having been surprised during the morning at several points, and many prisoners taken, 19 German batteries opened a vigorous fire at 7.00 p.m., from the ground to the south, west, and north of the fortress; after an hour it was, however, discontinued, as the pouring rain made it impossible to observe the effect of the fire. The bombardment took place in the evening, because, in view of the superior fortress artillery, it was only under the cover of darkness that the field batteries could be brought near and be subsequently withdrawn without considerable losses.[2]

Bazaine could expect, therefore, that any fresh breakout attempt would be met with stiff resistance. As to the most suitable sector to choose, nothing had really changed, although the possibility of reaching out to a relief force had disappeared. The northern sector, towards Thionville, would still have some advantages. An advance due east-ward would take the army nowhere in particular. Due south, towards Nancy, an attack still offered the chance of striking a blow at the German lines of communication, but after that it was difficult to see a worthwhile course to follow. And on the west side, in the direction of Verdun, there still lay the largest part of the investing army.

None of these options, therefore, at the moment were appealing. A campaign of minor actions against the lines of investment, which Bazaine had intended, had not really got under way, due to the heavy rain throughout the first part of September. Although, therefore, time was not on his side, Bazaine for the moment held his hand.

He did, though, start making efforts to contact the Government of National Defence. His first attempt to do so was to send out Debains, in disguise, to penetrate the German lines. His mission was to assure the new government of the Marshal's fidelity to his military obligations, and to seek instructions. Unfortunately Debains

---

1   *Official History*, Vol. III, pp. 177-178.
2   *Official History*, Vol. III, p. 177.

French soldiers buying provisions in the covered market at Metz. (*The Graphic*)

was intercepted, and sent back into Metz, although not before he had had an opportunity to talk to some German officers and to read their newspapers.[3]

Bazaine made further attempts to get in touch with the government, drafting a pressing request for information and instructions:

3   Ruby & Regnault, p. 206.

It is urgent for the army to know what is happening in Paris and in France. We have no news from outside, and rumours have been brought in by prisoners exchanged with the enemy which are both strange and alarming. It is important for me to receive instructions and news. We are surrounded by considerable forces which we have vainly tried to break through after two fruitless battles, on August 31 and September 1.[4]

Bazaine entrusted this dispatch, uncoded, to two cuirassiers of the Guard, who were local to the area. After a lengthy and perilous journey they only reached Montmédy on October 13, by which time their mission had been overtaken by events. The second dispatch, dated September 23, was given to a local peasant to take through German lines, which did not reach its destination.[5] For their part, Leon Gambetta, the new Interior Minister, and General Le Flô, the War Minister, also sent several emissaries to try to get through to Metz, but none of them were able to do so.

The situation was certainly not yet sufficiently clear for Bazaine to make a public statement to the army or the city, but he did take his senior commanders into his confidence. He appears in the first instance to have given them in writing the news which he had received, and Ladmirault and Leboeuf both claimed that his note understated the morale of his troops. He followed this up with a meeting with his generals on September 12.

The civil authorities were, however, anxious that the population of Metz should be informed about the grim situation outside the city. On September 13 a proclamation, which bore the signatures of General Coffinières, as governor of the fortress, Paul Odent, the Imperial Prefect and Felix Maréchal, the Mayor of the city. Announcing the establishment of the new government in Paris, the proclamation called on everyone to remain at their post, and to work together for the defence of Metz: 'In this solemn moment, France, the Fatherland, this word which symbolises all our feelings, all our affection, is at Metz, in this city which has so many times resisted the attacks of the country's enemies.' The announcement concluded that the army would not leave them: 'It will resist with us the enemies which surround us, and this resistance will give the government the time to create the means of saving France,'[6]

General Palat observed that it was permissible to suppose that this proclamation did not accord with Bazaine's views. There is really no reason to suppose this; but what it did do was to force his hand in making a public statement to the army about the situation. This took the form of an Order of the Day issued on September 16, in which Bazaine formally confirmed the situation following the capitulation at Sedan, with the internment of the Emperor in Germany, the departure of the Empress and the

---

4   Bazaine, *Episodes*, p. 178.
5   Ruby & Regnault, p. 208.
6   Palat, General Barthélemy, *Une grande question d'histoire et de psychologie, Bazaine et nos désastres en 1870* (Paris, 1913), p. 95.

German troops besieging Metz, drawing
by Becker. (Lindner)

Prince Imperial, and the setting up of the Government of National Defence in Paris.
He also gave the names of those comprising the new government and:

> Our military obligations towards the country remain the same. Let us then
> continue to serve her with devotion and the same energy, defending her land
> against the foreigner, the social order against evil passions. I am convinced that
> your morale, of which you have already given such proof will rise to the height
> of the circumstances, and that you will add new claims upon the admiration of
> France.[7]

Commenting on the wording of this, Palat concluded that it revealed Bazaine's
embarrassment. He wanted to avoid a public recognition of the new government,
while not taking a position against it. This was, Palat considered, understandable on
the part of a high dignitary of the Empire, as indeed it was. He went on, though, to
find it sinister that Bazaine should tack on to his phrases about defending the national
territory, which should have been his only concern, a reference to defending the social

7   Bazaine, *Episodes*, p. 178.

order against evil passions. He also noted, sarcastically, that Bazaine's suggestion that the army would add fresh claims upon the admiration of France was made at a time when he was doing almost nothing.[8]

Not unreasonably seeking all the information that he could get, at a time when the situation was so confused, Bazaine addressed a letter to Frederick Charles in an effort to find out what was going on. He asked him candidly what was the significance and the importance of the events which had occurred. This letter was taken to the Prussian headquarters by General Boyer who had always been one of Bazaine's most trusted aides.

To this, Frederick Charles wrote a courteous and informative reply on September 16, confirming the capitulation of the army of Châlons, and the capture of the Emperor, who as a result was no longer able to exercise any authority. He described the proclamation of a republic, noting that it did not derive from any action on the part of the Corps Législatif, adding that it had not been recognised internationally. The Empress and the Prince Imperial had, Frederick Charles told Bazaine, gone to England. Meanwhile the German army had resumed its march on Paris, where it would arrive on the following day. Finally, he enclosed a cutting from the *La Patrie* newspaper, which contained details of the new government.[9]

This letter was taken into the fortress personally by an officer on Frederick Charles's staff, and probably reached Bazaine on September 17. Palat observed, no doubt correctly, that it could not fail to have an effect on Bazaine's state of mind. If it was clearly premature to consider it as the beginning of a negotiation, it was certainly possible, reading between the lines, to see it as opening the door. It seems that on the German side there were those that hopefully perceived Bazaine's letter as having the same effect, though there is no reason to suppose that this was his intention.

The reply from Frederick Charles was written on instructions from Moltke, and the care with which it was drafted reflected Bismarck's wish to keep all his options open when it came to negotiations to end the war. A significant indication that those options might include a deal involving Bazaine and his army was to be found in the proclamation of September 11 by the newly appointed German governor general of Reims, which ended with the following words:

> The German governments could enter into negotiations with the Emperor Napoleon, whose government is still recognised at present, or with the Regency established by him. It could equally negotiate with Marshal Bazaine, who holds his command from the Emperor. But it is impossible to see how the German governments could properly negotiate with an authority that represents no more than part of the left of the former Corps Législatif.[10]

8   Palat, pp. 96-97.
9   Bazaine, *Episodes*, pp. 176-177.
10   Palat, pp. 92-93.

General Palat claims that the text of this proclamation reached Metz at some time between September 15 and 21 and observes that its terms could only confirm the conclusions which Bazaine drew from the letter from Frederick Charles.

After he had received that letter, Bazaine convened a further meeting at his headquarters, to which he invited the corps commanders, the divisional generals and the officers commanding the artillery and engineers. His purpose was to acquaint them with the letter which he had received, and in his memoirs he recollected his comments:

> In the present circumstances, and ignorant of the operations, let alone their importance, of the armies in the interior, we must remain on the defensive, but each corps commander must launch strikes in his sector to disturb the enemy, obliging him to deploy as many troops around us as possible and, at the same time, try to augment our resources. In communicating to our troops the distressing news, you must emphasise to them that discipline, the honour of the army, loyalty towards the imprisoned sovereign, must remain intact, so that we may not break our military oath.

Given all that is known about what was going on in Metz at the time, there is no reason not to accept that Bazaine did make a statement of this kind, which militarily speaking was perfectly appropriate. He also recorded that he made an offer to give up his command, and revert to his former status, but this prompted no response from those present, which is hardly surprising.[11]

As a pillar of the Second Empire Bazaine may well have been reluctant formally to acknowledge the authority of the new government, but he did so indirectly, ordering the removal of the Imperial coat of arms from official documents.[12] His uncertainty as to the line to take appears in the fact that some days later he changed his mind about this. In all the circumstances, it is perhaps understandable that he was very conflicted about symbols of power, and the anomalous position of his military authority. He wrote to Coffinières to comment on the publication of articles inside Metz that were hostile to the fallen Emperor: 'I will never permit those suffering misfortune to be insulted, or to make ridiculous in the eyes of our soldiers those whom we recently swore to obey.'

If his account is to be accepted, and there is no reason why it should not be, Bazaine was by September 16 already edging towards the effective recognition of the new government. Looking back, he remarked in *Episodes:*

> I considered this government to be an executive power to organise the resistance of the country, but not a political power. The Regency was still legally the government, in accordance with the constitution. We must continue to work together

11   Bazaine, *Episodes*, pp. 177-178.
12   Fermer, Douglas, *France at Bay* (Barnsley, 2011), p. 45.

for the defence of the national
territory with the executive power
without breaking the oath which
we swore to the Emperor.[13]

The binding nature of the military oath
and the extent to which it determines a
soldier's conduct, has been examined many
times. It must, however, be accepted that
for Bazaine and most of his officers, if
not always for his men, the oath was an
absolute obligation from which they could
not regard themselves as released. It was,
therefore, something that remained with
the Marshal as a significant factor in his
decision making. And, as Ruby & Regnault
point out, the presence at the head of the
new government of General Louis Trochu
did nothing to make Bazaine, or indeed
many of the officers of French army, look
more favourably upon it. For many of
them, Trochu's name did not inspire trust
and confidence, and he was seen as a man
who had deserted the sovereign, whom
he had sworn to defend, at a moment of
extreme danger.[14]

It was while Bazaine brooded over
his impossible situation that there was
an unexpected and extremely improbable entry onto the stage of history. This
was to play its part in the way in which
Bazaine came to be perceived as a result of
the subsequent course of events in Metz.
Edmond Regnier was born in Paris in
1822. He had been engaged in various
employments, and claimed to have studied
medicine and the law, though without
intending to practise. In 1870 he was living
with his second wife, an Englishwoman,

General Trochu, President of the
Government of National Defence.
(Rousset/*Histoire*)

Eduard Regnier. (Private collection)

13   Bazaine, *Episodes*, p. 250.
14   Ruby & Regnault, p. 210.

and their three children. With the imminent approach of the German armies towards Paris, he decided to take his family to London. There, convinced that something must be done to bring the war to an end, he concluded that he was the man to do it. For many years it was supposed in France that his proceedings pointed to his being a Prussian agent; Michael Howard wrote memorably that he might more justifiably have been thought a buffoon:

> Yet there is something which commands respect about this man who had the energy, the pertinacity and the self-confidence to gate-crash into the field of high diplomacy, like some member of the audience wandering onto the stage during a grand opera and boldly taking a hand.[15]

Regnier was devoted to the Second Empire and was determined to do something to bring about its re-establishment. He believed that in negotiations to end the war Bismarck would prefer to deal with the Emperor rather than the parvenu government that had set itself up in Paris. Guedalla wrote of Regnier that 'his subsequent proceedings were inspired by that happy blend of loose thinking and good intentions which is readily comprehensible to Anglo-Saxons.'[16] Regnier's efforts were to be thwarted not so much by his lack of any authority, but ultimately by the lack of flexibility of the parties concerned. Even had he been, for instance, a member of the former Imperial government, it is doubtful that his efforts would have enjoyed any greater success. He certainly was not an agent employed by Bismarck, or by the Prussian government, although the suggestion that he was lingered on, notably in a biography of the Empress published in 2004.[17] It is more than a little surprising that the idea that Regnier was an agent should recur in a modern biography. Palat refers to a letter written by Count Paul Hatzfeldt to his wife on November 20. He was a key member of Bismarck's foreign office staff, and intimately involved in the Chancellor's diplomacy. He wrote that he had received a pamphlet published by Regnier in London on his negotiations with Bismarck:

> As he does me the honour of making me play a part in them, I send it to you and bid you to take great care of it. In my opinion he is a fool, as I have always said from the beginning; but a good sort of fellow, badly rewarded by his attached but very clumsy friends. What he says of the Empress proves again what I have always said that she is a clever woman but incapable of coming to a decision on her own account.[18]

15   Howard, p. 269.
16   Guedalla, p. 207
17   Seward, Desmond, *Eugénie: The Empress and her Empire* (Stroud, 2004), p. 260.
18   Hatzfeldt, Count Paul, *The Hatzfeldt Letters* (London, 1905), p. 184.

The existence of such a letter would appear to explode the theory that Regnier was an agent. If that were not enough, Ruby & Regnault effectively disposed of the notion by quoting the whole of the text of a supportive letter written by Bismarck to Regnier on October 20, 1874, after the latter's conviction by a French court in his absence, pointing out that the Chancellor could have had no reason to write such a letter to a former spy.[19]

Regnier's first move, reasonably enough, was to endeavour to involve the Empress in the negotiations which he proposed to commence. Hearing that she was now at Hastings, where she was temporarily staying at the Marine Hotel, he went on September 14 to put before her his suggestions. These involved, inter alia, the denunciation of the Government of National Defence, and return to French territory by means of the French fleet, presumed to be still loyal to the Emperor. He set out these ideas in considerable detail in a letter which he delivered to her before calling to seek an audience. When he arrived at the Marine Hotel, he was disappointed to learn from Mme Lebreton, the Empress's reader and faithful friend (and sister to General Bourbaki) that Eugénie would not receive him. He was told that she had read his letter carefully, but would not act upon it, as she had 'a horror of anything that would bring about a civil war.'[20]

Regnier was not put off by this, writing several further letters to Mme Lebreton intended for the eyes of the Empress. Then, undaunted by the continued lack of response, he resolved to try his luck with the Emperor in his captivity at Cassel. Accordingly, having struck up an acquaintance with Augustin Filon, the Prince Imperial's tutor, he prevailed on him to obtain from the young prince a note to his father written on the back of a picture of the seafront at Hastings, which was the best he could do by way of a letter of introduction to Napoleon. He then travelled to France in order to obtain from Bismarck a pass to enable him to visit the Emperor.

On the face of it, Regnier's credentials were distinctly unimpressive, but when he arrived at Ferrières Bismarck saw in him a possible opportunity. Although his negotiations with Jules Favre had already begun, the possibility of an alternative solution to the problem of ending the war appealed to the Chancellor, and he willingly gave Regnier the chance to expound his proposals. One significant possibility concerned the Imperial forces shut up in Metz and Strasbourg. In due course, no doubt, they would be obliged to capitulate; Regnier offered to go to Metz to persuade Bazaine to do so in the name of the Empire. Following this, under the protection of his army, the Emperor would return to France and recall the Senate, the Corps Législatif and the Council of State, and resume the government of France. On any view, this proposal by Regnier represented a pretty long shot, but from Bismarck's perspective it might be easier to do a deal with the Imperial power than with the Government of National Defence. If the Empire was restored, peace might be more securely made

19   Ruby & Regnault, p. 215.
20   Palat, p. 116.

French troops in Metz before the statue of Marshal Ney. (*The Graphic*)

with a regime that possessed the necessary legal authority. In any case, the existence of this option might be a useful stick with which to beat Jules Favre, who had already grandiloquently announced that France would yield not an inch of her territory nor a stone of her fortresses.

Bismarck therefore provided Regnier with the necessary formal permission to enter Metz, and instructions went to Frederick Charles that he be given every facility to do so. On September 23 Regnier arrived at Corny, where Frederick Charles had now based his headquarters, and was then conducted to the outposts of Cissey's division. From here he was taken to Bazaine's headquarters, where he was announced by Captain Garcin of the general staff as being a messenger from the Emperor. When he was ushered into Bazaine's office, he gave his name, and said that he came from the Empress with Bismarck's consent. He showed Bazaine the Prince Imperial's signature on the message to Napoleon and asked him to countersign it as a souvenir of their meeting, which he did. Regnier went on to explain that the message he brought was entirely verbal; it was to propose that either Canrobert or Bourbaki should go at once to England and put himself at the disposition of the Empress. Regnier gave enough information about his relationship with the Empress and her household to convince the Marshal that his mission was authentic. Coming as it did with Bismarck's authorisation, Bazaine concluded that he must take the approach seriously. He later set out his recollection of the discussion:

> He explained to me his regret that there had been no treaty of peace nor an end to the war after Sedan; that the continued presence of German troops on French territory was ruinous for the country; that it would be a great service for him to bring about an armistice to lead to peace; that in this respect the army at Metz remained the only one organised which could give guarantees to the Germans if it had freedom of action, but that, without doubt, they insisted, as a pledge, on the surrender of the city of Metz. I replied that, certainly, if we were able to get out of the impasse in which we were, with the honours of war, that was to say with arms and baggage, in a word entirely assembled, we would maintain order in the interior, and ensure that the terms of the convention were honoured, but that there could be no question of the fortress of Metz, whose governor, appointed by the Emperor, could only give it up to him.[21]

This was, Bazaine said, merely a straightforward conversation to which he attached only a secondary importance, since Regnier had nothing in writing from either the Empress or Bismarck. The day being well advanced by the end of the interview, Regnier went to spend the night at Moulins les Metz before going on the following morning to the headquarters of Frederick Charles, to whom he gave an account of his meeting with Bazaine. The Prince told him that the surrender of Metz was an absolute condition of any negotiation. In this, he was expressing the views of the military, and of the King, but they differed from those of Bismarck.

At noon Regnier returned to Metz to discuss the arrangements for Canrobert or Bourbaki, as officers trusted by the Empress, to leave Metz and travel to England to discuss the proposals. He first saw Canrobert, who as usual declined the responsibility, on the grounds, he said, of his health. Regnier then saw Bourbaki, who at Bazaine's insistence agreed to go. The Marshal urged him to set off as soon as possible, adding a request that Bourbaki should keep him informed of the state of things elsewhere in France. The only instructions which he gave were that Bourbaki should explain the moral and military situation of the army in Metz; to ask what the position was of the Regency government both politically and diplomatically; and if it no longer existed to ask that they be released from their oath. What, Bazaine asked rhetorically in his memoirs, could be more loyal than that?[22]

21 Bazaine, *Episodes*, p. 180.
22 Bazaine, *Episodes*, p. 182.

19

Bourbaki

Thus it was that on September 25, disguised in the marshal's civilian suit that was much too big for him, and wearing a Red Cross brassard, Bourbaki set off on his journey to the Empress. He left the fortress among a party of doctors from Luxembourg and travelled to England by way of Brussels. During the first part of the journey, the party was escorted by a young subaltern on Frederick Charles's staff, Lieutenant von Dieskau, who had the opportunity of a candid discussion with Bourbaki, which he duly reported. Dieskau expressed his sympathy with Bourbaki's misfortune; the general replied, with tears in his eyes, that he deplored the war, with the declaration of which the Emperor had nothing to do. In the course of their discussion, he remarked that the heavy losses of the French infantry had been due to the great range and precision of the German artillery. He went on: 'I don't know why they have sent me from Metz to the Empress. Canrobert would have been better suited to this mission. I am not a political man, I am just a soldier.' Dieskau asked him if Bazaine was entirely devoted to the Imperial cause, and if he had any difference of opinion with the Emperor. To this, Bourbaki replied that 'if any such differences existed, they have not been expressed, since in his heart Bazaine is devoted to the Emperor, and the best proof of that, I tell you here, is that he pressed me to undertake this mission, knowing my complete devotion to the Imperial dynasty, and I am ready to do all I can to preserve the army in Metz for the Imperial cause.' He ended his conversation with Dieskau by saying that he did not know if Frederick Charles would remember him, 'but I beg that you will remind him of me.'[1]

Naturally those who wished to tarnish every aspect of Bazaine's conduct examined Bourbaki's mission with minute attention for signs that might support their relentless attack on the Marshal's probity. One such was Alfred Duquet, who described Bourbaki's visit to the Empress as being that of 'a corrupt general following a Prussian agent.' Not only were both statements completely false; Duquet went on to contradict himself twice, claiming that Regnier was an agent of Napoleon and that Bourbaki

---

1   Ruby & Regnault, pp. 219-220.

was sent by Bazaine to England as a means of getting rid of the one general whose opposition he feared.[2]

Before agreeing to undertake the mission to England Bourbaki had insisted on a number of conditions, which were, essentially, that Bazaine should expressly order him to go and that, once his mission was concluded, he would be allowed to return to Metz and resume his command of the Imperial Guard. These conditions, and the nature of his conversation with Dieskau, and particularly his final remark, completely put paid to another false allegation which was the unfounded suggestion that Bourbaki's departure from Metz was without the knowledge of the Germans and that he doubted if he would be able to return to the fortress when he came back from England.[3]

Later, when speaking of his mission at Bazaine's trial, Bourbaki defended the Marshal, saying that it was a small thread that might have led to the saving of the army, and that he did not believe that Bazaine had wanted to send him away: 'I believe only that he seized the opportunity to save the army from the sorrow of being reduced by starvation to capitulate.'[4] One witness at the trial was Commandant Samuel; it is difficult to know what to make of his evidence of a conversation with Bazaine later on, before the capitulation, in the course of which the Marshal is supposed to have said that he believed that he had been deceived by an individual purporting to come from the Empress. Given that Regnier's intervention led nowhere, it is certainly possible that Bazaine might thus have spoken of him.

Meanwhile, as Bourbaki was making his way to England, Regnier returned to Ferrières, without again seeing Frederick Charles. He was received there by Bismarck, to whom he again showed the message from the Prince Imperial, now countersigned by Bazaine, in order to demonstrate the effectiveness of his interview with the Marshal. Bismarck could certainly see the value of taking further the kind of proposition that Regnier appeared to have discussed with Bazaine, but it was evident to him that the question of the surrender of Metz was a potential sticking point. He sent a telegram, via Frederick Charles, to be passed to Bazaine, seeking clarification of his position as to the surrender of Metz. Bazaine wrote a letter to Frederick Charles in reply to this, which the Prince summarised in a telegram to Bismarck, quoting Bazaine as saying that he could not reply affirmatively to the Chancellor's question, but that he had said to Regnier that he could not deal with the capitulation of the city of Metz. His letter to Frederick Charles, however, was somewhat less categorical: 'The only thing that I would be able to accept is a capitulation with the honours of war, but without including the fortress of Metz in the convention to be negotiated. These are, effectively, the only conditions that military honour permits me to accept and they are the only conditions that M. Regnier is able to put forward.'[5] He went on to suggest that

2   Duquet, p. 170; Ruby & Regnault, pp. 220-221.
3   Ruby & Regnault, pp. 219-220.
4   Ruby & Regnault, p. 221.
5   Ruby & Regnault, p. 224.

General Boyer, his principal aide-de-camp, should visit Frederick Charles to explain further. At his trial Bazaine declared that his use of the word 'capitulation' in the letter was a simple error; he meant to use the word 'convention'. In any event, the issue of the surrender of the city was not resolved and could not be until the outcome was known of Bourbaki's visit to the Empress.

If anything useful was to be obtained from Regnier's intervention, it was obvious to Bismarck that it was Bourbaki's mission to England. Although he spent some time with Regnier before the latter returned to England to make another attempt to interview the Empress, he saw nothing more to be gained from him. Regnier then did go back to England and travelled to Chislehurst, where the Empress had taken up residence, arriving there after Bourbaki. For the general, his meeting with the Empress had been a shattering experience. He was shocked by the astonishment, real or simulated, which the Empress displayed at his arrival; he said later that he was 'so flabbergasted, even stunned' that he was quite unable to respond articulately to the questions which the Empress put. She told him that she refused to play the game of negotiations which had been suggested to her. She was, however, evidently deeply moved by the fate of the army, and she wrote to the Austrian Emperor Franz Joseph to ask him to intervene as a mediator. She also wrote an emotional letter to King William appealing for an end to the war:

> The sentiments which I have expressed to your Majesty must inspire the heart of a King. I am ready to make any personal sacrifice in the interest of my country, but I ask your Majesty if I could possibly sign a treaty which would impose an irreparable sorrow on France.[6]

Her letter was undated; but William replied on October 15 courteously explaining that in the present situation and 'the uncertainty which we have found in respect of the political dispositions of the army of Metz as much as in the French nation' he could not act in the spirit of her letter.

The hapless Bourbaki, meanwhile, returned to France. His mission had been a total and humiliating failure. He had not even obtained for the army a release from the military oath to the Empire. He made his way back to Metz, where he sought to be allowed to re-enter the fortress. When he presented his pass, however, it was found to have been misdated, and hence no longer valid. The decision as to whether nonetheless to let him pass belonged to Frederick Charles, and he opted to take an absurdly legalistic view, and refused to permit Bourbaki to proceed. This was in large part due to the fury on the part of the Prussian military at the way in which Bismarck seemed to be acting so as to deprive the army of its victory. It was a view with which Moltke had a good deal of sympathy, writing to Major General von Stiehle, Frederick Charles's chief of staff, on September 27:

6   Ruby & Regnault, p. 359, Annexe I.

In my opinion, it is only after a capitulation, or better still a peace with a government we can trust, that Marshal Bazaine's army can get out of its present situation ... In any case, the operations of our army at Metz have cost us too much to lead to a result which, from a military point of view, would be absolutely negative.[7]

Bismarck, however, was furious, and in the King's name sent a direct instruction that Bourbaki should be allowed to pass. He wrote a vigorous protest to Stiehle about military interference in a purely political matter:

I appeal to your Excellency's clear judgment and to your own perception, so that you will understand how discouraging it must be for me when, through this kind of failure to execute Royal orders, the danger arises that in the whole constellation of political calculations one single cog, which is necessary in its place, will refuse to do its work. How can I have the courage to proceed with my work if I cannot count on Royal orders ... being faithfully executed?[8]

Held up in Luxembourg in this way, awaiting the necessary permission, Bourbaki soon became discouraged. Although the instructions to let him through arrived at the headquarters of the Second Army, they arrived too late. On October 9 he left the hotel in which he had been waiting and made his way to Tours to offer his services to the Government of National Defence, where he was warmly received when he arrived there on October 15.

At Tours he met with Lord Lyons, the British ambassador, to whom he gave a very pessimistic view of the military situation:

He did not think that an army capable of coping with the Prussians in the field in anything like equal numbers could be formed in less than five or six months, even with first rate military organisers at the head of affairs, instead of the present inexperienced civilians. According to him, the Army of Metz was in admirable condition and might perhaps break out, but even so, where was it to go? Its provisions and ammunition would be exhausted long before it could get to any place where they could be replenished. As the surrender of Paris was only a question of time, the most prudent thing to do would be to make peace whilst these two fortresses were holding out, and it would be to the interest of Prussia to do so, because if Metz fell, Bazaine's army would disappear, and there would be no government left in France with whom it would be possible to treat, and

---

7   . Moltke, *Correspondence Militaire*, II, p. 301.
8   Quoted in Gordon Craig, *The Politics of the Prussian Army* (Oxford, 1955), pp. 207-208.

the Prussians would, therefore, be forced to administer the country as well as occupy it.[9]

Lord Lyons reported that the Government of National Defence had offered Bourbaki the command of the Army of the Loire, but that he had declined it, because he would not be given unlimited military power.

At Chislehurst, Regnier did get the audience with the Empress which he sought, and he was allowed to expound his proposals. She was not, however, prepared to commit herself to the bold course of action which he advocated, and with the ending of this interview he passed from the stage of history, although he did make an unsuccessful attempt to visit Napoleon at Cassel. The whole episode left Bazaine with all his problems, complicated by the remorseless passage of time towards starvation. Its real significance perhaps lies in the effect on the Marshal's thinking. He had had no choice but to consider the proposals when they were made to him; and if the question of his army being responsible for the maintenance of good order in France had not previously been a priority, it was clearly a possible way of extracting his army from its impasse. Without the support of the Empress, however, this was going to be even more difficult, even if Bismarck was disposed to keep it as an option on the table.

What was entirely clear to Bazaine was that there was no clear political or military precedent for the situation of his army or, indeed, for that of France or Prussia. For a man who was perhaps not particularly imaginative, this added to the intellectual difficulty of the problem which he faced. As always, the impact on history of the personalities of those making it was considerable. So far as Bazaine was concerned, it was not in his nature to be rash; it was not in his nature to disregard an oath of allegiance to his Emperor; and it was not in his nature to go out of his way to seek advice or to delegate the authority entrusted to him.

Militarily speaking, Bazaine could calculate with reasonable accuracy how long the army could hold out. He had not imposed strict rationing on the troops at the start of the investment, in order not to diminish their fighting power. Nor, whether out of negligence or weakness, had he obliged Coffinières to impose rationing on the civilian population of Metz. This policy inevitably had to be changed. Originally the allocation per day had been 750 g of bread, but this was cut on September 15 to 500 g, to 300 g on October 8 and finally on October 10 to 250 g. The army's horses, that could not themselves be fed, provided a supply of horsemeat; coffee and sugar were also rationed. Bazaine was also perfectly well aware of the almost insurmountable risks in endeavouring to force a passage through the German lines. Even a successful breakthrough would mean more casualties than the available facilities could cope with. Frederick Charles summarised the position:

9   Newton, Lord, *Lord Lyons* (n.d.), pp. 233-234.

If Bazaine had successfully broken out, what would have ensued? He would be pursued as if he were a defeated enemy and would be obliged to stand and fight. Since he could not take with him any trains, by the end of the second or third day he would have run out of munitions and then would be wiped out or would capitulate.[10]

To the political aspects of his situation Bazaine naturally brought the attitude of a Marshal of the Empire. Although it is certainly true that he had commanded the admiration of members of the opposition, he personally had no time for the actual leaders of the new government. He had endeavoured to get in touch with them to seek instructions as well as information but had got no response. He was completely in the dark as to what was being done to organise resistance in the provinces or what the new government expected of him. Nor was he sure that the government would survive for long; with no legal basis for its existence it might very well be vulnerable to a fresh upheaval on the streets of Paris. Taking all these matters into account, he was coming round to the idea that some kind of convention negotiated on the sort of terms that Regnier had put forward might be the least bad option. As for the willingness of the army to exercise political control of the country, he may have deceived himself as to the extent of its loyalty to the dynasty. The Guard, and the cavalry, could certainly be relied on, but this might not necessarily have been the case with the rest of the army. This, in its turn, raised the question of whether his authority over the troops was suffi- cient to lead them into non-military fields of action. And in working out how the army might be released from Metz, to whatever end, he must also consider that this would release something approaching a quarter of a million German troops.

Bazaine, therefore, knew that at best he had only until the end of October in which to arrive at a solution. The Government of National Defence, or at least its military advisers, could make the same calculation, and could see that it was only a matter of time before Metz must capitulate. There was, therefore, a rapidly closing window of opportunity if the government wished Bazaine to launch an attack to break out at whatever cost; but if that was what the government wanted, it made no effective attempts to order it, or indeed to propose any alternative line of action.

Having no means of knowing the strength of the forces on which the govern- ment could count, it may well be that Bazaine underestimated them. It was, though, a consideration that he must take into account, since if there was to be a conven- tion on the lines which Regnier had put forward, it might very well be the case that Bazaine's men might have to fight the forces of the Government of National Defence to achieve a restoration of the Empire. Many years later Bazaine had a final opportu- nity to explain his position. When he did so, the publication of his memoirs in 1883 was to provoke a fresh wave of hostility towards him. One of his sympathisers, the Comte d'Herisson, had been endeavouring to put the record straight, and had written

10   Ruby & Regnault, p. 222.

to a large number of those who had played a key part in the events of 1870. He was dismayed by the fact that many of those who replied to the questions which he had posed had insisted that they could only do so in confidence. This followed the letters which he had previously written to Leboeuf, Canrobert and MacMahon, none of whom was prepared to give any substantive reply. Accordingly, d'Herisson wrote to Bazaine, who replied on October 14, 1887:

> I have always been persuaded that a Marshal of France, commanding an army, had more right than a revolutionary movement to oppose an insurrection against the authority conferred by universal suffrage, and to put an end to a war which was being continued by a party that wished to take power.[11]

Unlike Canrobert, Bazaine had not shirked the responsibility of taking the command of the army when the Emperor pressed him to do so; but when he did, he could not have foreseen the intricate paths into which his duty would lead him. His tragedy was that none of those paths led to a favourable solution of the problem by which he was confronted.

Although the focus had always been on the reaction of the Empress to the situation, the publication in 1930 of the recollections of General Castelnau, who had been in attendance on the Emperor at Cassel, revealed that Napoleon had had much to say about the events at Metz, and on September 20 discussed with Castelnau what if anything should be done in the light of the information which he had gleaned from the issue of the Reims newspaper which carried the details of the German Governor-General's proclamation. Castelnau recollected Napoleon's reaction to the plight of Bazaine's army:

> Now, this is the only serious force we have today in France; it would thus be in Prussia's interest as in ours, not to make it prisoner but to preserve it until, once peace is made, so that it is in hand as the means, perhaps the only means, of maintaining order if, as is doubtless the case, it is threatened.[12]

Napoleon went on to suggest that in order to achieve this, there could be an armistice, enabling Bazaine's army to be resupplied until a peace treaty was negotiated. As Ruby & Regnault point out, his thinking coincided remarkably with that of Regnier. Castelnau, however, was sceptical. The two men discussed how to reach Bismarck, and Napoleon decided that it should be by way of an anonymous letter which Castelnau would give to Monts, the governor of the castle of Wilhelmshöhe in which Napoleon was held, for onward transmission to Bismarck. It was sent on by Monts by telegraph to Bismarck on September 22, and was, in all probability, communicated to Regnier

11   d'Herisson, Comte, *La Legende de Metz* (Paris, 1888), p. 76.
12   Quoted in Ruby & Regnault, pp. 227-228.

Prussian and French troops fraternising during the siege, drawing by Röchling. (Lindner)

who was then at Ferrières. It would thus have been perfectly possible, say Ruby &
Regnault, for this in turn to have been communicated by Regnier to Bazaine, who
would thus, in his considerations, have been aware of this 'idea' of the Emperor.[13]

A few days later Napoleon heard from Count Clary, sent to him by the Empress, of
the curious mission of Edmund Regnier, and he tried to find out if it was undertaken
at Bismarck's request; he subsequently heard from the Chancellor that he understood
him to have come from the Empress. 'All this', he wrote to Eugénie, 'is very extraordinary.' In due course Castelnau received an unsigned letter from Bismarck's office (the
Chancellor was being careful not to be seen to be opening negotiations direct with
the captive Emperor) to the effect that the proposal to allow Metz to be resupplied
would be for the Germans to renounce their military advantage. It would be possible
only if Germany could receive in exchange guarantees of peace on which it could rely
– which would effectively mean a blank cheque signed by a government able to meet
German terms, whatever they were. Napoleon sadly remarked to Castelnau that there
was nothing to be done on their side.

Although Regnier had departed from the scene, there were other important contacts
intended to kick start the peace process, even though Bazaine was unaware of them.
Chief among these was the intervention of the Duc de Persigny, a former ambassador to London and a confidant of the Emperor, whose Bonapartist credentials were

13   Ruby & Regnault, p. 228.

unimpeachable. Towards the end of September Persigny had an important conversation with Count Albrecht von Bernstorff, the Prussian minister in London. Persigny, of course, had an optimistic belief that there was in France a popular sympathy for the Empire, and his proposals, much in line with what Regnier had put forward, were based on this. To avoid anarchy in the country, Bazaine and his army should be released to retire beyond the Loire, while a government that was legally based negotiated peace. Neither the Emperor nor the Empress could return to the throne, but the Prince Imperial would be acceptable; Persigny was even prepared to accept an Orleanist restoration.

The key question, however, was that which Bernstorff put to Persigny: was Bazaine still loyal to the Empire, or did he recognise the new government? As Bernstorff reported on September 29 to Bismarck, Persigny could not answer that.[14] However, a further meeting between the two men on October 10 suggested that there was still some mileage in the possibility, and Bismarck set out in a letter to Bernstorff his thoughts on the way matters might proceed. For there to be any progress, however, the Bonapartists would have to appreciate the realities of the situation and these, it seemed, they had so far failed to grasp. Bismarck's letter went by courier to Bernstorff on October 15; it was followed next day by an urgent telegram informing the ambassador of a development requiring an immediate response. After a long period of silence, there was important news from Bazaine.

14   Ruby & Regnault, Annexe IV, p. 362.

20

Ladonchamps

The limited sorties which Bazaine had ordered to be undertaken by each corps commander in his respective sector had continued to be seriously hampered by the weather. Heavy rain fell, especially during the first fortnight of September. The failure to carry out such operations irked the Marshal, who frequently complained of the lack of initiative being shown by the corps commanders. Jarras heard the closing stages of a conversation between Bazaine and Changarnier on the subject, in the course of which he made plain his discontent that his orders to mount such operations had not been carried out. Jarras, who was always dissatisfied with what he regarded as the ambiguous nature of Bazaine's orders, reckoned that the corps commanders would have done more if they had been given specific instructions. He sadly recorded that this approach by the Marshal was either deliberate or was simply part of his nature.[1]

On September 22, however, an operation was undertaken with the objective of collecting all the available supplies of garden produce in the farms to the north-east and east of the French lines. At noon, the guns of Fort St Julien opened fire on the Prussian outposts at Noisseville and Sevigny, and under cover of this bombardment detachments of Leboeuf's 3rd Corps moved forward and occupied the villages of Nouilly, Lavallier and Colombey, and collected all the produce found there, loading it into wagons brought with them. Bodies of skirmishers entered Villers de l'Orme, while other troops, supported by gunfire from Fort Queuleu, captured La Grange aux Bois and Mercy le Haut and pushed on towards Peltre. The Prussian outposts here fell back to their main defensive positions, while two batteries shelled the villages which had been occupied. The French troops in this sector finally returned to the fortress at about 4:30 p.m.

Next day a similar sortie was mounted, when at about 1.00 p.m. a division of the 3rd Corps advanced towards Vany and Chieulles, and another division occupied Nouilly and Villers de l'Orme, while skirmishers pushed forward towards the vineyard at Failly. These advances were supported by gunfire, to which the Germans responded

1   Jarras, pp. 189-191.

Houses held by the Prussian at Ars-la-Quenexy, near Metz. (*Illustrated London News*)

with the artillery of the I Corps and the 3rd Reserve Division. In the face of this, the French were unable to get beyond Vany and Chieulles. Other advances towards Rupigny and Malroy failed. The German artillery response was sufficiently heavy to make it impossible for the French to collect any produce on this occasion, and they were obliged to return to the fortress with empty wagons. As on the previous day, there had also been a demonstration towards Peltre, but this made little progress.[2]

Since this latest sortie had been unsuccessful, the French planned a more elaborate operation intended to collect the stores of produce still remaining at Peltre and Colombey and, to the north of the fortress, at La Maxe. The operations to the south east would be carried out under the direction of the 3rd Corps, while that to the north was under the control of the 6th Corps. On the evening of September 26 there began a continuous exchange of light signals between Metz and Thionville in anticipation of the northern sortie. It was, however, in the southern sector that the action first got under way. At about 9.00 a.m. both Fort St Julien and Fort Queuleu began to fire on the German outpost positions, following which Duplessis's brigade advanced on Mercy le Haut. After occupying the village, Duplessis brought up two batteries, with which he opened fire on Peltre, which the guns of Fort Queuleu continued to bombard. Lapasset's brigade now came forward, three battalions advancing on Peltre and two on Crepy. At risk of being cut off, the defenders of Peltre retreated southwards into the Bois de l'Hopital. However, one company of the 55th Regiment did not receive the order to retire, and was surrounded; only its commander and 30 men were

---

2 *Official History*, Vol. III, p. 182.

Ambulance wagons at Metz. (Rousset/*Histoire*)

able to get away, and the rest were taken prisoner and marched into the fortress. After occupying the village, Lapasset's men carried off all the provisions and forage which they found there, before withdrawing to Metz at 11:30 a.m. after a successful operation. Meanwhile Montaudon's division, which had advanced on Colombey, was also successful in occupying the village and carrying off the stores there, before retreating to the fortress; this, in spite of a heavy bombardment by the German artillery.

To the north of Metz, the action of the 6th Corps began much later. It was not until noon that the French field artillery posted between Woippy and the Moselle, and the fortress guns of Fort St Julien, opened fire on the German positions held by the X Corps on either side of the river. After this the divisions of Tixier and Levasseur-Sorval advanced through the Bois de Woippy against La Maxe and Franclorchamps. Within an hour they had taken St Agathe, Bellevue and La Maxe, and at once occupied themselves with filling the wagons which they had brought with them with the produce and stores in these places. By 2.00 the operation had been successfully completed and, shepherded by a rearguard of skirmishers, the French infantry withdrew with their booty.[3]

These operations, which had involved a considerable number of troops, had mostly achieved their objectives. This had been, however, at a not inconsiderable cost. According to Bazaine, total French casualties in killed, wounded and missing amounted to 603 men over the period September 22-27.[4] The Germans had also

3   *Official History*, Vol. III, p. 185.
4   Bazaine, *Episodes*, p. 186.

suffered quite seriously, losing a total of 462 men during the same period. These engagements, therefore, had been serious affairs.

Operations such as these could, if successful, bring in supplies that were desperately needed, but they could only scratch the surface of the problem of feeding the garrison and population of Metz. And, in any case, the Germans took steps to ensure that such stores could not be accessed in the future, by removing all that remained and burning the villages within reach of any further attempts. For those inside Metz, the problem of malnutrition was considerable. In addition, both military and civilian doctors were struggling to care for the large number of sick and wounded. On September 24, Bazaine's chief medical officer had provided him with a report which made grim reading. He estimated that there were over 14,000 sick and wounded in hospitals, including the many temporary facilities that had been established, with another 2,000 being cared for in private houses. Illness was rife, and was increasing, due to a general diet lacking in salt and vegetables. He noted the incidence of scurvy, smallpox and typhoid fever, and was profoundly concerned that the serious lack of medical supplies could not be made good.[5]

All too plainly, the clock was ticking more and more loudly. The civilian population, not unnaturally, wanted something, anything, to be done, and there was a growing lack of confidence in Bazaine's ability to do it, whatever that might be. On the same day that he received his medical officer's report, a civilian deputation had come to Bazaine to appeal for some effective action, submitting a petition which read: 'We believe that the army assembled beneath our walls is capable of great things, but we also think that it is time it did them.'[6] Meanwhile the rain which had poured down steadily during the first half of September, but which had then lifted, returned at the end of the month. Nor was there any news from outside the city to raise the spirits; on September 29 Frederick Charles sent in to Bazaine a courteous letter to tell him that Strasbourg had capitulated.

Against this background, and the complete uncertainty of the situation in the rest of France, Bazaine turned again to the idea of a serious attempt at a breakout from Metz. His plan was for an advance northwards towards Thionville, on either side of the Moselle. One reason for selecting this direction appears to have been the possibility of collecting some or all of the stockpile of rations that it was said had been accumulated at Thionville. On October 1 he began a series of movements to prepare for the assault by occupying Lessy and Chalet Billaudel, both of which were at once entrenched in order to protect the left flank of the army when it advanced. During the night of October 1/2, the landwehr picket occupying the Château Ladonchamps was driven out, retreating to St Remy. The French also occupied St Agathe. During the morning of October 2 the Germans launched an unsuccessful attempt to recover Ladonchamps. The French now sought to push their advance forward to St Remy, but

5   Bazaine, *Episodes*, pp. 192-193.
6   Quoted Howard, p. 268.

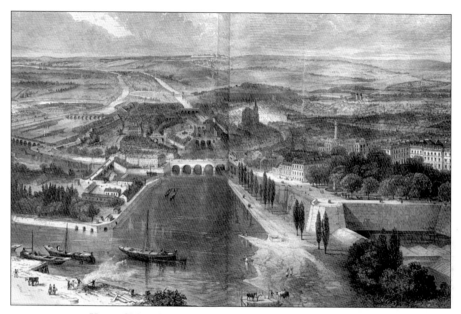

View of Metz from the south-west. (*Illustrated London News*)

were unable to do so. A stalemate having been reached, there followed a stationary contest between the two sets of outposts in which the artillery on both sides took part. The exchange of gunfire continued until nightfall. This engagement had been quite serious; the Germans suffered losses of 168 men killed and wounded and French losses were much about the same.

Operations continued on October 3, when the French pushed forward in advance of Ladonchamps in order to cover the position which they had taken up there. There was a continuous exchange of artillery fire, supported on the French side by the guns of the larger forts. The Germans endeavoured to set on fire with their artillery the villages in the front line of the French positions, but failed in this, since as a precaution all inflammable material had been removed.

Preparations for the assault continued; those troops which were to remain behind for the defence of Metz were told off, and the army's doctors inspected every man who was to take part in the operation in order to check his fitness to march. Each corps was required to deliver a report by October 6 of its readiness for the sortie. Orders were issued that all sick men were to be brought into the city. Bazaine consulted Colonel Marion, the commander of the *pontonniers*, who would be responsible for building any bridges required for the advance. He asked if several boats laden with the necessary bridging material could move down the Moselle at the same time as the army advanced, in order to be on hand to effect the crossing of the river Orme.

As these preparations for the assault continued, Bazaine convened a meeting of his corps commanders on the afternoon of October 4 to discuss his plan. Opening the discussion, he summarised the current position of the army, noting the inevitable deterioration in the supply situation, and the consequent effect of this, as well as the news trickling in from the outside, on the morale of the army. The corps commanders had plenty to say about this, believing that there were still considerable resources within the city that had not yet been taken up; their complaint was that not enough had been done with regard to this. Bazaine's response to this complaint was to say that this was the responsibility of the governor of the fortress, and any recriminations with regard to the matter should be addressed to him. He went on to review his plan. He intended that the 6th Corps and the Guard should advance up the left bank of the Moselle; the 4th Corps would follow on the heights which on this bank dominated the valley. At the same time, the 3rd Corps would advance up the right bank, protecting the movement from the side of the river. Finally, the 2nd Corps would follow as the rearguard.

Recording the discussion, Jarras noted Bazaine's evident diffidence about the operation which he proposed to undertake:

> In putting forward this plan, the Marshal did not impose it. He did not conceal the fact that it was possible that objections could be raised to it; but, having not been able to find another that was preferable, he asked that they examine it. If it was rejected, he asked what they would suggest in its place. He asked the corps commanders to make their views clearly known, because he intended to follow the advice which they gave him.[7]

The only objection actually raised came from Leboeuf, who was concerned about the heavy burden which the plan placed on his corps. Since it would be separated from the rest of the army by the Moselle, it seemed to him that even with five divisions, one of which was cavalry, it would be difficult to march very far without encountering, first in his front and on his right flank, and soon on his rear as well, very superior forces. However, Leboeuf promised to study the plan carefully, and to talk to Bazaine about it. In any case, he said, he was ready to carry out any orders which he was given. The only other comments raised at the meeting came from Ladmirault, who expressed grave doubts about the prospects of success. Bazaine then ended the discussion, remarking:

> Leaving our lines without fighting is impossible. I have put forward a plan of operations which seems to me to offer the least difficulty. If you do not accept it, please indicate to me an alternative which we will consider in its turn, and we can then go with whatever the meeting decides.[8]

---

7   Jarras, p. 235.
8   Jarras, pp. 235-236.

Thus the stage was set for another attempt to break out of the investment, but once again Coffinières interposed his views, on October 5 writing to Bazaine a letter protesting about the plan. He had been engaged in carrying out the order to bring all the sick men into the city, which was very difficult because all the barracks and hospitals were full. He complained that Soleille had called for two companies of *pontonniers*; these were men who had been serving the guns of the forts and must be replaced. He anticipated a total of 25,000 sick, for whom they had no medical supplies. He ended his letter with a grim warning: 'God grant that 150,000 inhabitants and garrison, as well as your own army, may not be the victims of the decision which you are about to take.'[9]

This was a moment in time when, as Bazaine was aware, there were negotiations in train at Ferrières between Bismarck and Jules Favre, which might lead to an armistice. The responsibility of launching an attack at this point, with only a very limited chance of success, but the certainty of heavy casualties, was very great. It was too great for Bazaine. Whether with the Ferrières talks in the front of his mind, or the letter from Coffinières, or Leboeuf's concerns about his operations plan, he abruptly decided to cancel the assault. Instead, taking advantage of the positions that had been occupied during the preceding days, he converted it into a large-scale raid in the sector north of Ladonchamps.

The suddenness of his decision to give up the operation led to the suggestion that he never seriously intended to carry it out. His planning for it, so the argument ran, was half-hearted at best. D'Andlau saw the letter from Coffinières as crucial in leading to the abandonment of the scheme, although also seeing the influence of Bazaine's immediate entourage, particularly General Boyer, in his decision.[10] Duquet and Palat cite as evidence that Bazaine had little intention of proceeding with the breakout the fact that he had been studying books withdrawn by Boyer from the library of the military school which dealt with the sieges of Genoa and Danzig, and also the capitulation of Baylen during the Napoleonic wars.[11] These capitulations might have had little to offer a way of a precedent, but that of Kléber at Mainz in 1793 did have features that were relevant to the situation of the army in Metz. Kléber's army had been permitted by the Prussians to leave Mainz with full military honours, having given its parole not to fight again against Prussia; and Kléber's army had gone on to be used by the French government to suppress the rising in the Vendée. It cannot be known if this example of a politico-military solution to the problem of ending a siege had any influence on Bazaine; but in the curious situation that existed in the autumn of 1870, it could not be said to be impossible for something on these lines to be negotiated.

Bazaine's orders for October 7 were for the seizure of all the supplies in the farmsteads north of Ladonchamps, which were still occupied by the advanced German outposts. 400 wagons were in readiness for the operation, which was to be carried

9   Bazaine, *Episodes*, pp. 190-191.
10   D'Andlau, pp. 275-276.
11   Duquet, p. 190; Palat, p. 197.

A Prussian siege battery before Metz. (*The Graphic*)

out by Canrobert's 6th Corps and by the Voltigeur Division of the Guard. On the left flank, the advance was to be supported by Ladmirault's 4th Corps in the woods north west of Woippy, and on the right flank, on the other side of the river, by Leboeuf's 3rd Corps, which was to move northward along the right bank of the Moselle towards Malroy. The operation was originally timed to commence at 11.00 a.m., but a delay in the issue of orders caused postponement until 1.00. At that time, with the support of the guns of Fort St Julien, the Voltigeur Division advanced towards Franclorchamps and St Remy and then, beyond those villages to Les Grandes Tapes and Les Petites Tapes. At the same time, a chasseur battalion moved on Bellevue. Levasseur-Sorval's division of the 4th Corps advanced towards Villers les Plenois and the Bois de Vigneulles. Strong reserves were concentrated at La Maison Rouge and Woippy. All of this added up to a very powerful advance, albeit one which could be for a very limited time.

Facing it, immediately in its path, stood the 3rd Reserve Division on the left bank of the Moselle, holding a position astride the railway line; it was soon pushed back by the advancing French infantry. At Les Grandes Tapes, where the farm buildings had been inadequately prepared for defence, and where the defenders tried to make a stand, the French soon surrounded them, and took a large number of prisoners. Much the same occurred at Les Petites Tapes, which by 2:30 was also in the hands of the Voltigeurs. At the same time, further detachments advancing from Ladonchamps and St Agathe and from the Bois de Woippy, drove the Germans out of Bellevue.

As usual, though, the advancing French infantry came under heavy fire from the German artillery. The guns of the 3rd Reserve Division as well as some from the X

Corps came into action in support of the ten heavy guns already in position north of Semecourt. From 1.00 there had been a stationary action limited to exchanges of rifle fire along the western side of the engagement, but the 5th Division from Alvensleben's III Corps now came up to check the French advance, moving to Villers les Plenois. There followed a vigorous struggle around a brick kiln a mile or so east of the village, where Grenier's division repulsed a German advance, before further reinforcements drove the French back into the Bois de Woippy and St Anne. Fresh German troops arriving now advanced to the attack of Bellevue and St Anne. Bazaine, in accordance with his usual practice, had gone up into the front line of his troops. A Voltigeur officer, Captain de Chasseloup-Laubat, reported that his men expressed both 'fear and admiration' for the Marshal, as he exposed himself to enemy fire: 'He's a tough one', they said.[12]

On the other side of the river Aymard's division had advanced towards Malroy and Charly before being halted by the artillery of the X Corps. This was, however, only intended as a feint attack, as the corps commander Voigts-Rhetz readily perceived, and he ordered one of his brigades to cross to the left bank to support the 6th Landwehr Brigade which was engaged in an attempt to recapture the farmsteads of Les Grandes Tapes and Les Petites Tapes. In this the landwehr were ultimately successful, occupying both sets of farm buildings by 5.00. Within an hour of this success, the Germans had also recaptured Bellevue and St Anne, as well as St Remy.[13]

Meanwhile another feint attack had been mounted by Metman's division over familiar ground in the direction of Lauvallier and Noisseville; Manteuffel, like Voigts-Rhetz, did not take it very seriously, reckoning that the outcome of the day's fighting would be settled on the left bank of the river. The French made temporary gains, only to be halted by the German artillery at Poix, Servigny and Noisseville, and by 6:30 they began to retreat into the fortress. Meanwhile fighting had continued around Château Ladonchamps, where a large force of infantry and artillery beat off a German attack from St Remy. A final attempt to capture the place, directed from the west, at about 8.00 also failed. After this, the fighting died down everywhere.

It had been a significant engagement. Total German casualties amounted to 1,782 men, of whom some 500 had been taken prisoner. French losses in total were 1,257. Bazaine should have had no complaints about the spirit of his men, most of whom had gone bravely into battle all day. The operation had not, however, been successful in achieving its principal object of gathering in supplies from the farmsteads in the area.

Jarras endeavoured to draw some limited comfort from the engagement:

> The operation, valiantly carried out by the Guard, produced no result in terms of the forage sort, but we took a considerable number of prisoners, and the enemy

12   Ruby & Regnault, p. 239.
13   *Official History*, Vol. III, p. 193.

also suffered serious losses in killed and wounded. Ours, although somewhat less, were out of proportion to the results obtained.[14]

Jarras also recorded Bazaine's reaction to the way in which the operation had gone:

On the following day Marshal Bazaine said that this attack had demonstrated the impossibility for the army to break through by the Moselle Valley in the direction of Thionville, the positions occupied by the enemy being too strong, furnished with considerable artillery and protected by the presence of numerous troops. In addition, the Marshal declared himself dissatisfied with the manner in which the movement of Marshal Canrobert had been supported, on the left by the 4th Corps and on the right by the 3rd. His intentions, he said, had not been followed and he had seen with his own eyes the feebleness with which the troops had acted, particularly those of the 4th Corps in the Bois de Vigneulles. There, the men had profited, the moment they were not under observation, to step behind a tree, take a drink, and then return to their bivouacs. The road they took, said the Marshal, was lined with men like a column of ants.[15]

14   Jarras, p. 237.
15   Jarras, pp. 237-238.

21

Boyer

Although in many respects the French had done well in the fighting at Ladonchamps, the engagement did nothing to alter Bazaine's opinion that there was no realistic likelihood of an attempt to break out succeeding. On the evening of 7 October he sat down to write a private letter to his corps commanders and Soleille and Coffinières. He was painfully aware that there was mounting discontent among the civil population, which had led to demonstrations against the Empire; Metz had always been a centre of republican sentiment. In one particularly serious incident, a delegation to Coffinières had forced their way into his office and smashed a bust of the Emperor. But this was not Bazaine's most serious concern; it was the inevitable approach of starvation that prompted his letter. He had freely expressed the view that provisions in the city could be exhausted by October 18, and so far as he knew there were no negotiations going on with the Prussians that could relieve the army's situation by that date. His letter, therefore, began with a blunt statement of the position:

> The moment is approaching when the Army of the Rhine will find itself in perhaps the most difficult situation to which a French army has ever been subject. Supplies are beginning to run short and in what can only be a very short time they will run out entirely ... Our resources are exhausted, our forces are starting to waste away and to disappear. In these grave circumstances I am calling on you to explain the situation and to share my thoughts with you.[1]

He went on to ask each of them to reply within 48 hours with their opinion and advice, after having consulted their divisional generals. When he had their responses, he would convene a Council of War to seek a definitive solution to the situation in which the army found itself.

They all did as he asked. Coffinières, after reviewing the sequence of events which had led the army into its situation, set out in remorseless detail the position

---

1   Bazaine, *Episodes*, p. 194.

as to the available supplies. On the basis of the rationing system currently being applied, there were sufficient to feed the army for less than 10 days, which could be extended by perhaps five days by taking part of the stores in the hands of the civil authorities. That would mark the absolute limit that was possible, and because of the difficulty of simultaneously feeding 230,000 people, it would in practice mean that the last day would be October 19. In conclusion, he said that the Marshal was the only person who could judge if his advice was sound, but as governor of the fortress of Metz he must assert that, with or without a battle, if there was no unforeseen event to change the position, the army and the fortress could not resist beyond Sunday, October 19.[2]

Desvaux, commanding the Guard in Bourbaki's absence, reported that, if the conditions which the enemy wished to impose were honourable, and conformed to the rights and usages of war, the generals whom he had consulted unanimously thought that the Army of the Rhine should accept those conditions. If, on the other hand, the honour of the army would be infringed by the enemy's stipulations, they considered that they should be rejected, and that honour and military duty required that the army should go out and fight.

A German parley at Metz, drawing by Becker. (Lindner)

In Frossard's opinion, it would be possible for an honourable capitulation to be agreed, which would leave the army complete, and organised, and ready to move to wherever it was necessary to safeguard social order. He considered that there were many precedents for such a convention, applicable in a case such as that of the Army of the Rhine to an army which had not been beaten and had maintained its honour and which was capable of inflicting severe losses on an enemy that sought to impose terms that were too rigorous or unacceptable. Like Desvaux, he thought that negotiations should begin as soon as possible.[3]

2   Bazaine, *Episodes*, pp. 196-199.
3   Bazaine, *Episodes*, pp. 199-201.

Leboeuf, on the other hand, took a different view. He and his generals believed that by having retreated into Metz, the army had saved the city from bombardment, and had also rendered the country a considerable service by effectively paralysing 200,000 men of the Prussian army. 'Up to now, the soldiers have not suffered privation; they are even better fed than the garrison; thanks to this, to the care of their leaders and the foresight of the military administration, the strength and health of the soldiers are in a perfect state; but the privations which are commencing will soon change that state of things.' If the army left Metz, it would not be long before the fortress fell. He was, he said, aware of the difficulties of launching an attack, but he and his generals were of the opinion, nevertheless, that the army should launch a fresh assault.[4]

For Ladmirault, the present state of the 4th Corps was that it was still capable of making a great effort if that was required of it. The discipline of the corps was good; the officers were respected, and their example still inspired courage and devotion among most of the soldiers, but each day the situation was getting worse. The cavalry and artillery would be greatly hampered by the condition of their horses. Each day the number of sick men increased. Nonetheless, the men of the 4th Corps would, he said, be ready to face whatever supreme task that Bazaine would require of them.

Canrobert and his generals believed that the time had come to see if it was possible for a convention to be concluded with the enemy on honourable terms, for the army to leave with their arms and baggage, on condition that it would not serve against Prussia for a period not exceeding one year. If the terms offered were not such as could be honourably accepted, then they were resolvedved to attack the Prussian lines, *coûte que coûte*. Canrobert went on, however to review the enormous difficulties facing a sortie.[5]

Bazaine's corps commanders had thus given him the considered opinions for which he had asked. In his *Episodes*, he remarked that it was sad to think that, three years later, the views expressed had been modified, both to the Commission of Enquiry and at his court-martial. Bazaine also commented on the criticism that he consulted his generals too often, pointing out that this had been done since the start of the campaign, and by the Emperor himself.

Having considered the replies which he had received, Bazaine now convened the Council of War for October 10, to be attended by the corps commanders, Soleille, Coffinières and Intendant General Lebrun. Convinced as he was of the impossibility of launching a successful breakout, Bazaine can have had little doubt of the way in which the deliberations would go.

The Council of War assembled at Bazaine's headquarters at Ban St Martin at 4:30 p.m. Jarras and Boyer were also in attendance, though neither took part in the discussion. Boyer acted as secretary and recorded a full note of the meeting. Until he heard Bazaine reading out the reports of the corps commanders, Jarras had no idea of their

4   Bazaine, *Episodes*, pp. 201-203.
5   Bazaine, *Episodes*, pp. 204-206.

contents.[6] Bazaine opened the discussion by briefly summarising the present position, and then asked Coffinières and Intendant Lebrun to explain the supply situation. The governor stated that on the basis of the existing rationing it was possible to feed the army until October 20. He was gravely concerned about the state of public health within the fortress, where there were 19,000 men sick and injured, without adequate shelter or bedding, and lacking the necessary medication; there was also a shortage of doctors. The chief medical officer had reported a growing number of cases of typhus, smallpox and dysentery, which was rapidly spreading into the civilian population. The governor's report provoked a heated discussion, and he was criticised for not having acted with sufficient energy; it was also suggested that he had been colluding with opposition elements among the civilian population. Coffinières vigorously defended himself, pointing out all the difficulties of his task, and saying that he had entirely devoted himself to his duty to the Army of the Rhine. For the first time during the siege, perhaps as a response to pressure from the civilian authorities, he expressed himself as sympathetic to the idea of launching a further assault.

After reading the written opinions which he had received, Bazaine invited discussion of the military situation. Following this, he put four questions the meeting. The first of these was whether the army should continue to hold out in Metz until the complete exhaustion of its provisions. To this, there was unanimous agreement; it would continue to detain 200,000 enemy troops and would gain time. Next, Bazaine asked whether operations should be continued around Metz in an endeavour to collect provisions and forage. No, said the corps commanders; these operations had been expensive and had produced little, and their lack of success damaged the morale of the troops. The third question was whether *pourparlers* with the enemy could be begun to negotiate the terms of a convention. The reply to this was unanimously in favour, provided that these should be begun no later than in 48 hours, with the object of obtaining terms which must be honourable and acceptable to everyone. Lastly, Bazaine asked whether the army should launch an attack to try to break through the enemy lines. This raised a further question; Coffinières, still in belligerent mode, suggested that it was preferable to launch such an attack before entering into discussions. This was rejected by the majority, but it was agreed that if the conditions demanded by the enemy were incompatible with their honour and military duty, then an attempt should be made to force a way out of the fortress.

Boyer's record of the proceedings was signed by all those present, perhaps because Bazaine wished to cover himself. However, although it was, as Ruby & Regnault point out, normal for a commander-in-chief to seek opinions from his subordinates, the responsibility remained his. At his trial, Bazaine always firmly maintained that this was the case.[7] At the end of the discussion it was agreed that Boyer should be sent on a mission to the King of Prussia.

6   Jarras, p. 242.
7   Ruby & Regnault, pp. 239-240; Bazaine, *Episodes*, pp. 207-209.

French cavalry dismounted as infantry during the siege. (Rousset/*Histoire*)

Jarras had taken no part in the discussion but felt strongly that sending Boyer on his mission to Versailles was a mistake. He regretted very much that the decision as to the course to be pursued had been the subject of discussion at the Council of War at all; in his opinion this was wrong:

> To my mind, General Boyer's mission could only have disastrous consequences. If it succeeded, it meant the division of the army as a prelude to a detestable civil war. If it failed, we would regret the loss of time, perhaps irreparable, causing the enfeebling of our soldiers' strength more and more with each hour that passed by reason of destitution and lack of food.[8]

Jarras was not alone in being sceptical about the possible use of the army in an attempt to restore the Imperial regime. Lieutenant-Colonel Charles Fay wrote in his diary that although it had been known for a victorious army to impose itself on a country, how could one conceive of the troops of a beaten army claiming to restore a dynasty which had only a few weeks previously been rejected by the nation.[9]

Although Jarras moaned a lot about Bazaine, sometimes with good reason, he could be fair minded in his comments. He wrote in his memoirs, on the subject of the discussions at the Council of War:

> It has been said that Bazaine's only object was to gain time, and thus to lead the army until the day came when, with the last of its rations, it would be forced to capitulate. I affirm that this thought never occurred to me, neither on October 10

8   Jarras, p. 256.
9   Fay, pp. 245-246.

nor in the following days, and I do not recall anything being said in my presence which suggested capitulation.[10]

This was no less than the honest truth. Bazaine had at all times aimed at preserving his army and turned towards negotiations with the enemy as the only remaining means by which he might achieve this.

General Napoleon Boyer, Bazaine's trusted principal aide-de-camp, was probably the best man to carry out the mission. It was not going to be easy. He was being sent to ask King William to agree to a military convention whereby the Army of the Rhine would be allowed to leave Metz with its arms, its baggage, its flags and all its materiel, and relocate in a neutral zone of France. He took with him a memorandum drafted by Bazaine, setting out the reasons why this should be allowed. It was, in substance, very much more political than military in its character. Notably, it did not suggest the restoration of the Empire. Bazaine concluded this note by setting out what a liberated Army of the Rhine could achieve:

> It would re-establish order and protect society in France, whose interests were in common with the rest of Europe. It would give Prussia at the same time a guarantee of pledges on which she could rely and then would contribute to the advent of a regular and legal power with which relations could be restored without upheavals and entirely naturally.[11]

Boyer's personality was the subject of widely varying opinions. Bazaine's detractors have seen in him the Marshal's evil genius; but these views, formed long after the events with which Boyer was concerned, were at odds with his record of service, in the course of which he received high praise from his superiors, including Le Flô, Saint Arnaud and others, who commented on his intelligence, his capability and his tact. There were, though, some contemporary views which were not so flattering. The Empress Charlotte had a poor opinion of him; General von Monts, when meeting him at Wilhelmshöhe, thought him intelligent though rather sly and sometimes lacking in tact; and according to M. Tachard, the French minister in Brussels, Pepita Bazaine hated him for his influence over the Marshal. On the other hand, Frederick Charles wrote: 'The general arrived during dinner, with his eyes bandaged; he appears intelligent and energetic.'[12]

The Prince may have formed a favourable opinion of Boyer when he arrived at his headquarters at Corny, but he was extremely hostile to the nature of his mission, suspecting that Bismarck might be looking for a political and not a military conclusion to the investment of Metz. Accordingly, at first he refused to allow Boyer to travel

---

10   Jarras, p. 258.
11   Bazaine, *Episodes*, pp. 209-211.
12   Ruby & Regnault, p. 243.

on to Versailles; when this was reported to Bismarck, he went at once to the King, who ordered that Boyer be allowed to proceed. Frederick Charles complied, but with a bad grace, writing to General Hermann von Tresckow, the Chief of the Military Cabinet:

> What is it that is hoped to be obtained from Boyer? I hope that it is merely to meet with him, because I alone have the right to conclude a military convention, and not Bismarck. At the start of September there could have been certain advantages. Now it would be disastrous, because six weeks of the siege have brought us nearer to the capitulation of Metz. Neither the army, which has suffered so much, nor I are willing to forego picking the ripe fruit that is ready to fall.[13]

The issue prompted a spirited discussion at the Royal headquarters in Versailles. The Crown Prince referred to it in his diary:

> Prince Frederick Charles is against receiving the French intermediary, for he is rightly enough afraid that in the end the capitulation will come to be signed at Versailles instead of before Metz, and he, after being detained there for months, will only be a looker on; however, he is now pacified on this point, having been assured that he is to sign the stipulations whatever they are.[14]

Bismarck's relationship with the upper echelons of the Prussian military was deteriorating. He had not endeared himself to them during discussions at the end of the Austro-Prussian War in 1866. The King and his leading generals had their hearts set on marching into Vienna; Bismarck asked sarcastically why they should stop there; why not pursue the Austrians into Hungary and, since they would be unable to maintain their lines of communication, 'why not go on to Constantinople, establish a new Byzantium and leave Prussia to its fate?'[15]

In his memoirs, which are not invariably reliable, Bismarck claimed to have overheard a conversation aboard the train taking the Royal headquarters to the front in 1870. Moltke's Quartermaster General, Lieutenant-General Theophil von Podbielski, addressing General Albrecht von Roon, the War Minister, said, according to Bismarck: 'So arrangements have been made this time that the same thing does not happen again.' Bismarck wrote that before the train started he had heard enough to know that Podbielski was referring to his participation in military discussions.[16]

Boyer finally left Metz on October 12 at 10.00 a.m.; his train was held up at Nanteuil, from where he left by carriage at noon next day. He finally arrived at Versailles at

13   Ruby & Regnault, pp. 241-242.
14   Emperor Frederick III, *War Diary* (London, 1928), pp. 155-156.
15   Craig, Gordon A., *The Battle of Königgrätz* (London, 1965), p. 180.
16   Bismarck, Prince Otto von, *Reflections and Reminiscences* (London, 1898), p. 103.

A view of the French camp at Vallières, near Metz, during the siege. (Rousset/*Histoire*)

5.00 a.m. on October 14 and met with Bismarck at 1.00 that day. The Chancellor received him affably; after Boyer had explained briefly the object of his visit, Bismarck reviewed the history of his discussions with Regnier, and Boyer told him that his purpose was to take up the conversation that Regnier had initiated. He explained that the telegram about the surrender of Metz had greatly disturbed Bazaine, and it was to dispel misunderstanding that the Marshal had sent him to the Royal headquarters. When Boyer mentioned Bazaine's note to Frederick Charles, Bismarck rose, and said: 'There are here, close by, people who understand French. Walls, as they say, have ears: let us go into the garden; we shall talk more freely.' Lighting a cigar, Bismarck led the way.[17]

Boyer went through the proposals contained in Bazaine's note. A key sticking point was still the question of the surrender of Metz which, he said, was in the hands of Coffinières; having been appointed as governor by the Emperor, it was only from him that he could obtain his release. The two men discussed the problem of controlling the army once it had emerged from Metz; this might be partly met by its public commitment to the Imperial Regency. Bismarck pointed out the risks involved, remarking: 'Note very carefully that if you cannot control the army your personal situation will become one of extreme danger. Your life, your fortune and your country are at stake, and you are risking exile at the very least.'[18] Bismarck made plain that his principal concern was with the eventual peace treaty. If the army in Metz was to be released,

17   Boyer diary quoted in Augustin Filon, *Recollections of the Empress Eugenie* (London, 1920) p. 204.
18   Boyer diary, Filon, p. 206.

he must have some guarantee that his ultimate conditions would be met. 'Go, then, to Hastings, general', he said, 'and obtain from the Empress the order for General Coffinières to deliver up Metz since Marshal Bazaine has not the power to do it. That will be already some guarantee for us.'[19]

Bismarck continued with his analysis of the current situation and remarked that the members of the Government of National Defence were 'mad men who did not even know the meaning of a republican state.' The meeting ended after some three hours with Bismarck's promise to put the matter before the King who, he said, would no doubt wish to consult Moltke and Rune; Boyer could expect his answer on the following day, after which he could return to Metz.

Next day Bismarck came to see Boyer at his lodgings. He told him that the generals were insisting on a capitulation on the same terms as that of Sedan, but that he had pointed out to the King the political and diplomatic aspects of the matter. Putting aside the question of capitulation for the moment, he said that the army in Metz must pledge itself to support the Imperial dynasty. Bazaine must publicly declare that he would do so. At the same time the Empress must, on the basis of this support, appeal to the nation for the confirmation of the Imperial regime by a vote.

Boyer accordingly returned to Metz to report on his discussions, arriving in October 17, having prepared a detailed note of his conversations with Bismarck.[20] Next day there was another Council of War to consider his report. Changarnier joined the meeting, of which Boyer took a formal note. After discussion of the proposals which Bismarck had made, the meeting turned once again to review the chances of success for a breakout attempt; it was unanimously agreed that in all likelihood it would fail. Several felt concern about the effect on the army of such a failure. The corps commanders each spoke in the same terms as previously. The key issue, however, was whether to continue negotiations with a view to agreeing an honourable military convention to lead to the re-establishment of a government with which the German governments could deal. There was no consensus; the majority were in favour, but Coffinières and Leboeuf were opposed; both still were prepared to launch an attack, even with all the difficulties it faced.[21]

The majority decision meant that Boyer should go at once to England to meet with the Empress. He took with him a letter from Bazaine: 'Some time ago I sent General Bourbaki to your Majesty. Having had no response, I am sending today General Boyer, my aide-de-camp, to assure you of our loyalty. Please have the goodness to give him your instructions, you may have confidence in him.'[22] Boyer also took a letter from General Frossard, appealing to Eugénie 'to listen to General Boyer, now sent by the Marshal, and to believe his words which reflect the feelings of us all.'[23]

19   Boyer diary, Filon, p. 206.
20   Bazaine, *Épisodes*, pp. 219-224.
21   Bazaine, *Épisodes*, pp. 216-218.
22   Bazaine, *Épisodes*, p. 218.
23   Filon, pp. 212-214.

Vedette of the Prussian 5th Uhlans before Metz. (*The Graphic*)

Boyer left Metz on October 19, and travelled to London en route to Chislehurst, arriving there on October 21. Filon described his appearance: 'The manners of General Boyer were grave and unassuming. His face just then was pale and haggard with hardship and suffering, and he looks like the ghost of that noble army of which he had been one of the leaders and whose fate he mourned. Seeing him thus our hearts bled.'[24]

Eugénie's position was extremely difficult. Concerned to do anything she could to help, she had no leverage. Following her discussions with Boyer, she authorised him to send a telegram to Bismarck asking for an armistice at Metz and for the army to be revictualled for fifteen days and asking to know what the conditions of peace were. To King William she sent a message appealing to him to be favourable to her request: 'Its acceptance is an indispensable condition if negotiations are to proceed.'

But there was really no way in which William, or his generals, would contemplate the revictualling of Metz, and on October 24 Bismarck sent a telegram to Bazaine with his response. In it, he forwarded at Boyer's request the text of a telegram recording his visit to the Empress, who was doing all she could to assist the army of Metz, 'which is the object of her profound solicitude and is in her constant thoughts.' Bismarck, however, further observed:

> I must observe, M. le Maréchal, that since my interview with General Boyer, none of the guarantees which I have explained are indispensable before negotiations can be begun with the Imperial Regency have been received, and that the future of the Emperor's cause has not been assured by the attitude of the nation and the French army; it is impossible to lend oneself to negotiations of which her Majesty alone would have to make the results acceptable to the French nation. The proposals which have reached us from London are, in the present situation,

24   Filon, p. 211.

Inhabitants from Metz trying to leave the city before its surrender. (*Illustrated London News*)

absolutely unacceptable, and I declare to my great regret that I can see no further chance of reaching a result by political negotiations.[25]

William wrote directly to Eugénie:

I desire with all my heart to restore peace to our two nations, but to secure this it would be necessary to establish at least the probability that we shall succeed in making France accept the result of our transactions without continuing the war against the entire French forces. At present I regret the uncertainty in which we find ourselves with regard to the political dispositions of the Army of Metz, as well as of the French nation, does not allow me to proceed further with the negotiations proposed by your Majesty.[26]

25 Bazaine, *Episodes*, p. 228.
26 Howard, p. 280.

Eugénie, while awaiting this response, had asked Bernstorff for a meeting with him in an effort to elicit what might be the shape of the final peace settlement, but got nowhere with this. Nor did the unofficial efforts made by Prince Richard Metternich, the Austrian ambassador, who had been talking to the members of the Government of National Defence at Tours, get anywhere. Boyer remained in London awaiting developments; on October 26 he asked Bernstorff for a safe conduct to enable him to return to Metz, but the ambassador discouraged him, saying that nothing was yet concluded. But it was in Metz that the crucial decisions were now to be taken.

22

Capitulation

It was raining again in Metz. The dry spell at the beginning of October had given way to cold miserable weather. Day after day the rain poured down, turning the camp sites into quagmires. Coffinières had on October 20 ceased to provide food for the army, and the army's own stocks had lasted only two days. The bread ration for the civilian population was down to 300 g per day. Not surprisingly, the decline in morale of the army was now beginning to accelerate.

As the days passed, Bazaine was criticised for not appearing more in public, bringing from one irate critic the accusation that he 'stayed shut up in his office at Ban St Martin – like a pasha in his seraglio.' Even if there had been any justification for this remark, it took no account of the circumstances. As Guedalla wrote: 'What temptation was there for him to parade before his starved and sullen troops in their waterlogged encampments or to encounter the reproaches of disappointed officers?'[1] In actual fact, all the time that he had been awaiting news of the outcome of Boyer's mission, he had also been actively seeking a solution to his impossible situation. On October 21 he tried again to elicit a response from the Government of National Defence by sending out six copies of a dispatch in the hands of separate emissaries:

> I have several times sent out men who have volunteered to give news of the army of Metz. Since then our situation has only got worse, and I have received not the least response from either Paris or Tours. It is however urgent that I know what has been happening in the interior of the country and in the capital, since before long famine will oblige me to take some step in the interest of France and of the army.[2]

No answer came. It certainly could not be said that the Government of National Defence was unaware of the desperate situation of the Army of the Rhine. On

---

1   Guedalla, p. 213.
2   Ruby & Regnault, pp. 260-261.

October 25 Bourbaki, who was by then at Lille, telegraphed Admiral Fourichon at Tours: 'General Boyer has said to one of my parents that provisions and munitions are running out at Metz, and that capitulation is imminent. I wrote to you yesterday; I await a response.'[3] Two days later Gambetta wrote to Bourbaki:

Leon Gambetta. (Scheibert)

> The supreme interest of the situation of Marshal Bazaine is that he should know that by holding out he can still save everything. You love your country too much not to imagine what can or cannot be done to reach him with advice dictated solely by feelings for the nation's glory and its safety. So send men from you, with your urgent advice, to explain the position. He must be made aware of the intervention of Europe and that he must prolong the resistance, on which we have the right to count.[4]

He added that Bourbaki should not skimp on money or rewards for the messengers. Interestingly, Gambetta made no suggestion that a breakout should be attempted.

Bazaine had not stopped thinking about the possibility, even though since Ladonchamps he had reached the conclusion that it stood little chance of success. On October 22, in conversation with General Lapasset, he discussed the possibility of a sortie in a southerly direction, remarking: 'Unfortunately, those who are injured or fall behind would be taken prisoner, for we would have to move without stopping.' Lapasset was enthusiastic about the idea; but the grim reality was that an assault by infantry without artillery would be doomed, as Bazaine well knew, even if making the attempt would redound to his personal reputation. He remarked in a candid discussion with Intendant Lebrun:

> I too would like to break out. It would be the most remarkable action of the war and I would be covered with glory ... But after one, two or three days of struggle, my army would be beaten, driven back, sabred by cavalry, dispersed and the

3   Bazaine, *Episodes*, p. 226.
4   Bazaine, *Episodes*, p. 227.

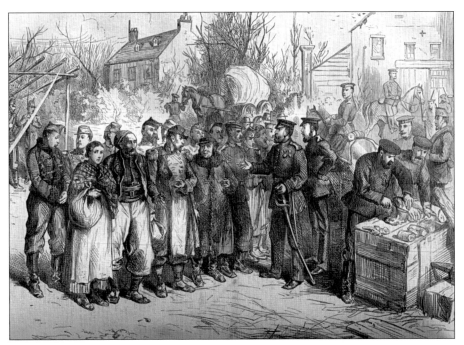

French prisoners from Metz at Remilly. (*Illustrated London News*)

wreckage made prisoners; in the end, a disaster. Before God, I would not take the responsibility of causing the death of 40,000 men.[5]

In this heart cry Bazaine explained, in a few words, the anguish which he felt for his situation and that of his men, as he constantly sought to find some alternative solution.

It was in this frame of mind that, on receiving the notification from Bismarck of the rejection of Boyer's efforts to obtain some kind of political settlement, Bazaine convened a further Council of War on October 24. The meeting assembled at 8.00 a.m; in addition to the corps commanders it was attended by Coffinières, Soleille, Lebrun, Changarnier and Jarras. Lieutenant-Colonel Willette took the minutes. It was naturally a difficult meeting, and passions ran high. Bazaine opened the meeting by reading the telegram from Bismarck and the information from Boyer, and then put the question as to whether a final effort should be made to break out from the fortress and if so at what part of the German lines of investment it should be directed.

The first to speak was Desvaux. He believed that an attack should be made to the westward, in the direction of St Privat and Amanvillers, which offered the best chance of success. He advocated an assault with a maximum force. His views, however,

5   Ruby & Regnault, p. 262.

commanded little support. Neither Ladmirault nor Frossard believed that their troops would follow them. Leboeuf, whose corps had, according to Jarras, unlike the rest of the army not ceased to receive regular provisions, was in favour of an attack to the west. He thought that his troops would do their duty, but much less energetically than at the start of the campaign. However, he also observed that an attack would be a heroic folly.

Canrobert dreaded a collapse that would bring no honour to the flag. Later, when giving evidence at Bazaine's trial, he asked graphically if honestly, if military honour would permit the leading of sheep to the slaughter house to have their throat cut.[6] Soleille thought that no one would get through; an attack would be useless and culpable. Coffinières, having previously been in favour of an attack, had somewhat cooled; he said that a better point of attack would be the Haute-Prevoye plateau, but the discussion was pointless if the men would not follow their officers. It was the Intendant Lebrun who brought this part of the discussion to a close, when he observed, flatly, that there were no more provisions.

The meeting then turned, as all must have known it would, to the question of opening negotiations with the enemy. Frossard still hoped that it would be possible to obtain the release of the army on condition that it gave its parole not to serve again during the war. Coffinières thought that the problem for the Germans of dealing with so many prisoners of war would be a valuable bargaining point and suggested that they should seek an armistice. Canrobert, more realistic, did not believe that the Prussians would consent to an arrangement that would be more advantageous to the French than to themselves. He suggested offering to recall the former Chamber to conduct the negotiations, while not consenting to recognise the Government of National Defence. Bazaine pointed out the difficulty of negotiating the fate of the army separatelyfrom that of Metz.

The final question to be decided was the selection of the individual to send to interview Frederick Charles. Bazaine suggested that it should be Desvaux; he, however, refused on the not unreasonable grounds that he did not agree with the majority view. As an alternative, Bazaine proposed that the intermediary should be Frossard; at this, Changarnier bluntly observed that Frossard was not sufficiently calm, nor had the right disposition to carry out such a negotiation. If Frossard would not do, suggested Canrobert, then Changarnier himself was the man; and this was generally agreed. The venerable general said that his devotion to the Army of the Rhine and to its commander compelled him to accept the task. The conditions which he was instructed to seek were, first, that the army should be allowed to call for the re-establishment of the former legislature, or for new elections; and, secondly, that the Army of the Rhine, and the fortress of Metz should be neutralised, so that the assembly might be convened to negotiate with the Germans.

6   Ruby & Regnault, p. 263.

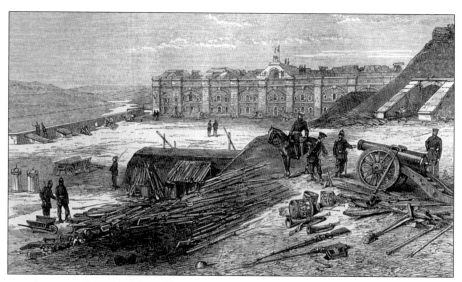

Interior of Fort St Quentin, Metz, following the surrender. (*Illustrated London News*)

During the discussions at the Council of War, Bazaine's generals had been given every opportunity to put forward their opinions as to the right course to pursue. There was, though, no question of their sharing the responsibility for the final decision. When it came down to it, therefore, it was Canrobert's blunt comment about leading sheep to the slaughterhouse that most aptly summarised Bazaine's situation. Ruby & Regnault effectively disposed of the suggestion that a refusal to do so could be accounted a criminal act:

> It is absurd to require a commander to deliver a battle that he has already esti-mated as lost, and this was the case. At most, it might have been possible, rather than to fight a battle, to take advantage of night and under cover of the woods to send out several small detachments of resolute men, adequately provisioned; those that got through might serve as cadres for the young levies of the Government of National Defence. Anything more ambitious could not reasonably be hoped for. But it should not be forgotten that Bazaine was entirely ignorant of Gambetta's intentions. The refusal of Bazaine to sacrifice his men was imputed a crime; it is ironic to note that Trochu was dragged through the mud by Villemesant, the editor of *Figaro*, who reproached him for fighting the battle of Buzenval to save his own reputation while knowing that defeat was certain and capitulation inevi-table. Trochu lost the action which he brought against the newspaper.[7]

7   Ruby & Regnault, pp. 263-264.

Frederick Charles agreed to a meeting with Changarnier 'as a mark of esteem for the illustrious general and as proof of his consideration for the valiant French army'. On October 25 at 11.00 a.m. the elderly general was received with proper respect and all due ceremony; but the courtesy of the Prussian commander reflected no reduction in the firmness with which he maintained his position. There was no question of the two sides meeting as equals. He listened politely to the basis of the convention that Changarnier put forward but said that he would not dare even to submit such proposals to Versailles. The fate of Metz must, he said, be linked to that of the army. It would be appropriate for Lieutenant-General von Stiehle, his chief of staff, to meet with the French general appointed for the purpose at Frescaty, to discuss the terms of a proposed convention. Frederick Charles added, casually, that he believed that France in future would be best served by restoration of the monarchy, preferring the Comte de Paris to the Orleanist Duc d'Aumale.

Changarnier accordingly made his way back into Metz to report to Bazaine the outcome of his discussions. That afternoon Cissey was designated to meet with Stiehle at Frescaty. As soon as they met, Stiehle made it clear that the terms of a capitulation would not be greatly different from those of Sedan. He repeated that the city must be surrendered and the army must give up its flags. In accordance with Bazaine's instructions, Cissey untruthfully said that these had been burnt after the revolution of September 4, in accordance with customary French practice. For the moment Stiehle accepted this, and did not point out that this was scarcely consistent with Bazaine's protestations of loyalty to the Empire. The final terms of a conven-

General von Stiehle, Chief of Staff of the German Second Army. (Pflugk-Harttung)

tion, Stiehle said, should be negotiated between the respective chiefs of staff. He gave Cissey a protocol outlining the clauses which should be included.[8]

A further Council of War accordingly met next day, October 26, to hear the reports of Changarnier and Cissey. It was a largely futile discussion. Coffinieres declared that left to itself the fortress could hold out until November 5 and that by reason of his oath he could not give it up until it had been reduced to the last extremity. Bazaine seems to have made an attempt to insist that the fate of the fortress should be settled

8   Jarras, p. 293.

The survivors of Lapasset's brigade burn their colours, Metz, 26 October, painting by Dujardin-Beaumetz. (Rousset/*Histoire*)

separately from that of the army, but all the rest declared that it must follow the army, which had protected it until then; Bazaine accepted this. Various other suggestions were made, of which perhaps the oddest was the proposal by Frossard that the library of the Army School of Engineers should be excluded from the surrender. There was some discussion of whether the officers would be permitted to retain their swords; if this was to be allowed only for the generals, they should refuse, so that it could not be said that they were being treated differently from the other officers. The meeting ended with the decision that Jarras, as chief of staff, should meet with Stiehle to settle the final terms of the capitulation.[9] Jarras regretted that he had not had a voice in the discussion, and had hence not been able to express his opinion although, having considered the discussion and the frame of mind of those taking part, it would not have been possible to obtain any other decision from them.[10]

The decision that Jarras should undertake the negotiations came as no surprise to him; before the meeting, Bazaine had told him that this was his intention. The chief of staff protested; the way in which Bazaine had treated him throughout the campaign

9   Bazaine, *Episodes*, pp. 233-235; Ruby & Regnault, p. 265.
10   Jarras, pp. 299-300.

'had persuaded me that this poignant mission would be given to someone else.' He pointed out that he had had no voice in the Council of War and had not contributed to the existing state of things. Bazaine would have none of that, abruptly telling Jarras that the task was one of the functions of a chief of staff, and that he must undertake it. That did not stop Jarras, when at the end of the Council of War Bazaine announced that he would be conducting the negotiations, from protesting again that someone else should do so, as he had taken no part in deciding the principles of the convention. When Frossard then made a number of vehement remarks, Jarras murmured to Bazaine that Frossard would accept the mission and asked him to suggest this. Bazaine did so, and Frossard seemed inclined to accept; but the rest of the Council were of the view that the matter had been decided, and Frossard withdrew. Jarras, Bazaine declared, had the authority to speak for all the Council of War, which had complete confidence in him, and he then briefed Jarras as to the detailed terms of the convention to be negotiated.[11]

There was never any question of the responsibility for the decision to capitulate belonging to anyone but Bazaine, but it is not insignificant that his senior generals were solidly behind the decision. That was a consideration that should have weighed heavily at Bazaine's trial; it might have been a different matter if he had taken the decision in the teeth of opposition at the Council of War, but, as it was, he was morally entitled to feel, from the support which he received, that he was doing the right thing. At his trial, though, this aspect of the matter was brushed aside, and it was suggested that the Councils of War were only meetings which had no authority.[12]

Following the end of the meeting, Bazaine wrote to Frederick Charles to ask when and where Jarras could meet with Stiehle, and at 4.30 the Prince's reply came, proposing that the meeting take place at 6.00 a.m. next morning at the Château de Frescaty. Jarras decided to take with him two members of his staff, Fay and Samuel. During the night, Intendant Lebrun discovered four days' worth of food, and came to Bazaine to tell him. Bazaine was much upset, saying that negotiations were under way, and that the position would not be changed. In fact, the additional provisions were consumed before the surrender took place or left for the wounded. Jarras appears to have left before Lebrun's revelation.

Arriving at Stiehle, Jarras was courteously received, but ran into an immediate problem; the Prussian chief of staff refused to authorise the French officers to retain their swords. He also refused another request which Jarras had been instructed to make, which was to allow a token detachment to return to France, on giving its parole, as a symbol of the capitulation. Neither of these terms had been provided for in the protocol that Stiehle had given to Cissey, and Stiehle said that the King's orders were that the terms put forward could not be varied. Jarras replied that he too had express instructions and outlined the terms which he had been instructed to raise. Stiehle

11   Jarras, pp. 303-304.
12   Ruby & Regnault, p. 265.

listened to him without interruption, but when Jarras had finished, said that he could not discuss the terms in dispute. Jarras tried again; perhaps the omission of the terms allowing the officers to keep their swords was a mistake? No, said Stiehle, it was intentional. One matter that had annoyed the King, he said, was that a general of the army at Sedan had violated his parole. This was a reference to General Ducrot, who had given his parole after Sedan, and then turned up in Paris. Jarras argued that this as an isolated instance; but Ducrot had been in command during the battle, albeit only briefly, and King William took the matter seriously.

Confronted with the intractable position taken by Stiehle, Jarras did his best. Fay records him as bursting out at this point:

> It is true; we are your prisoners. Famine obliges us to surrender, but we have the right to ask all the honourable adjustments possible in the first article of the convention, because we are the masters of the second. It provides that the fortress will be given up with all its materiel, and that rifles, cannons, eagles and flags et cetera will be surrendered. If you will not amend the first article by including the terms for which we have asked, what is there to prevent us from blowing up the forts, destroying our gun carriages, spiking our guns, smashing our rifles, burning our powder and our flags and, this destruction completed, opening the gates and saying: Enter, you are the masters? What will you do then, faced with our bare chests, defenceless? You would not dare open fire, humanity would not allow it, the civilisation on which you count. You treat us harshly, you subject the officers to the same regime as the soldiers, depriving them of their rights. Well, what would be the result? And who would come out best?

Jarras went on to complain that Stiehle was justifying his position on the basis of an alleged and isolated action. He should be careful, he said, not to exasperate the French army; it was giving up, beaten by hunger, but still had its arms and munitions: 'You want to impose on us a grave humiliation, which we do not deserve, and which could have serious consequences.'[13]

Following this, Jarras proposed to withdraw. Stiehle then said that notwithstanding his refusal to sign that day, they could discuss the detailed text, and then produced a document which Frederick Charles had issued giving him full powers. Jarras could not do likewise, since, preoccupied with his mission, it had not occurred to him that this would be necessary, but in the event the absence of such a document was not important. Stiehle then returned to the issue of the officers' swords, saying that in recognition of the courage shown by the French army, those who gave their parole not to serve again during the war would be permitted to return to France with their swords and personal effects. At this Fay interrupted; if the Germans wished to recognise the courage of the French army, the best way to do so would be to allow this to

13   Fay, pp. 261-263.

all officers and not just a few. He thought also that the army should be permitted to march out in front of their conquerors and then deposit their arms before becoming prisoners of war.

The protests of the French delegates were not without their effect on Stiehle. The King, he said, had said that he did not wish the officers to retain their swords; the most he could do was to ask Frederick Charles to telegraph the King in order to refer the matter to him, and he would do this. Jarras and his colleagues withdrew; the meeting had lasted three hours. They took away with them the amended terms for which they had asked and reported to Bazaine. Nothing had been said about the flags. Jarras, on returning to headquarters, obtained the document investing him with full powers to sign the capitulation. Bazaine approved of the stance that had been taken, with the exception of the suggestion that the army should march out in front of the German army with the honours of war; this, he considered would be humiliating.[14]

For this, Bazaine was subsequently criticised. It was suggested that his reason for not accepting the honours of war in this way was because he did not wish to show himself to his troops. In his defence at his trial, however, it was pointed out that these honours had been refused by Gouvion St Cyr in 1813, and nor had they been accepted by Uhrich at Strasbourg, Wimpffen at Sedan, Denfert-Rochereau at Belfort or Trochu at Paris. It was merely one more stick for Bazaine's detractors to beat him with.

Bazaine instructed Jarras to confirm to Stiehle the explanation that Cissey had given with regard to the regimental flags, namely that in France it was customary for these to be burnt after a revolution, and to say that the process had already begun. Jarras observed that it was unwise in this way to draw attention to the issue, and that he did not suppose that Frederick Charles or Stiehle would believe it anyway.[15]

While waiting for further news from the German headquarters at Corny, Bazaine gave Jarras some further instructions. First, as to Changarnier, he was to explain that he had joined the army's headquarters as a private individual and was not even part of the reserve. He should, therefore, on no account be made a prisoner of war. Next, he was to seek permission for Prince Murat, commanding a cavalry brigade, to go, albeit as a prisoner of war, to join the Emperor at Cassel. Finally, Jarras was to make the necessary arrangements for Bazaine to leave Metz on the day of the surrender, and to visit Frederick Charles at Corny.[16]

During the course of the morning Stiehle sent in a message to say that the King had authorised Prince Frederick Charles to agree that the French officers could retain their swords; and that the provisions in the convention which Jarras had inserted with regard to the honours of war would also be accepted. At 6.00 p.m. on August 27 Jarras, accompanied again by Fay and Samuel, made his way to the Château Frescaty. This time Jarras brought with him the formal authority enabling him to sign the convention

14   Ruby & Regnault, p. 260.
15   Jarras, p. 300.
16   Jarras, p. 321.

on behalf of Bazaine. Stiehle was surprised to be told that although the provision for the honours of war to be accorded was to be incorporated in the protocol, the French army would not be taking advantage of this. The final terms of the surrender provided that each corps would be conducted to a particular point, and the officers would then return to Metz to await their departure for Germany. Those who gave their parole not to serve again against Germany during the war would not be made prisoners. After signing the protocol, Jarras and his colleagues returned to Metz at about 10:30, as the rain continued to beat down. Here and there inhabitants of the city stood in front of posters containing the proclamation by Coffinières announcing the intention to capitulate. As the coach carrying Jarras went by there was no disturbance; no one who saw it doubted that its journey marked the end of their city and of the army.[17]

The protocol having been signed, Bazaine turned to the mournful task of preparing a final Order of the Day to the Army of the Rhine. Subsequently, as with everything else that Bazaine did, it was minutely examined for any comments that might put him in a bad light; but there was nothing that he could have written that would have avoided such treatment:

Defeated by famine, we are obliged to submit to the laws of war and become prisoners. At various times in our military history brave soldiers led by Masséna, Kléber, Gouvion St Cyr etc have experienced the same fate, which did not tarnish their military honour when, like you, they had also done their duty to the limit of human endurance.

All that it was loyally possible to do to avoid this end has been done, without success. As for renewing a supreme effort to break the enemy's fortified lines, in spite of your courage and the sacrifice of thousands who gave their lives for their country, it has been rendered fruitless by the armament and the crushing forces which have held those lines. The consequence would have been a disaster.

Retain your dignity in adversity, respect the honourable conventions that have been agreed, if we are to be respected as we deserve. And above all, for the sake of the army's reputation, avoid acts of indiscipline such as the destruction of arms and materiel, so that in accordance with military custom, the fortress and its armament may be returned to France when peace is signed.

In leaving the command, I want to express to generals, officers and soldiers my appreciation of their loyal support, their brilliant courage in battle, their resignation in privation, and it is with a broken heart that I leave you. [18]

News of the imminent capitulation prompted wild talk among a number of officers who sought to overthrow Bazaine. D'Andlau was among them. Two engineer captains, Rossel and Boyenval, were involved. Arrested and brought before Bazaine, Rossel was

17   Fay, pp. 266-267.
18   Bazaine, *Episodes*, p. 248.

released, the Marshal having accepted his candid replies; Boyenval was imprisoned. Rossel was to come to a sad end, executed as an officer of the Commune by Versaillist forces in 1871. The problem for the plotters was to find someone to take the command. Ladmirault and Changarnier were approached, and indignantly refused. Clinchant, whom Montaudon, his divisional commander called his best brigade commander, turned out to have no sense of proportion; he had attended several public meetings at which he had had the most extravagant things to say. He asked that he be given 15-20,000 men with which to launch a breakthrough; only a few hundred could be found. The project, as Ruby & Regnault note, was both undisciplined and absurd; it could not but fail.[19] To his credit, Clinchant later wrote to Bazaine to express his respect for the Marshal's stoicism in the face of misfortune. Four months after the surrender of Metz, Clinchant would find himself leading another beaten French army into internment in Switzerland.

The question of the regimental colours prompted violent recriminations against Bazaine for his conduct with regard to their fate. It was a usual term of a capitulation that the regimental colours of the defeated army should be surrendered, and this symbolic gesture was, to a victorious army, very important indeed. Everyone knew this. It was therefore inevitable that the sequence of events which led to the colours of the Army of the Rhine, or most of them, falling into the hands of the Germans, should be scrutinised minutely. As a result Bazaine was subjected to the most extravagant accusations as to the part he played. Even Howard accepted some of the criticisms of the way in which he managed the terms of the capitulation. He noted that 'Bazaine's alacrity in enforcing obedience to these conditions earned him perhaps more odium than any other episode in the entire campaign.' He described how Bazaine had given particular orders for the colours to be stacked at the Arsenal; and he went on to comment that the Marshal's later protests to the effect that he intended them to be burned but that his orders were not carried out, and that the Prussians then forbade it, did him even less credit.[20]

However, Ruby & Regnault, mindful of the significance of the accusations made against Bazaine in respect of the colours in creating a generalised climate of hatred and contempt, devoted an entire chapter to the question. So convincingly did they refute the charges against Bazaine that Howard, in a footnote, accepted that they had done 'much to explain his apparently equivocal attitude over the burning of the colours.'[21]

It was in anticipation of the term that would be included in the protocol of the capitulation that, on October 26, Bazaine gave orders that they be collected and burned. According to the evidence of Captain Mornay-Soult at Bazaine's trial, the order was first given to d'Andlau to pass on to corps commanders and he refused to

19   Ruby & Regnault, p. 296.
20   Howard, p. 282.
21   Howard, p. 283n.

The colonel of the 1st Grenadiers, French Imperial Guard, destroys their colours on the surrender of Metz, painting by Lucien Mouillard. (Rousset/*Histoire*)

The surrender of Metz, painting by Freyberg. (Rousset/*Histoire*)

do so. As had been foreshadowed in Stiehle's meeting with Cissey, the protocol did indeed refer to their surrender, together with all the other military property of the army. Unfortunately, there was a further serious delay on the part first of the corps commanders and then of Soleille, who was to oversee the carrying out of the mournful task at the Arsenal. One exception was Desvaux, who had the colours of the Imperial Guard burnt before him. When the capitulation was signed, therefore, the colours, or most of them, were still in existence, and it would thereafter have been a flagrant breach of the convention for them not to be handed over, and the Germans were entitled to insist on this. Both sides were bound by the curious code that applied to the military conception of honour and neither, once Jarras had signed the capitulation, could have been expected to behave any differently. Thanks to Cissey's improbable claim that the colours had been destroyed after the revolution, which was not believed from the outset, the Germans were on their guard, and had every right to require their surrender.

On October 29, with the rain still beating down, the French soldiers made their way out of the city to the locations assigned to them. To the very great surprise of the Germans, there were far more of them than had been realised. Including the garrison, a total of 173,000 men surrendered, a figure which included 6,000 officers, over 15,000 sick and wounded, as well as *gardes mobiles* and customs officers. A total of 56 imperial eagles had survived their attempted destruction; perhaps more importantly, 622 field guns, 876 fortress guns, 72 mitrailleuses, 137,000 chassepots, 123,000 other small arms, a large quantity of ammunition and a great deal of other stores passed into German hands.[22]

During the course of the campaign, the Army of the Rhine had suffered total casualties of the 42,460 killed and wounded, among whom were 26 generals and some 2000 officers.[23]

Fay recalled the scene on the morning of October 29. He was impressed by the demeanour of the soldiers of the Imperial Guard:

> Not being able to contain my emotion, I mounted my horse and rode, eyes cast down, trying not to see the bereavement of the whole country. But at Ban St Martin, what a spectacle came into view. The place was encumbered with horses and carriages to be delivered to the enemy; the rain, which had fallen without ceasing for 48 hours, had formed a thick pall of mud. Along the glacis of the fortress, there marched forward, into the mist, the troops of the Guard; they were heading, calm and resigned, for the road to Nancy, where they would be passing in front of our enemies, and then seeking a damp bivouac, waiting to be sent to Germany. This attitude of our soldiers, so well tried, so enfeebled by their suffering and by the appalling weather, seemed as a consolation among so much misery. They went without complaint, without abuse for their leaders, carrying out their final orders and marching regularly to the inevitable rendezvous.[24]

On the morning of October 29 Bazaine rode out with some of his immediate staff to await notification that Frederick Charles was ready to receive him. The German

---

22   *Official History*, Vol. III, p. 297.
23   Ruby & Regnault, p 297
24   Fay, pp. 269-270.

Bazaine's army surrenders. (*Illustrated London News*)

Prisoners from the French Imperial Guard after the surrender at Metz.
(*Illustrated London News*)

The German troops enter Metz. (*Illustrated London News*)

commander was not immediately available, having gone to watch his troops enter the city, after the French army had marched out. Standing in the rain, the Prince, like Colonel Fay, was impressed by the soldiers of the Guard as they passed by. It was not until the afternoon that he sent a message to Bazaine, who then made his way to the German headquarters at Corny for the interview. There is a glimpse of Bazaine on this miserable journey from the pen of Archibald Forbes, the distinguished British journalist who had accompanied the German armies:

It was the day of the formal capitulation of Metz. A vast throng of infuriated citizens and of French soldiers not yet formally surrendered, was fermenting boisterously on the Ban St Martin road, on the opposite side of the Moselle from the city. Suddenly an open carriage dashed down the road, scattering the crowd to right and left. In it sat a short fat man with a heavy determined face, in the lines of which it seemed to me that there lurked some scorn. It was Marshal Bazaine ... At the sight of him there arose from the crowd a wild unanimous yell of execration. 'Down with the traitor!' 'Curse him!' 'Kill him!' were the angry cries; and infuriates dashed at the carriage and at the horses' heads only to be hustled aside by the cavalry escort. Bazaine's face never changed or blenched, and he looked down upon the people who were clamouring for his blood as if they had been dirt.[25]

Bazaine's meeting with Frederick Charles was, inevitably, awkward. The Prince did say that if ever he should need a testimonial to his loyal conduct, he would be happy to supply it.

Meanwhile, at dinner that night at Versailles Bismarck was in expansive mood, observing that the number of prisoners taken at Metz exactly doubled the previous total. He had heard that Napoleon had requested that the three marshals taken at Metz should be sent to join him at Wilhelmshöhe: 'That would make a whist party. I have no objection and shall recommend the King to do so.'[26]

25   Forbes, Archibald, *Memories of War and Peace* (London, 1895), p. 243.
26   Busch, Moritz, *Bismarck: Some Secret Pages of his History* (London, 1898), I, p. 271.

23

D'Andlau

The storm of recrimination broke over Bazaine's head as soon as the capitulation of Metz became known. Gambetta set the ball rolling. Ever since Bourbaki, prevented by Frederick Charles from returning to Metz, had on October 15 arrived at Tours to report for duty, members of the Government of National Defence had been under no illusion about the state of things at Metz. However, Gambetta's only response to the situation had been his belated letter of October 27 to Bourbaki urging him to send emissaries into the city to explain the importance of holding out as long as possible. The news of the capitulation, therefore, came as no surprise to him.

Gambetta's response was to seize the opportunity to publish a violently worded proclamation denouncing Bazaine as a traitor. In doing so, he had several motives. It was a means of demonstrating that it was the Second Empire that had brought this further catastrophe on France, following that of Sedan. It would, he hoped, serve as a rallying cry to inspire the nation to make still greater efforts in the prosecution of the war, led as it was by a government with the moral purity of republicanism. And by explaining that the capitulation was not due to a defeat for the French army, but to the personal treachery of an individual, it would bolster the people's confidence in their soldiers in the struggles to come.

His first draft was even more extravagant in its terms than what finally appeared. Even this version, however, was too much for Admiral Fourichon, who refused to sign it. The other two members of the delegation at Tours, Crémieux and Glais-Bizoin, dutifully added their names to that of Gambetta. Thiers, when he heard of it, described it as 'abominable.' It began:

> Metz has capitulated. The general on whom France counted, even after Mexico, has just deprived the nation in danger of more than 100,000 of its defenders. Marshal Bazaine has betrayed us. He has made himself the agent of the man of Sedan, the accomplice of the invader; and, contemptuous of the honour of the army of which he held the command he has given up without even making a supreme effort, 120,000 soldiers, 20,000 wounded, their rifles, their cannons, their colours and the strongest fortress in France: Metz, until

now undefiled by the stain of the enemy. Such a crime is beyond the penalties of justice.[1]

And so it went on. It was a disgraceful document; Guedalla was prepared to concede that it was 'good politics':

> It was essential, as Gambetta saw it, for Frenchmen to believe that they had not been defeated, that it was all due to some dark transaction between the Marshal and the enemy, in which the Emperor had somehow been involved. If they could only be brought to take that view, seeing in Bazaine 'l'agent de l'homme de Sedan, le complice de l'envahisseur,' all would be made plain. For then France would realise that the Empire was solely to blame for their unhappy situation and rally cheerfully to the Republic.[2]

The proclamation did not, however, go down well outside France. In England, the veteran Field Marshal Sir John Burgoyne, who could look back on a career that stretched all the way to the battle of Corunna with Sir John Moore, and who had fought in the Crimea with Bazaine, was moved to write to *The Times* to protest:

> The violent attacks against Marshal Bazaine and his condemnation for having surrendered Metz cannot fail to arouse the indignation of any impartial observer. For one thing, to accuse such a man of treason is absolutely incomprehensible. After a long and honourable life, he had nothing to gain by an act contrary to the interests of his country.[3]

Adolphe Thiers, first President of the French Third Republic.
(Private collection)

Burgoyne went on to review the circumstances in which France found herself, and the situation of the army in Metz, pointing out the impossibility of it successfully breaking out of the investment. He ended his letter:

---

1   Ruby & Regnault, p. 304.
2   Guedalla, p. 223.
3   D'Herisson, pp. 65-66.

Having served with the Marshal in the Crimea, I feel it my duty to resist the attacks made against a brave companion in arms, whose military reputation has been compromised in so inconsiderate a manner by his political enemies.[4]

But before leaving the question of Gambetta's proclamation, and its calculated dishonesty, it is instructive to note the dispatch which he sent to Crémieux, Freycinet and Laurier on Christmas Day 1870: 'Who has set up a council of enquiry to judge Bazaine? The enquiry has already been made; nobody has consulted me. I am absolutely opposed to this, and I wish you to stop these things. Reply immediately.'[5]

As d'Herisson observed, this was the language of a dictator. There had of course been no enquiry; but by this time Gambetta had no further interest in judging Bazaine. His character assassination of the Marshal had served its purpose, and a public trial would be going much too far.

Even without the stimulus of Gambetta's proclamation, there would be plenty of Frenchmen ready to seek some explanation that would excuse the comprehensive military defeats of 1870. It fell, therefore, on ears ready to accept its basic premise of treachery, and all the later critics of Bazaine could be sure of a ready audience. There were many voices raised against Bazaine even before the war ended, adding copious if mendacious detail that snowballed as time went on. Among those who hounded him in this way, it was Colonel d'Andlau's malevolent allegations, with their appearance of military verisimilitude, which would above all drive public opinion and would lead the Marshal ultimately to his trial at the Grand Trianon.

Gaston d'Andlau was born into the minor nobility on January 1 1824, and at the age of 18 went to St Cyr, passing out in 1844. He was made lieutenant in 1847, captain in 1850, lieutenant-colonel in 1864 and full colonel in 1869. He distinguished himself in the fighting before Sebastopol in 1855. On his return from the Crimea he was attached to Napoleon's staff as an orderly officer. In 1859, in the Italian campaign, he took part in the battles of Magenta and Solferino, where his service was acknowledged by being entrusted to take the Austrian colours captured during the fighting to Paris. At the end of the war he was appointed as a military attaché in Vienna, where his aristocratic background went down well. Returning to France, he was sent on a mission to Germany, where he formed a strong impression of Prussia's intentions. He wrote a book aimed at preparing the French cavalry for a conflict that appeared more and more likely. When it came, he was in due course appointed to the general staff of the Army of the Rhine.

Thereafter, so sustained was the malignancy which he was to display towards Bazaine that it calls for an explanation; and this, Ruby & Regnault were entirely convincingly able to provide. As they observed, d'Andlau was a man whose moral worth was not at the level of his intellectual capacity. He did not, it appears, enjoy a

4   D'Herisson, pp. 65-66.
5   D'Herisson, p. 171.

high reputation in the army. At the start of the campaign there occurred an incident which affords a convincing reason for d'Andlau's subsequent conduct. At that time, when Bazaine had been provisionally appointed to the command of the Army of the Rhine, d'Andlau sought a position on his personal staff. He believed it would be useful to obtain a recommendation, through the intervention of his parents, from the Countess Martel, who was close to Bazaine's wife Pepita. Some days later the countess received from the Marshal a reply scribbled in pencil:

> Pepita has sent me your message. When one is launched on such a formidable adventure, one wants only honourable and dependable people around me. This is not the case of Colonel d'Andlau. I see that you are not aware of his reputation. If you are sufficiently at ease with M.de Ludre to speak openly, tell him this. Otherwise say that my staff is complete.

Subsequently, in the course of a heated discussion, de Ludre showed the note to d'Andlau.[6] As events were to show, d'Andlau never forgot and never forgave Bazaine for this rejection. He turned next to the possibility of finding a place on the Emperor's staff, on which he had previously served, asking for a position as aide-de-camp. He met with another refusal but did manage to get appointed to the general staff, under Leboeuf. As a result he naturally found himself under Bazaine's orders after August 12.

Practically all the contemporary writers and journalists were prepared to accept at face value that d'Andlau was outstanding as a member of the general staff for his intellectual qualities and his military competence. A more clear-sighted view came from Colonel Fix, who was very familiar with the members of the staff, with whom he was in regular contact. In his view, without denying d'Andlau's intelligence, this concealed 'under the serene and indifferent ease of the epicurean that eating well had perhaps made a little heavy, a violent and passionate temperament.' Fix also noted that d'Andlau's principal occupation appeared to consist of getting his secretary to make copies of all the documents that he might be able to make use of later, without having obtained any authorisation to do so.[7]

D'Andlau was a chancer, and a thoroughly dishonest one. His later career was entirely consistent with the devious self-promotion of his military service. He entered politics, and succeeded in getting elected to the Senate in January 1876 for the Department of the Oise. There he sat on the centre-left; for all that he proclaimed himself as a Republican, he voted more than once with the right, or abstained. He had, previously, been a professed supporter of the Orleanist cause. In 1878 he was one of a group of senators who made tentative approaches to the left, although it appears that no formal links were established. In 1879 he was re-elected and continued as a

---

6   Ruby & Regnault, p. 308.
7   Ruby & Regnault, p. 309.

member of the Senate until 1886, during which time he oscillated between right and left. In 1879 he was promoted to the rank of *géneral de brigade*.

He was, however, perpetually short of money, and as time went by he began to devote himself more and more to his business affairs rather than to politics. It was his continuous search for ready cash that was in due course to prove his undoing. In 1887 it came to light that he was an active participant in a conspiracy for the sale of honours, taking money from gullible individuals who sought to be admitted to the Legion d'Honneur. It is not difficult to see d'Andlau as an extremely proficient confidence trickster. Daniel Wilson, the son in law of President, Jules Grevy, a deputy who had been allowed to have an office in the Elysee Palace, had been using it for the sale of honours on an enormous scale. D'Andlau was heavily involved in the traffic, which it was estimated had involved several thousand decorations of the Legion d'Honneur sold at some Fr.25,000 apiece. Charges were brought against d'Andlau for his part in the affair; he was not immediately arrested and was able to flee to Belgium before the case came to court. In his absence he was convicted, and sentenced to 5 years imprisonment, and fined the sum of Fr.3000. He subsequently made his way to Argentina, where he subsisted off the profits of a gambling club. He died in Buenos Aires in January 1892. Bazaine was to live long enough to hear of d'Andlau's disgrace; he would have been entitled to permit himself a wry smile when he received the news of the downfall of his nemesis.

After the fall of Metz Bazaine had proceeded, as requested, to Cassel to join the Emperor in his captivity. Napoleon had written to him on October 31, the day of his arrival there:

> I feel true satisfaction in my misfortune to learn that you are near to me. I shall be happy to express to you the warm feelings which I have for you and for the heroic army which under your orders fought so many bloody battles and perseveringly endured such unprecedented privations.[8]

MacMahon had also been invited to join the Emperor at Wilhelmshöhe but declined. Possibly he did not feel comfortable about a discussion with Napoleon of his strategy in the days leading up to Sedan, about which the latter had written to the Empress on the night before the battle: 'We have made a march contrary to all principle and commonsense; this will bring disaster.' As it was to turn out, MacMahon's military career had not ended, as he might have supposed; and he certainly could not have foreseen the role that in due course he would play in the political life of his country.

General Monts described Bazaine's appearance and demeanour on his arrival at Cassel:

8   Bazaine, *Episodes*, p. 251.

His fair hair, sparse and somewhat grizzled, and his lacklustre gaze give the aspect not of an old soldier nor the appearance of a man endowed with great energy. Nevertheless he has often shown that he does possess it. His attitude is calm and dignified.[9]

After all that Bazaine had endured it is hardly surprising that he should exhibit signs of his ordeal.

Pepita, who was heavily pregnant, soon joined him at Cassel. Eugénie, who had paid a brief visit to Wilhelmshöhe and was there when Bazaine arrived, subsequently wrote a letter warmly sympathising with him in respect of the unjustified accusations which he had to bear. Canrobert and Leboeuf did not long remain with the Emperor, who suggested that it was perhaps not in their own best interest that they extend their stay. Monts accordingly found them alternative accommodation. Bazaine, however, remained. The suggestion that he was living in considerable luxury while his men languished in prison camps embittered some of them and added to his unpopularity. In fact, Monts had installed Bazaine and his family in a small villa in a suburb of Cassel.

The Marshal faced stoically the public odium in which he was held. He had been inclined to publish an immediate and detailed refutation of the allegations made against him, but Canrobert urged him to wait until public feeling was less aroused.[10] He did however write a letter to Trochu in his capacity as head of the government, strongly protesting about the terms of Gambetta's proclamation which he said was intended 'to blacken the reputation of a Marshal of France who had served his country loyally for 40 years and whose name has never been associated with intriguing politicians of parties which divide us.'[11] Passed by the Germans to Jules Favre, Bazaine's letter seems never to have reached Trochu.

In December 1870 there came before Bazaine the most hostile denunciation that he had so far received. This was in the form of an anonymous letter which was extraordinary for the bitterness and contempt which it displayed, and remarkable for the ludicrous but apparently detailed accusations which it made against him. Published in the *Independence Belge*, it was dated November 27, from Hamburg. Ruby & Regnault set out almost in full this outrageous document 'in order to give some idea of the madness which had taken over some minds.'[12]

The author was, of course, Colonel Gaston d'Andlau, as he admitted at Bazaine's trial. Tenderly treated by the Duc d'Aumale, the president of the court, who told him that he was not obliged to answer the question, d'Andlau said that he wrote the letter at Hamburg: 'After having been dragged across the middle of Germany,

9   Ruby & Regnault, p. 302.
10   Bazaine, *Épisodes*, p. 253.
11   Bazaine, *Épisodes*, pp. 255-256.
12   Ruby & Regnault, pp. 305-308.

after having seen our arms and our cannon, I was in a state of exasperation easy to understand.'[13] Quite why he felt the need to offer an explanation is not apparent, since by the time of the trial he had written the book which had made him famous. He bluntly accused Bazaine of treason in a correspondence:

> This grief has not been spared us, and we have witnessed this shameful spectacle of a Marshal of France wishing to make his shame the steppingstone of his greatness, our disgrace the basis of his dictatorship; delivering his soldiers, without weapons, like a herd taken to the abattoir and then to the butcher, giving up their arms, their cannon, their flags to save his money and his plate.[14]

Duc d'Aumale, President of the Court Martial of Marshal Bazaine. (Private collection)

He went on at considerable length in the same vein. He claimed the 'honour of being one of the authors of the conspiracy which was formed in the first days of October to force Bazaine to march or be deposed,' listing those generals and colonels who were party to the plot and explaining that they lacked only a leader of sufficient seniority who would be able to rally the army.

D'Herisson records that this effusion caused an outcry in the army held prisoner in Germany, and that a number of officers to their honour sent letters of protest to the *Independence Belge* and other newspapers. He quoted one such from Captain de la Bégassière, who considered that the letter that had been published could only have been the work of a madman and was astonished that the newspaper should have been prepared to print it.[15] To the ensuing public controversy Bazaine contributed by publishing his official report.

With the ending of the war when Paris capitulated in January 1871, Bazaine was released. In the uncertain situation that existed in France, he took his family to live for the time being in Geneva. Cissey, who had in the meantime become War Minister,

---

13   D'Herisson, p. 176.
14   Ruby & Regnault, pp. 305-306; d'Herisson pp. 177-180.
15   D'Herisson, pp. 181-182.

advised him to remain there for the moment, as feelings against him were still running high in France. In the election that had followed the armistice, the Republicans were unsuccessful, and the new government was headed by Thiers, who had the task of negotiating the terms of peace. These were harsher than might have been obtained before the fall of Metz, but Thiers was in no position to stand out against the implacable Germans.

He soon had another fearful problem to deal with, when in March revolution broke out in Paris with the seizure of power there by the Commune, plunging France into civil war. Thiers had to find a general to lead his government's army in its war against Paris. Guedalla recounts that he was overheard reviewing possible candidates. One soldier, he thought, would have fitted the role perfectly: 'Malheureusement, il s'appelle Bazaine.'[16] Thiers had always held a high opinion of the Marshal, and he continued to look out for his interests in the months that followed. Meanwhile, it was MacMahon who was appointed to crush the revolution.

Colonel de Villenoisy was one of the officers who had been up in arms against Bazaine in the closing days at Metz; he got up a petition, which he had signed by a number of officers, calling for a court martial of those generals responsible for the surrender of Metz. The matter came before the new Assembly. On March 29, 1871 Changarnier went to the rostrum 'to avenge an army wrongly calumnied.' In a passionate address, he outlined the history of the brave army of which Prince Frederick Charles had spoken so warmly, and defended Bazaine against the allegations made. There followed subsequently a discussion as to whether there should be a Commission of Enquiry. Thiers intervened; he did not want to relive the drama of Marshal Ney, but the law which required the enquiry should be followed. It would give Bazaine the opportunity to obtain the justice which he sought, 'having had the honour to command, and to command gloriously, one of the country's most noble armies.'[17]

Unfortunately it was decided that the Commission of Enquiry should be headed by the elderly Marshal Baraguey d'Hilliers, who was not wholly dispassionate in his feelings towards Bazaine, dating from the incident in the Italian campaign of 1859 when he had forbidden Bazaine to march to the sound of the guns and been reproached by Napoleon for so doing. Nor was he any longer well-disposed to the Second Empire, to which Bazaine had remained so faithful; the Empress had accused Baraguey on September 4, when he gave up command of the troops in Paris, of having profited from the Empire in happy days only to abandon it in its adversity. Baraguey's conduct of the enquiry was regrettably to demonstrate his lack of impartiality. What was more, two members of the commission, Generals d'Aurelle de Paladines and de Sévelinges, had served under Bazaine and should, properly, have recused themselves. Worse still, its proceedings were not heard in camera, as should have been the case, and the Assembly's stenographers, who took the minutes, sold their notes to the newspapers;

16   Guedalla, p. 288.
17   Ruby & Regnault, p. 311.

and as Ruby & Regnault point out, 'it went beyond its remit by dealing with the facts which led to the capitulation of the army without it being decided if it was integrated with the fortress.'[18] Finally, Bazaine was called on only one occasion to give evidence.

No surprise, then, that the commission came down firmly against Bazaine, censuring him on four counts:

- for having entered into discussion with the enemy which led to an unprecedented capitulation;
- for not having destroyed the army's materiel;
- for not seeking to ameliorate the lot of the soldiers and of the wounded;
- for having surrendered the colours.

This judgment was pronounced in the spring of 1872. In the meantime the appalling d'Andlau had published at the end of 1871 his account of the events of 1870 under the title *Metz: Campagne et Negociations* which was an immediate success, running into nine editions by the following year. It made an immediate and substantial contribution to the public feeling against Bazaine, as d'Herisson observed:

> Colonel Count d'Andlau's book, full of false insinuations, deceitful hypotheses, illegally copied documents, the whole presented appropriately, in a facile style, fully achieved its object. This book, by itself, prepared and insured the marshal's condemnation.[19]

Written passionately and extravagantly, the book was 'a work of supreme inelegance, even indecency; in the case of disagreement with his chiefs, an officer who had profited from all the advantages of his enviable situation close to the Emperor as a member of the general staff should have remained silent. D'Andlau was embarrassed by no such scruple.'[20] The book even sought to cast blame on Bazaine for the capitulation of Sedan; to French public opinion, seeking to explain away its catastrophic military failures, it was especially convenient to concentrate all the responsibility for them on the head of one man. The influence of the book was, then, enormous; Bazaine even observed a copy of it on the table of Baraguey d'Hilliers.

The Emperor was following events closely, and wrote Bazaine on August 17, 1872 to acknowledge his birthday wishes:

> We think of you often and cannot understand how you are able to bear the accusation to which you have been subjected. I hope that your tribulations will

18   Ruby & Regnault, p. 312.
19   D'Herisson, p. 173.
20   Ruby & Regnault, p. 309.

soon be over. This trial will prove that you did all that was in your power to do. Remember me to la Maréchale and believe in my sincere friendship.

Thiers was still in power when the Commission of Enquiry published its report; intending to dismiss the proceedings in due course, he raised the possibility that Bazaine might demand a court martial, telling Pepita that he still regarded the Marshal as 'notre premier général.' Publicly, Thiers said: 'No, I will not fling the country into a disturbance like that aroused in 1815 by a trial of bitter memory, and I shall only submit the Marshal to the judgment of his peers if he demands it himself.'[21]

In his memoirs Thiers wrote that Bazaine consulted him and General du Barail, the current War Minister. He asked them what they considered he should do; 'but when he had learned that the government would not take any responsibility in answering this request, in the end he yielded to the outcries of public opinion, and in a letter which I made public, demanded a trial.'[22]

Bazaine would have been wiser to have left matters as they stood. The Assembly demanded that there be a full investigation into the events at Metz, and General Séré de Rivières was appointed to compile a report. Although the general public were displaying such violent hostility towards him, fanned by the Press, Bazaine might reasonably hope for more support from those at the head of

General du Barail, commander of French Reserve Cavalry Division. (Private collection)

the government and the army. He had, for instance, a conversation with MacMahon, who said: 'I have always stood up for you here.' To this, Bazaine replied: 'And so you ought, as you know better than anyone why we fell back on Metz.'[23] As an oblique reference to Weissenburg and Wörth, however, it was perhaps a little tactless.

Séré de Rivières was an engineer, who in the years before 1870 had been influential in the design and development of French fortresses. During the war he served as chief of the engineers of the 24th Corps in the Army of the East. Having performed well

21 Adolphe Thiers, *Memoirs 1870-1873* (London, 1915), p. 219.
22 Thiers, p. 219.
23 Guedalla, p. 230.

in the early part of the campaign, he was promoted to be chief of the army's engineers. When the war ended he took a prominent part in the operations against the Commune in Paris. When appointed to the task of preparing the report on the operations at Metz, he, having previously served under Bazaine, should also have recused himself. It was thought that he might be favourably disposed to the Marshal; but in the event he showed himself to be a furious critic, fussy and mean minded. When interviewing Bazaine he made no secret of the fact that he had made up his mind as to Bazaine's motives, frequently observing that the Marshal, believing that Paris could not hold out long, wanted to preserve his army in order to be able to impose himself on France.[24] The report which Séré de Rivières produced was extremely long, and took on the character of an indictment.

All might still have been well, had Thiers not, in May 1873, left office. One person whom he certainly would not have expected to succeed him was Marshal Patrice MacMahon, who some time earlier had in conversation with Cissey said: 'As for me, having received the command from M. Thiers, I will not go to take M. Thiers' place as President. Say so to him in order that he may not believe the absurd sayings that are being put about.'[25] By the spring of 1873 the Marshal had evidently forgotten this high-minded sentiment, and when on May 24 Thiers resigned, it was MacMahon who took his place. Thus it was a new administration that had to take the decision as to whether to proceed with the court martial, and after a short pause it was decided to do so.

There followed some considerable debate as to who should constitute the court. It was decided, by the terms of a new law passed by the Assembly that the court should consist of *généraux de division* who had commanded an army, a corps, or the artillery or engineers of an army, a decision which meant that Bazaine would be judged not by his peers but by subordinates. The debate continued over whether the court should be selected on the basis of seniority. For the Orleanists, this meant that it should be presided over by the Duc d'Aumale – or, in other words, that the July Monarchy would sit in judgment on the Second Empire. This was agreed; but many of the senior generals declined to serve on various pretexts, frequently citing ill health. Chanzy, for instance, refused to have anything to do with it, giving no reason. In the end the court consisted of Generals de la Motte-Rouge, de Chabaud-Latour, Tripier, Princeteau, Ressayre and de Malroy. Most of them were Orleanists; they were on the whole a rather moth eaten lot.

To conduct the prosecution the government assigned General Pourcet. It was not a distinguished choice. 60 years of age, he had served as Changarnier's aide-de-camp and on the general staff during the Italian campaign. When war broke out in 1870 he was serving in Algeria. Returning to France, he was appointed to the command of the 16th Corps on the Loire. This command did not last long, Freycinet writing five

24   Bazaine, *Episodes*, p. 287.
25   Thiers, p. 221.

days later that he had not been confirmed: 'He lacks initiative, he drowns himself in details; in addition, his health is poorly. In our grave situation, perhaps on the eve of a decisive battle, it is necessary to act promptly.' He was succeeded by Chanzy. Pourcet later briefly commanded the 25th Corps in a skirmish near Blois at the beginning of 1871. When due to retire he tried unsuccessfully to argue that his war service entitled him to continue on the active list regardless of his age. He did not go quietly; his farewell order to his soldiers was considered by the War Ministry to be an act of indiscipline, and it was revoked.

There was a question of whether the Duc d'Aumale had actively sought the presidency of the court. His seniority was due solely to his having been appointed as *général de division* by his father King Louis Philippe at the age of 21. Now, what he wanted was apparently a corps command; according to du Barail, he had a lot of difficulty in persuading the duke to accept the assignment. Once appointed, however, he made a great meal of it, doing all he could to demonstrate what a considerable task it was.

To defend him, Bazaine appointed the very high profile lawyer Charles Lachaud. Known for his Bonapartist sympathies, Lachaud was by some way the best-known member of the Paris Bar, renowned for his passionate addresses to juries in criminal cases. One contemporary observer remarked that his eloquence was more suited to impress 'the collection of cowards and imbeciles of which a jury is usually composed' than to convince military judges.[26]

It was at first considered that the trial might take place at Compiègne, but it was finally decided that it should be held in the Grand Trianon at Versailles, a building that had for some time been redundant, and which was accordingly fitted out for the purpose. A house in Versailles was found for Bazaine and his family, since pending the court martial he was technically under house arrest, and there, with his lawyers, he prepared his defence and received distinguished and sympathetic visitors. Notwithstanding the inordinate length and hostile conclusions of the report of Séré de Rivières, he remained confident of acquittal.

26   Ruby & Regnault, p. 319.

24

Trial

The hearing commenced on October 6, 1873. The charges which Bazaine faced were encompassed in four questions to which the court would be required to provide an answer:

First, was Marshal Francois-Achille Bazaine, ex-commander-in-chief of the Army of the Rhine guilty of having on October 28, 1870 at the head of an army in the field signed a capitulation?

Second, had this capitulation had the result of giving up the arms of this army?

Third, had Marshal Bazaine violated the law which requires that he had, before signing the capitulation, done everything called for by duty and honour?

Fourth, was Marshal Bazaine guilty of having, on October 28, 1870, capitulated to the enemy and surrendered the fortress of Metz, of which he had the supreme command, without having exhausted all the means of defence of which he disposed and without having done everything called for by duty and honour?

The charges against Bazaine were brought under two articles of the Code of Military Justice, which addressed the question of capitulations:

Article 209: Every governor or commandant is punishable by death with military degradation who, tried following an opinion of a commission of enquiry, is found guilty of having capitulated to the enemy and surrendered the fortress entrusted to him without having exhausted all the means of defence at his disposal and without having done all that was required of him by duty and honour.

Article 210: Every general and every commander of a unit of the army who capitulates in the open field is punishable:

1. By death, with military degradation if the capitulation resulted in the surrender of his troops or if, before negotiating verbally or in writing, he had not done all that was required of him by duty and military honour:
2. By dismissal in all other cases.

Article 209 was of course much the less absolute of the two, since it lets in the opinion of a commission of enquiry and does not exclude an acquittal. Article 210, on the other hand, means that any capitulation in the open field must at least merit dismissal. This was introduced by Napoleon I by Imperial decree in 1812. He had been outraged and dismayed by the capitulation of General Dupont at Bailen in 1808. It had never previously been applied. In the case of Bazaine, so significant a military disaster was the surrender of Metz that it was inevitable that a guilty verdict would bring with it the death penalty.

Such a verdict, of course, required the court to make a subjective judgement as to what was meant by the exhaustion of every means of defence or what was required by duty and military honour. There was no precise yardstick by which a court could measure such a circumstance. It may be that here, perhaps, lay the reason for the optimism with which Bazaine faced his trial, since from his point of view he could believe that no commander, in the situation of his army at the end of October 1870, could have done any more. He should, though, have reflected that in the feverish climate of public opinion that had been created in France, there would be enormous pressure on the court to convict.

As the trial proceeded and the unending procession of witnesses (there were no less than 365 in all) came and went, many of them openly hostile, the spiteful aggression of the prosecution and the demeanour of the court must surely have led Bazaine to doubt whether his early confidence in the outcome had been justified.

There was no reference to treason in the wording of the four questions. There did not have to be, since the suggestion that this might have been Bazaine's motivation for his conduct hung like a cloud over the proceedings. A number of witnesses were called expressly to give evidence of the Marshal's treasonable activities. The testimony of many of these was frankly absurd, and their evidence was exposed for what it was worth. Guedalla cites the evidence of one such, for instance: 'A French schoolmistress, who swore that she had overheard some German generals suggesting (at the tops of their voices, it would appear, and in French) that it would be a good idea to bribe Bazaine.'[1] Other witnesses claimed that Bazaine was in the habit of crossing from the French lines to the German, presumably there to engage in treacherous discussions with the enemy. These allegations were comprehensively rebutted by the evidence of General de Place, the commander of the advanced French positions at Moulins, and by Commandant Danloux, the commander of Bazaine's cavalry escort, who dismissed these tales as a 'popular fable;' and by Captain Mornay-Soult, who

---

1   Guedalla, pp. 241-242.

invariably accompanied Bazaine when he left his headquarters. Then again there was a maidservant who testified to having served dinner several times to Bazaine and Frederick Charles at the latter's headquarters at Corny. In spite of the obvious absurdity of this, the Duc d'Aumale allowed her evidence to be heard. The fact that grotesque allegations such as these could be seriously put forward illustrates the extent to which the authorities had allowed themselves to be swayed by the feverish atmosphere of hate and suspicion that had built up around Bazaine. Attention seeking individuals found in the prosecution a ready market for their wares. However, by the end of the hearing none of this nonsense carried any weight.

The verbatim record of the proceedings was made available by the prosecution to private publishers, who brought out editions of this, accompanied by comments, before and after each day's hearing. These, such as the edition published by Auguste Ghio in Paris in 1874, were almost uniformly hostile to Bazaine, making comments about him as the trial went on. They also noted the names of the great and the good, from France and from abroad, who attended each day's hearing, and the reactions of the audience to the evidence being given. On October 17, for instance, it was suggested that there was much discussion among the public about the lack of contact between Bazaine and the Government of National Defence. The commentator went on to observe that 'the replies of the Marshal appeared to have made an unfortunate impression on the members of the court.'[2]

The hearing began, after the reading out of Bazaine's service record, with a reading by a clerk of Séré de Rivières' interminable report. Once this had been done, the court heard Bazaine's rejoinder. Very much shorter, it nonetheless addressed the central facts of Bazaine's plight and that of his army. One sentence of this document summed up Bazaine's case:

> When the final moment came and it was clear that a last effort was impossible, I sacrificed myself with the memory of my own feelings as a private in Africa forty years ago. I did not feel that I had the right to make a vain sacrifice for empty glory of those lives that were so precious to their country and their families.[3]

It was not until October 13 that the trial reached the point where Bazaine was to be cross-examined by the Duc d'Aumale. The president of the court was anxious to demonstrate that he had fully mastered his brief; his questions contained much detail and were usually very much longer than the Marshal's replies. By October 17 the cross examination, conducted more or less chronologically, had reached the time of the capitulation of Metz:

2   *Procès* p. 88.
3   Guedalla, p. 236.

D'Aumale: Do you believe that the situation at September 29 was such that you could confer on yourself the right to treat with the enemy?

Bazaine: I believe that I had that right from the moment that I no longer was in communication with the lawful government or with the Government of National Defence. I believed myself to be free, I was not merely the commandant of the fortress and, as commander-in-chief I was, by acting in this way, serving my country.

D'Aumale: You believe that this right belongs to the commander-in-chief – I do not speak of the commandant of the fortress – who has the honour to command and to defend the fortress of Metz and would not have been below a Marshal of France? We find numerous and glorious examples in our history. I ask you if, as commander-in-chief, on September 29, you judged that the situation was such that you could give yourself the right to conclude a military convention when, according to you, it is necessary to read 'military convention' into the words 'capitulation with the honours of war.'

Bazaine: There was no precedent for my situation. I no longer had a government. I was, you might say, my own government; there was no one to direct me, I was directed only by my conscience.

D'Aumale: Was this preoccupation with negotiation, then, of greater weight in your mind than the strict execution of your military duty?

Bazaine: Yes: I perfectly accept that military duty is binding when there is a legal government, which has taken power recognised by the country, but not when one is faced with an insurrectionary government. I do not accept that.

D'Aumale: There was always France.[4]

This crisp reproach made a considerable impression; but, as Ruby & Regnault point out, what did it amount to?

What would the duke have replied if his interlocutor had asked him to be more precise? The part of France that was occupied, or the part under the orders of a government which a soldier of the Empire could not recognise and which had not been in touch with him? Bazaine would have been entitled to reply that he had never ceased to take as one the interest of France with that of the Empire.[5]

Public attention was of course focused on the more senior ornaments of France's defeated army who came to give evidence after that of Bazaine:

The prisoner was followed by an endless line of witnesses, as marshals tramped into the box to give warm testimonials to themselves, but rarely to each other; and

4   *Procès*, p. 90.
5   Ruby & Regnault, p. 324.

spectators were regaled with Canrobert's vivacity and the solemnity of Leboeuf. At one stage the evidence took an exciting turn, when it appeared to indicate that MacMahon might actually have been responsible for his own defeat; and it was quite dramatic when Palikao crossed the court to shake Bazaine by the hand.[6]

Palikao had insisted on giving his evidence standing. Much that he had to say concerned the march of the Army of Châlons; he was asked by Lachaud whether the army had in his opinion been in any danger during the night of August 25/26. Not at all, he replied: 'I had good reason to believe the contrary having regard to the positions of the enemy.'[7]

With the completion of the evidence, the time came for the closing speeches. First came that for the prosecution. From one session to the next General Pourcet had shown himself as aggressive, bitter and petty. His attitude had been entirely consistent with the tone of the document produced by Séré de Rivières. When he came to deliver his summing up, he read it in a flat monotone. That one hears what one wants to hear may be shown by du Barail's reference to it in his memoirs as having been delivered with 'passion.' The legal journal Le Droit, on the other hand, claimed that it had been delivered 'without passion, simple without being dry, dignified without emphasis.'[8]

Lachaud remarked that he had never, in his whole career, heard an indictment like it. Another to comment was Paul Lenoir, the author of a book on the capitulation of Metz. Pourcet's summing up was, he wrote, 'a veritable tissue of malicious insinuations, unjustified statements and colossal mistakes; it was the most monstrous charge to which any man, above all a soldier, even if ambitious, even if acting under orders, could attach his name.'[9] According to Lenoir, the author of this poisonous diatribe was Challemel-Lacour, a confidant of Gambetta. Ruby & Regnault find this not improbable. It had evidently been prepared somewhat earlier, since the most absurd allegations given in evidence had long since been exploded, but still appeared in Pourcet's summing up.

This performance continued from December 3 until December 6; it occupied 164 pages of the text of the verbatim report of the proceedings and ended predictably for a call that Bazaine be convicted under Articles 209 and 210. The courtroom was completely full to hear Lachaud rise on December 7 to give his closing address:

> Lachaud's plaidoirie, extremely noble to read, perhaps insufficiently precise, must have been extraordinarily compelling. It occupied four sessions. Among the finest passages, it is necessary to cite that in which the orator took Gambetta to task, who had known for a fortnight that the Army of Metz was doomed,

6   Guedalla, p. 239.
7   Procès, p. 221.
8   Procès, p. 401.
9   Lenoir, Paul, Le Maréchal Bazaine et la Capitulation de Metz quoted in Ruby & Regnault, pp. 324-325.

did nothing to assist it and insulted its leaders, heaping on them ignominious abuse that the prosecutor was content to dismiss as 'suspicions' ... Lachaud's great effort naturally pointed out that Bazaine, with no room to manoeuvre, surrounded by the works and batteries of the enemy, could not be considered a combatant in the open field.[10]

Lachaud also spoke at considerable length, concluding on December 10. In reply, Pourcet called for the death penalty as being the first lesson, for the 140,000 recruits just now putting on their uniform, of the severe and noble duty that it imposed on them. To this Lachaud responded, magnificently:

I had thought that it would have been enough to demand the head of a Marshal of France, that there was no satisfaction to be had in wanting to decapitate the army. I was wrong ... My last word will also be addressed to those soldiers, those 140,000 young men to whom, in order that they may learn discipline, it is necessary to show that a Marshal of France is a traitor. Ah! You consider that this is a fine example. It would be better, to my mind, it would be better for them to learn that calumny does not avail when it is aimed at the innocent, that the army does not blush for shame or fear to raise its head; that if one of its leaders was unfortunate, he was not unworthy, and that the honour of the army was unscathed save for this ordeal ... I have faith in justice, I have faith in God, I have faith in you, and I do not fear an act of iniquity.[11]

When Lachaud sat down there was a general murmur of approval, which was quickly stilled.

Bazaine was then asked by the duke if he had anything to add. He rose, the medal of the Legion d'Honneur prominent on his chest, and in a firm voice said: 'I have in my heart two words: 'Honneur et Patrie,' which have guided me throughout my military life. I have never departed from this noble motto, neither at Metz or anywhere else, during the forty two years I have loyally served my country. I swear this here, before Christ.'[12]

The court rose at 4:35 p.m.. It returned at 8:55 p.m., and the Duc d'Aumale announced the court's conclusion on the four questions which had been posed. Bazaine and his lawyers were not present as the answers were read out before a hushed audience. To each question the answer was, unanimously, 'yes.' The duke went on to state that in view of Articles 210 and 209 the court ' unanimously sentences François-Achille Bazaine, Marshal of France to death, with military degradation.' The audience was stunned; many women burst into tears.

---

10   Ruby & Regnault, p. 327.
11   *Procès*, pp. 630-635.
12   *Procès*, p. 635.

After announcing that the accused had 24 hours in which to lodge an appeal, the court rose. The sentence was communicated to Bazaine in an adjoining room, in the presence of Colonel Willette, his aide-de-camp; Pourcet ordered the clerk to read the sentence. Bazaine asked if that was all; Pourcet replied that it was, and Bazaine, who had remained entirely impassive said: 'Shoot me as soon as possible; I am ready.' He at once intimated that he would not appeal.

What was striking about the judgment was that it gave no reasons. Presumably, if there had been an appeal, these must have been provided, since the alternative to an appraisal of the reasons for the verdict would have had to be a rehearing. Where a decision was made that an accused had not done all that duty in military honour required, the reasoning for a decision based on vague and cloudy concepts of that kind was all the more necessary if it was to be accepted as fair. And this, in the present instance, was very far from being the case.

That night Bazaine sat down to write a letter to Charles Lachaud:

> My dear and valorous defender,
> At this supreme moment, I write to thank you with all my soul for the heroic efforts you have made in upholding my cause. If such great eloquence as you have drawn from the expression of the truth, and the dedication of your noble heart, could not convince my judges it is because they were not to be convinced; because in your admirable words you did more than was humanly possible.
>
> I shall not appeal. I do not want to prolong before the whole world a spectacle so mournful, and I ask you not to take any step in my favour.
>
> It is no longer from men that I seek justice; it is from time; it is in the moderating of passions that I hope will bring my justification.
>
> I await, firm and resolute, strong in my conscience that I have done nothing with which to reproach myself, the execution of the sentence.[13]

When she heard the news, the Empress was quick to respond, telegraphing to Rouher: 'I am distressed by the sentence. Make known to Marshal Bazaine that I wish I could soften his cruel moments.'

From London, Sir John Burgoyne wrote a warmly sympathetic letter to Bazaine, with whom, he said, he had the honour and pleasure to serve, and to tell him that among all classes in England there was profound sympathy for their former allies in their misfortune.

Bazaine had always been a believer, and in his misfortune sought consolation in his religion. His letters to his younger son, published in 1905, demonstrate a profound faith. During his period of house arrest at Versailles Bazaine saw the local curé daily, to whom he regularly made his confession. On December 12 the Bishop of Verdun wrote movingly to the curé to express his sorrow at the appalling news of the sentence:

13   *Procès*, p. 639.

With the Marshal, I protest against a condemnation that disavows impartial history. For the last twenty four hours I have shared all the anguish, all the heartbreak of the family and friends of the illustrious and innocent condemned man. With him, I forgive his judges; but I regret that they could not rise above the passionate impulses of opinion, for their responsibility appears to me to be harder to bear than that of the victim.

Thank you, dear friend, for all the tenderness, all the respect, all the devotion that you have given. I join with all your sentiments; please say to the unfortunate Marshal, for whom I pray constantly, that he remains always a Christian soldier and confident in the justice of God, which unlike that of man never fails and which compensates a hundredfold for what death takes from us.

The Bishop was entirely certain of Bazaine's innocence, not least because the Marshal had authorised the curé to communicate his confessions to him.[14]

However, the court, immediately after sentence had been pronounced, delivered a letter to the War Minister calling on President MacMahon to commute the sentence. The reasons given for this were Bazaine's long and distinguished service since 1831; the wounds that he had suffered; his actions which had merited the award of his baton as Marshal; and the fact that he was not responsible for the disastrous start to the campaign.

That night Pepita, following up the appeal from Bishop Dupanloup to MacMahon that he should exercise clemency, went to the Elysée Palace, and demanded an audience. Assured that a reprieve would be granted, she withdrew. Nothing more was heard all next day; but at midnight a messenger came to the Trianon to tell Bazaine that the president had commuted the sentence to twenty years' imprisonment. Commenting on this, Ruby & Regnault observed that perhaps MacMahon, the former commander of the 1st Corps and of the Army of Châlons, saw in the condemnation of Bazaine an absolution for his own mistakes, weaknesses and hesitations. Had he, after all, done all he could to come to Bazaine's aid? And what of his previous disorderly retreat after Wörth, which had obliged Bazaine himself to retreat on Verdun? Asked many years later about the case, MacMahon said that he had expected that Bazaine would be acquitted, and added: 'Was he really guilty? He did not defend himself.'[15]

After learning of the commutation of the sentence, which also cancelled the offensive provision for military degradation, Bazaine wrote to MacMahon politely acknowledging his decision and suggesting, perhaps ironically, that MacMahon had let his heart rule his duty. Little time was wasted in packing Bazaine off to prison; it was decided that he should be incarcerated in the citadel of Ste Marguerite, on the largest of the Iles de Lerins, off the coast between Antibes and Cannes. The citadel was made famous by Alexandre Dumas who located it as the prison which housed the

14   Ruby & Regnault, p. 333.
15   Ruby & Regnault, p. 333.

'Man in the Iron Mask.' Willette accompanied him in his imprisonment; and so did Pepita, bringing with her their younger children.

The conditions in which Bazaine was held were not unpleasant; there were several rooms to accommodate him and his family, together with Colonel Willette and two maids. The governor, M. Marchi, was not an unreasonable man. The climate was all that might be expected from an island just off the coast of southern France. There was no restriction placed in the way of visitors to the island. But Bazaine quickly became bored, while Pepita had soon made up her mind that he should make his escape. This was a project which the Marshal at first resisted, but she continued to press the idea on him. D'Herisson, writing of the period of Bazaine's imprisonment, described her as 'pretty, seductive, devoted, with a courage almost manly at certain moments, and fundamentally ambitious.' It was not long before Bazaine yielded to her persuasion, and they began to plan the escape.

Before, however, putting this into effect, Pepita made a final effort to secure Bazaine's release, travelling to Paris with her brother-in-law to seek an audience with MacMahon. According to d'Herisson, the president received the two supplicants coldly:

> La Maréchale reminded him that her husband was his former comrade, his chief, who had gloriously worn his epaulette for forty two years; that, if they had the right to shoot him, they did not have the right morally to torture him for the rest of his days. But nothing helped. Marshal MacMahon remained inflexible.[16]

He understood, he said, why such an appeal was made, but he could do nothing. However, it was possible to have some hope for the future. Hope, Pepita replied tartly, belonged to God; he gave it to everyone. So saying, she withdrew, and returned to the Ile Ste Marguerite to finalise her plans with Colonel Willette and Captain Doineau, one of Bazaine's officers from his African days.

This involved chartering a steamer at Genoa, which was to lie off the island. A rowing boat, hired from the Croisette at Cannes, would arrive at the foot of the 75 foot cliff, down which the portly Marshal, suspended on a rope attached to a convenient gargoyle on the wall of the citadel, would lower himself. On the evening of August 9, 1874 the plan was put into effect. Half an hour before Bazaine's rooms were due to be secured by the guards, Willette let him down to the beach below, where the rowing boat was waiting. All went well; by midnight the party was aboard the steamer *Ricasoli*, and next morning Bazaine went ashore in Italy. Willette now left the island and took the train to Paris. Subsequently he and Doineau, with Marchi and the three guards were put on trial; Marchi and two of the guards were acquitted, but Willette and Doineau (who were represented by Charles Lachaud) and the third guard were convicted and sentenced to a few months' imprisonment.

16   D'Herisson, p. 299.

The decision to escape was, in the opinion of Ruby & Regnault, a mistake. Sooner or later, they reckoned, he would have been released. Locked up, Bazaine was a nuisance to the government; having escaped, even though he had not given his parole not to do so, he revived memories of his supposed wrongs. On the other hand, it must be said that popular feeling against Bazaine had not subsided, and it would have been a bold French government that would fly in the face of popular opinion and release him.[17]

He and Pepita had naturally discussed what he might do once he was again a free man; she believed strongly that he should seek a military command from the Carlists, who once again were rising in revolt in Spain. This suggestion, however, he was not prepared to entertain in any circumstances; he had served Queen Isabella in his younger days when a member of the Foreign Legion, and would always remain loyal to her, as indeed she had been to him. For once, he did not succumb to Pepita's insistent persuasion. In the first instance, Bazaine and his family travelled to Switzerland, where the recently widowed Empress Eugénie was staying with the Prince Imperial. From there, Bazaine went on to Cologne; he wrote to the War Minister in an effort to exonerate Willette and Marchi, and his servant Auguste Bareau, in connection with his escape.[18] He then travelled to Belgium. While there he wrote a long letter for publication in the *New York Herald* which contained a very much more hard-hitting defence of his actions at Metz than he had put forward previously.

He was thereafter a very busy correspondent, writing many letters in which he restated the iniquity of his conviction. He was disappointed by what, as he saw it, had become the forgetfulness of the Imperial family, observing to a correspondent in 1876 that his conduct towards the Empress 'could not have been more loyal, and her ingratitude is manifest.'[19] He did, though, remain in touch with the Imperial circle in England, to a member of which he wrote in March 1879: 'What a mess the Government of our country is in. I hope they are beginning to understand the conduct of the loyal 'modern Bayard,' the defeated hero; and what a gang of crooks our parliamentarians are! When is the clean sweep coming? I am all ready for it.'[20] His reference to MacMahon as the 'modern Bayard' was underlined in red pencil.

Above all, however, he devoted his time to writing a detailed account of the events of 1870. This was published in Madrid in 1883 with the title *Episodes de le Guerre de 1870 et le Blocus de Metz*. He dedicated the book movingly to Queen Isabella, acknowledging her constant goodwill towards him in bad times as well as in good. It is a book about which there are two views. For Philip Guedalla, 'the whole unhappy story was set out in detail without bitterness, and he closed with a good Frenchman's prayer for his country, which was met with abuse.'[21] Ruby & Regnault, on the other hand, found it confused, badly written, and thought that it did not silence the controversy, but

---

17   Ruby & Regnault, p. 338.
18   Bazaine, *Episodes*, p. 298.
19   Ruby & Regnault, p. 342.
20   Guedalla, p. 254.
21   Guedalla, p. 255.

rather the reverse. He did, though, make a firm response on the subject of Canrobert, Ladmirault and Frossard, and above all on the silence of MacMahon.[22]

In the many letters which Bazaine received, there were significant phrases used by former Bonapartist ministers and others such as Rouher, Schneider, Bourgoing and the Duc de Gramont, which were by no means merely simple and banal expressions of sympathy. In their letters to him are to be found expressions such as 'fidelity in captivity,' as well as 'abnegation' and 'future reparation.' Ruby & Regnault ask themselves whether these comments do not indicate that 'in all the tortuous negotiations of Metz, in the face of an extraordinary situation, he was a man who sacrificed to his sovereigns his life and his honour and who in their interest, did not defend himself?'[23]

Bazaine's exile was certainly lightened by the constant support of some at least of his former colleagues, who, to their credit, remained in touch with him. Notable amongst them was General Desvaux, who wrote regularly to assure him of his support and respectful sympathy in the Marshal's misfortune. So too did General Justin Clinchant, notwithstanding that he had been one of those involved in the agitation among senior officers in the last days at Metz. Another was Commandant Magnan, the officer on Bazaine's staff chosen to bring news of the Army of the Rhine after the battle of Vionville-Mars la Tour. Above all, there was the faithful Willette, who cheerfully sacrificed his career to his belief in the Marshal's innocence.

Archibald Forbes, who had seen Bazaine on the day of the capitulation of Metz, saw him next at the Trianon, 'arraigned on a capital charge before a tribunal that could scarcely dare to acquit him even if he should prove his innocence; yet he confronted fate here with the same impassive phlegm as he had faced the populace of Metz.'[24] Forbes wrote that he had never believed in the accusations of treachery, holding Bazaine 'to have been a heavy, unenterprising, plodding, fairly honest sort of man,' who had done what he believed was best. In his opinion, had Bazaine had subordinates 'honest and capable of cooperating with him,' and had his army's morale not been so damaged before he took command, 'it might have been that the chroniclers of the war would have had a different tale to tell.' Forbes published a vindication of Bazaine's conduct, in which he wrote: 'The French nation, which sought to be relieved of all the injustices suffered by a people bitterly ashamed, tortured by a humiliated pride, was possessed of a furious desire to have a scapegoat.' He later received in 1883 a grateful letter from the Marshal:

> I feel that I must express to you my gratitude for your article on my iniquitous trial. It certainly is very late to attempt to influence public opinion, purposely prejudiced as it has been by all parties, in order to save the national vanity, as well as the several responsibilities of the Governments of the Empire and of that of

---

22   Ruby & Regnault, p. 339.
23   Ruby & Regnault, pp 340-341; Bazaine, *Episodes*, pp. 291-293.
24   Forbes, pp. 343-344

the National Defence. But truth always prevails in the end, and your conscientious article should have a great effect. There are many things I could say, not to defend myself – my conscience as general in chief has no reproaches to make to me; but to enlighten upright men and open their eyes to their own shortcomings at that epoch. A scapegoat was searched for, who offered himself up; and the French nation, reckoned so generous, relieved itself of all responsibility by transferring it to the head of the soldier, a self-made man, who having spent forty years of his life in campaigning in the four quarters of the earth, had no personal friends among the politicians in power; and who had no supporters once the Empire was overthrown and the Republic took its place. Again thanks, and a hearty clasp of the hand.[25]

Each year, the grim recollection of the months of August, September and October, which he called his 'season of black memories' brought renewed sadness. In 1887 Bazaine suffered an injury to his face when he was attacked with a knife by a crazed commercial traveller; his assailant was sentenced by a Spanish court to a lengthy term of imprisonment. But the Marshal's health was deteriorating. In the autumn of 1888, Pepita was in Mexico with her daughter when Bazaine's heart failed; he died on September 25. Only a small party of Spaniards, his sons and a French priest followed his coffin to a grave in the foreign cemetery.

25   Forbes, p. 344.

25

Conclusion

Helmuth von Moltke, in his history of the Franco-Prussian War first published in 1891, expressed the way in which Bazaine's situation had been generally perceived abroad:

> There is no doubt that Bazaine was influenced, not wholly by military, but also by political considerations; still it may be asked whether he could have acted differently in the prevailing confusion of France. From the correspondence referred to, and his behaviour in the battles before Metz, his reluctance to quit the place was evident. Under its walls he could maintain a considerable army in unimpaired condition till the given moment. As the head of the only French army not yet shattered, he might find himself in a position of greater power than any other man in the country. This army must, of course, first be freed from the bonds which now confined it. Even if it did succeed in forcibly breaking out, it would be greatly weakened; and it was not inconceivable that the Marshal, as the strongest power in the land, might be able to offer a price which should induce the enemy to grant him a passage ...That the Marshal, if his plans had come to fulfilment, would have acted otherwise than in the interest of France is neither proved nor to be assumed ... That he was subsequently charged with treason obviously arose, no doubt, from the national vanity of the French, which demanded a 'traitor' as a scapegoat for the national humiliation.[1]

One of the most influential of those to have reviewed in detail the question of the capitulation of Metz was General Bartholémy Palat. He was a very well respected French historian, who produced a number of authoritative books on the Franco-Prussian War. He usually wrote under the pseudonym Pierre Lehautcourt. In 1908 he published volume 7 of his *Histoire de la Guerre de 1870,* which dealt with the capitulation of Metz. He returned to the subject, this time dealing particularly with Bazaine,

---

1   Moltke, p. 104.

in 1913, when he published *Une Grande Question d'Histoire et de Psychologie: Bazaine et nos Désastres en 1870*. In both works he is extremely critical of the Marshal; his views reflect the opinions that were still generally held at the time. His writing is so authoritative that it is only with great diffidence that his opinion can be questioned.

Palat's final conclusions in the later book were more concerned with Bazaine's attempts to negotiate a settlement than with his military decisions during the investment. He accepts the standard view that in his retreat after the battle of Vionville-Mars la Tour, Bazaine had already made up his mind to seek refuge in Metz rather than to make a final attempt to defeat the enemy. Palat considers that by offering battle in the Amanvillers position Bazaine was merely justifying his decision to retreat. After that, with the definitive retirement of the army under the guns of Metz, Palat's view was that Bazaine, in military terms, did nothing and awaited events.

In considering the subsequent negotiations, Palat dismissed some of the more ludicrous allegations, such as the suggestion that Bazaine treasonably accepted a bribe to surrender Metz, or that he held secret meetings with Prince Frederick Charles. But he finds the Marshal guilty of political ambition in his dealings through Regnier, Bourbaki and Boyer: 'His dishonest compromises are sufficiently explained by the desire to play a role in a restoration which he believed to be imminent.'[2] That is one way of looking at it; but what Bazaine was doing accorded with his military oath, and preserving the army was his first concern. If offering Bismarck the chance to negotiate a stable peace was the way to achieve this, then so be it.

Palat concluded his latter study by repeating a savage personal denunciation of Bazaine:

> Bazaine, who was neither very intelligent nor very perceptive, as is often claimed, whose military and moral value was very thin, was not up to the situation into which circumstances had elevated him. Egoistic calculations led him to the worst mistake a commander of an army can commit: to make domestic politics one of his actions against the enemy.[3]

And he brushes aside what he calls 'timid attempts at rehabilitation,' such as the books published by d'Herisson and Elie Peyron.

But Bazaine's mistake, if it was a mistake, was to look at his situation as a whole. Merely to put his head down and treat his responsibility as solely a matter of military calculation would have been to ignore his wider duty to France. Once he had become aware of Regnier's intervention, which brought the possibility of negotiation with Bismarck, he would have been delinquent to have disregarded it. Thereafter, events did not work out favourably, and were to show that negotiations were a dead end; but he could not have known that this would be the case.

2   Palat, p. 343.
3   Palat, pp 345-346

Turning to the most shrill of Bazaine's subsequent critics, for Alfred Duquet there was of course virtually no limit to the Marshal's crimes, and it is scarcely necessary to say more than that Duquet entirely endorsed the prosecution's case at the Trianon and regretted that the sentence was not carried out. He does not, however, stop with the Marshal. He quotes with satisfaction comments made and repeated by Séré de Rivière and Pourcet to the effect that it was not only Bazaine who was guilty: 'The documents which we have had in our hands are damning of a number of general officers.'[4] Nor does Duquet spare MacMahon:

> As for Marshal MacMahon, if one cannot charge him with a crime as defined by the law, he had, nevertheless, in the course of his unfortunate campaign committed so many mistakes, giving proof of his incapacity, which brought with them so many disasters, that it was uncomfortable for him to be severe on others, or to call for the legal action which several of his friends feared.[5]

An English author, Captain Henry Brackenbury wrote, following the ending of the Franco-Prussian War, a book under the title *Les Maréchaux de France,* which was published in 1872, but which, almost at once, he caused to be withdrawn in view of Bazaine's forthcoming trial. Since his book was extremely critical of the Marshal, he felt it would be inappropriate to publish a work which extensively dealt with matters that were *sub judice.* He displayed a clearer sense of the proprieties than the French authors who had, one after another, cumulatively added to the strength of public feeling against Bazaine. Regrettably, it should be added, Captain Brackenbury appears to have swallowed whole a large number of d'Andlau's assertions, quoting extensively from the latter's book.

Among the contemporary voices that were raised in protest against Bazaine's treatment was that of Comte d'Herisson. His book was one of a not inconsiderable number which were so slightingly dismissed by Palat as 'timid attempts'at the Marshal's rehabilitation. The scheme of *La Legende de Metz* is not chronological, and is therefore somewhat confusing, but it is most certainly not 'timid,' and mounts a robust defence of Bazaine while unsparing of his detractors such as d'Andlau and the moving spirits of the prosecution. It was d'Herisson's intention to allow the many documents which he cited to speak for themselves. It was, he considered, a patriotic duty 'not to leave weighing heavily on one head the whole weight of all the mistakes which were made, and to establish an exact account of the responsibilities, whoever may be affected.'[6]

Subsequent historians might have been expected to have some measure of detachment, but, as has been seen, this was not always the case. It is therefore a relief to turn away from the rancid bile of such as Alfred Duquet to a more modern assessment

---

4   Duquet, p. 328.
5   Duquet, p. 328.
6   D'Herisson, p. viii.

of Bazaine and the events surrounding the fall of Metz. Generals Ruby & Regnault produced an outstanding piece of research and analysis. Writing in 1960, they had the benefit in particular of the publication in 1932 of the memoirs of Napoleon III's aide, General Castelnau and the post-war release of the German Foreign Ministry archives. They succeeded in comprehensively demolishing the allegations of treachery against Bazaine, and painstakingly set out his story in the confused context of the time. They demonstrate that, as to his honour, the Marshal most certainly deserves rehabilitation. On the other hand, they recognise that he was blameworthy for various failings, weaknesses and error. They put their conclusions thus:

> Was Bazaine a traitor? No. This suggestion is rejected as being absolutely absurd.
>
> Was he incapable? No, but the situation he inherited on August 13 was more than compromised; the army he took over was inferior in every respect to the enemy. He succumbed to the difficulties of his task and the burden of his command. Poorly supported, poorly obeyed, he did not wield the iron fist which alone could redress his tragic situation.
>
> At Metz, was he a victim of his obedience and his loyalty to his sovereigns? The documents recently revealed show that his conduct in the course of the negotiations was in accordance with the intentions of the Emperor and the Empress, and that his attitude at the Trianon was inspired by the noble desire that these not be disclosed.[7]

The most authoritative study of the Franco-Prussian War is still in many ways that of Michael Howard. Ruby & Regnault's *Bazaine: Coupable ou Victime?* was published while his own book was already in the press, and he was therefore unable to make use of some of the material which it contained. As previously noted, he was, however, able to incorporate a brief reference to its conclusions:

> The book is an ably argued defence of Bazaine, which not only destroys completely the charge of treachery but does much to explain his apparently equivocal attitude over the burning of the colours. But it does nothing to clear him of the charge of military incompetence.[8]

Howard does, however, make the point that other soldiers have faced situations no less agonising, 'and not all have emerged from the ordeal with any great credit than Marshal Bazaine.'

There is really no convincing reason to suppose that any of the higher commanders of the French Imperial army would have done significantly better. Canrobert's reluctance to accept responsibility does not suggest that he could have wielded the

---

7   Ruby & Regnault, p. 356.
8   Howard, p. 283n.

necessary 'iron fist,' while MacMahon's record in 1870 was arguably rather worse than that of Bazaine. There was nothing in the performance of the other senior corps commanders to indicate that they would have improved on the Marshal's discharge of his responsibilities. Bazaine is frequently cited as a classic example of a man promoted beyond the level of his abilities. The fact is that neither Bazaine nor MacMahon ever expected to exercise supreme command. During the years of peace, as well as during the first weeks of war, the only supreme commander contemplated was the Emperor himself. This principle was well established; when, for instance, Canrobert, Bazaine and Failly were in command of expeditionary forces, they had been closely supervised by Napoleon from home.[9]

It is for his conduct of the battle of Vionville-Mars la Tour that Bazaine has been most heavily criticised. He displayed, it has been contended, a lack of urgency; it was a characteristic that he shared with other prominent French generals, most notably MacMahon. It was partly due to excessive caution. On August 16 neither he nor Canrobert ever appreciated the actual strength of the German forces with which they were immediately engaged. Both were sufficiently deceived by Alvensleben's bold front.

In hindsight, the time factor is immediately apparent, and writers have been impatient with the failure of Bazaine and his senior commanders to have grasped the need for haste. Another criticism, which also applies with as much force to his staff and his divisional and corps commanders, is of his failure to do more to locate the actual position of the enemy. It is astonishing, for instance, that Forton, neither late on August 15 nor on the morning of the battle, did not attempt any effective reconnaissance. Once battle was joined, the same criticism applies to all those senior commanders facing, or about to face, the enemy.

Nor, it appears, did Jarras do anything by way of calling for reconnaissance to be undertaken. The result was that Bazaine fought the battle in more or less complete ignorance of the position of his adversaries. Nevertheless, in ordering first Leboeuf and then Ladmirault to advance on his right wing, Bazaine created a real opportunity for a victory. He was perfectly aware of this, as was shown by his observation that once Ladmirault appeared 'all would be swept away.'

Throughout the day Bazaine certainly was cautious; justifiably so, since he had seen Frossard's corps on his left badly beaten, and it is unsurprising that he should have taken steps to bolster his position there, or that he should have been uneasy that Steinmetz might get in behind him. The battle brought out the best and the worst in Bazaine. All day he had displayed the courage for which he was famed and which served as a major inspiration to his men; but he exercised little control over the battle until the time came to determine what should follow.

9   Holmes, *The Road to Sedan*, p. 59; Aronson, Theo, *The Fall of the Third Napoleon* (London, 1970), p. 244.

By nightfall his plan to take up the Amanvillers position was almost certainly the army's best option. Analysing its situation, General Bonnal pointed out that even if the army had pressed on, and had, improbably, been able to reach Verdun, it would have been trapped a few days later between the Meuse and the Argonne: 'Marshal Bazaine's solution was the only wise one, given the inadequacy of the high command and the waste of time between August 7 and 12.'[10] Bazaine was entirely convinced of the stopping power of the modern rifle, and particularly of the chassepôt; wherever possible, it was his intention to use the advantage which this gave to the defence, and in taking up the Amanvillers position he had a perfect opportunity to exploit the weapon's superiority.

Having selected a defensive position that was extremely strong, it is certainly true that on August 18 Bazaine was content to play a largely passive role, leaving the conduct of the battle for much of the day to his corps commanders. Once defeat became apparent, he had no choice but to retreat under the guns of the fortress of Metz. Thereafter, the key decisions which he had to make concerned the attempts to break through the German lines which surrounded his army. He correctly concluded, after Noisseville, that a successful breakout was impossible, since even if the army forced itself through the enemy defences, it would have stood no chance in open country against the forces that the Germans would have brought against it.

It was to his negotiations to secure the release of his army that the severest criticism was attached. It is worth observing that in the years before the war, after his return from Mexico, Bazaine was never considered to be *un homme politique*. There is no reason to suppose that he harboured any political ambition (although the same might have been said of Marshal MacMahon, who three years after the proclamation of a Republic had taken the place of Adolphe Thiers as its president). Bazaine was not motivated by personal aspirations, but by his loyalty to the Emperor and the Empress, and to his military oath of allegiance.

It is unnecessary to add much on the subject of Bazaine's trial. The pressure for a conviction was considerable, not only from the almost hysterical Press and public opinion, but also among some elements of the government and the army. Bazaine certainly ought to have realised that in the face of this it was at least probable that he would be convicted. And even if he was acquitted, he was wrong in assuming that in the eyes of the people of France he would have cleared his name. The members of the court would simply have been execrated for failing in their duty by letting a guilty man walk free. And as the trial progressed, the ultimate outcome should perhaps have become more apparent to him, as the court heard witness after witness whose evidence was wholly irrelevant to the charges faced by Bazaine, but who were called in order to put all his actions, and indeed his thoughts, in the worst possible light. Since the court gave no reason for its decisions, it is impossible to say what consideration was given to the repeated consultations in which Bazaine engaged with his senior

10   Quoted Guedalla, p. 181.

commanders. Of course these did nothing to lessen his ultimate responsibility for the capitulation, and to his credit he never suggested that they did, but the endorsement by the Council of War of the decision to surrender was, or should have been, nevertheless a significant mitigating factor.

Years later, when he came to write his memoirs, General Francois du Barail, who as War Minister had supervised Bazaine's trial, acknowledged what had been done: 'And then we needed a scapegoat, we needed an expiatory victim who bore the weight of all our misfortunes, which allowed our pride to be unburdened upon him.'[11]

In his conduct during 1870, therefore, Bazaine was guilty on the one hand of no more than a number of errors of military judgment, and on the other of grasping at what seemed a possible means of saving his army by attempting negotiations which, in the context of his situation, were destined to go nowhere. He was, at the last, guilty only of being mindful of the fate of his men if he embarked on a final, doomed attempt to escape. He lacked the spark of military genius that might, improbably, have brought his army success against an adversary that was quite simply always its superior. But his patriotism, his courage and his fidelity to his military oath deserved better of the French people for whom he fought and whose persecution of him was to their lasting discredit.

11   Quoted in Ruby & Regnault, p. 354.

Bibliography

Adriance, Thomas J., *The Last Gaiter Button* (Westport, Connecticut, 1987)

Anon, *La Dépèche du 20 Aout 1870* (Paris, 1872)

Aronson, Theo, *The Fall of the Third Napoleon* (London, 1970)

Ascoli, David, *A Day of Battle* (London, 1987)

Baryy, Quintin, *The Franco-Prussian War 1870-1871* (2 Vols.) (Solihull 2007)

Bazaine, Marshal F.A., *Episodes de la Guerre de 1870 et le Blocus de Metz* (Madrid 1883)

Bazaine, Marshal F.A., *L'Armée du Rhin depuis le 12 Aout jusqu'a 29 Octobre 1870* (Paris, 1872)

Bell, Harry, (ed.) *St Privat: German Sources* (Fort Leavenworth, Kansas, 1914)

Bibesco, Prince G, *Campagne de 1870: Belfort, Reims, Sedan* (Paris, n.d.)

Bismarck, Prince Otto von, *Reflections and Reminiscences* (2 Vols.) (London, 1898)

Boguslawski, A von, *Tactical Deductions from the War of 1870-71* (London, 1872)

Bonie, Lieutenant-Colonel, 'The French Cavalry in 1870' in *Cavalry Studies from Two Great Wars* (Kansas City, 1896)

Bonnal, General, *La Manoeuvre de St Privat* (Paris, 1904)

Brackenbury, Captain H, *Les Maréchaux de France* (Paris, 1872)

Bury, J.P.T. & Tombs, R.P., *Thiers 1797-1877: A Political Life* (London, n.d.)

Bury, J.P.T., *Gambetta and the National Defence* (London, 1964)

Busch Moritz, *Bismarck in the Franco-German War 1870-1871* (London, 1879)

Busch Morris, *Bismarck: Some Secret Pages of His History* (2 Vols.) (London, 1898)

Caemmerer, General von, *The Development of Strategical Science* (London, 1905)

Cartier, Vital, *Le General Trochu* (Paris, 1914)

Chabert, F.M., *Journal du Blocus de Metz* (Metz, 1871)

Cox, G.P., *The Halt in the Mud: French Strategic Planning from Waterloo to Sedan* (Boulder, Colorado, 1994)

Craig, Gordon A., *The Battle of Königgrätz* (London, 1965)

Craig, Gordon A., *The Politics of the Prussian Army* (Oxford, 1955)

D'Andlau, Colonel Joseph, *Metz: Campagne et Negociations* (Paris, 1872)

D'Herisson, Comte, *La Legende de Metz* (Paris, 1888)

Daily News, *War Correspondence* (London, 1871)

De Lonlay, Dick, *Francais et Allemands* (Paris, 1888)

Des Godins de Souhesmes, G, *Blocus de Metz en 1870* (Paris, 1872)

Du Cane, Brigadier General J.P., *The Campaign in Alsace* (London, 1912)

Duquet, Alfred, *Les Derniers Jours de l'Armee du Rhin* (Paris, 1888)

Elliot-Wright, P, *Gravelotte-St Privat* (Westport, Connecticut, 2005)

Etat-Major de L'Armee, *La Guerre de 1870: L'Investissement de Metz* (Paris, 1907)

Etat-Major de L'Armee, *La Guerre de 1870-71: L'Armee de Châlons* (Paris, 1905)

Fay, Colonel Charles, *Journal d'un Officier de l'Armée du Rhin* (Brussels, 1871)

Fermer, Douglas, *France at Bay* (Barnsley, 2011)

Filon, Augustin, *Recollections of the Empress Eugénie* (London, 1920)

Fitzmaurice, Lord Edmund, *The Life of the Second Earl Granville* (London, 1905)

Forester, W, *Prinz Friedrich Karl von Preussen* (Stuttgart, 1910)

Forbes, *Archibald, Memories and Studies of War and Peace* (London, 1895)

Forbes, Archibald, *My Experiences of the War between France and Germany* (2 Vols.) (London, 1871)

Frederick III, Emperor, *War Diary* (London, 1928)

Frossard, General Charles, *Rapport sur les Operations du Deuxième Corps* (Paris, 1872)

German General Staff, *Official Account of the Franco-German War 1870-1871*, trans. Captain F.C.H. Clarke (5 Vols.) (London, 1874)

Ghio, A. (ed) *Procès du Maréchal Bazaine* (Paris, 1874)

Grouard, A, *Wörth et Forbach* (Paris, 1905)

Guedella, Philip, *The Two Marshals* (London, 1943)

Hale, Major Lonsdale A, *Tactical Studies of the Battles of Colombey-Nouilly and Vionville* (London, 1877)

Haslip, Joan, *Imperial Adventurer* (London, 1971)

Hatzfeldt, Count Paul, *The Hatzfeldt Letters* (London, 1905)

Henderson, Colonel G.F.R., *The Battle of Spicheren* (London, 1891)

Henderson, Colonel G.F.R., *The Battle of Wörth* (Yorktown, Virginia, 1899)

Hoffbauer, Captain E, *The German Artillery in the Battles near Metz* (London, 1874)

Hohenlohe-Ingelfingen, Prince Kraft zu, *Aus Meinem Leben* (Berlin, n.d.)

Holmes, Richard, *The Road to Sedan* (London, 1984)

Hooper, George, *The Campaign of Sedan* (London, 1908)

Howard, Michael, *The Franco-Prussian War* (London, 1961)

Howes, Colonel P., *The Catalytic Wars* (London, 1998)

Hozier, Captain H.M. (ed), *The Franco-Prussian War: Its Causes, Incidents and Consequences* (London, n.d.)

Hyde, H. Montgomery, *Mexican Empire* (London, 1946)

Hönig, F., *Tactics of the Future* (London, 1899)

Hönig, F., *Twenty Four Hours of Moltke's Strategy* (Woolwich, 1895)

Jacoby, J.C., *1870: La Guerre en Moselle* (Metz, 2014)

Jarras, General Louis, Souvenirs (Paris, 1892)

Kaehler, Major, 'The German Cavalry in the Battle of Vionville-Mars la Tour' in *Cavalry Studies from Two Great Wars* (Kansas City, Missouri, 1896)

Kunz, Hermann, *Le Maréchal Bazaine pourrait-il en 1870 sauver la France?* (Paris, 1896)

Lebrun, General Bartholémy, *Souvenirs Militaires*, 1866-1870 (Paris, 1895)

Lenoir, Paul, *Le Maréchal Bazaine et la Capitulation de Metz* (n.d.)

Martiny de Riez, M., *La Guerre de 1870-71* (Laon, 1871)

Maurice, Major General F., *The Franco-German War 1870-71* (London, 1900)

May, Major E.S., *Field Artillery with the Other Arms* (London, 1898)

May, Major E.S., *Guns and Cavalry* (London, 1896)

Moltke, Field Marshal Helmuth von, *Correspondance Militaire* (5 Vols,) (Paris, n.d.)

Moltke, Field Marshal Helmuth von, *Military Correspondence 1870-71*, ed. S Wilkinson (Oxford, 1923)

Moltke, Field Marshal Helmuth von, *Strategy: Its Theory and Application* (Westport, Connecticut, 1971)

Moltke, Field Marshal Helmuth von, *The Franco-German War of 1870-71* (London, 1907)

Newton, Lord, *Life of Lord Lyons* (London, n.d.)

Palat, General Bartholémy, (Pierre Lehautcourt) *Histoire de la Guerre de 1870: La Capitulation de Metz* (Paris, 1908)

Palat, General Bartholémy, *Grande Question d'histoire et de Psychologie: Bazaine et nos désastres en 1870* (Paris, 1913)

Pelet-Narbonne, General, *Cavalry on Service* (London, 1906)

Porch, Douglas, *The French Foreign Legion* (London, 1991)

Pratt, Lieutenant-Colonel S C, *Saarbruck to Paris 1870* (London, 1914)

Rich, Elihu, *Marshal Bazaine Before the Tribunal at Versailles* (London, 1873)

Ridley, J., *Napoleon III and Eugénie* (London, 1979)

Robinson, G.T., *The Fall of Metz* (London, 1871)

Rot, F., *Le Dernier Siège de Metz* (Metz, 2013)

Ruby, General Edmond and Regnault, General Jean, *Bazaine: Coupable ou Victime?* (Paris, 1960)

Rustow, W., *The War for the Rhine Frontier* (3 Vols.) (London, 1871)

Schiebert, J, *The Franco-German-War 1870-71* (Chatham, 1891)

Schell, A. von, *The Operations of the First Army under General von Steinmetz* (London, 1873)

Semur, F.C., *Mac-Mahon: ou la Gloire Confisquée* (Paris, 2005)

Sencourt, Robert, *Napoleon III: The Modern Emperor* (London, 1933)

Seward, Desmond, *Eugénie* (Stroud, 2004)

Stevenson, Sara Yorke, *Maximilian in Mexico* (New York, 1897)

Stoffel, Colonel Baron Eugene, *Rapports Militaires* (Paris, 1871)

Stone, Captain F.G., *Tactical Studies from the Franco-German War of 1870-1871* (London, 1886)

Thiers, Adolphe, *Memoirs 1870-1873* (London, 1915)

Thompson, J.M., *Louis Napoleon and the Second Empire* (Oxford, 1954)

Verdy du Vernois, Colonel Julius von, *With the Royal Headquarters* (London, 1897)

Vincler, J., *Le Maréchal Bazaine: Coupable ou Victime 1870-73* (Metz, 2013)

Wawro, Geoffrey, *The Franco-Prussian War* Franco- (Cambridge, 2003)

Wellesley, Sir Victor and Sencourt, Robert, *Conversations with Napoleon III* (London, 1934)

Williams, Roger L., *Napoleon III and the Stoffel Affair* (Worland, Wyoming, 1993)

Wood, Field Marshal Sir E., *Achievements of Cavalry* (London, 1897)

Wylly, Colonel H.C., *Magenta and Solferino* (London, 1907)

Index

People

Places

Formations & Units

The period 1815-1914 is sometimes called the long century of peace. It was in reality very far from that. It was a century of civil wars, popular uprisings, and struggles for Independence. An era of colonial expansion, wars of Empire, and colonial campaigning, much of which was unconventional in nature. It was also an age of major conventional wars, in Europe that would see the Crimea campaign and the wars of German unification. Such conflicts, along with the American Civil War, foreshadowed the total war of the 20th century.

It was also a period of great technological advancement, which in time impacted the military and warfare in general. Steam power, electricity, the telegraph, the radio, the railway, all became tools of war. The century was one of dramatic change. Tactics altered, sometimes slowly, to meet the challenges of the new technology. The dramatic change in the technology of war in this period is reflected in the new title of this series: From Musket to Maxim.

The new title better reflects the fact that the series covers all nations and all conflict of the period between 1815-1914. Already the series has commissioned books that deal with matters outside the British experience. This is something that the series will endeavour to do more of in the future. At the same time there still remains an important place for the study of the British military during this period. It is one of fascination, with campaigns that capture the imagination, in which Britain although the world's predominant power, continues to field a relatively small army.

The aim of the series is to throw the spotlight on the conflicts of that century, which can often get overlooked, sandwiched as they are between two major conflicts, the French/Revolutionary/Napoleonic Wars and the First World War. The series will produced a variety of books and styles. Some will look simply at campaigns or battles. Others will concentrate on particular aspects of a war or campaign. There will also be books that look at wider concepts of warfare during this era. It is the intention that this series will present a platform for historians to present their work on an important but often overlooked century of warfare.

Submissions

The publishers would be pleased to receive submissions for this series. Please contact series editor Dr Christopher Brice via email (chrismbrice@yahoo.com), or in writing to Helion & Company Limited, Unit 8, Amherst Business Centre, Budbrooke Road, Warwick, Warwickshire, CV34 5WE.

Books in this series:

1. *The Battle of Majuba Hill: The Transvaal Campaign 1880-1881* John Laband (ISBN 978-1-911512-38-7)*

2. *For Queen and Company: Vignettes of the Irish Soldier in the Indian Mutiny* David Truesdale (ISBN 978-1-911512-79-0)*

3. *The Furthest Garrison: Imperial Regiments in New Zealand 1840-1870* Adam Davis (ISBN 978-1-911628-29-3)*

4. *Victory over Disease: Resolving The Medical Crisis In The Crimean War, 1854-1856* Michael Hinton (ISBN 978-1-911628-31-6)*

5. *Journey Through the Wilderness: Garnet Wolseley's Canadian Red River Expedition of 1870* Paul McNicholls (ISBN 978-1-911628-30-9)*

6. *Kitchener: The Man Not the Myth* Anne Samson (ISBN 978-1-912866-45-8)

7. *The British and the Sikhs: Discovery, Warfare and Friendship (c.1700–1900)* Gurinder Singh Mann (ISBN 978-1-911628-24-8)*

8. *Bazaine 1870: Scapegoat for a Nation* Quintin Barry (ISBN 978-1-913336-08-0)

* Denotes books are paperback 246mm × 189mm, other books are hardback.